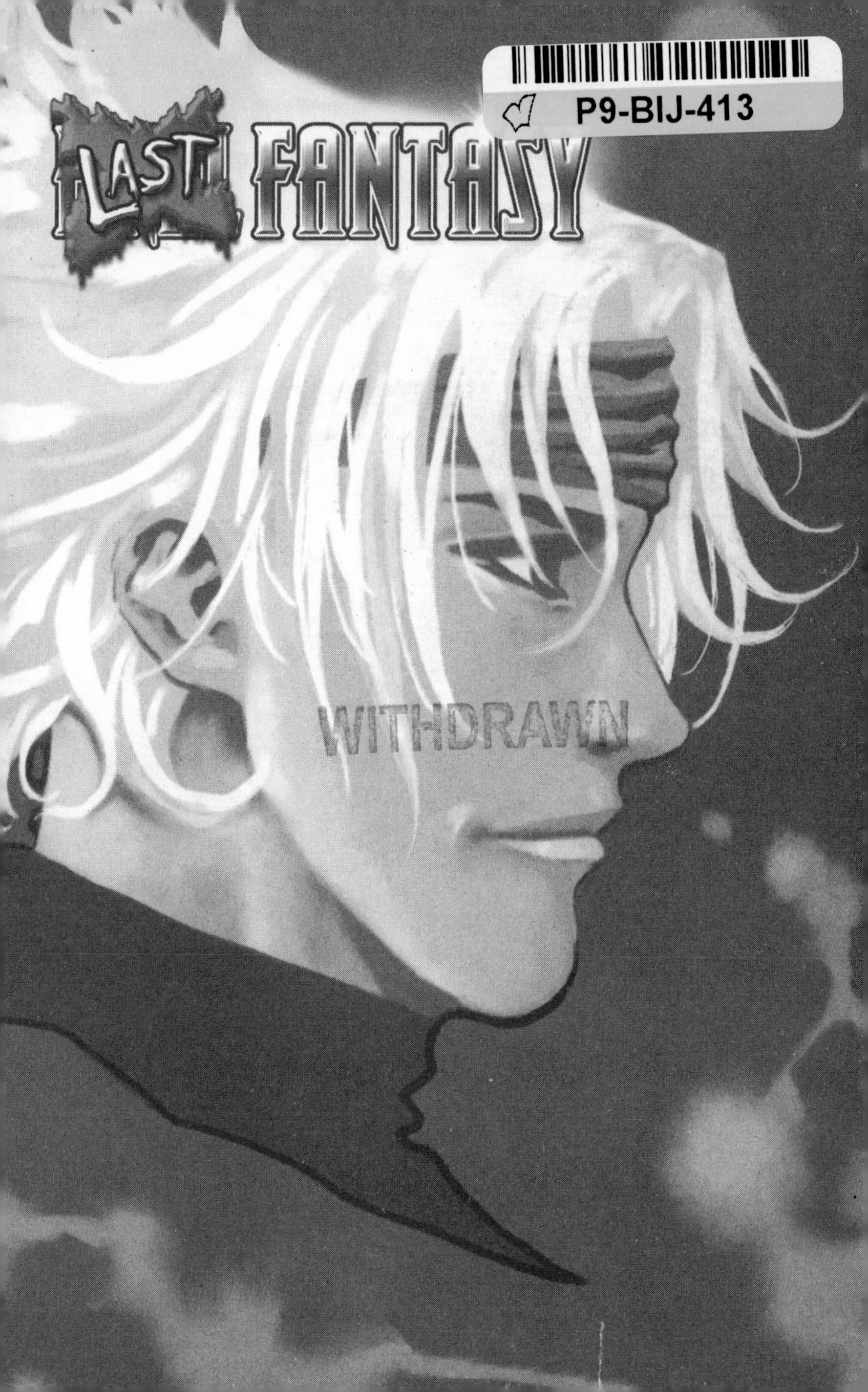
LAST FANTASY

Last Fantasy Vol. 3
Written by Creative Hon
Illustrated by Yong-Wan Kwon

Translation - Sora Han
English Adaptation - Mike Wellman
Copy Editor - Stephanie Duchin
Retouch and Lettering - Dongjin Oh
Production Artist - Jihye "Sophia" Hong
Cover Design - Kyle Plummer

Editor - Luis Reyes
Digital Imaging Manager - Chris Buford
Production Manager - Liz Brizzi
Managing Editor - Vy Nguyen
VP of Production - Ron Klamert
Editor in Chief - Rob Tokar
Publisher - Mike Kiley
President and C.O.O. - John Parker
C.E.O. and Chief Creative Officer - Stuart Levy

A  Manga

TOKYOPOP Inc.
5900 Wilshire Blvd. Suite 2000
Los Angeles, CA 90036

E-mail: info@TOKYOPOP.com
Come visit us online at www.TOKYOPOP.com

ISBN: 1-59532-528-X

First TOKYOPOP printing: November 2006
10 9 8 7 6 5 4 3 2 1
Printed in the USA

VOLUME 3

STORY BY CREATIVE HON
ART BY YONG-WAN KWON

HAMBURG // LONDON // LOS ANGELES // TOKYO

CONTENTS

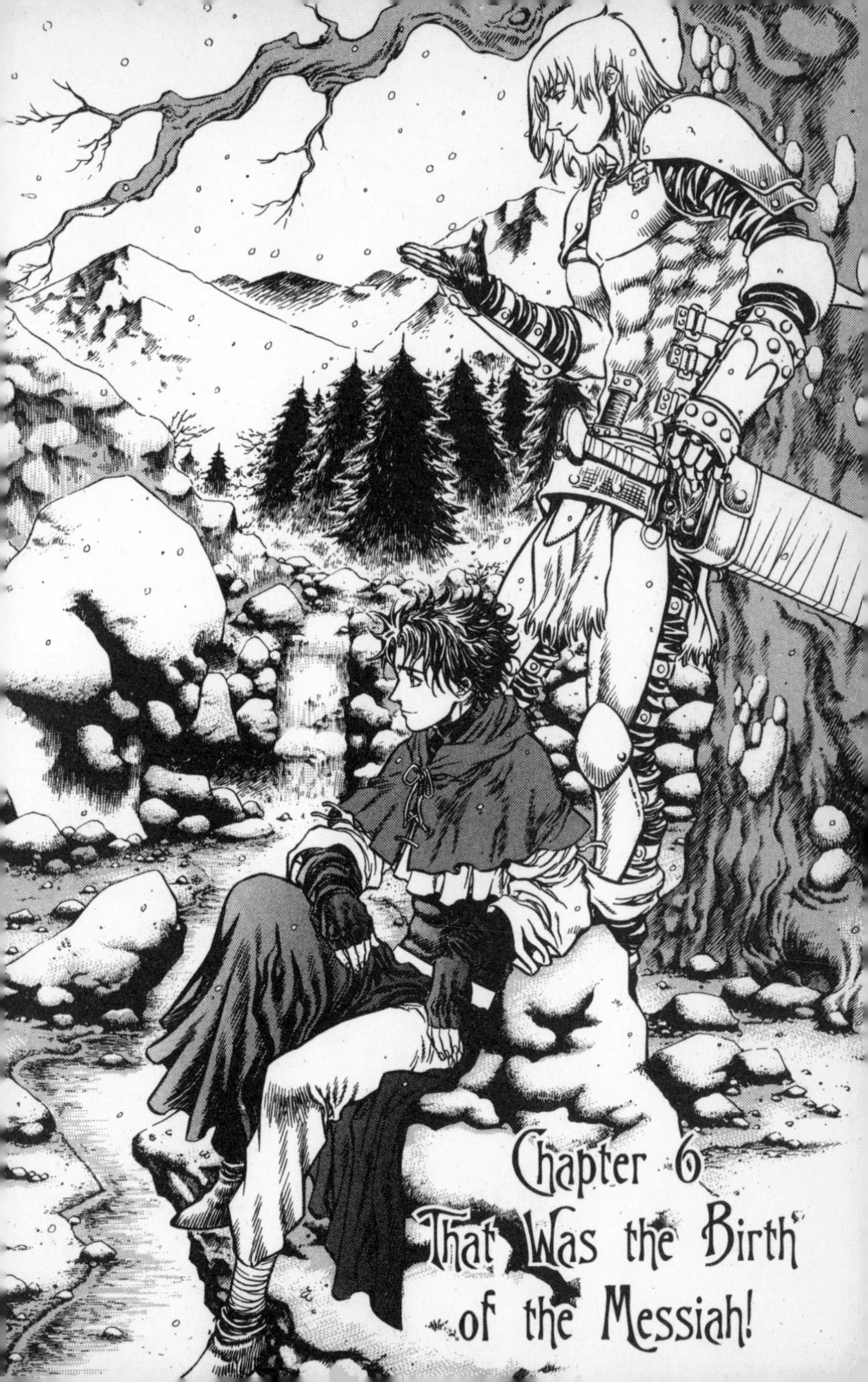
Chapter 6
That Was the Birth of the Messiah!

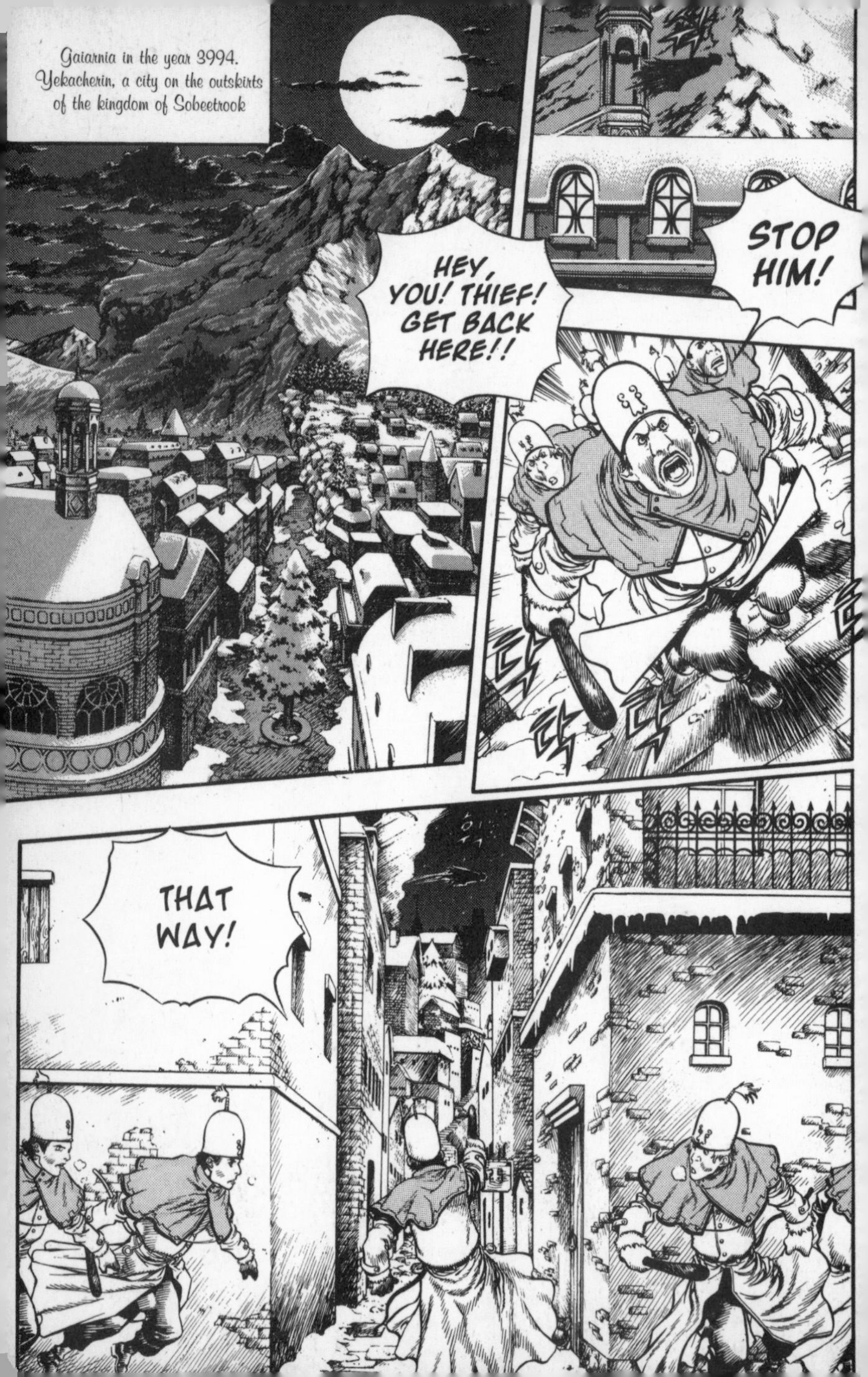
Gaiarnia in the year 3994.
Yekacherin, a city on the outskirts of the kingdom of Sobeetrook
HEY, YOU! THIEF! GET BACK HERE!!
STOP HIM!
THAT WAY!

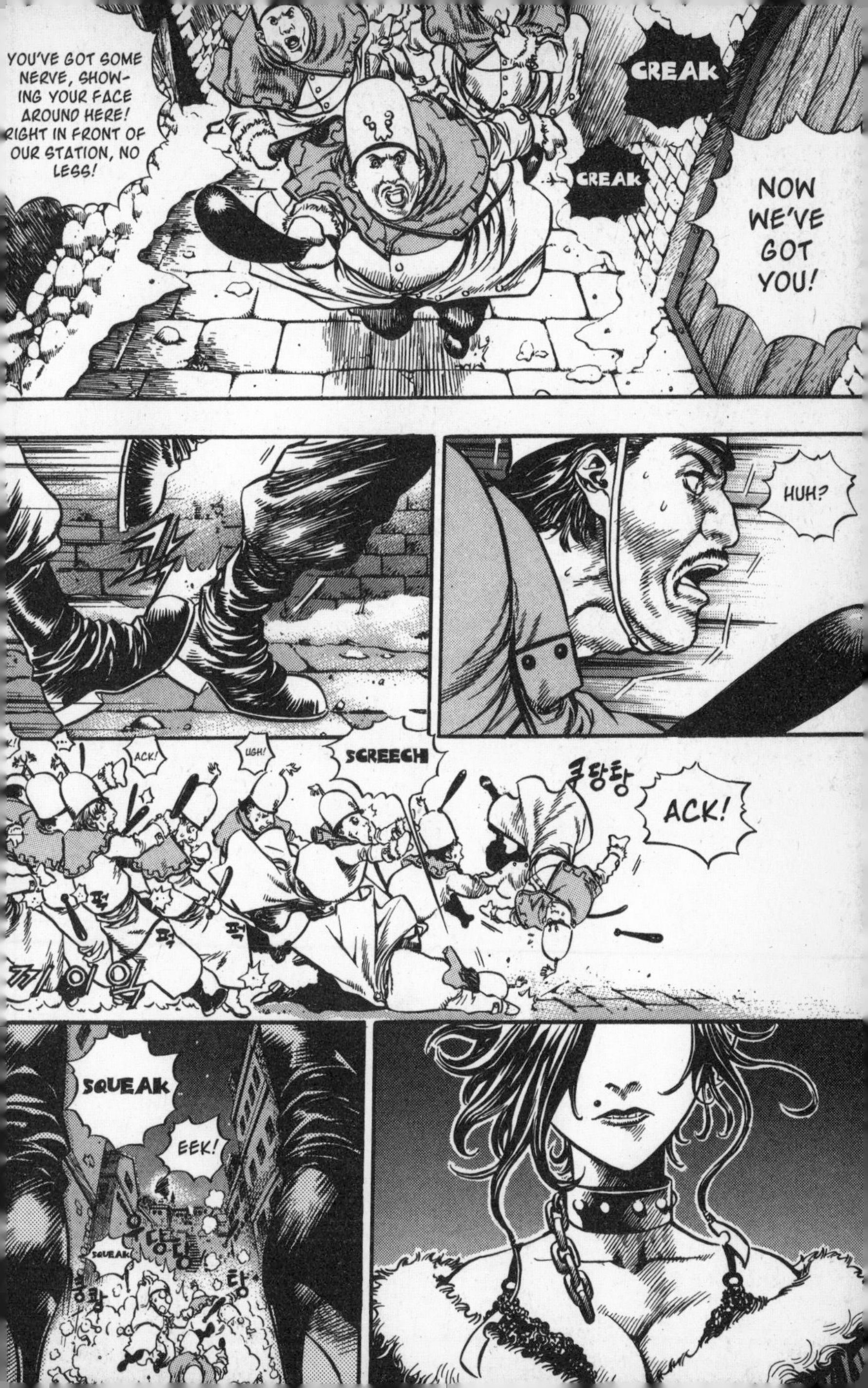
YOU'VE GOT SOME NERVE, SHOWING YOUR FACE AROUND HERE! RIGHT IN FRONT OF OUR STATION, NO LESS!
CREAK
CREAK
NOW WE'VE GOT YOU!
HUH?
ACK!
UGH!
SCREECH
쿠당탕
ACK!
SQUEAK
EEK!
SQUEAK

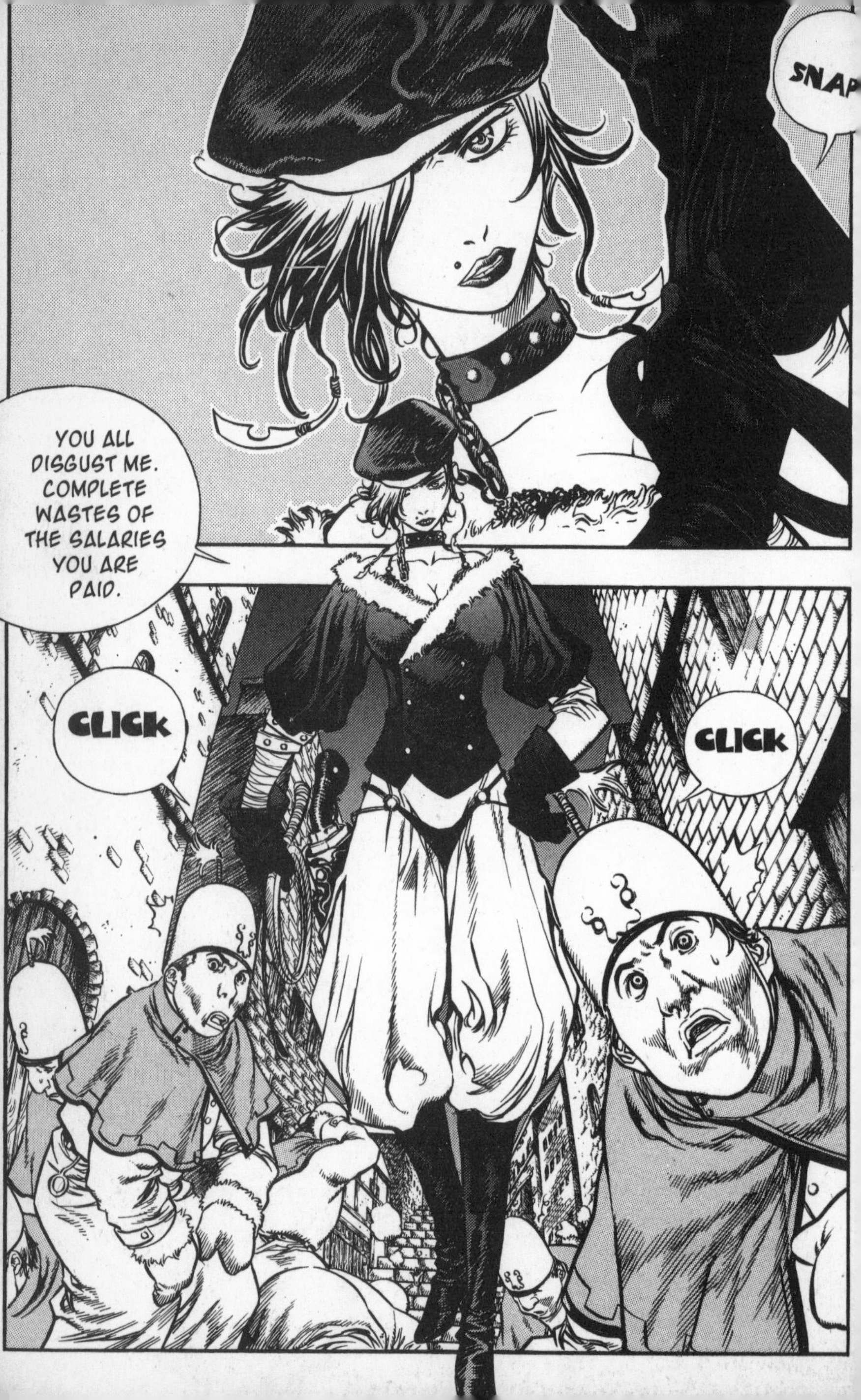
SNAP
YOU ALL DISGUST ME. COMPLETE WASTES OF THE SALARIES YOU ARE PAID.
CLICK
CLICK

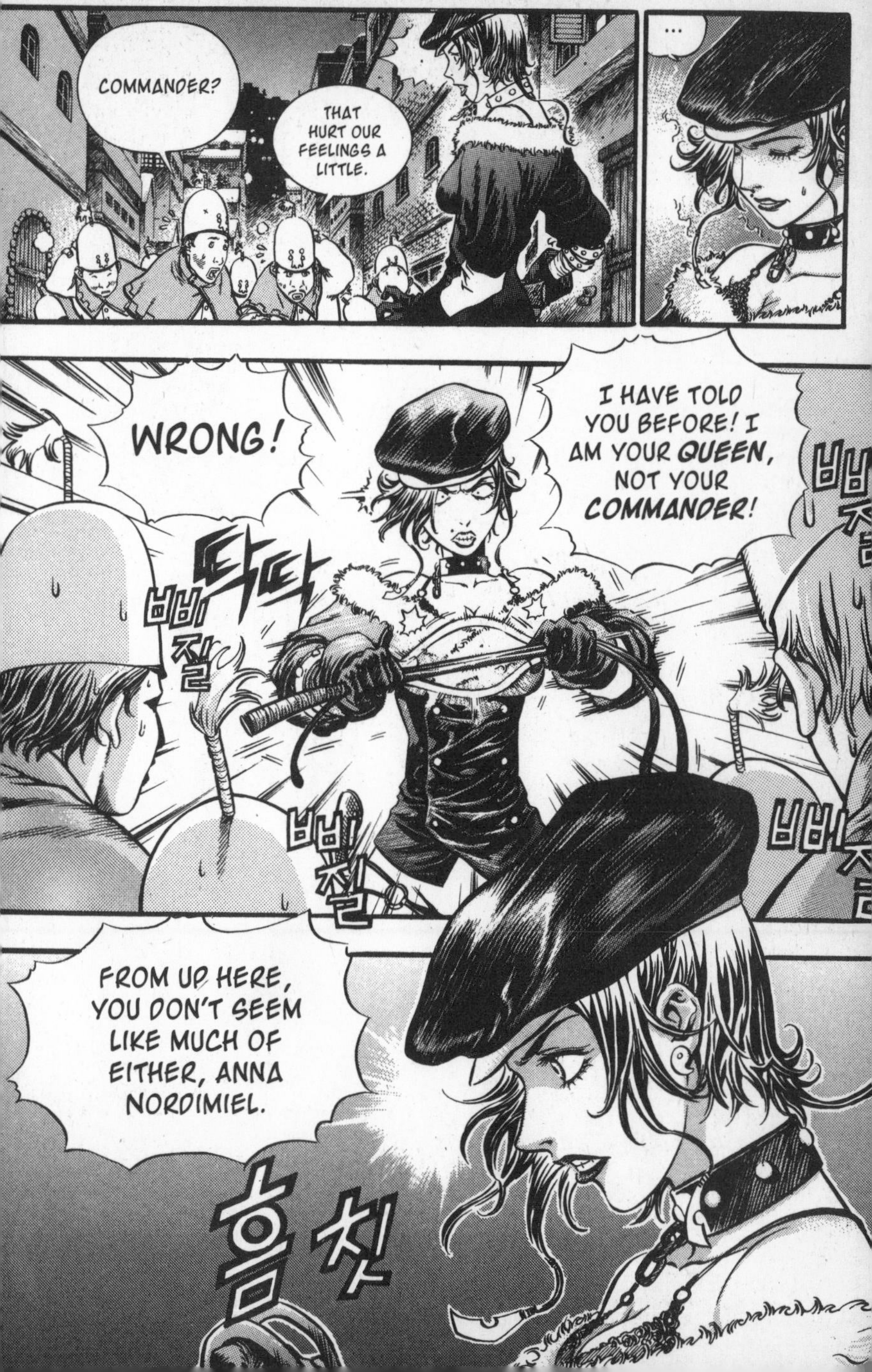
COMMANDER?
THAT HURT OUR FEELINGS A LITTLE.
...
WRONG!
I HAVE TOLD YOU BEFORE! I AM YOUR QUEEN, NOT YOUR COMMANDER!
딱딱
삐질
삐질
FROM UP HERE, YOU DON'T SEEM LIKE MUCH OF EITHER, ANNA NORDIMIEL.
흠칫

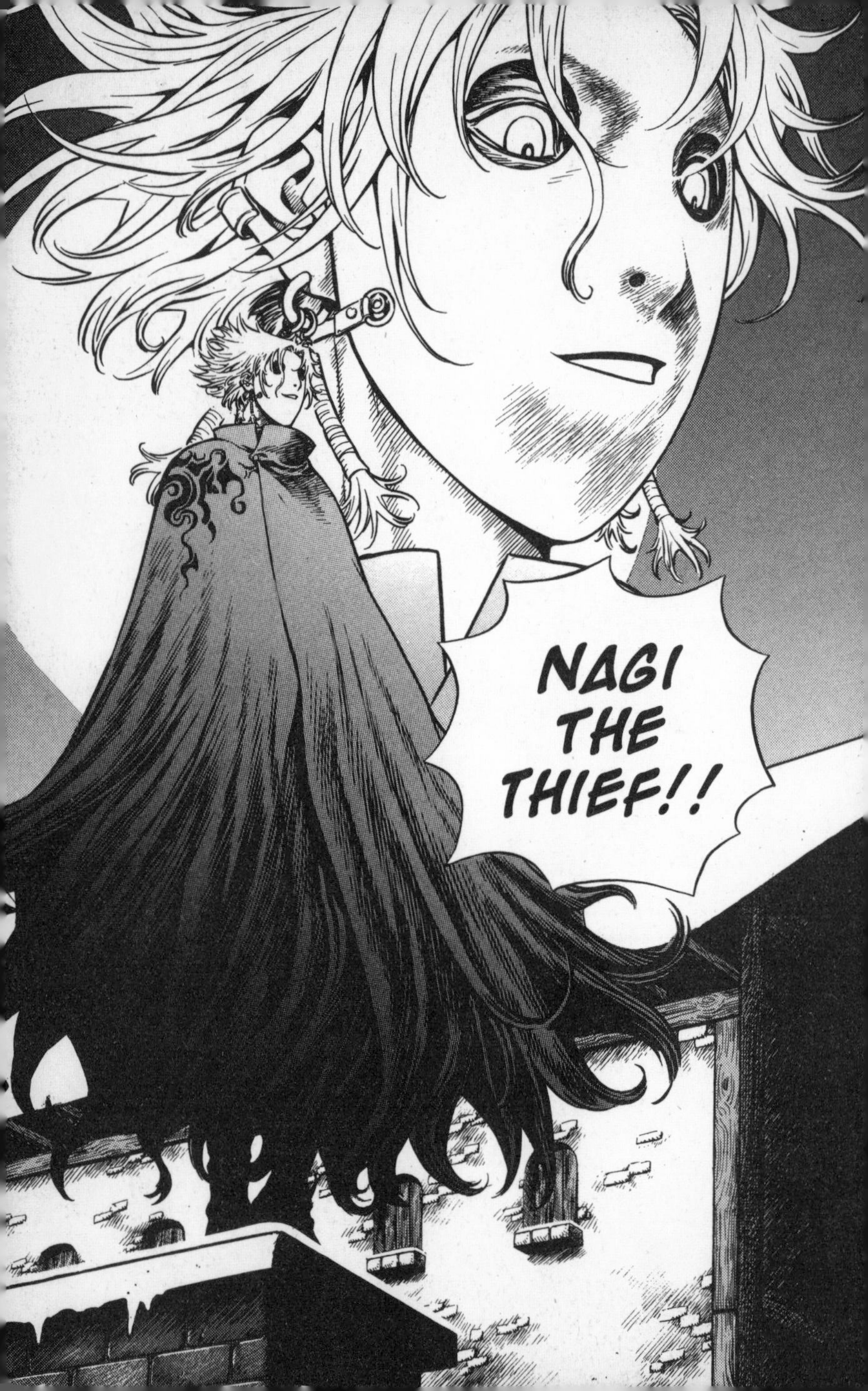
NAGI THE THIEF!!

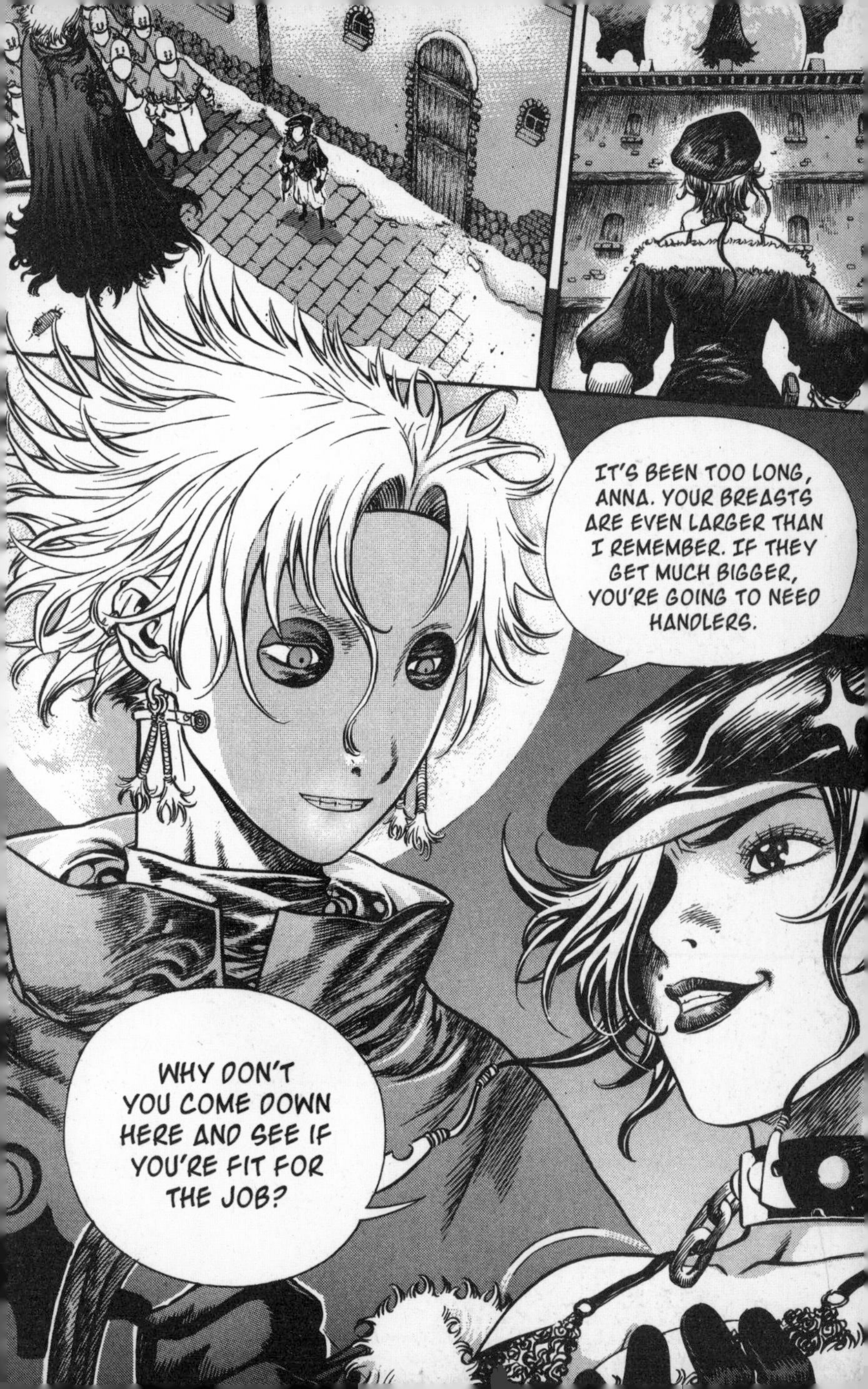
IT'S BEEN TOO LONG, ANNA. YOUR BREASTS ARE EVEN LARGER THAN I REMEMBER. IF THEY GET MUCH BIGGER, YOU'RE GOING TO NEED HANDLERS.
WHY DON'T YOU COME DOWN HERE AND SEE IF YOU'RE FIT FOR THE JOB?

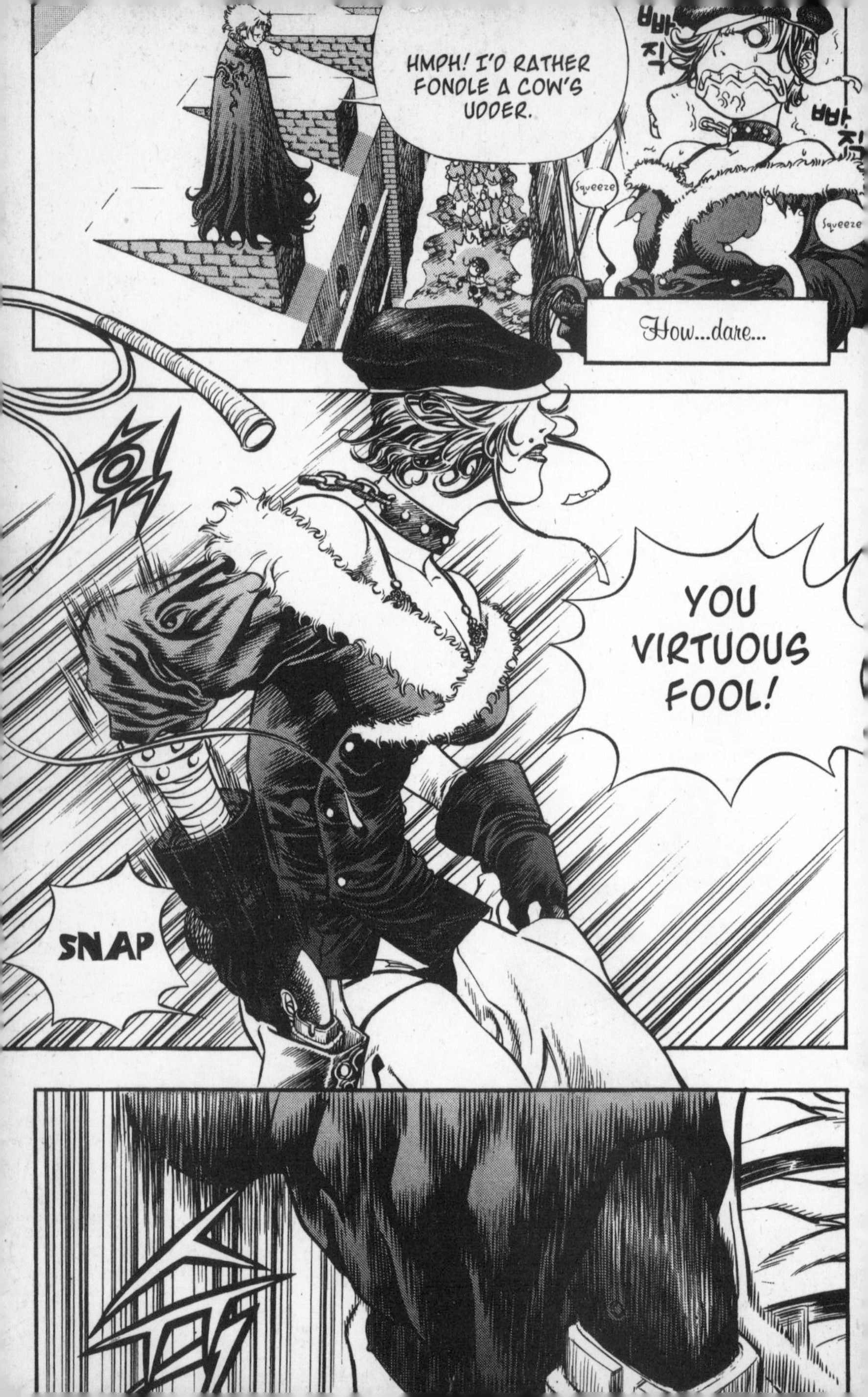
HMPH! I'D RATHER FONDLE A COW'S UDDER.
빠직
빠직
Squeeze
Squeeze
How...dare...
YOU VIRTUOUS FOOL!
SNAP

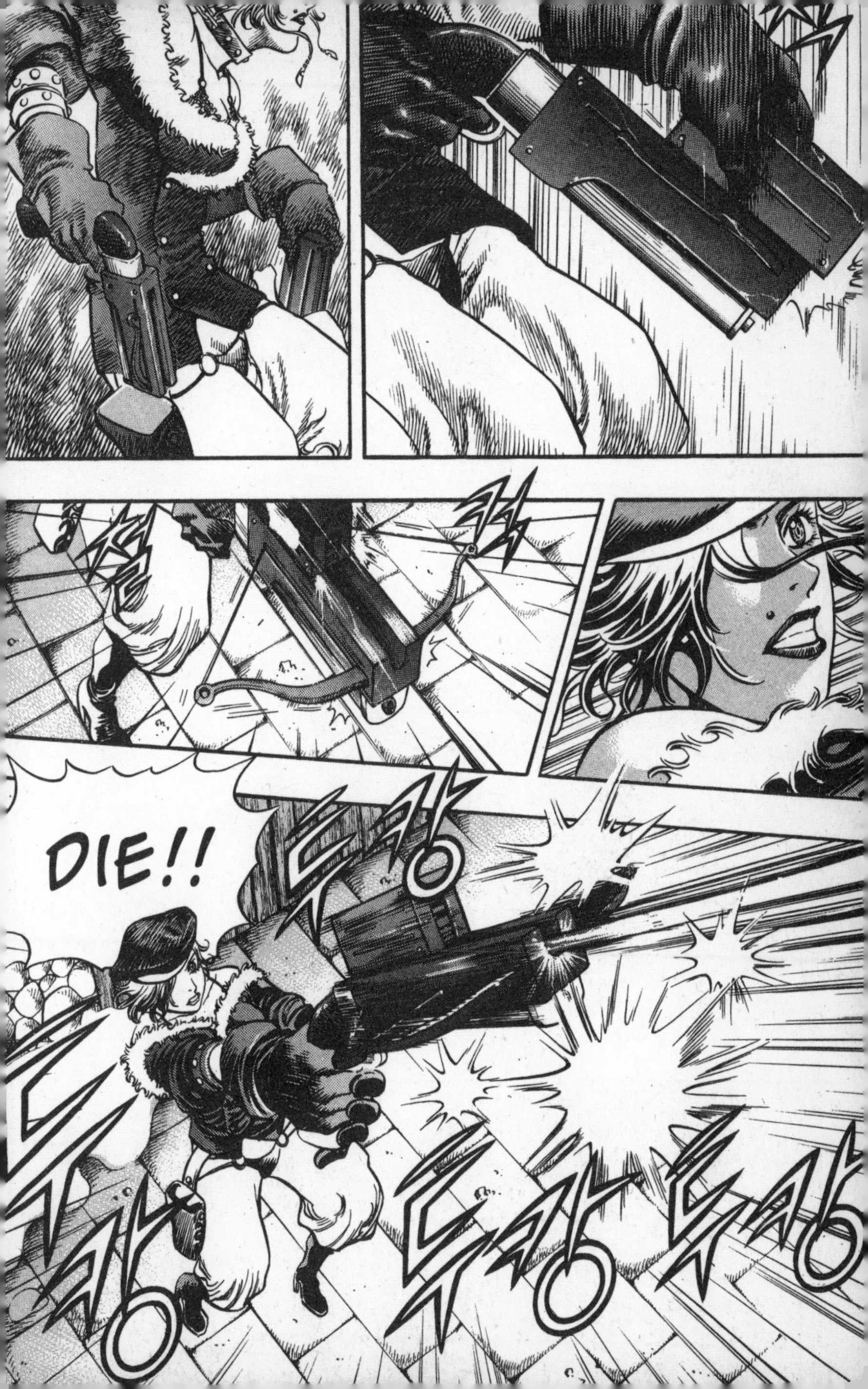
DIE!!

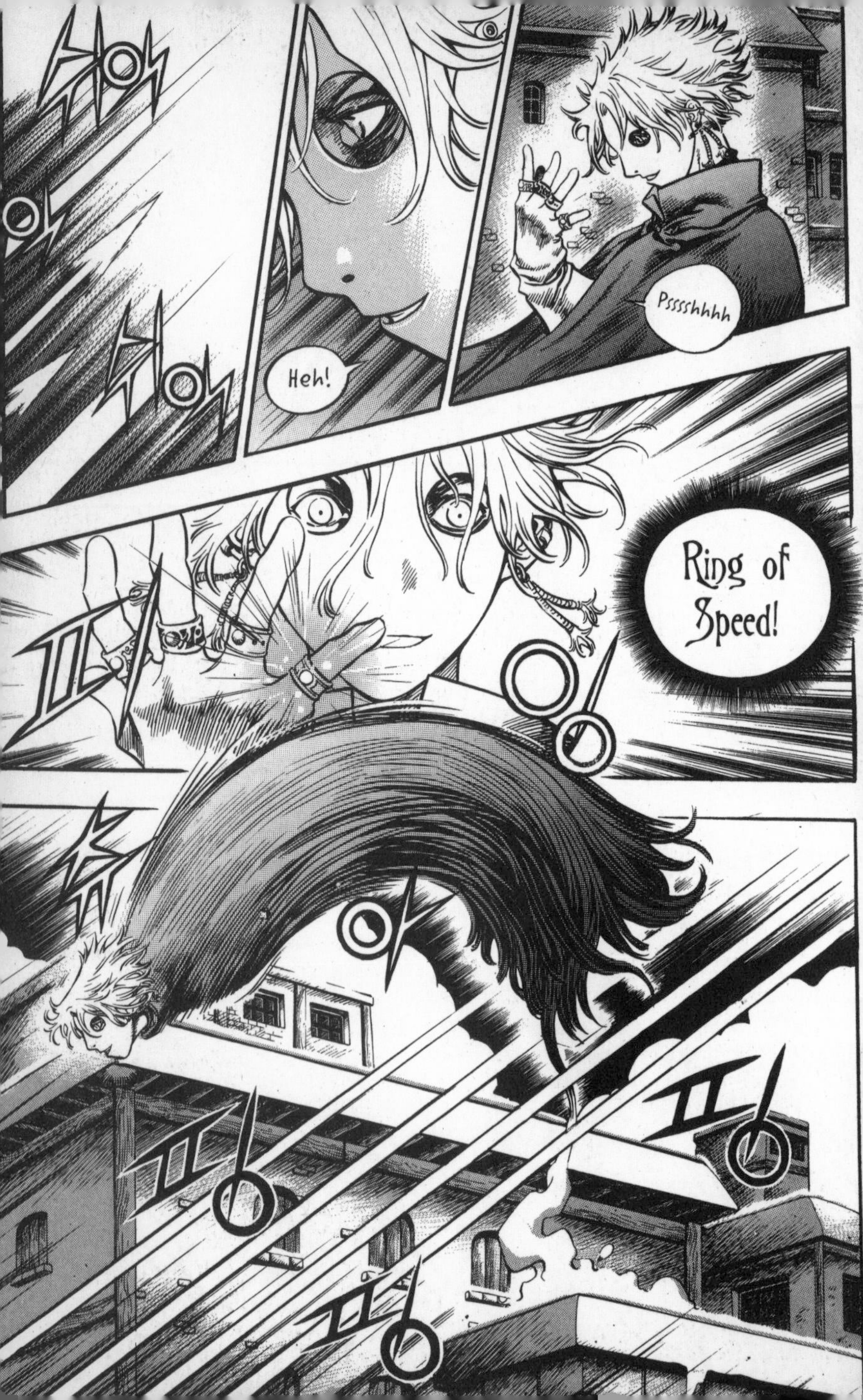

Heh!
Pssssshhhh
Ring of Speed!

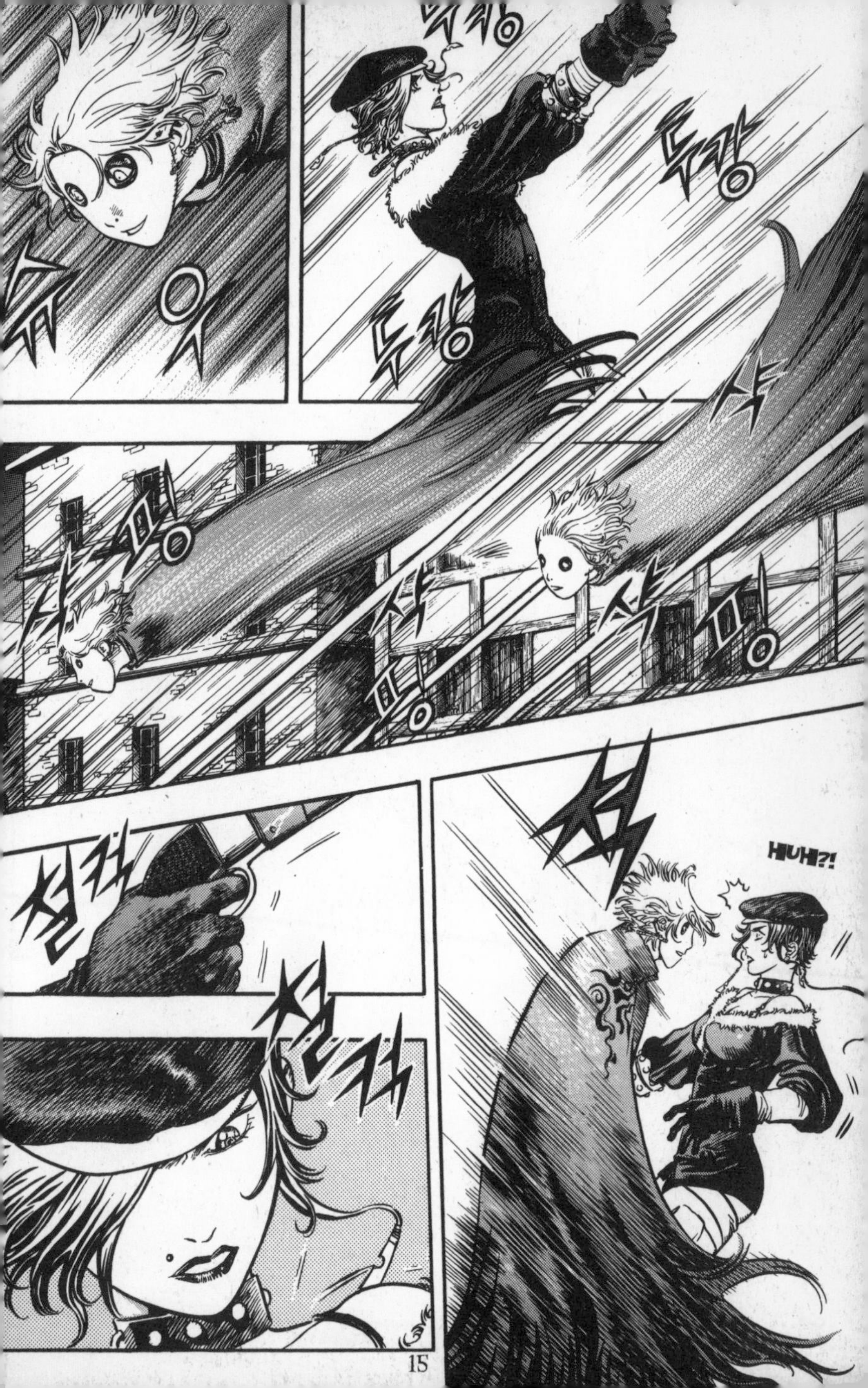
철컥
철컥
HUH?!

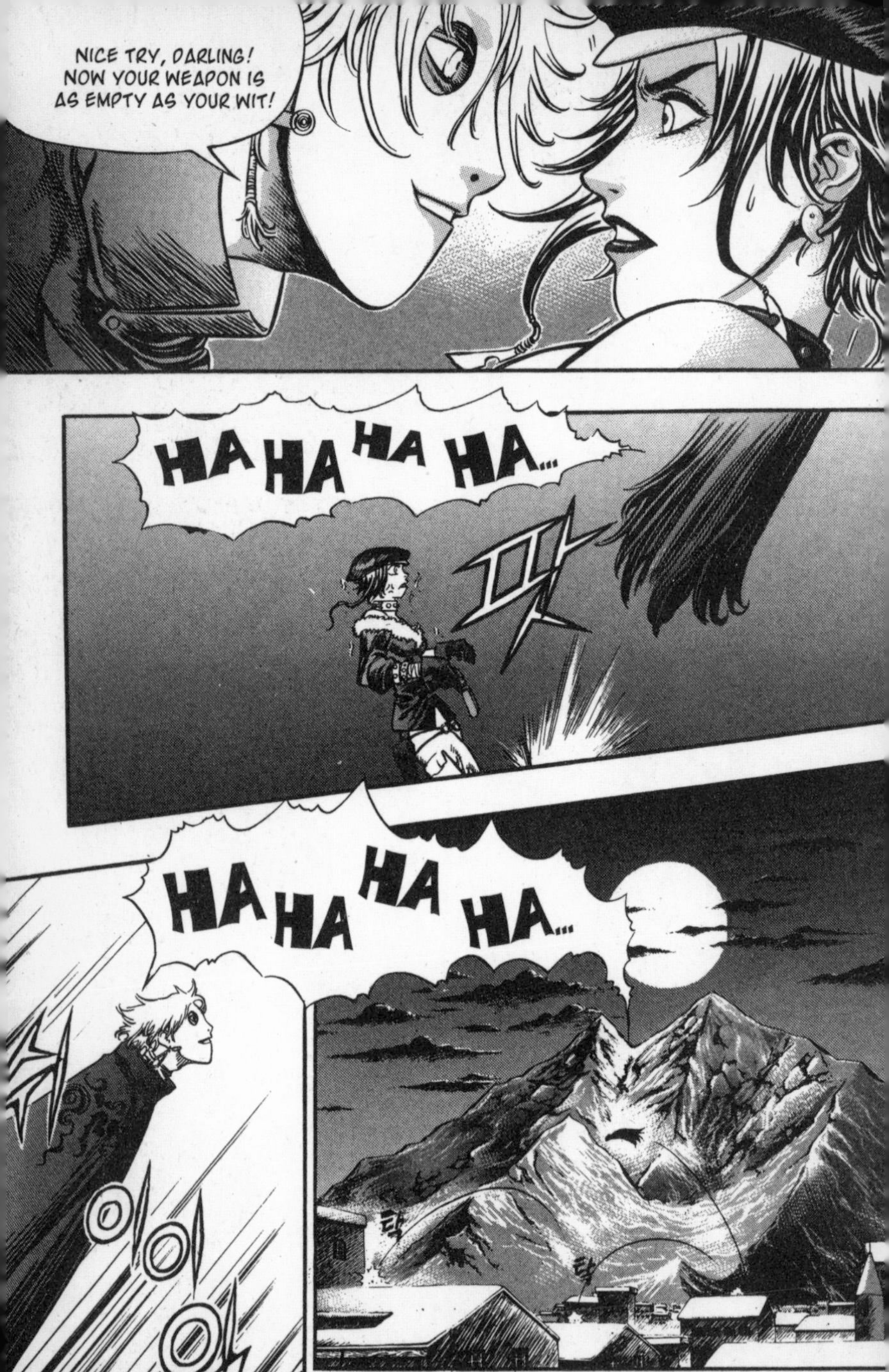
NICE TRY, DARLING! NOW YOUR WEAPON IS AS EMPTY AS YOUR WIT!
HA HA HA HA...
HA HA HA HA...

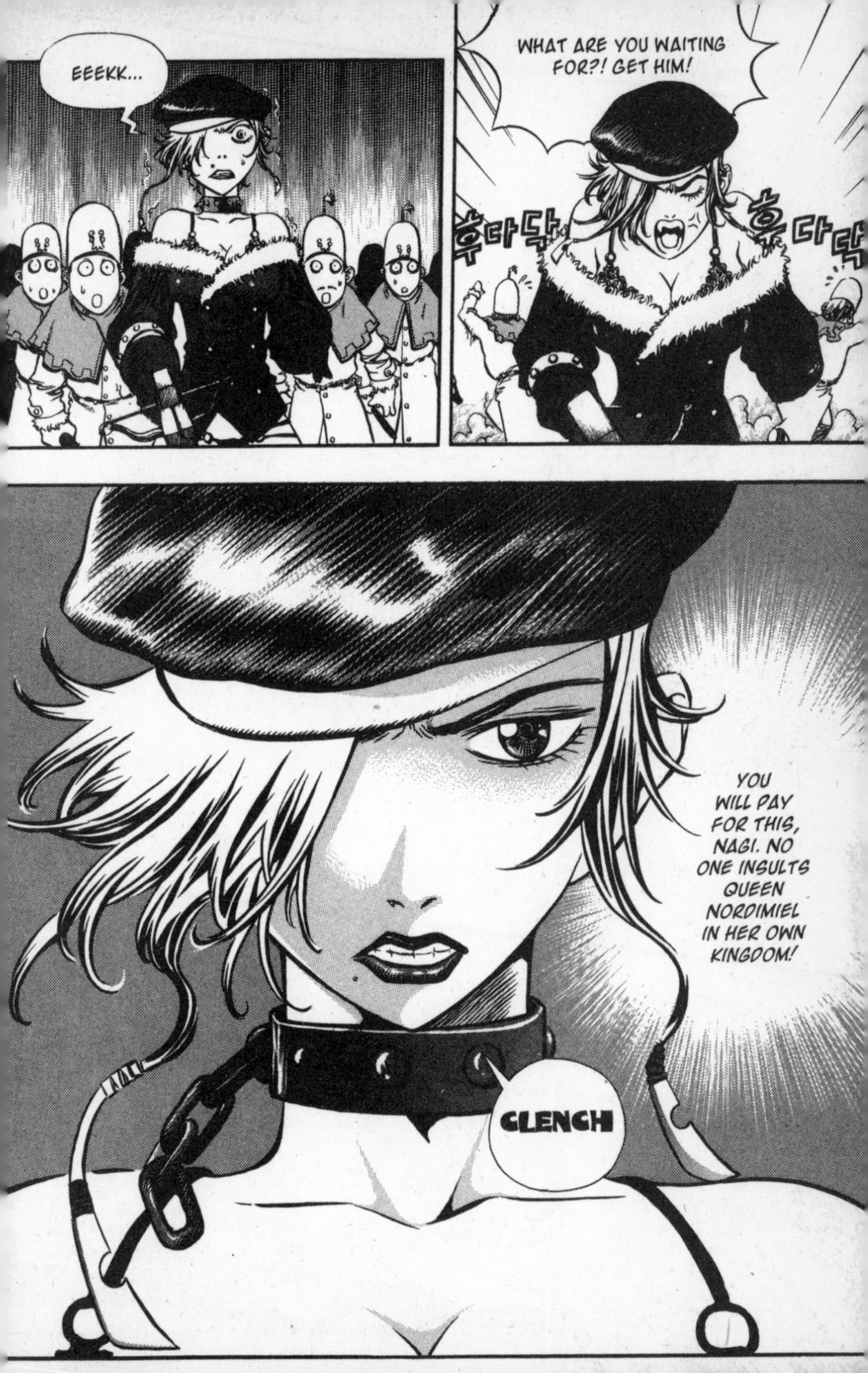
EEEKK...
WHAT ARE YOU WAITING FOR?! GET HIM!
후다닥
후다닥
YOU WILL PAY FOR THIS, NAGI. NO ONE INSULTS QUEEN NORDIMIEL IN HER OWN KINGDOM!
CLENCH

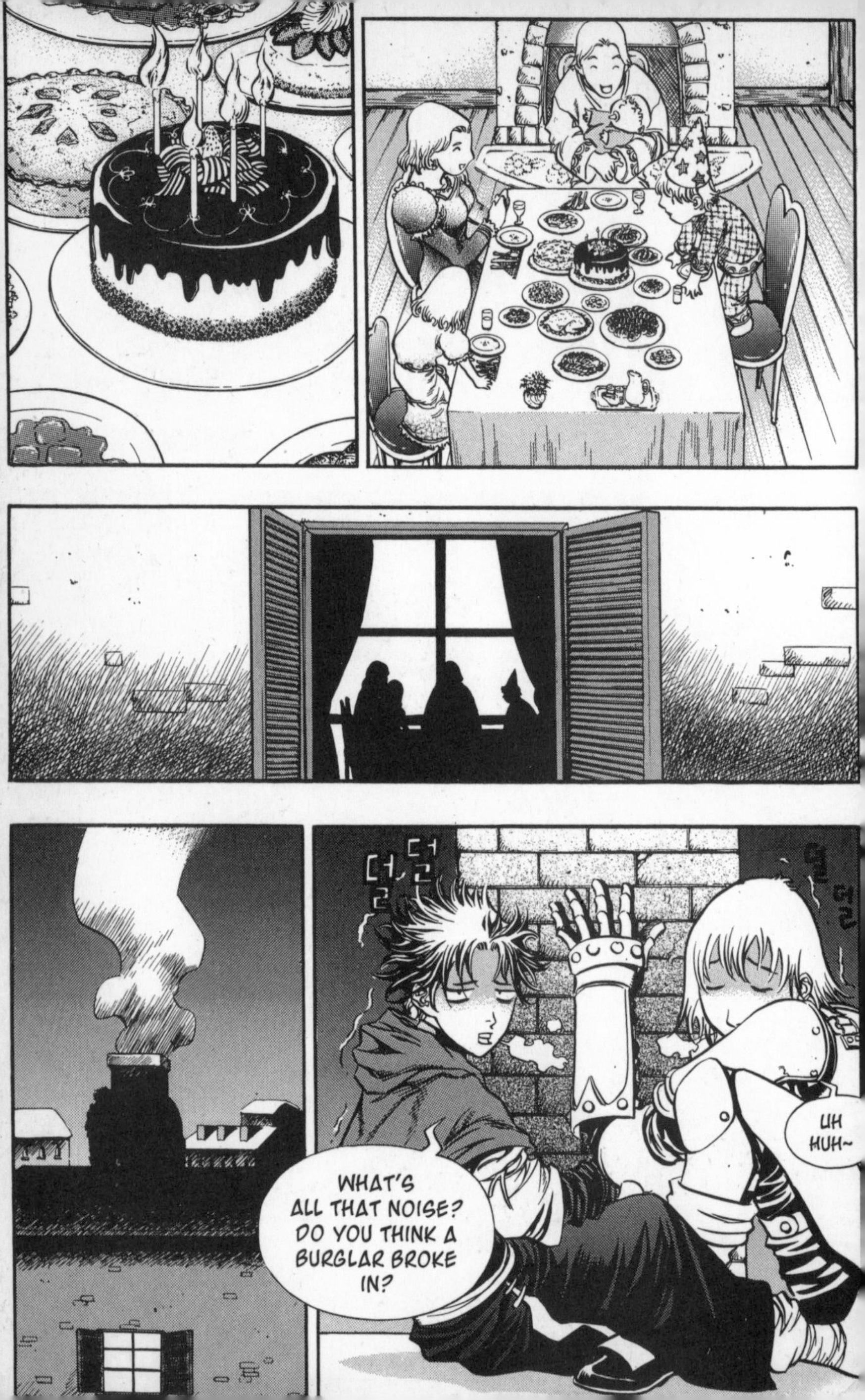
WHAT'S ALL THAT NOISE? DO YOU THINK A BURGLAR BROKE IN?
UH HUH~

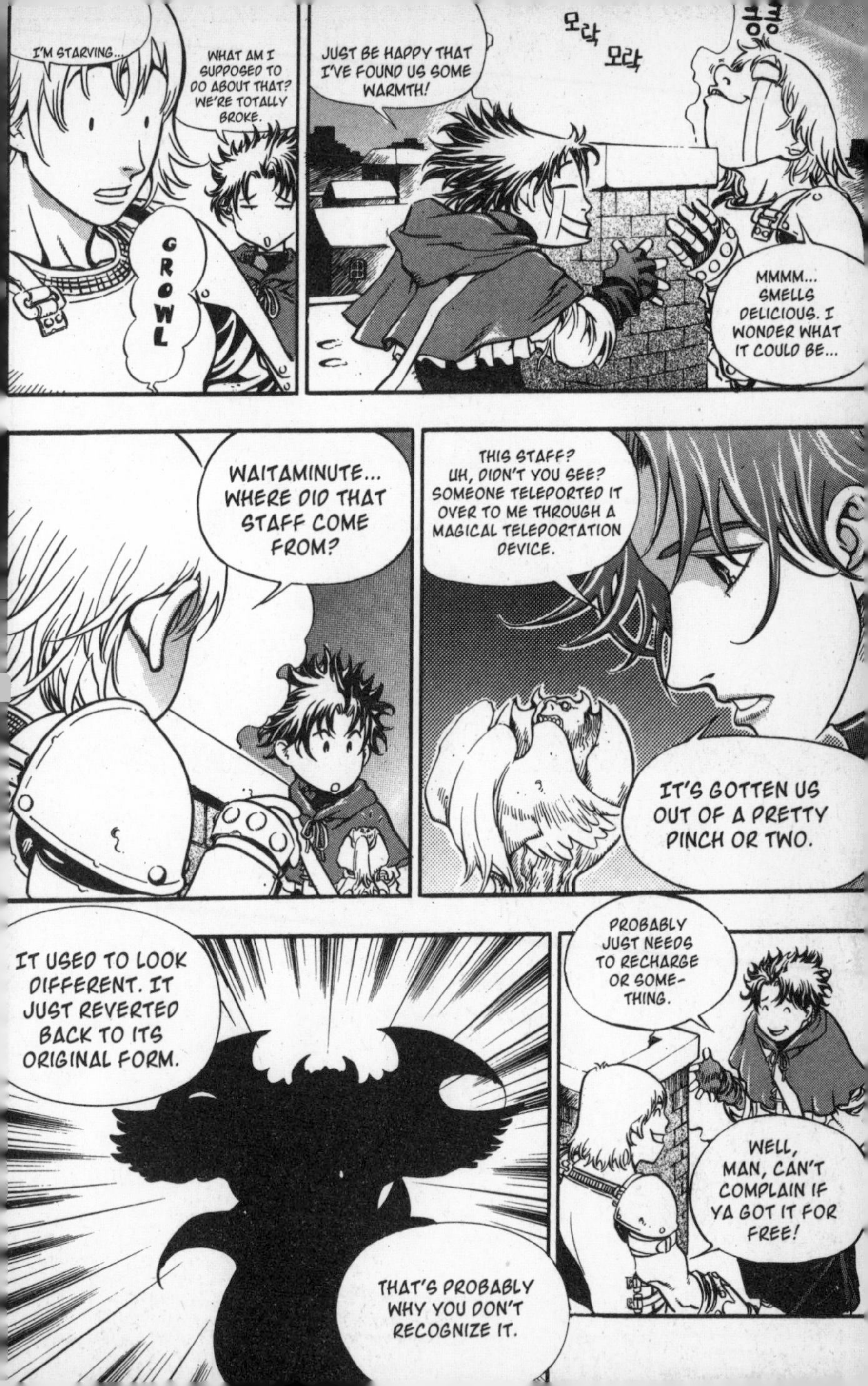

I'M STARVING...
GROWL
WHAT AM I SUPPOSED TO DO ABOUT THAT? WE'RE TOTALLY BROKE.
JUST BE HAPPY THAT I'VE FOUND US SOME WARMTH!
모락 모락
킁킁
MMMM... SMELLS DELICIOUS. I WONDER WHAT IT COULD BE...
WAITAMINUTE... WHERE DID THAT STAFF COME FROM?
THIS STAFF? UH, DIDN'T YOU SEE? SOMEONE TELEPORTED IT OVER TO ME THROUGH A MAGICAL TELEPORTATION DEVICE.
IT'S GOTTEN US OUT OF A PRETTY PINCH OR TWO.
IT USED TO LOOK DIFFERENT. IT JUST REVERTED BACK TO ITS ORIGINAL FORM.
THAT'S PROBABLY WHY YOU DON'T RECOGNIZE IT.
PROBABLY JUST NEEDS TO RECHARGE OR SOME-THING.
WELL, MAN, CAN'T COMPLAIN IF YA GOT IT FOR FREE!

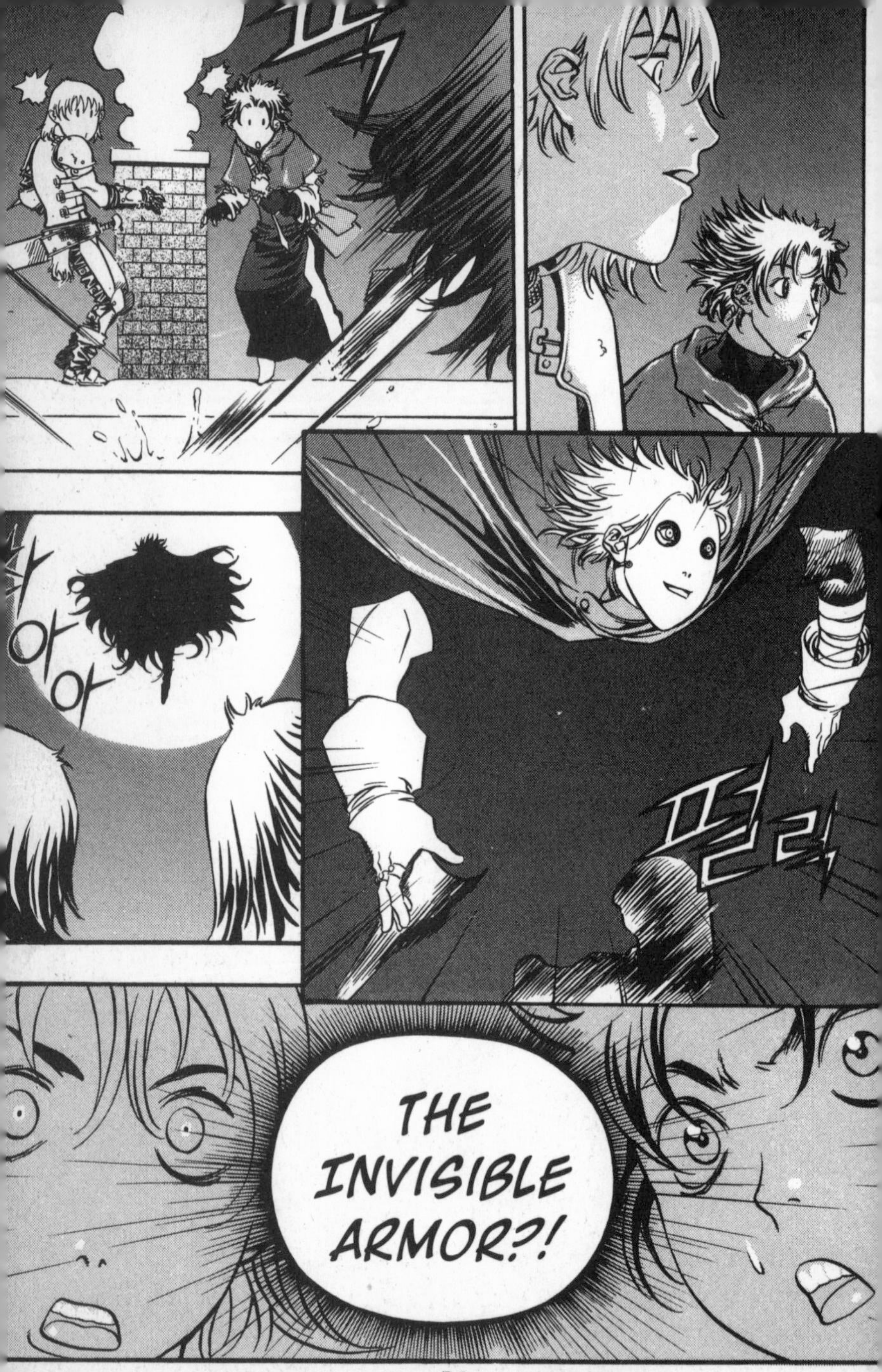
THE INVISIBLE ARMOR?!

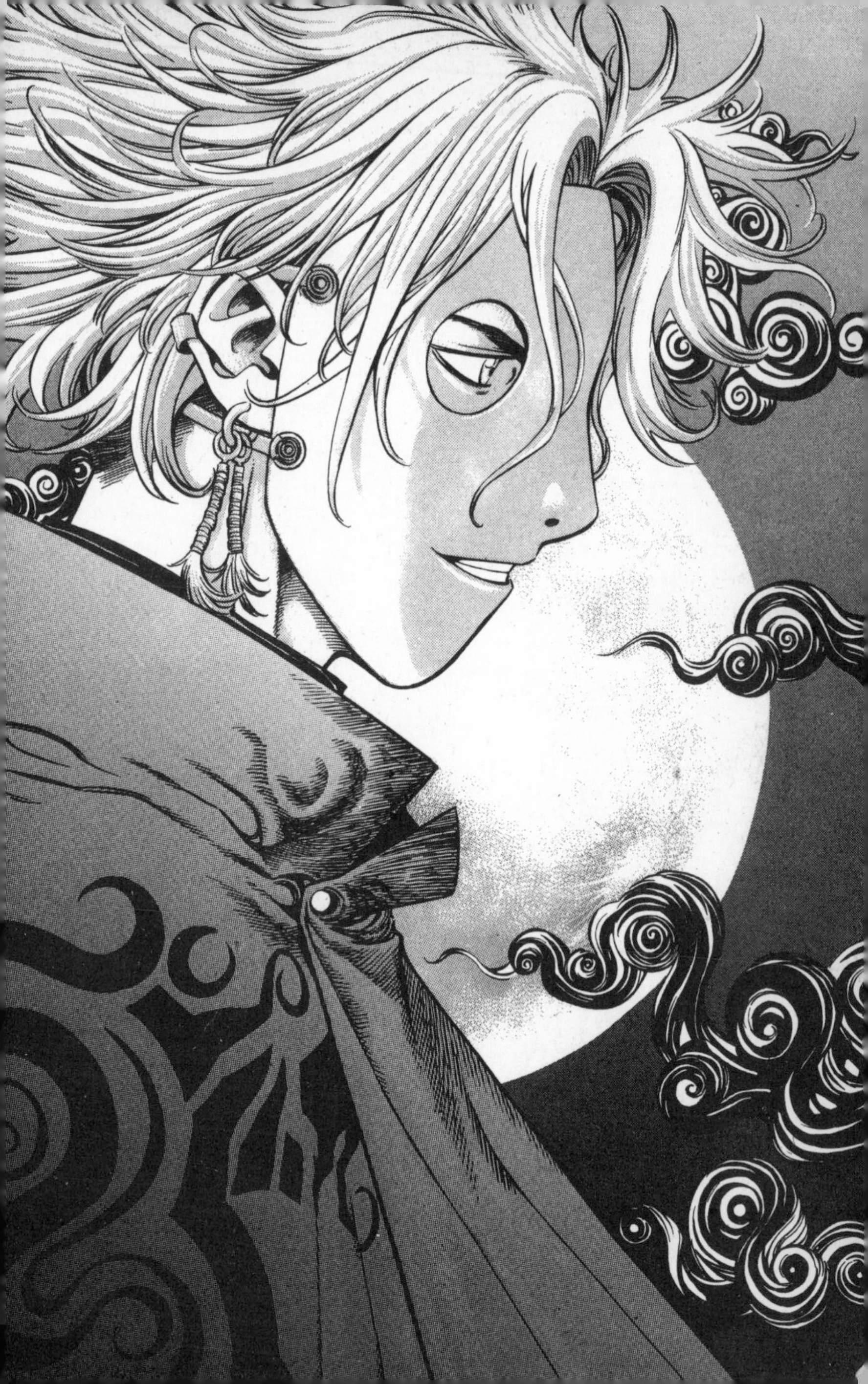

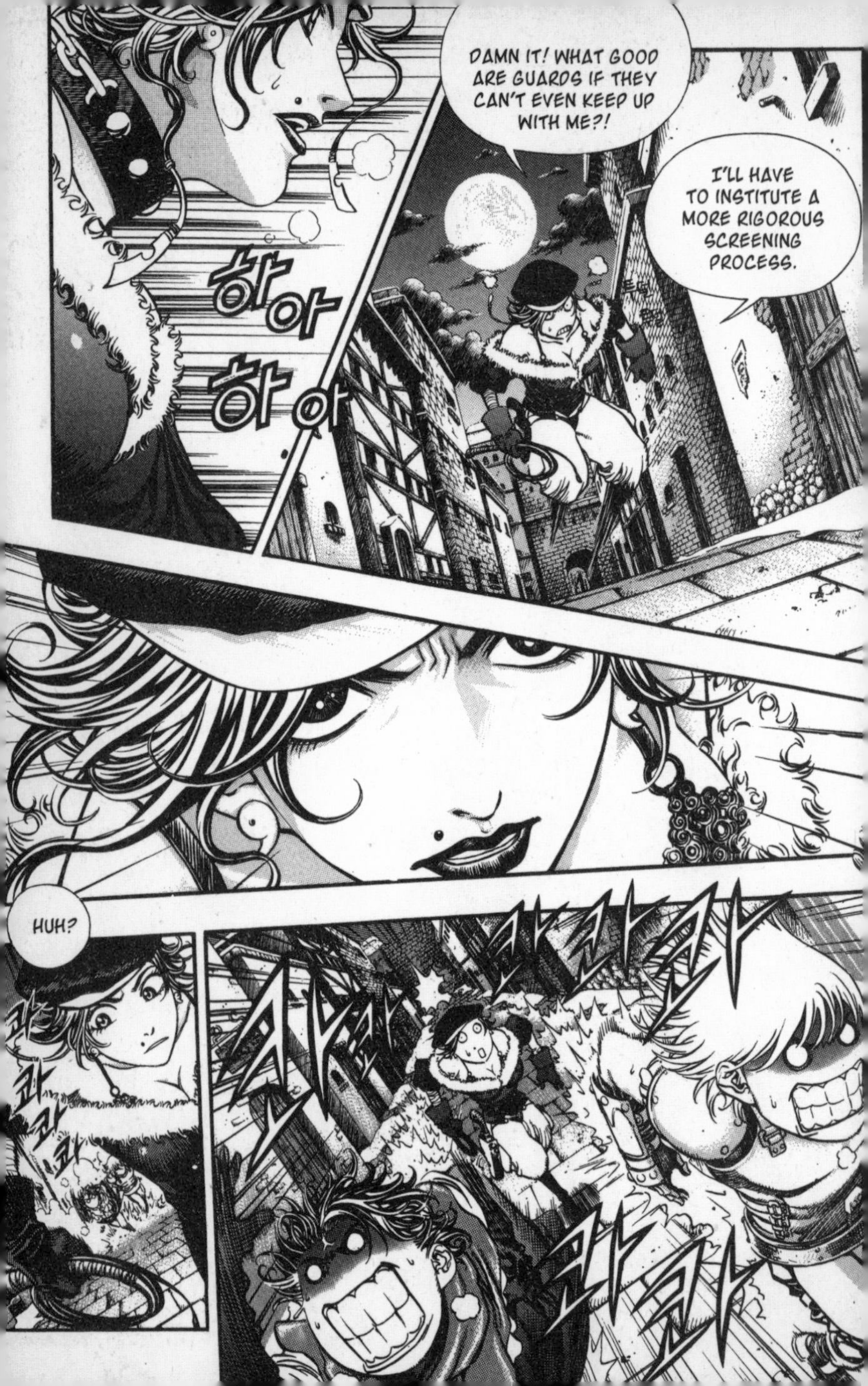
DAMN IT! WHAT GOOD ARE GUARDS IF THEY CAN'T EVEN KEEP UP WITH ME?!
I'LL HAVE TO INSTITUTE A MORE RIGOROUS SCREENING PROCESS.
하아
하아
HUH?

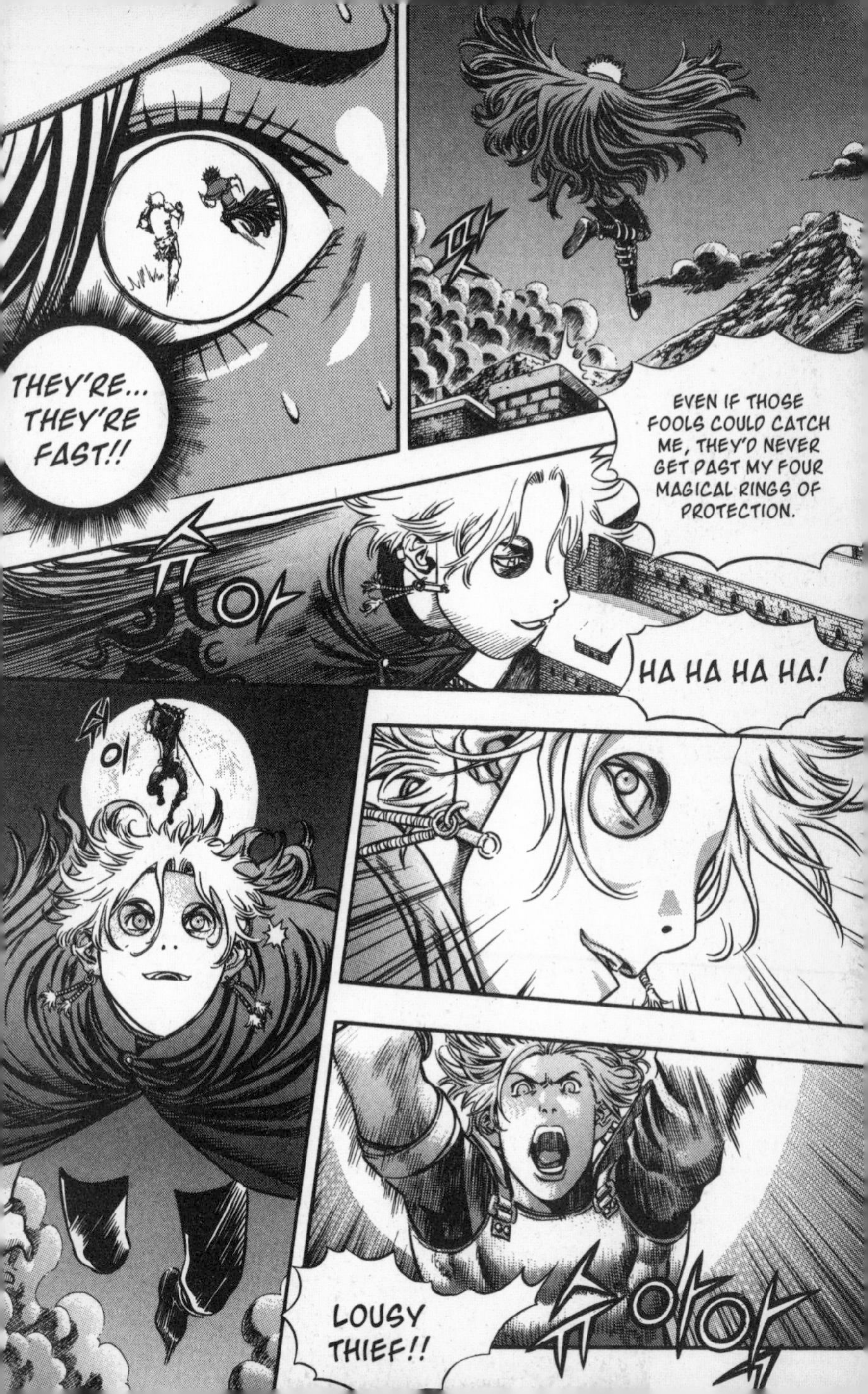
THEY'RE... THEY'RE FAST!!
EVEN IF THOSE FOOLS COULD CATCH ME, THEY'D NEVER GET PAST MY FOUR MAGICAL RINGS OF PROTECTION.
HA HA HA HA!
LOUSY THIEF!!

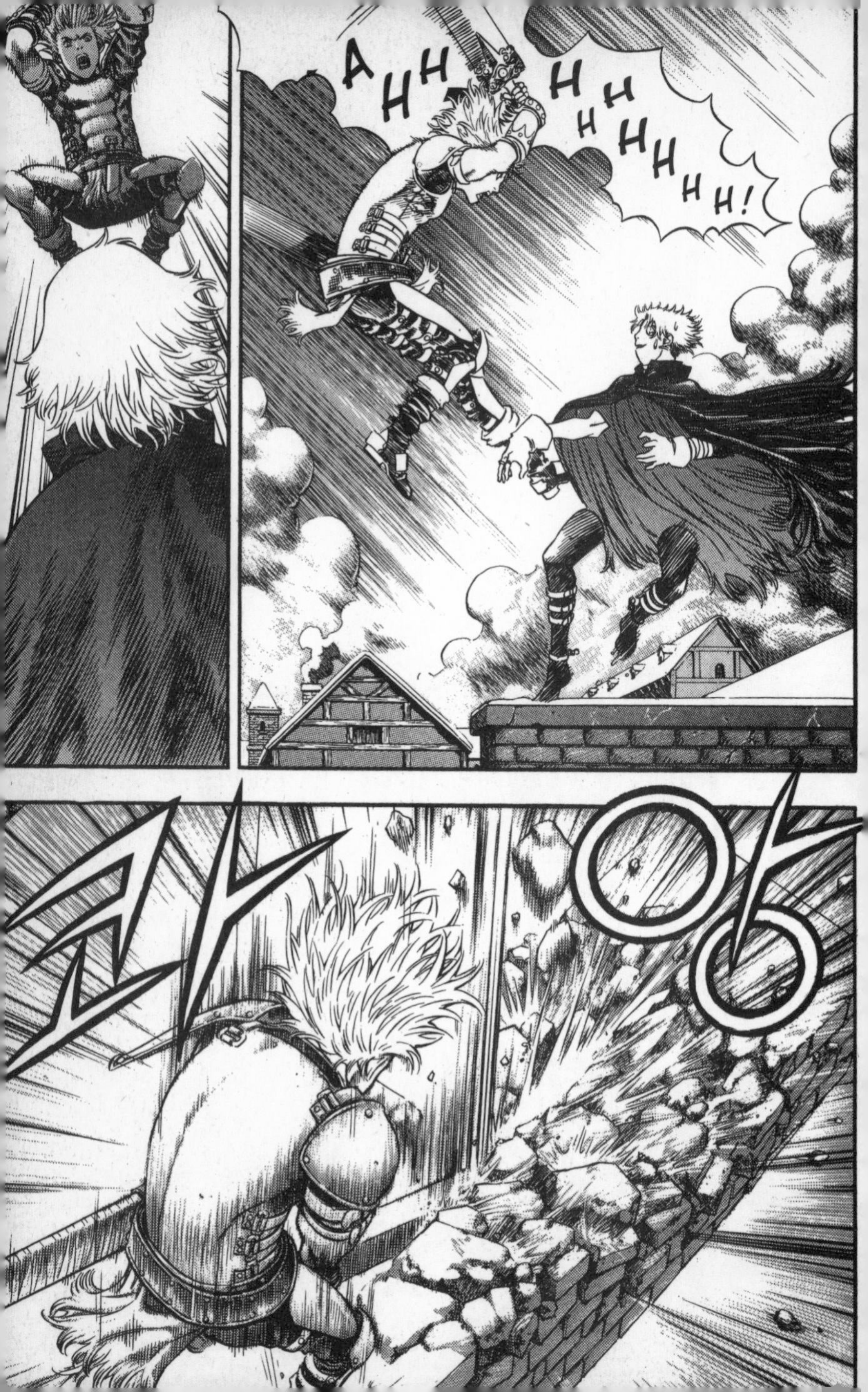
AHHHHHHHHHHH!

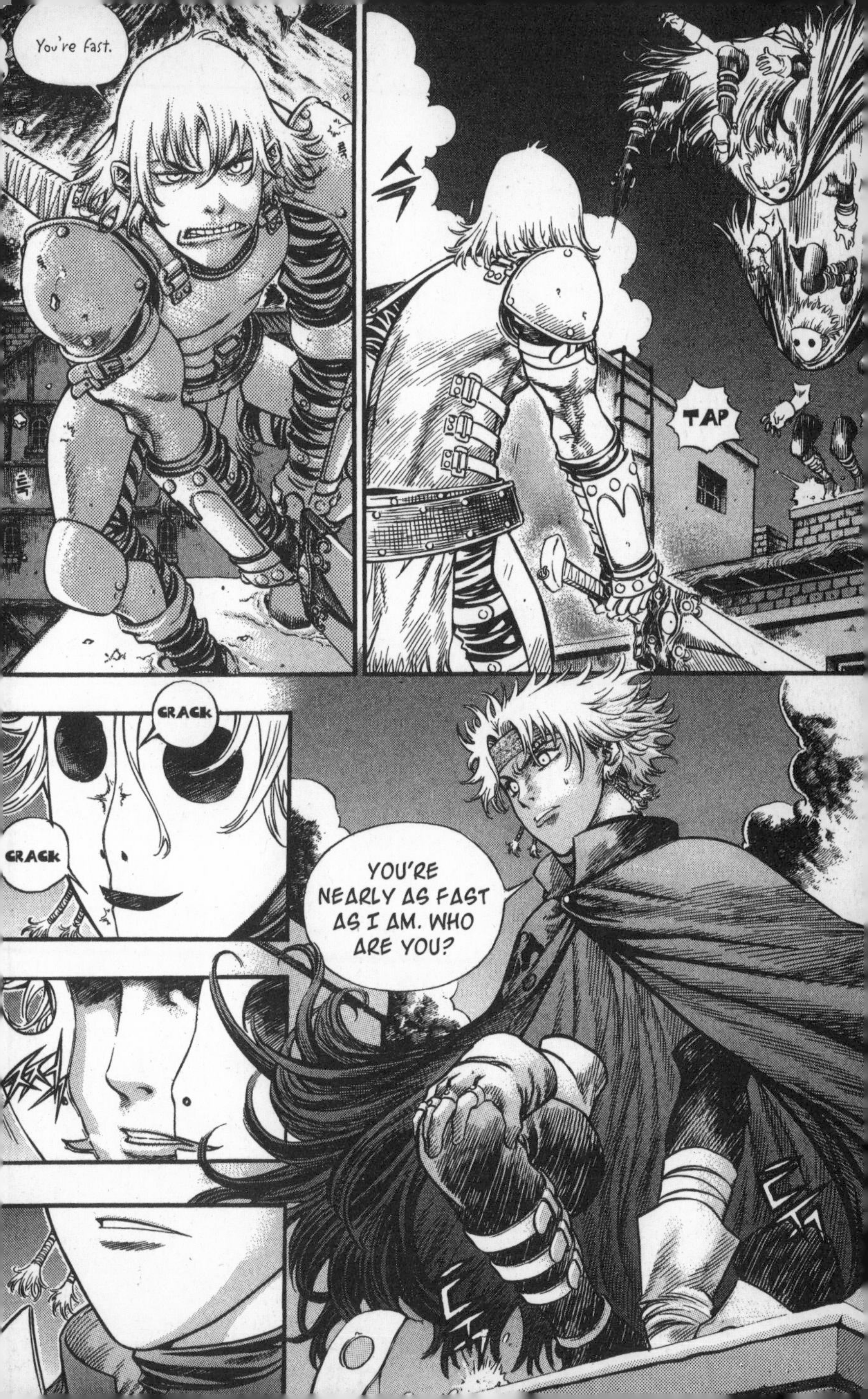
You're fast.
TAP
CRACK
CRACK
YOU'RE NEARLY AS FAST AS I AM. WHO ARE YOU?

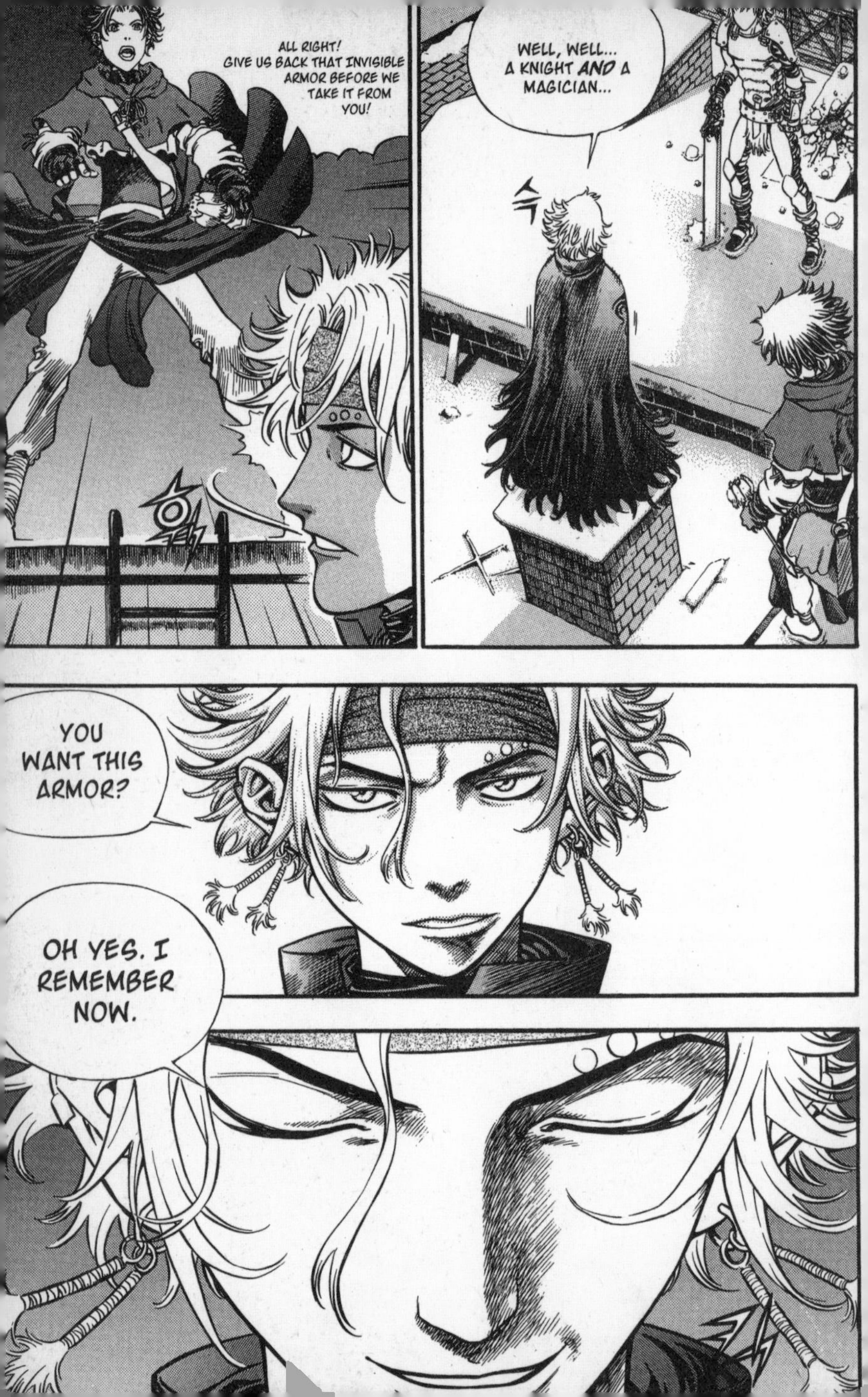
ALL RIGHT! GIVE US BACK THAT INVISIBLE ARMOR BEFORE WE TAKE IT FROM YOU!
WELL, WELL... A KNIGHT AND A MAGICIAN...
YOU WANT THIS ARMOR?
OH YES. I REMEMBER NOW.

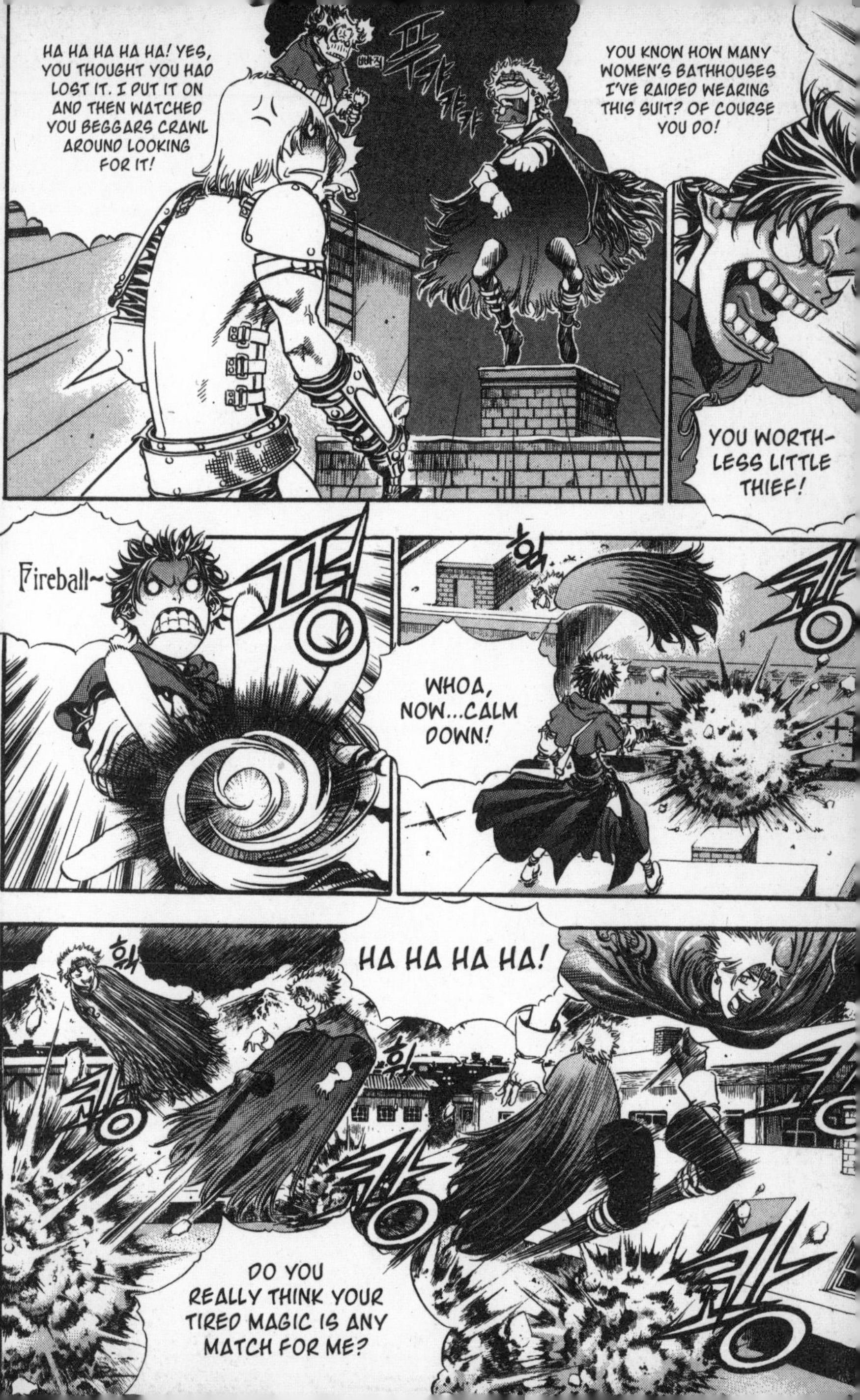
HA HA HA HA HA! YES, YOU THOUGHT YOU HAD LOST IT. I PUT IT ON AND THEN WATCHED YOU BEGGARS CRAWL AROUND LOOKING FOR IT!
YOU KNOW HOW MANY WOMEN'S BATHHOUSES I'VE RAIDED WEARING THIS SUIT? OF COURSE YOU DO!
YOU WORTHLESS LITTLE THIEF!
Fireball~
WHOA, NOW...CALM DOWN!
HA HA HA HA!
DO YOU REALLY THINK YOUR TIRED MAGIC IS ANY MATCH FOR ME?

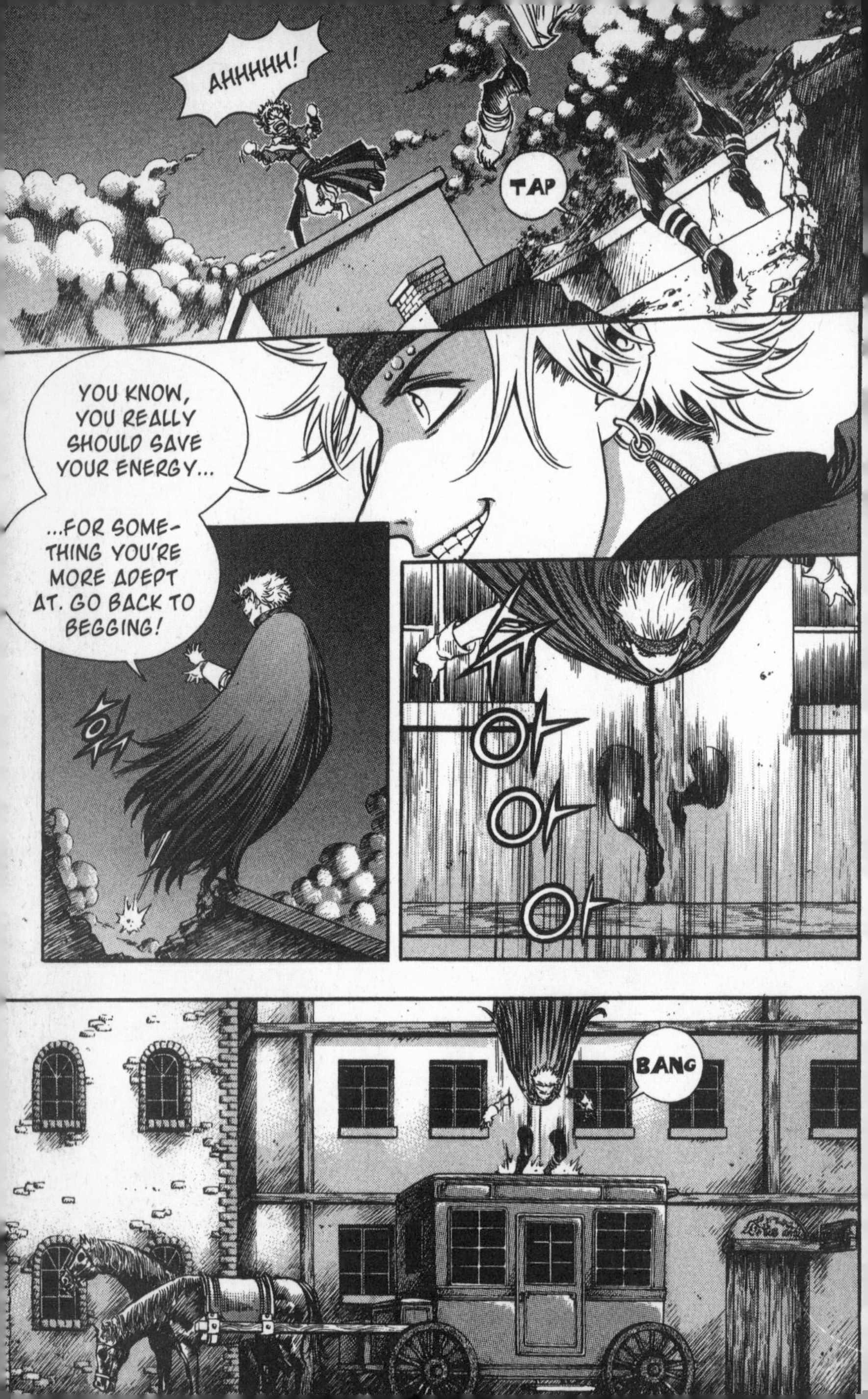
AHHHHH!
TAP
YOU KNOW, YOU REALLY SHOULD SAVE YOUR ENERGY...
...FOR SOME-THING YOU'RE MORE ADEPT AT. GO BACK TO BEGGING!
BANG

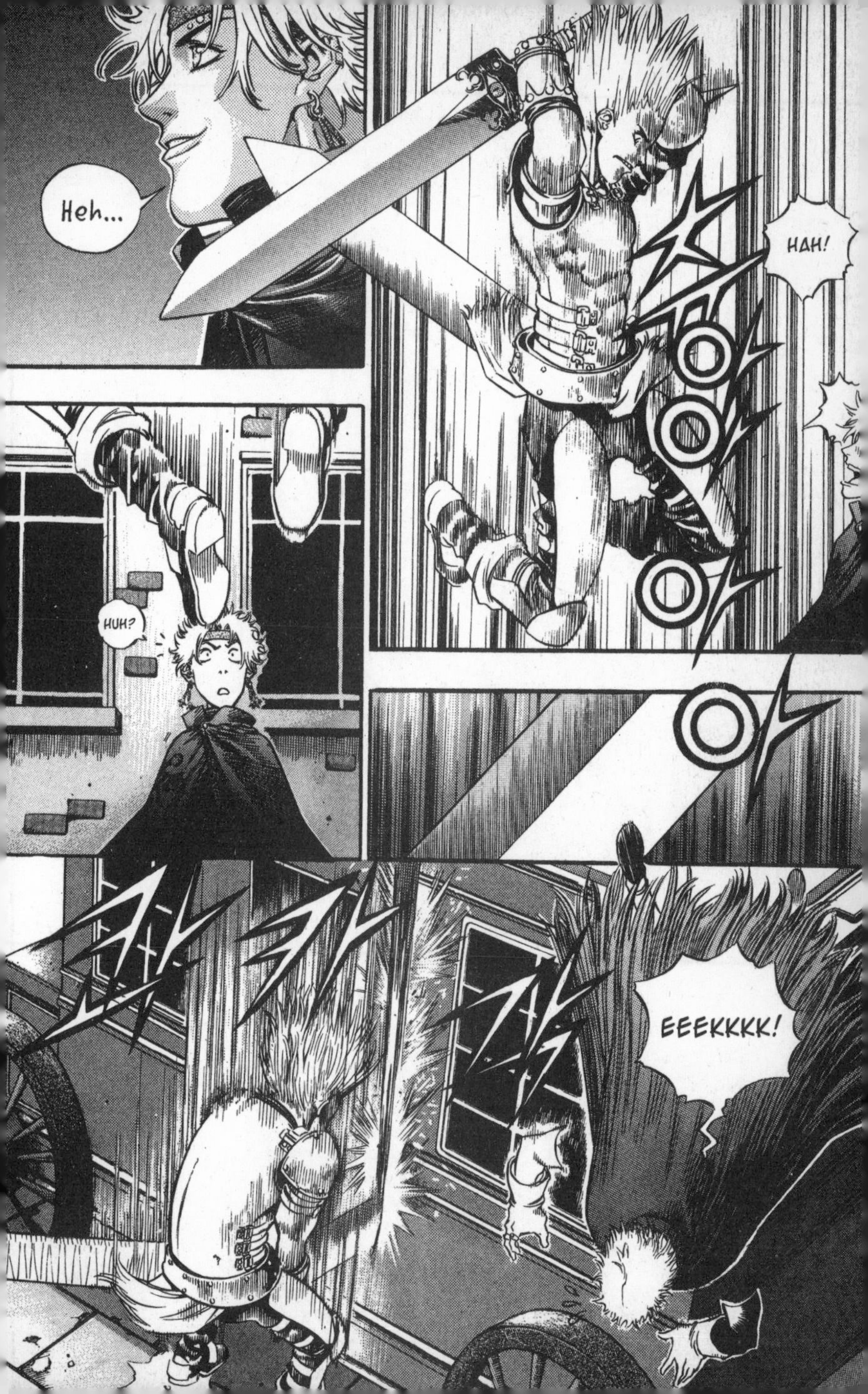
Heh...
HAH!
HUH?
EEEKKKK!

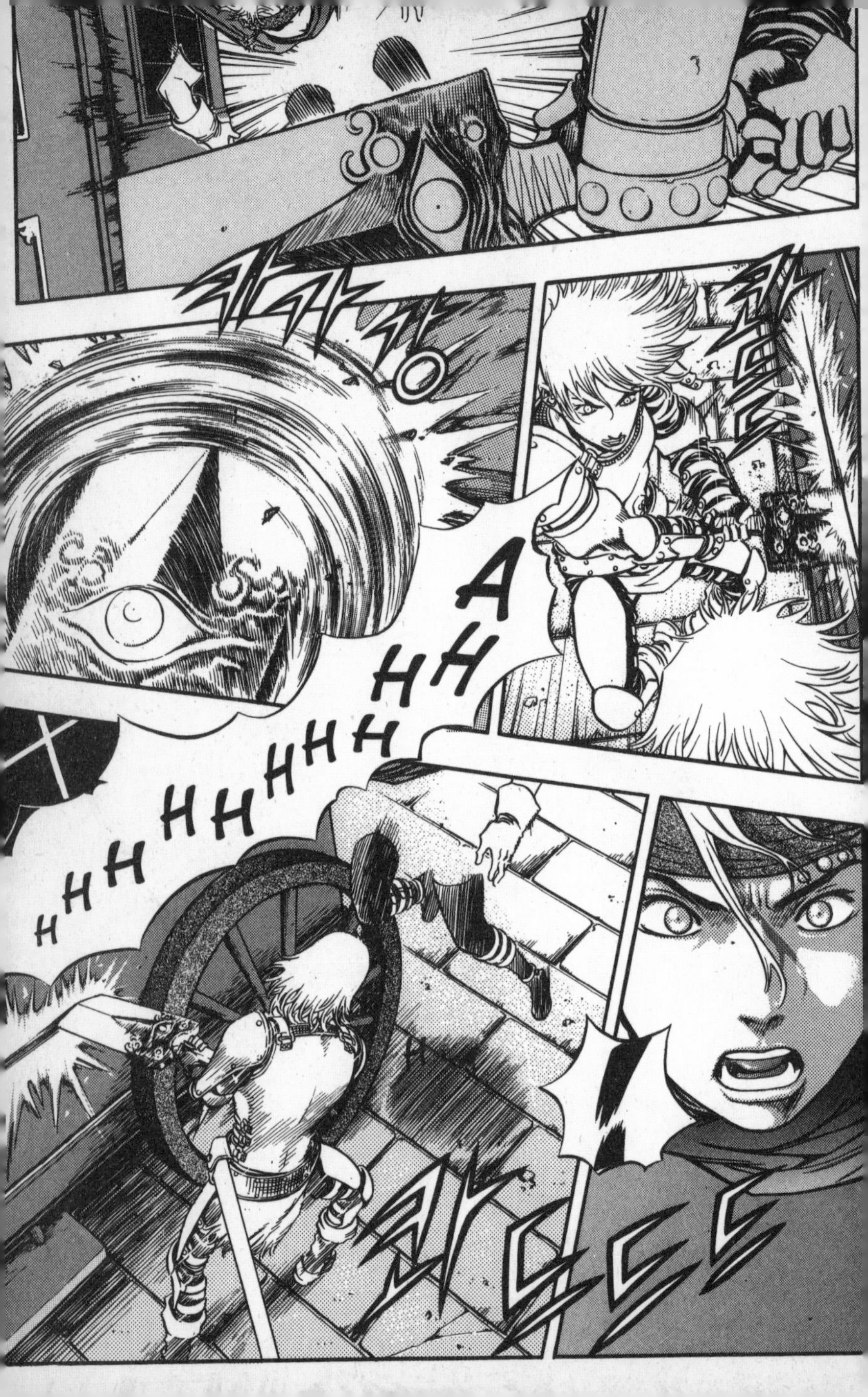
AHHHHHHHHHHHHHH

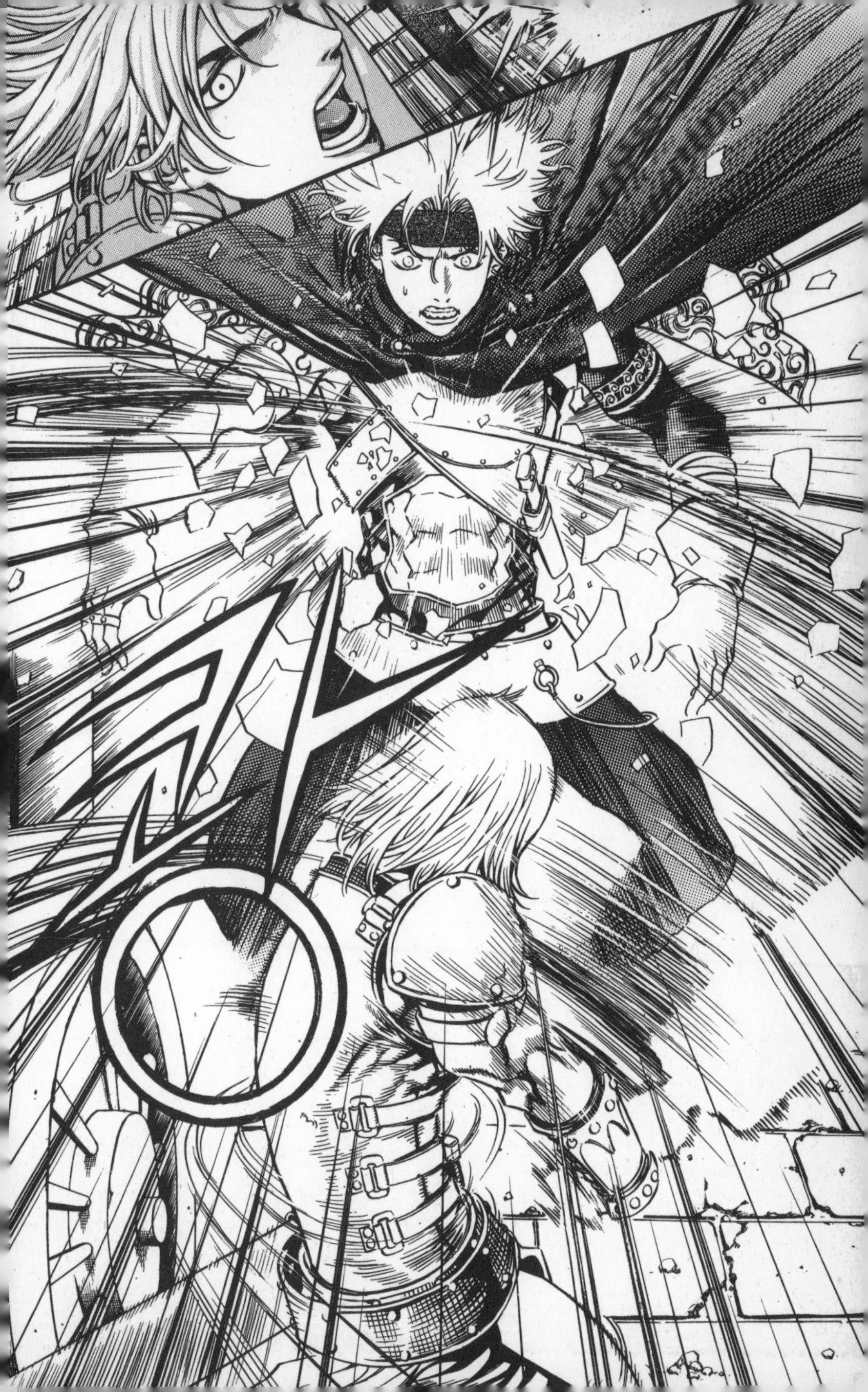

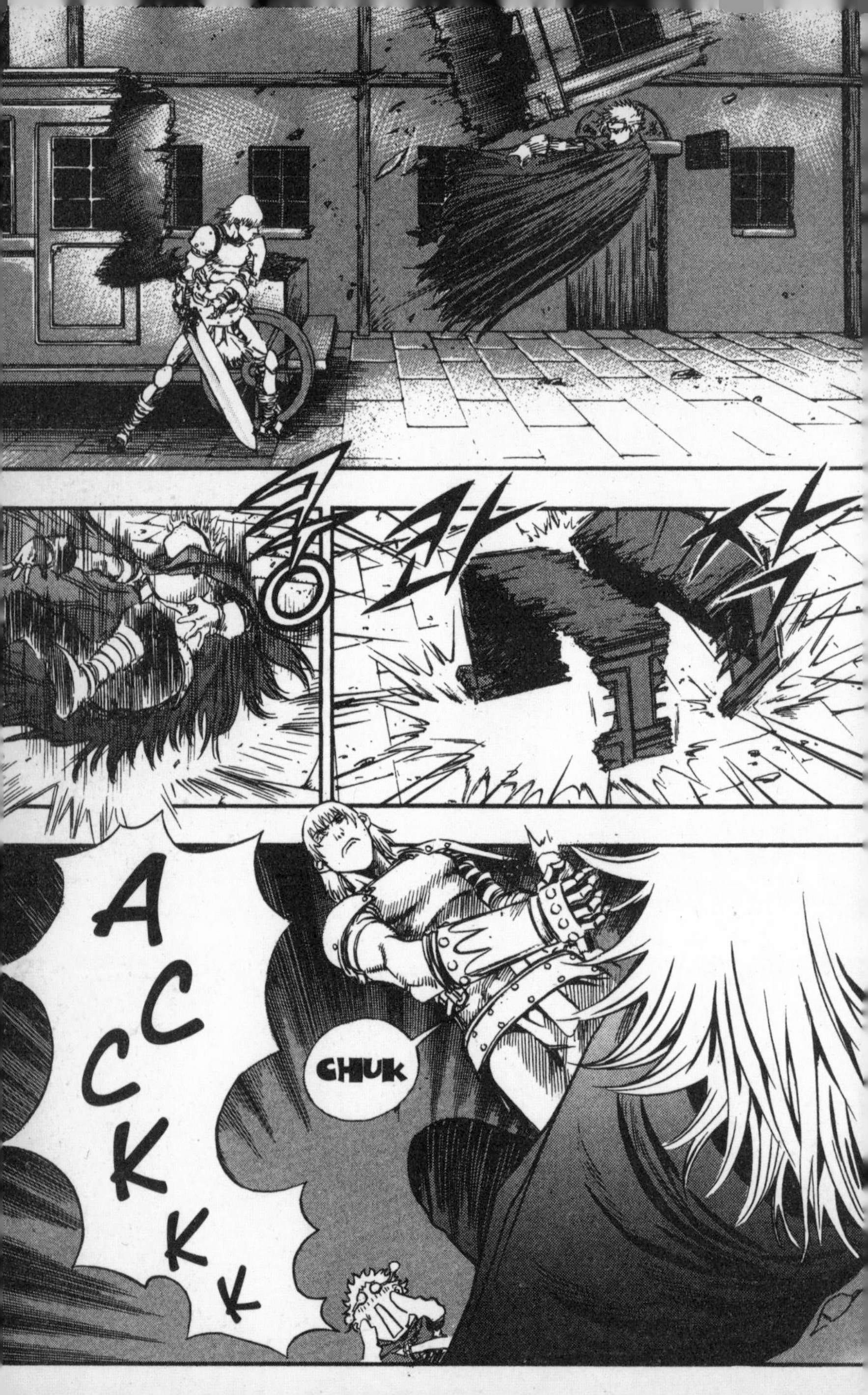
CHUK
ACCKKK

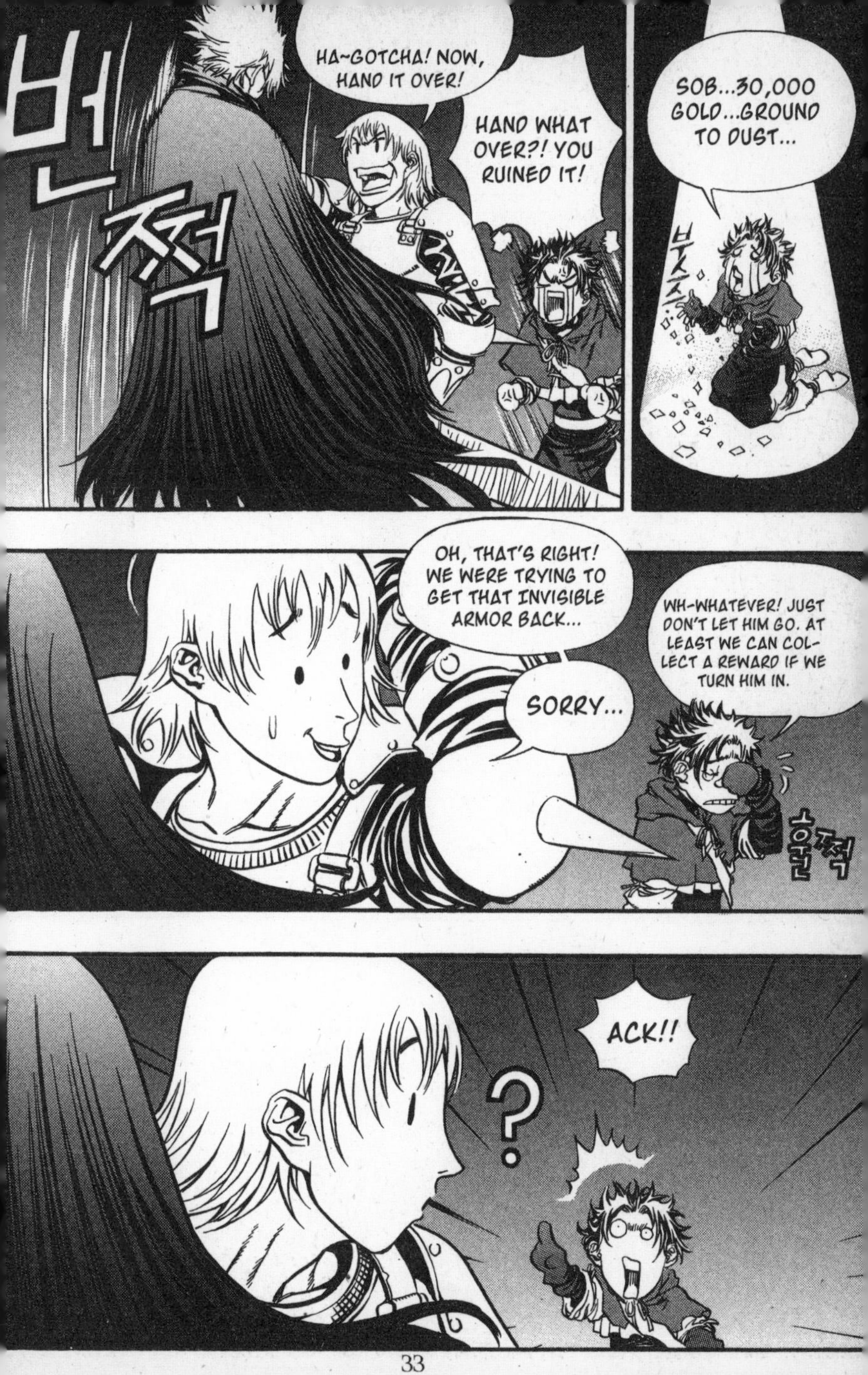

번쩍
HA~GOTCHA! NOW, HAND IT OVER!
HAND WHAT OVER?! YOU RUINED IT!
SOB...30,000 GOLD...GROUND TO DUST...
OH, THAT'S RIGHT! WE WERE TRYING TO GET THAT INVISIBLE ARMOR BACK...
SORRY...
WH-WHATEVER! JUST DON'T LET HIM GO. AT LEAST WE CAN COLLECT A REWARD IF WE TURN HIM IN.
훌쩍
?
ACK!!

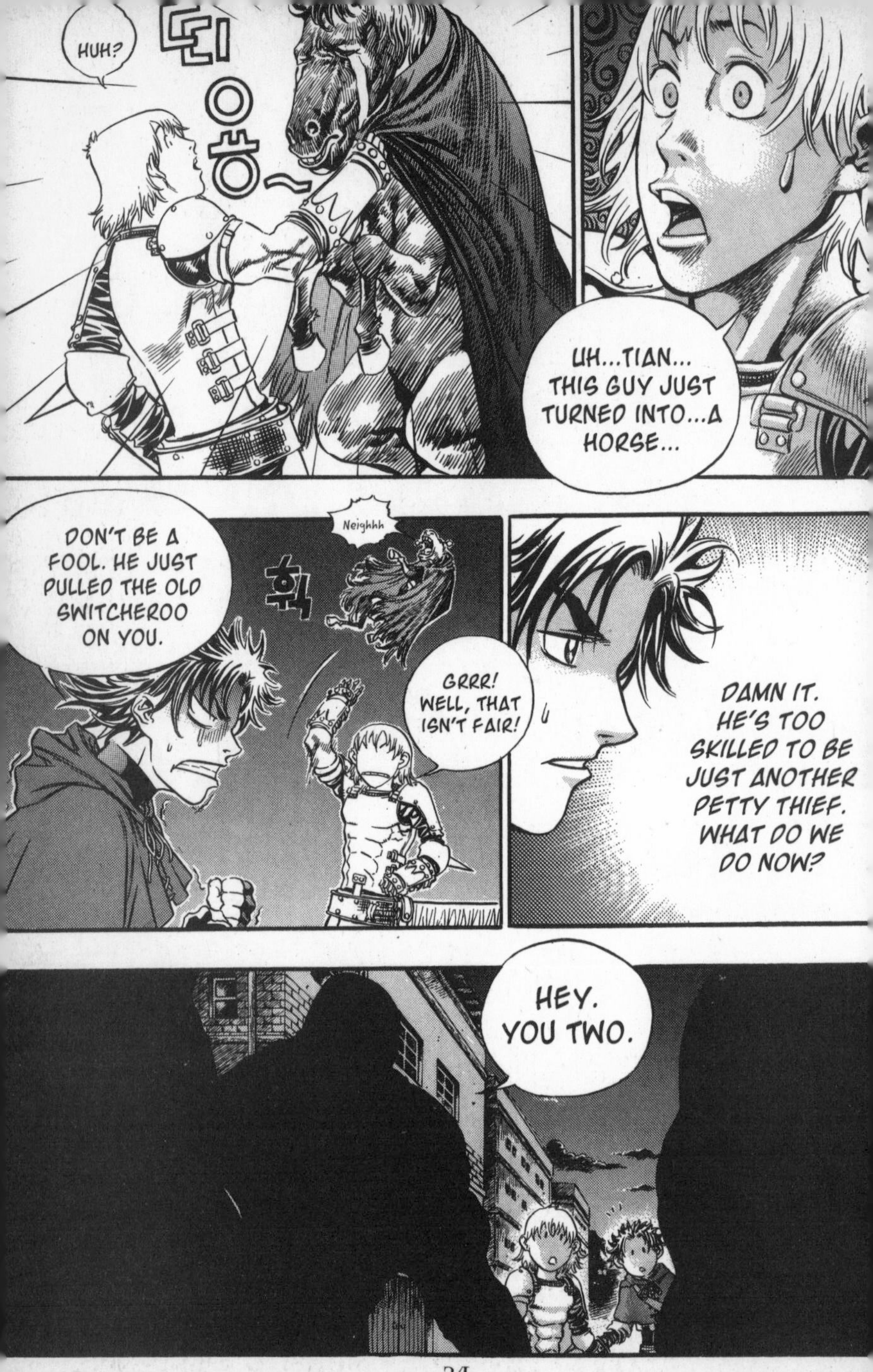
HUH?
띠용~
UH...TIAN... THIS GUY JUST TURNED INTO...A HORSE...
DON'T BE A FOOL. HE JUST PULLED THE OLD SWITCHEROO ON YOU.
Neighhh
휙
GRRR! WELL, THAT ISN'T FAIR!
DAMN IT. HE'S TOO SKILLED TO BE JUST ANOTHER PETTY THIEF. WHAT DO WE DO NOW?
HEY. YOU TWO.

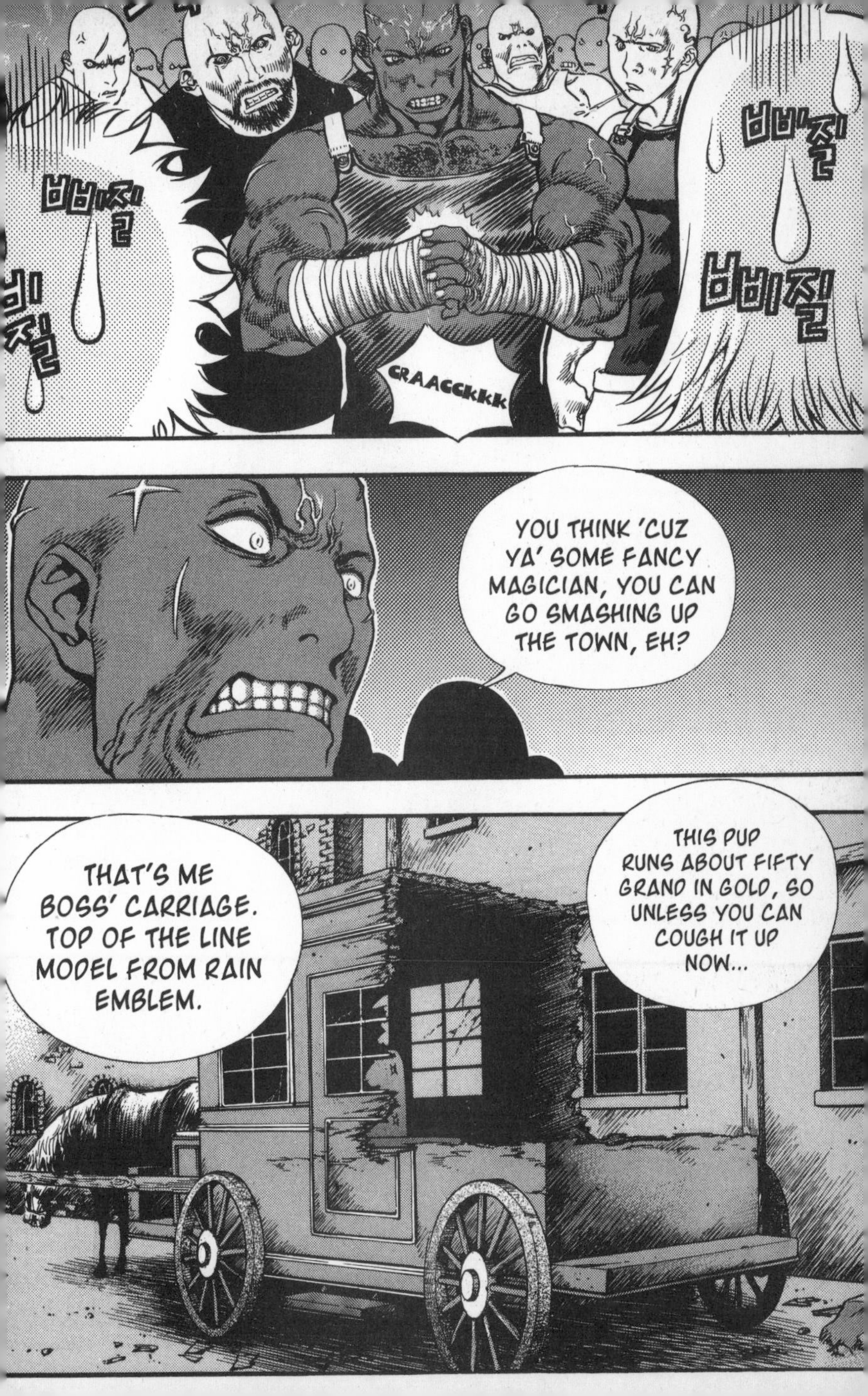
CRAACCKKKK
YOU THINK 'CUZ YA' SOME FANCY MAGICIAN, YOU CAN GO SMASHING UP THE TOWN, EH?
THAT'S ME BOSS' CARRIAGE. TOP OF THE LINE MODEL FROM RAIN EMBLEM.
THIS PUP RUNS ABOUT FIFTY GRAND IN GOLD, SO UNLESS YOU CAN COUGH IT UP NOW...

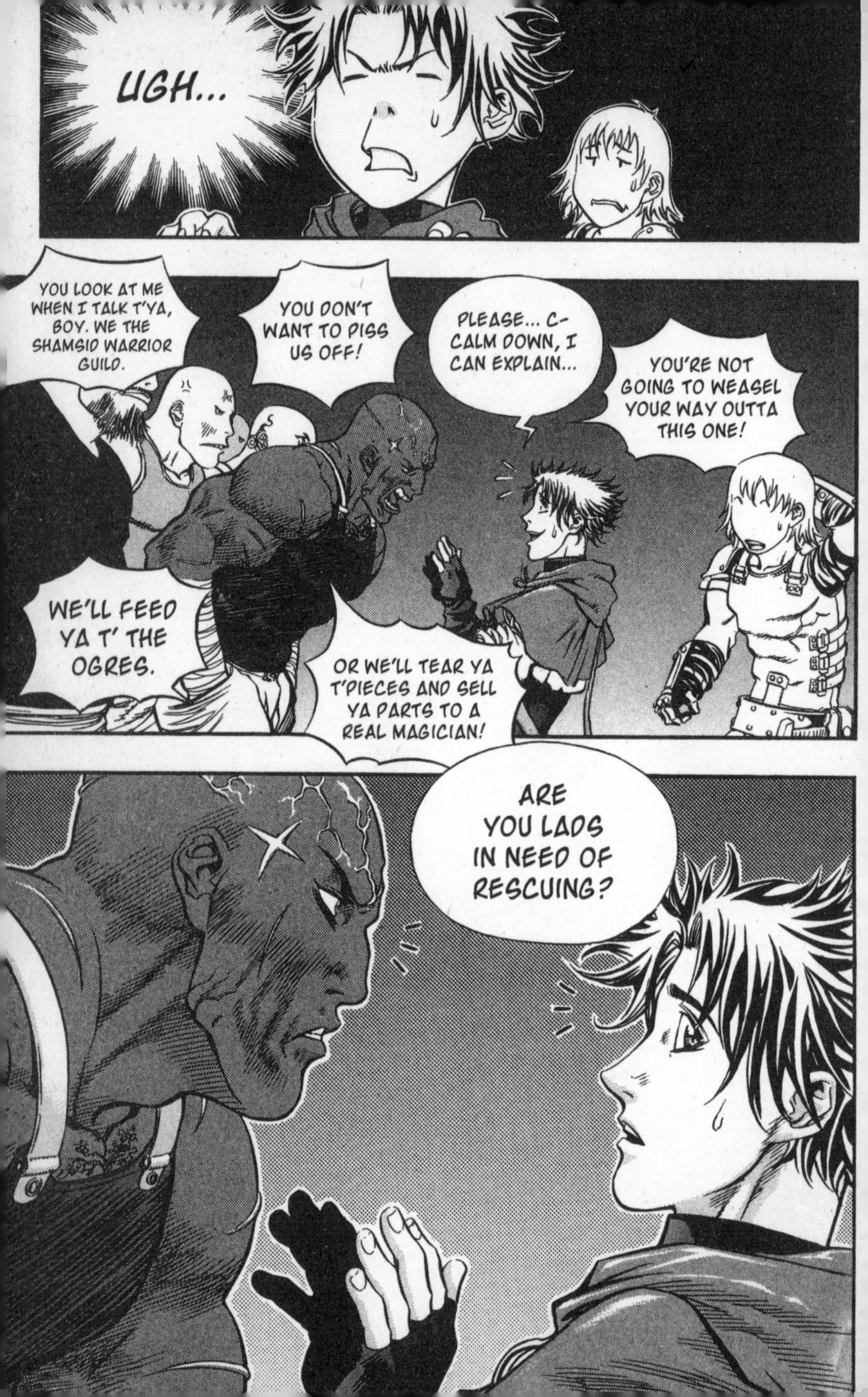
UGH...
YOU LOOK AT ME WHEN I TALK T'YA, BOY. WE THE SHAMSID WARRIOR GUILD.
YOU DON'T WANT TO PISS US OFF!
PLEASE... C-CALM DOWN, I CAN EXPLAIN...
YOU'RE NOT GOING TO WEASEL YOUR WAY OUTTA THIS ONE!
WE'LL FEED YA T' THE OGRES.
OR WE'LL TEAR YA T'PIECES AND SELL YA PARTS TO A REAL MAGICIAN!
ARE YOU LADS IN NEED OF RESCUING?

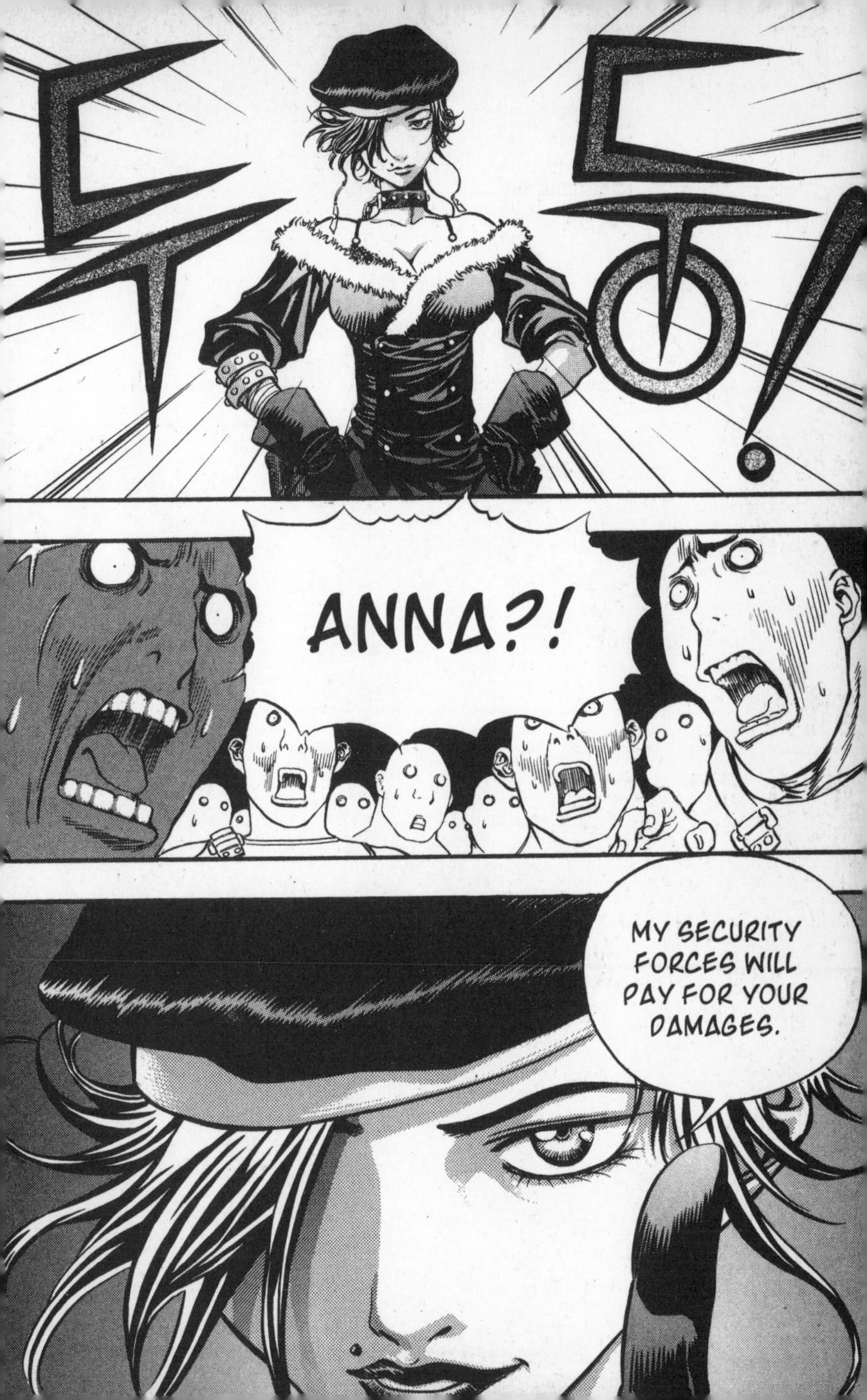
ANNA?!
MY SECURITY FORCES WILL PAY FOR YOUR DAMAGES.

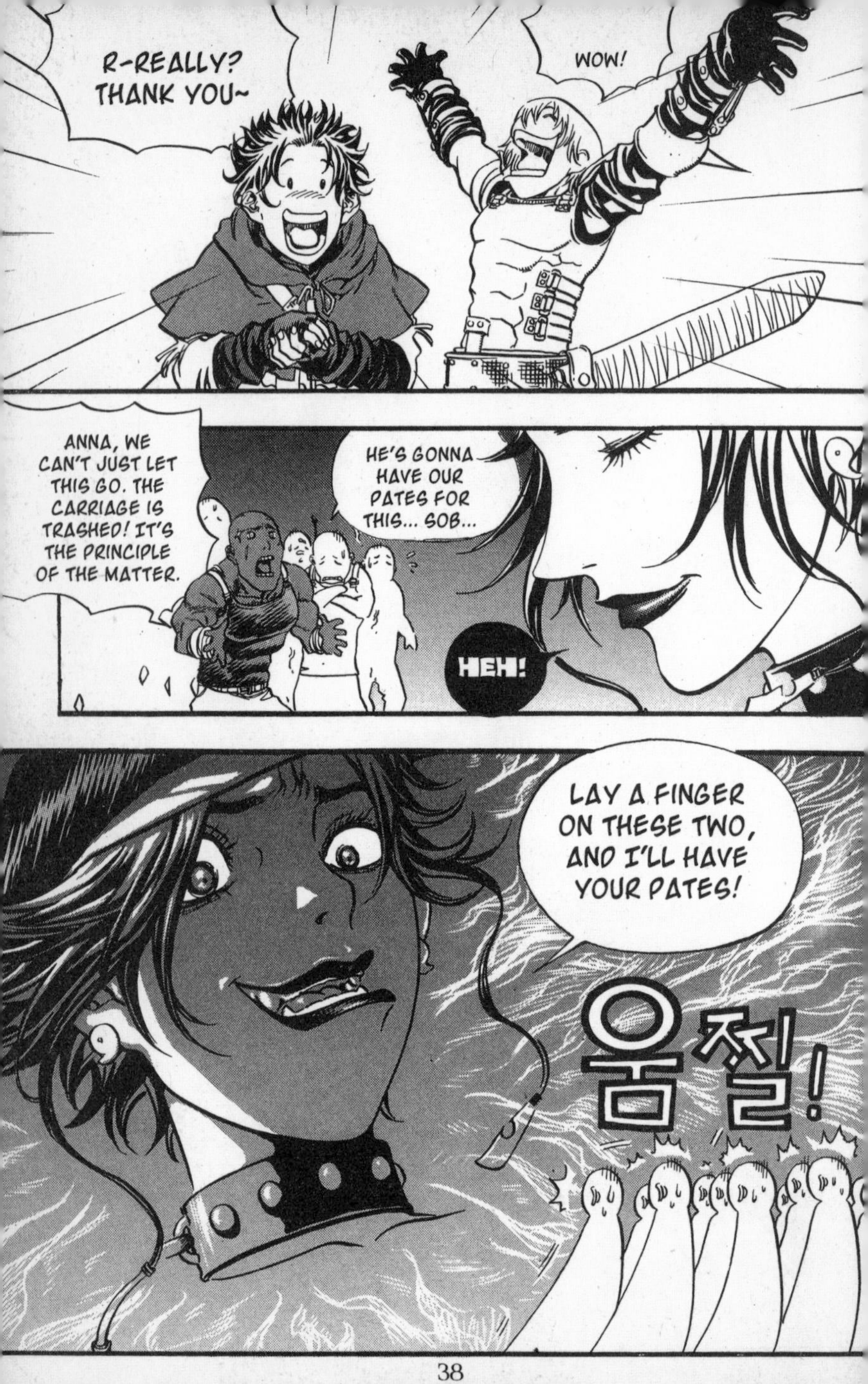
R-REALLY? THANK YOU~
WOW!
ANNA, WE CAN'T JUST LET THIS GO. THE CARRIAGE IS TRASHED! IT'S THE PRINCIPLE OF THE MATTER.
HE'S GONNA HAVE OUR PATES FOR THIS... SOB...
HEH!
LAY A FINGER ON THESE TWO, AND I'LL HAVE YOUR PATES!
움찔!

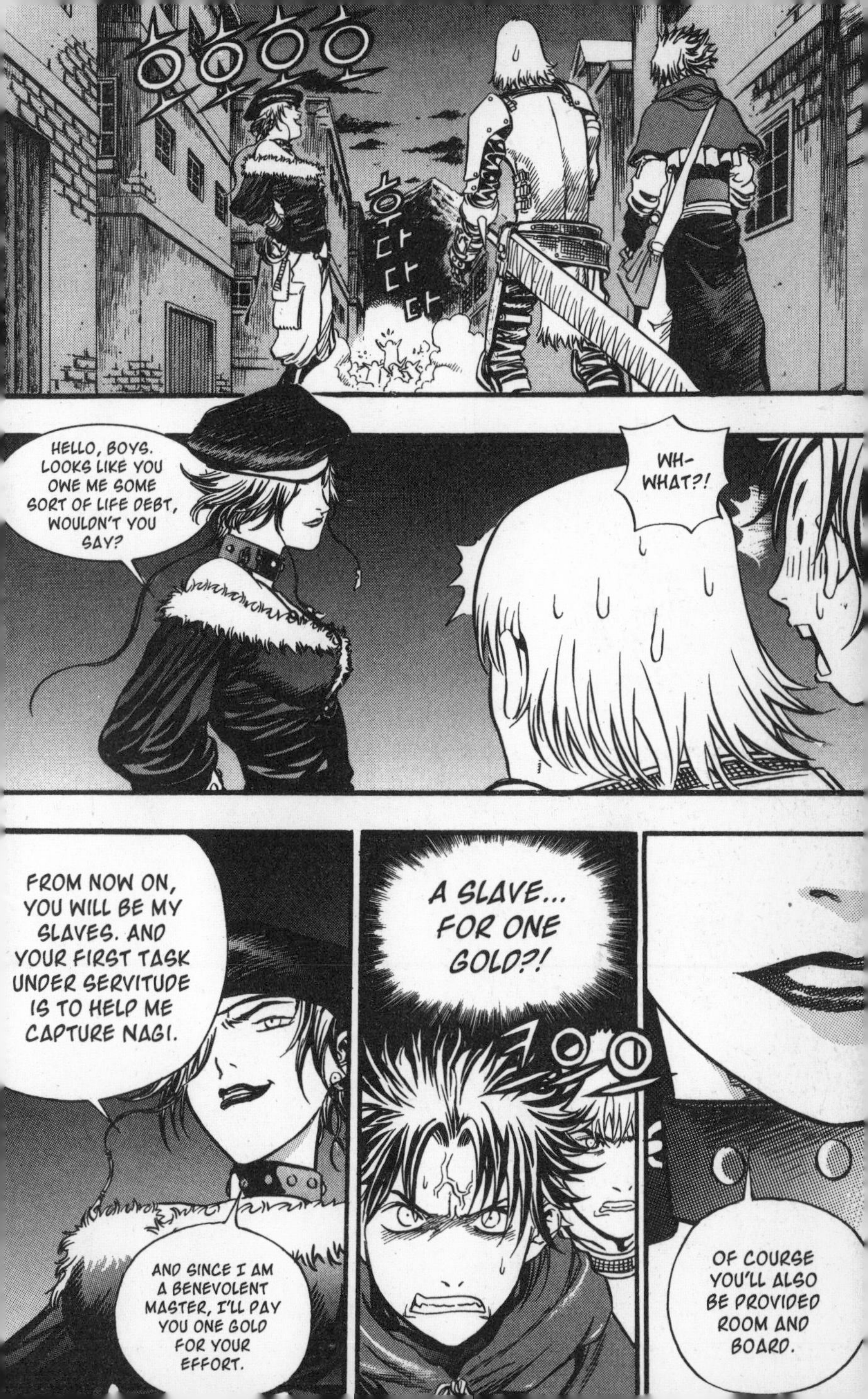
후다다다
HELLO, BOYS. LOOKS LIKE YOU OWE ME SOME SORT OF LIFE DEBT, WOULDN'T YOU SAY?
WH- WHAT?!
FROM NOW ON, YOU WILL BE MY SLAVES. AND YOUR FIRST TASK UNDER SERVITUDE IS TO HELP ME CAPTURE NAGI.
AND SINCE I AM A BENEVOLENT MASTER, I'LL PAY YOU ONE GOLD FOR YOUR EFFORT.
A SLAVE... FOR ONE GOLD?!
OF COURSE YOU'LL ALSO BE PROVIDED ROOM AND BOARD.

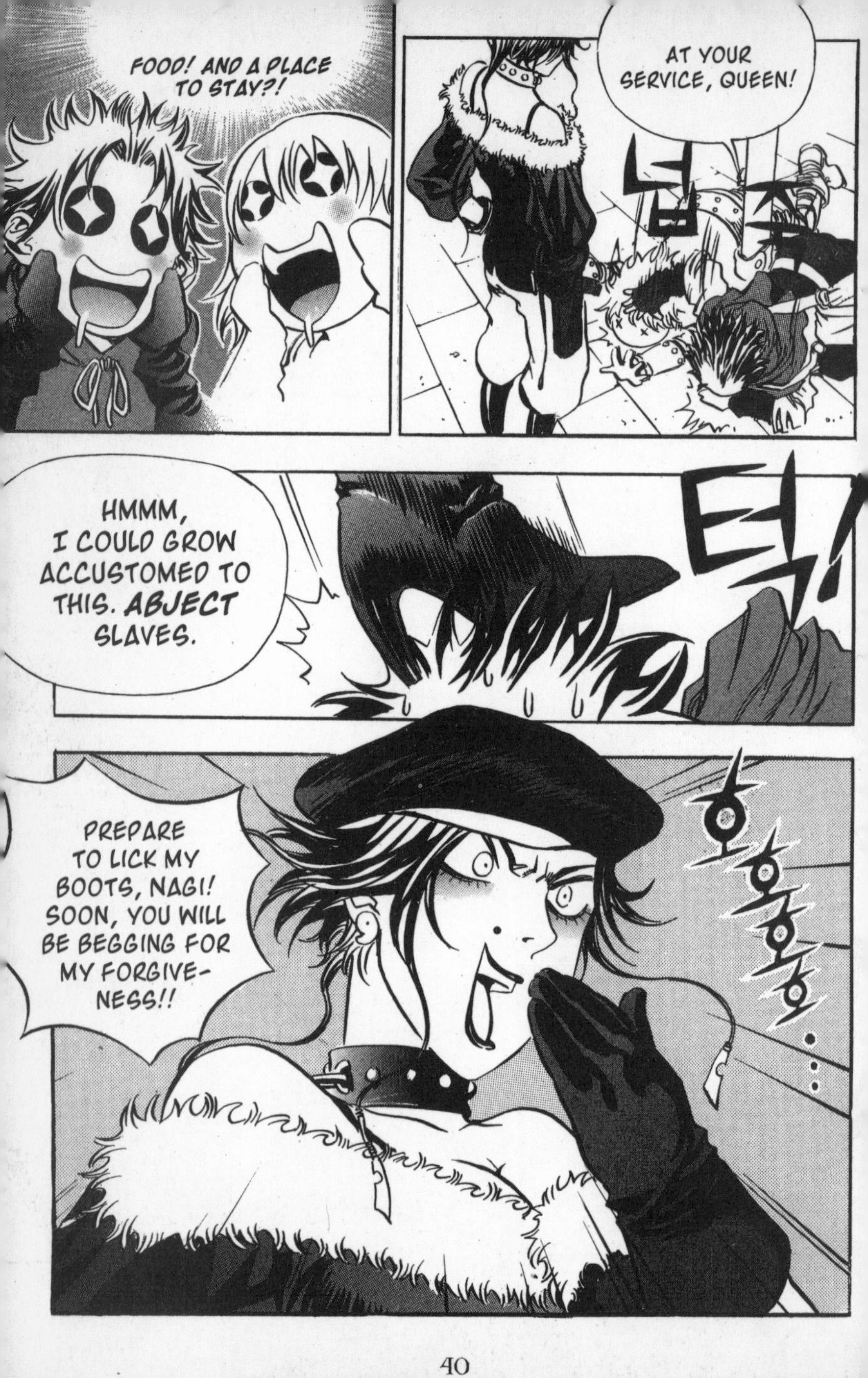
FOOD! AND A PLACE TO STAY?!
AT YOUR SERVICE, QUEEN!
넙죽
HMMM, I COULD GROW ACCUSTOMED TO THIS. **ABJECT** SLAVES.
턱!
PREPARE TO LICK MY BOOTS, NAGI! SOON, YOU WILL BE BEGGING FOR MY FORGIVE- NESS!!
호호호호...

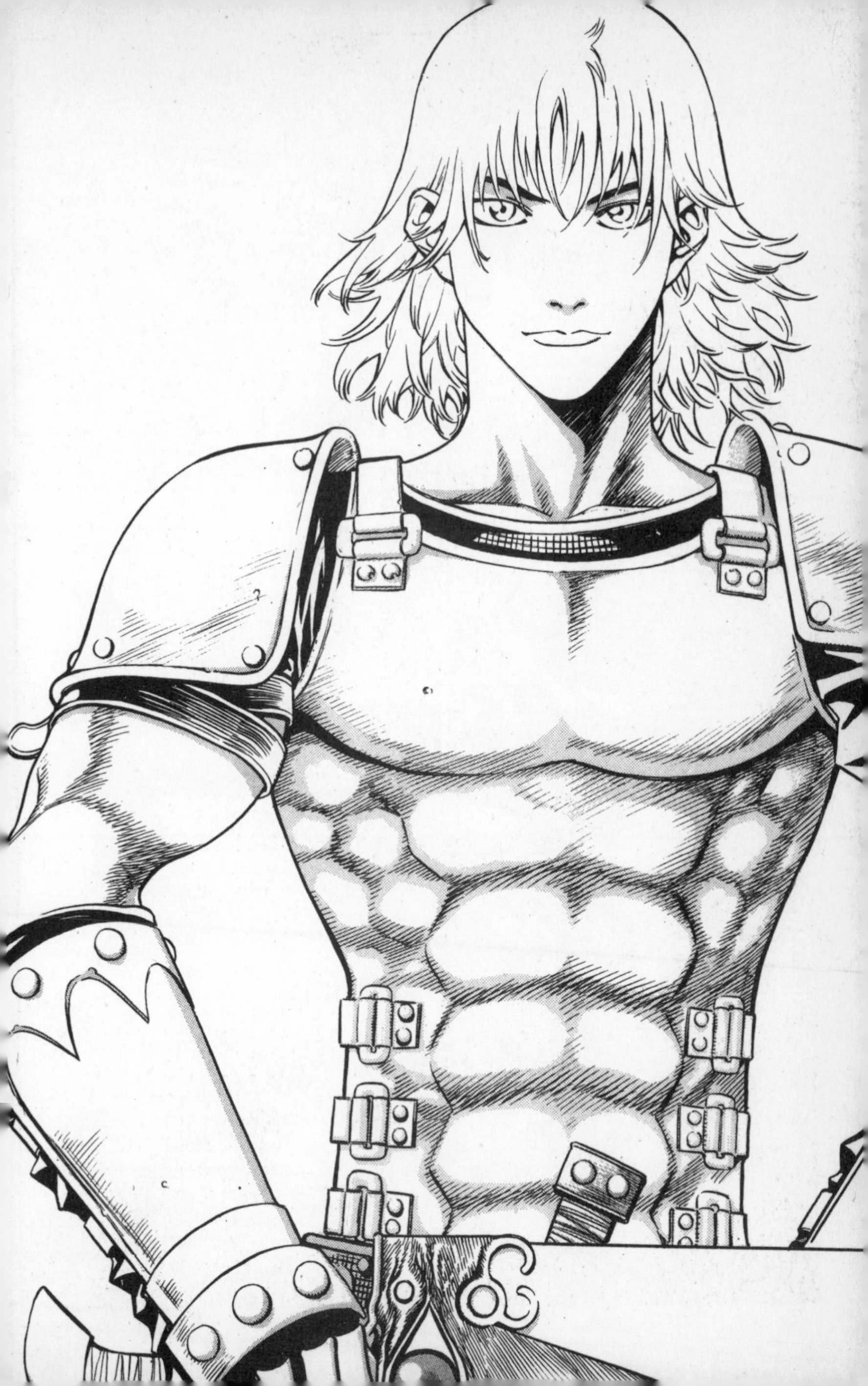

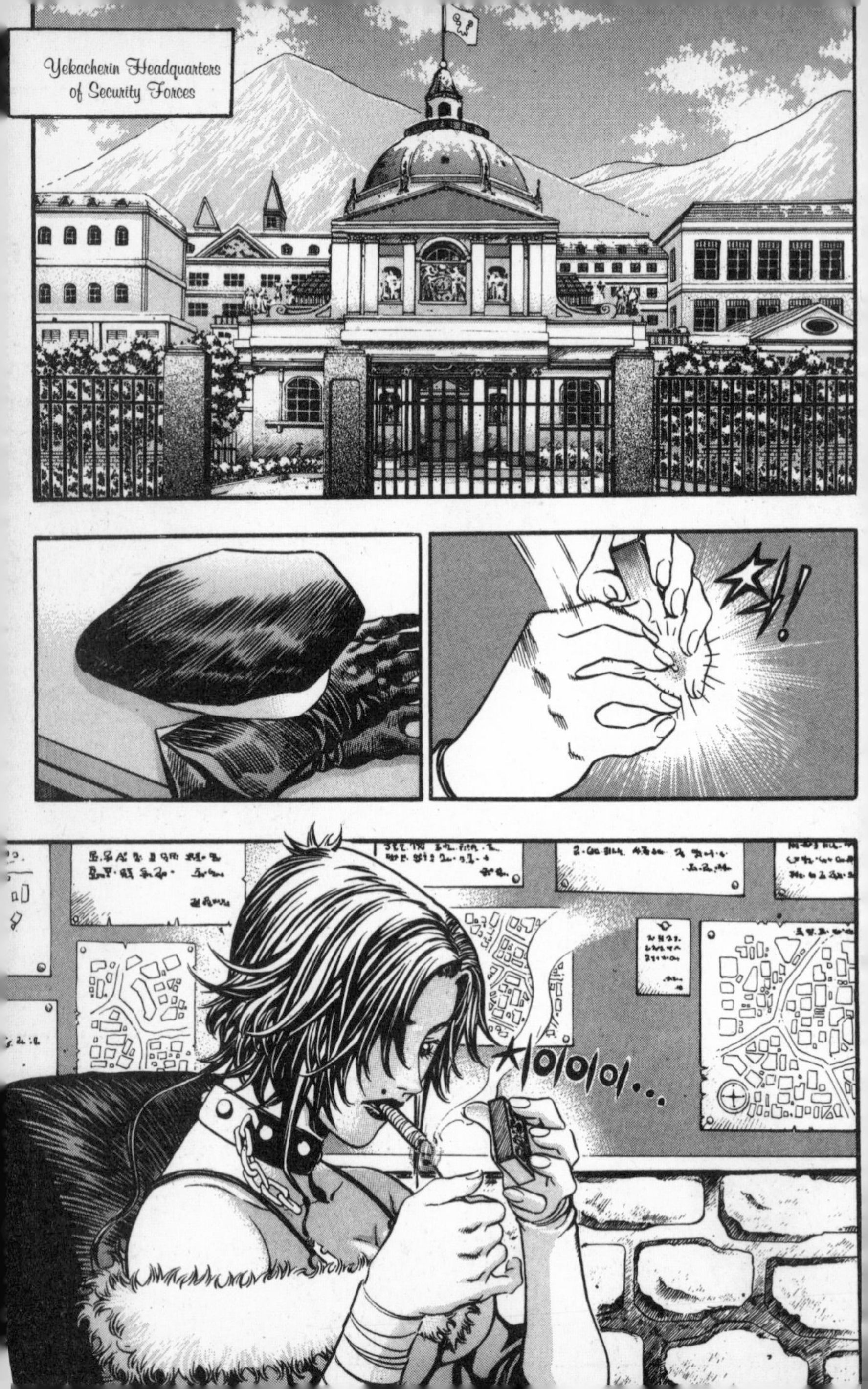
Yekacherin Headquarters of Security Forces
치이이이...

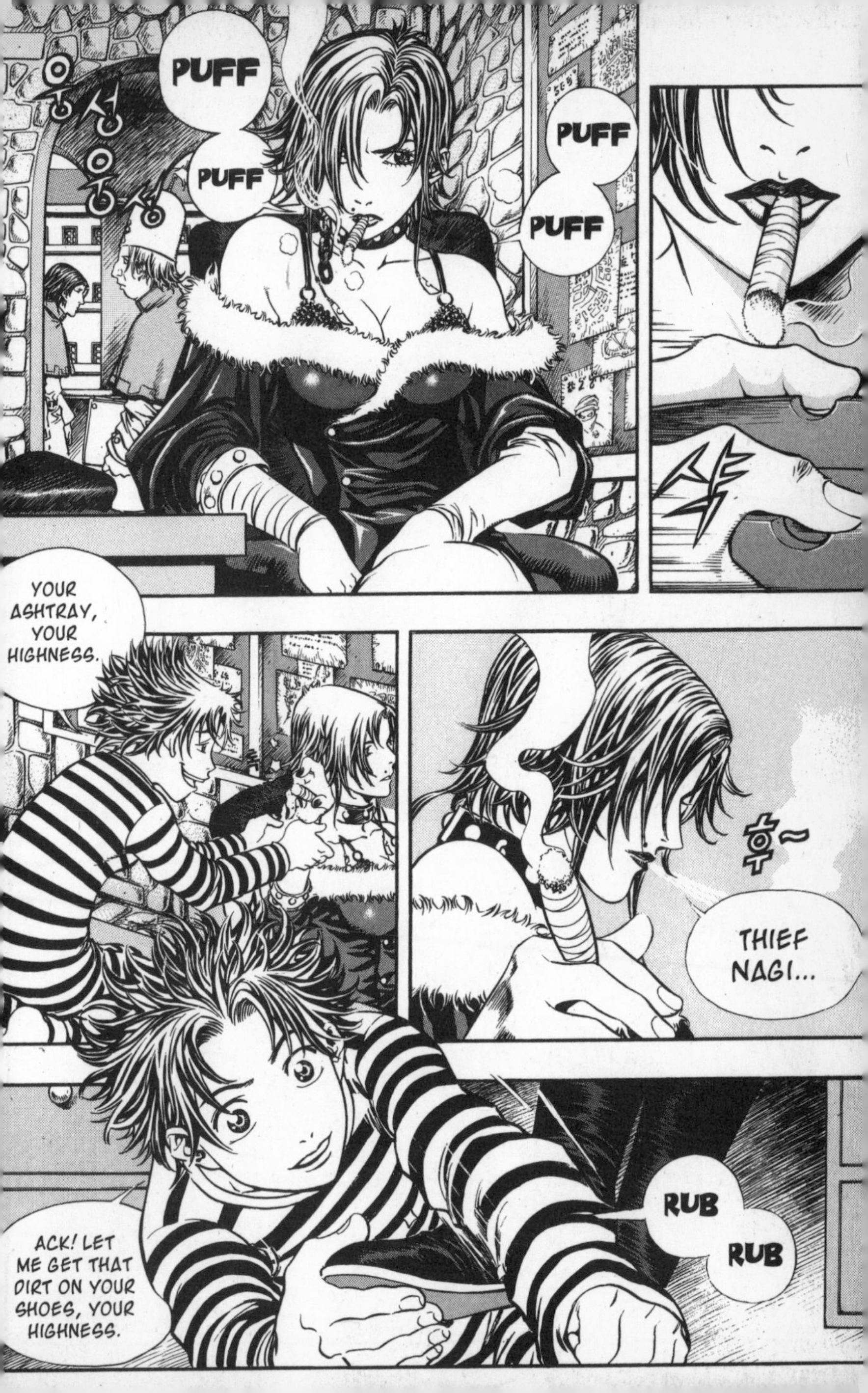
PUFF
PUFF
PUFF
PUFF
YOUR ASHTRAY, YOUR HIGHNESS.
THIEF NAGI...
ACK! LET ME GET THAT DIRT ON YOUR SHOES, YOUR HIGHNESS.
RUB
RUB

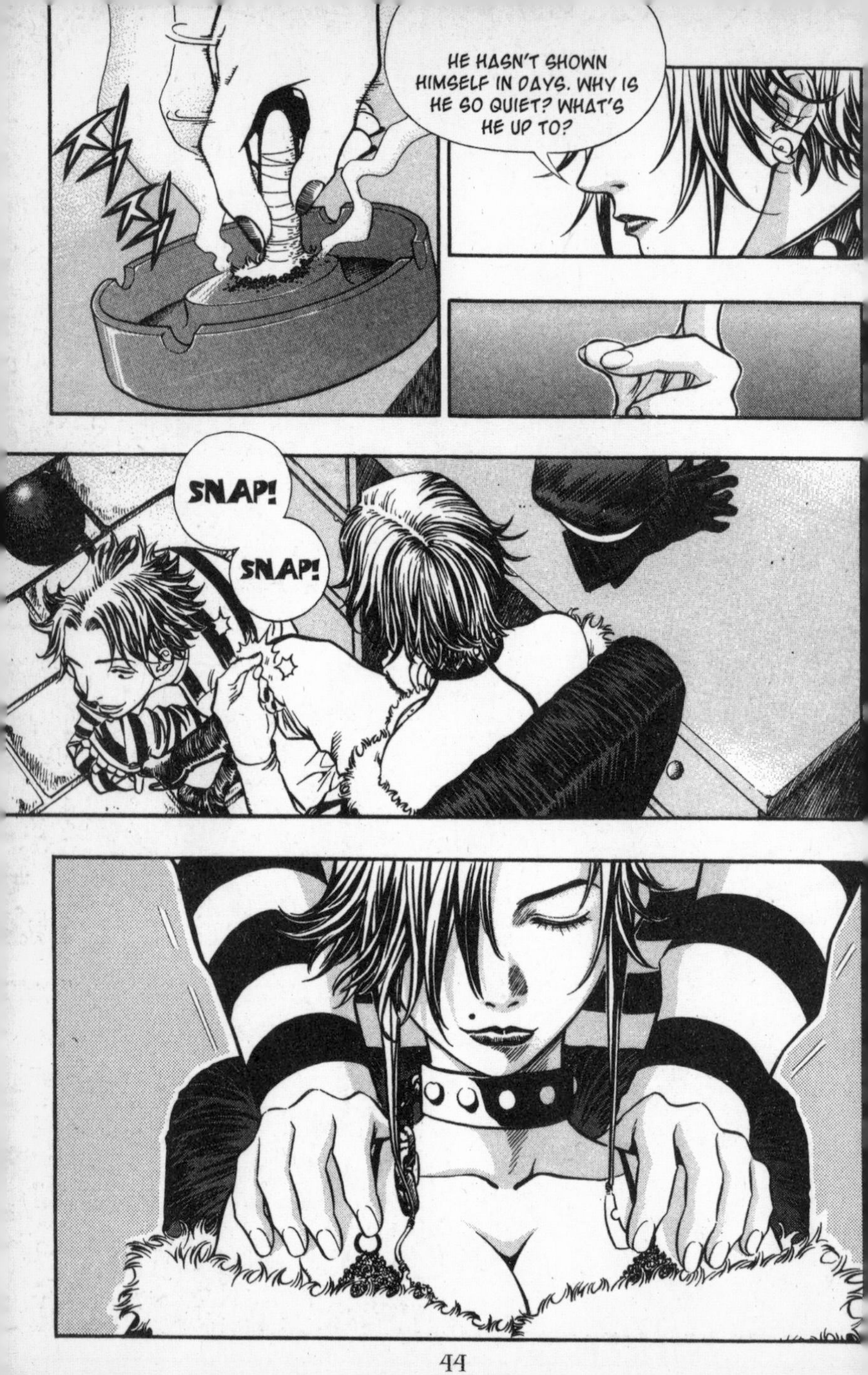
HE HASN'T SHOWN HIMSELF IN DAYS. WHY IS HE SO QUIET? WHAT'S HE UP TO?
SNAP!
SNAP!

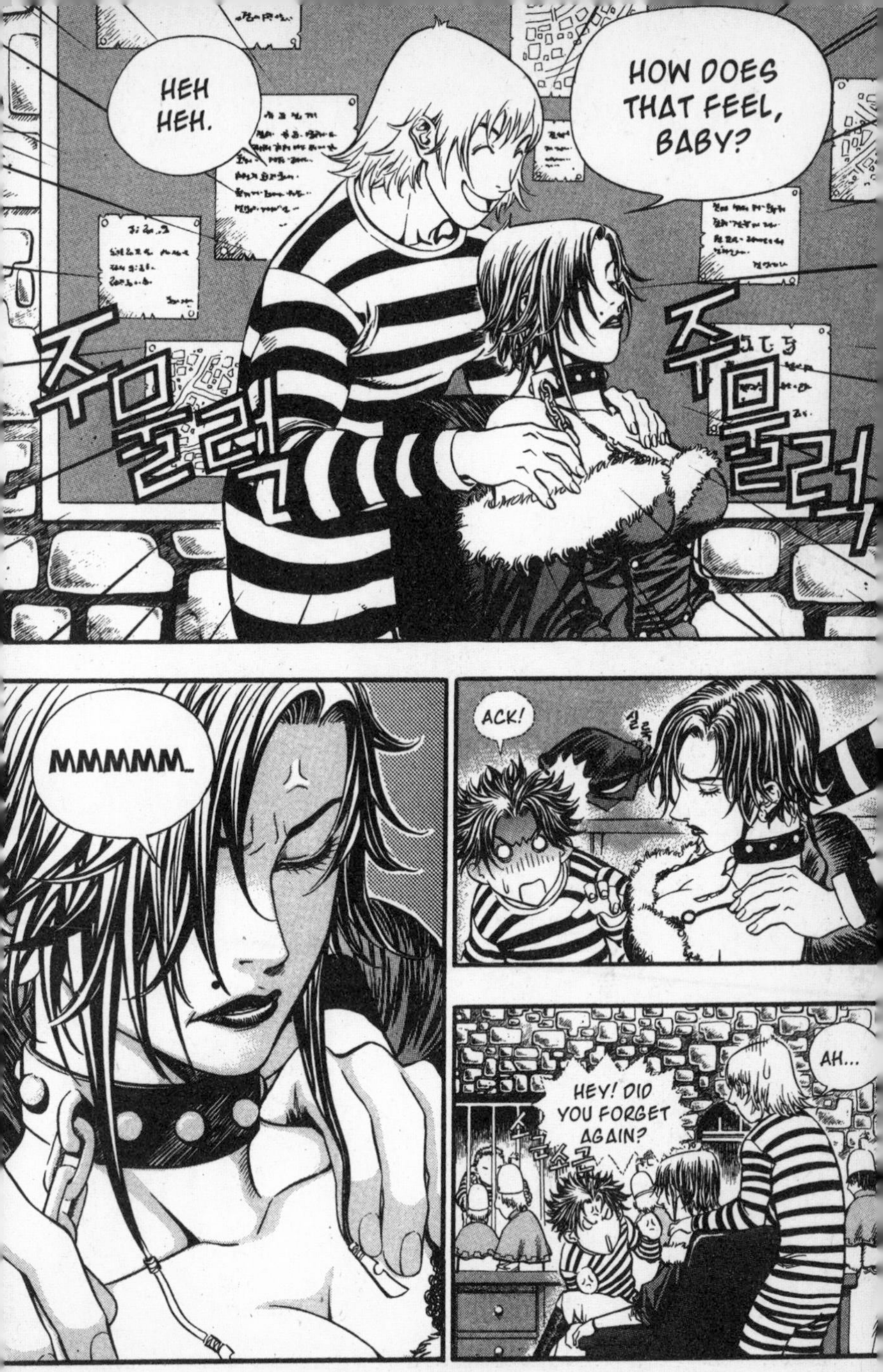
HEH HEH.
HOW DOES THAT FEEL, BABY?
MMMMM...
ACK!
HEY! DID YOU FORGET AGAIN?
AH...

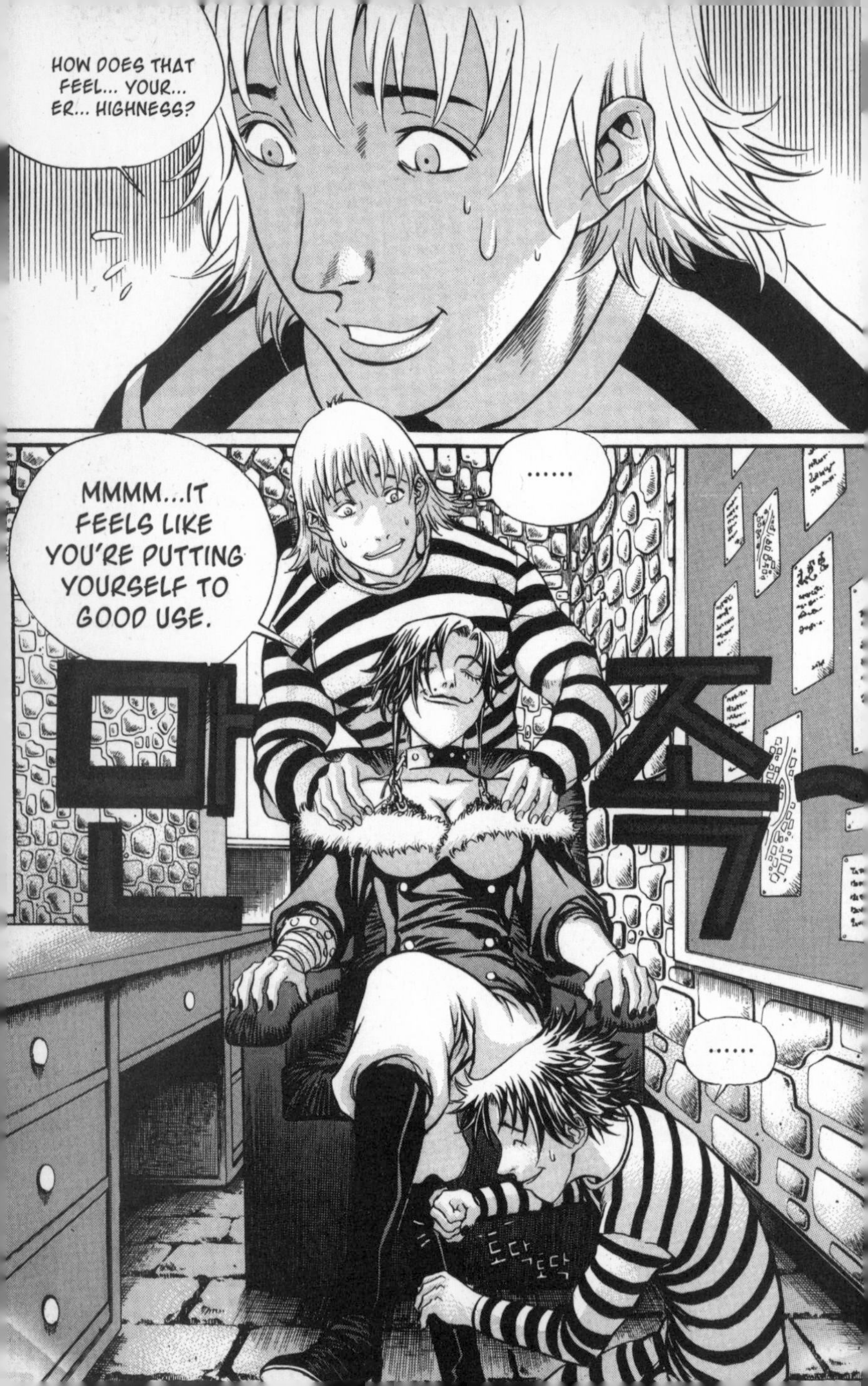
HOW DOES THAT FEEL... YOUR... ER... HIGHNESS?
MMMM...IT FEELS LIKE YOU'RE PUTTING YOURSELF TO GOOD USE.
......
만족~
......
토닥토닥

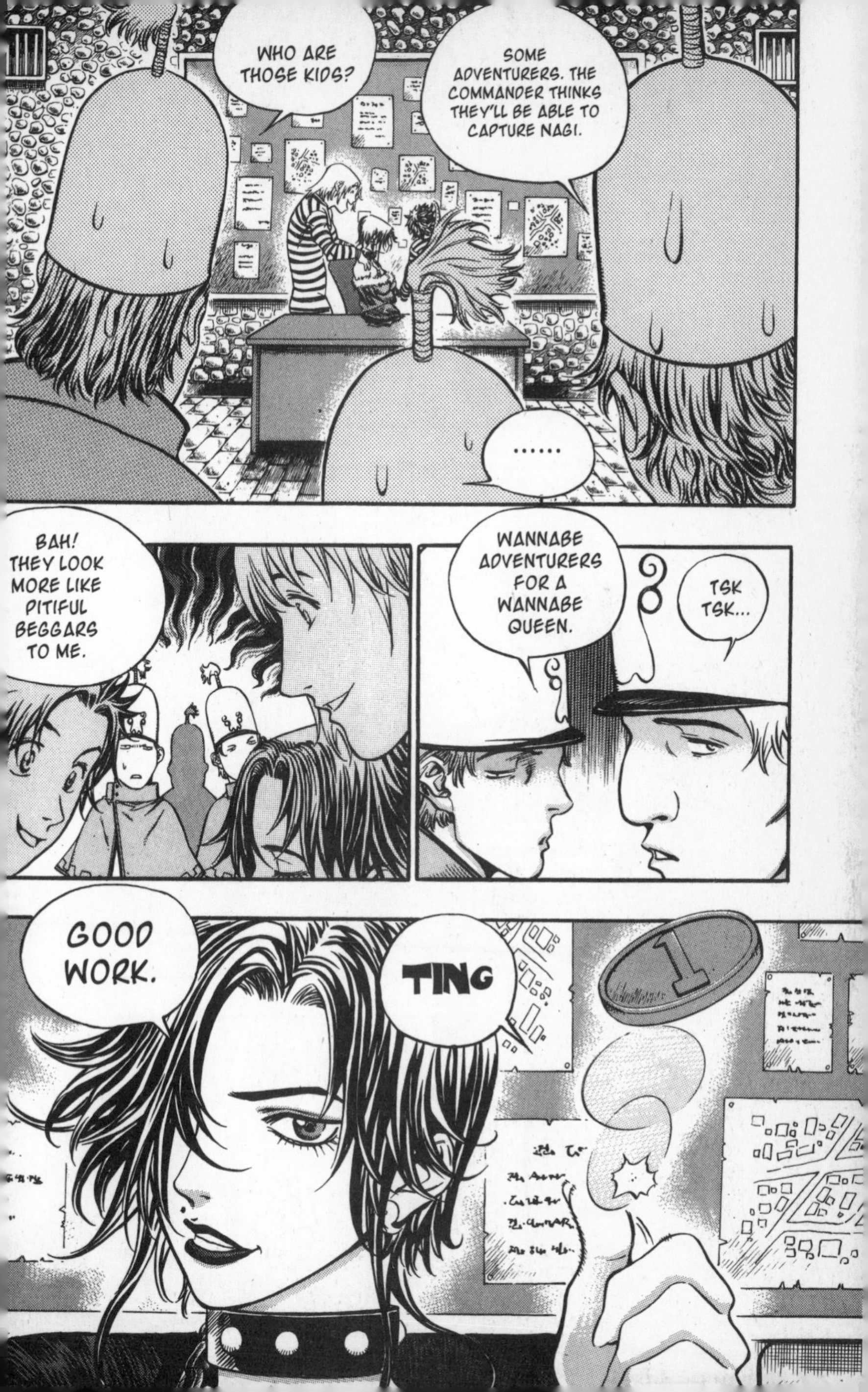
WHO ARE THOSE KIDS?
SOME ADVENTURERS. THE COMMANDER THINKS THEY'LL BE ABLE TO CAPTURE NAGI.
......
BAH! THEY LOOK MORE LIKE PITIFUL BEGGARS TO ME.
WANNABE ADVENTURERS FOR A WANNABE QUEEN.
TSK TSK...
GOOD WORK.
TING

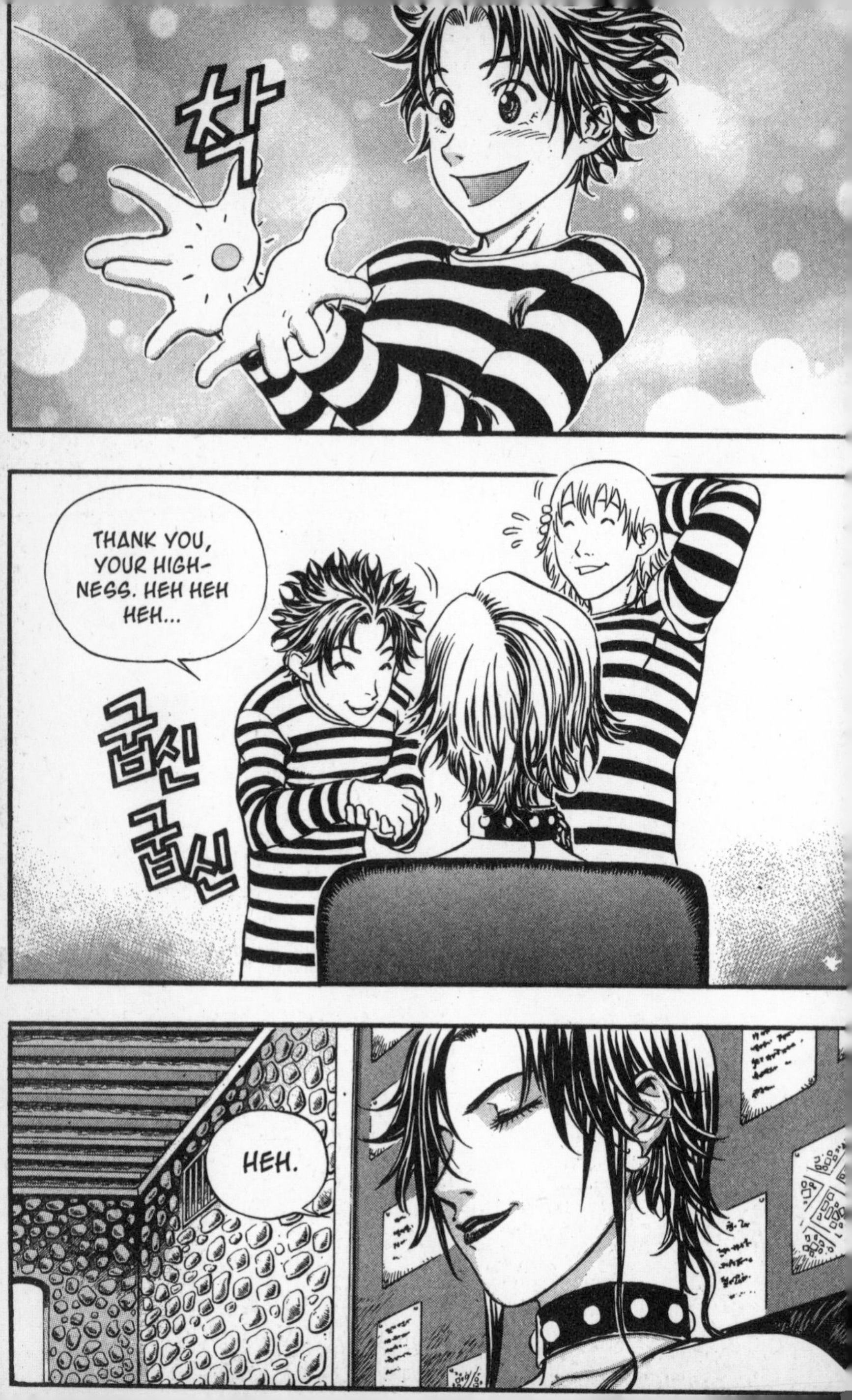
착
THANK YOU, YOUR HIGH-NESS. HEH HEH HEH...
굽신 굽신
HEH.

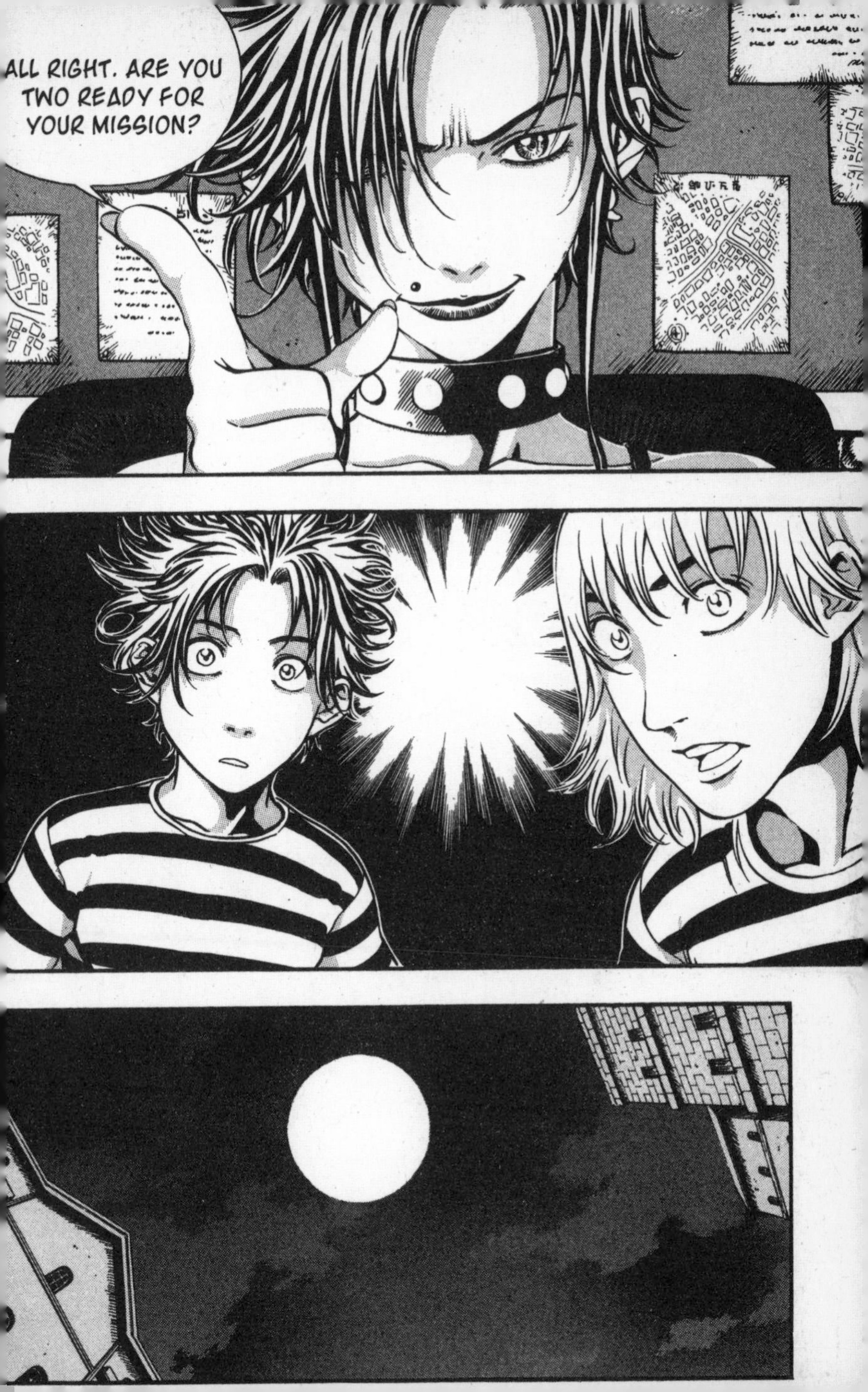
ALL RIGHT. ARE YOU TWO READY FOR YOUR MISSION?

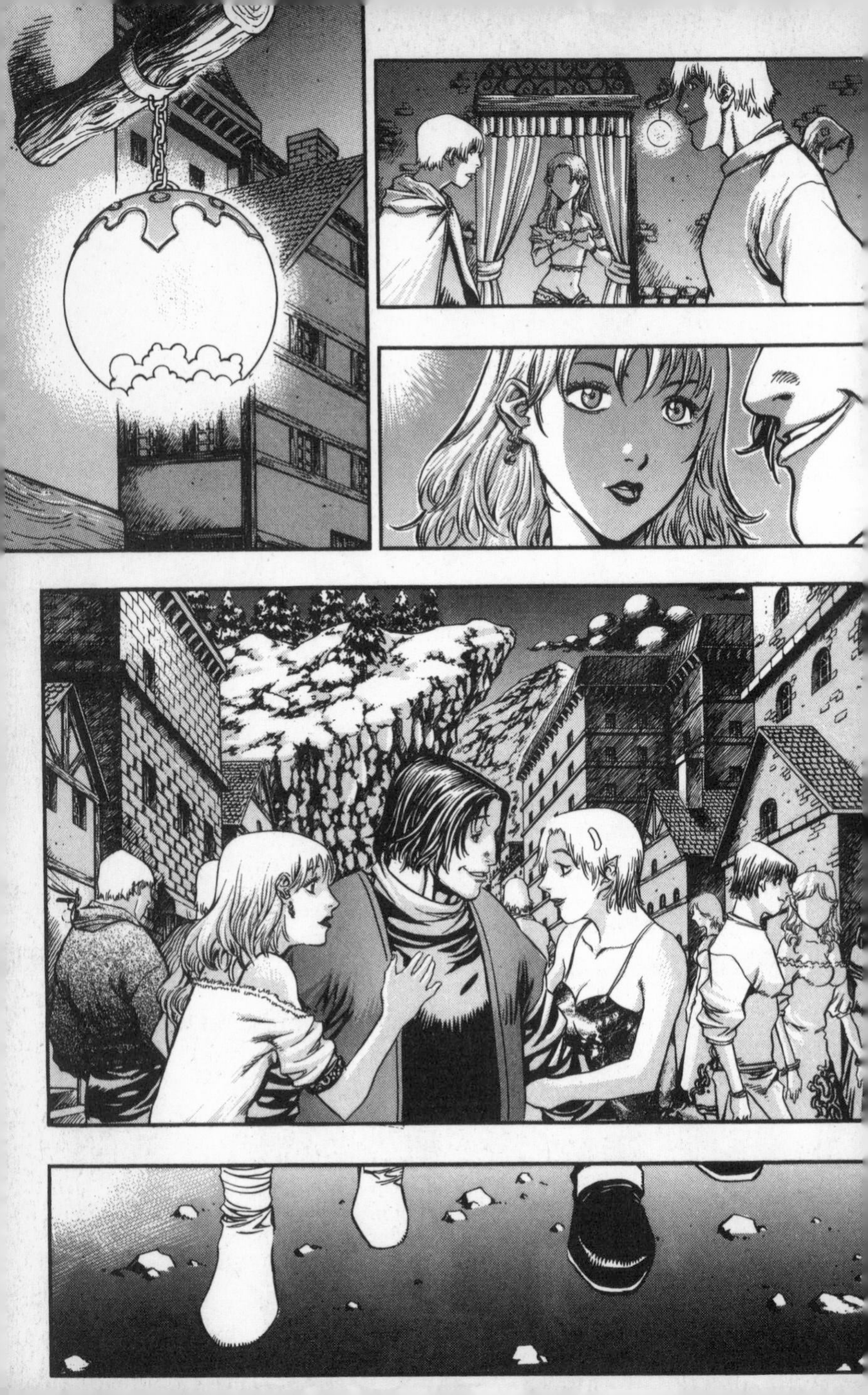

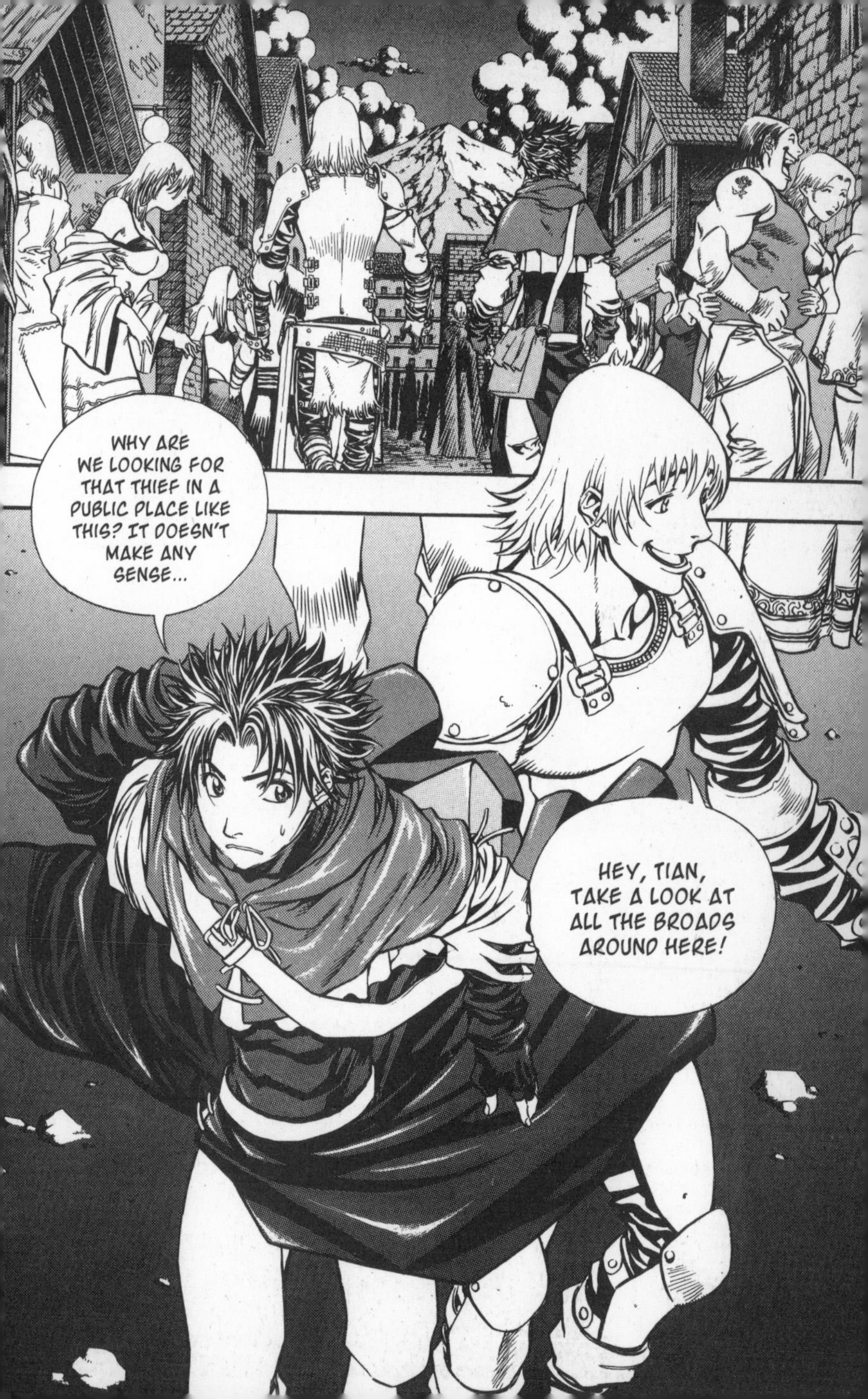
WHY ARE WE LOOKING FOR THAT THIEF IN A PUBLIC PLACE LIKE THIS? IT DOESN'T MAKE ANY SENSE...
HEY, TIAN, TAKE A LOOK AT ALL THE BROADS AROUND HERE!

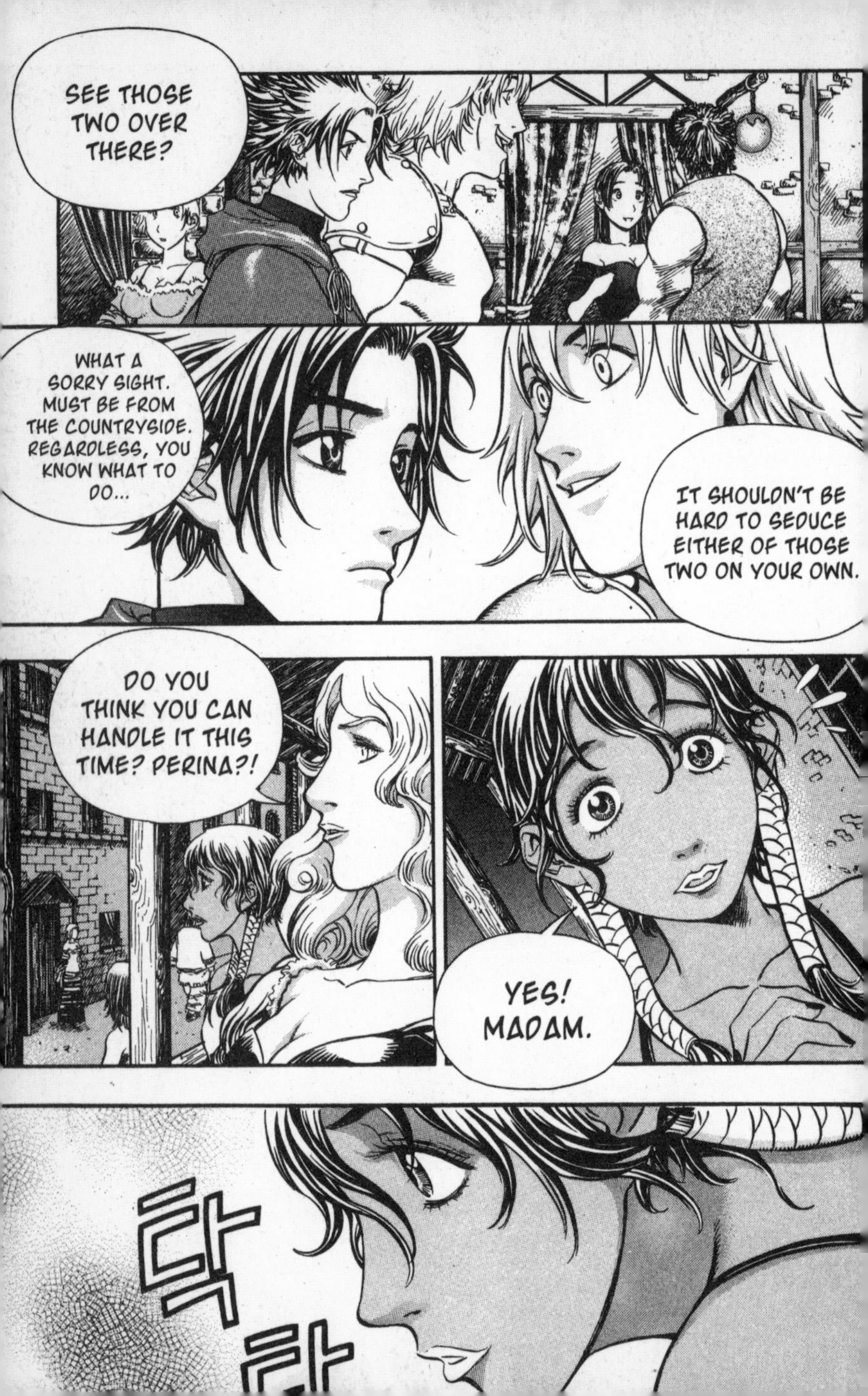
SEE THOSE TWO OVER THERE?
WHAT A SORRY SIGHT. MUST BE FROM THE COUNTRYSIDE. REGARDLESS, YOU KNOW WHAT TO DO...
IT SHOULDN'T BE HARD TO SEDUCE EITHER OF THOSE TWO ON YOUR OWN.
DO YOU THINK YOU CAN HANDLE IT THIS TIME? PERINA?!
YES! MADAM.

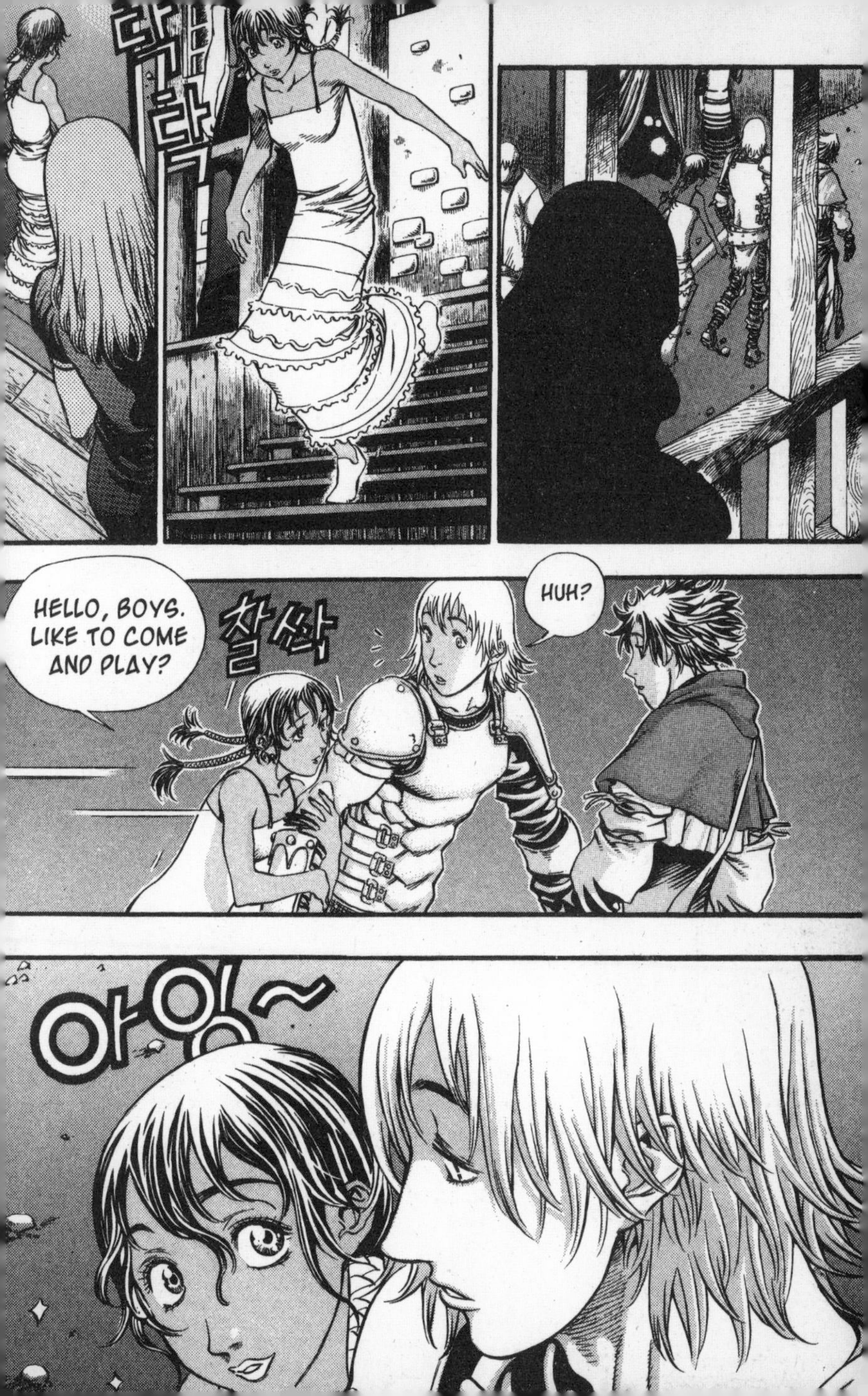

다 다 닥
HELLO, BOYS. LIKE TO COME AND PLAY?
찰싹
HUH?
아잉~

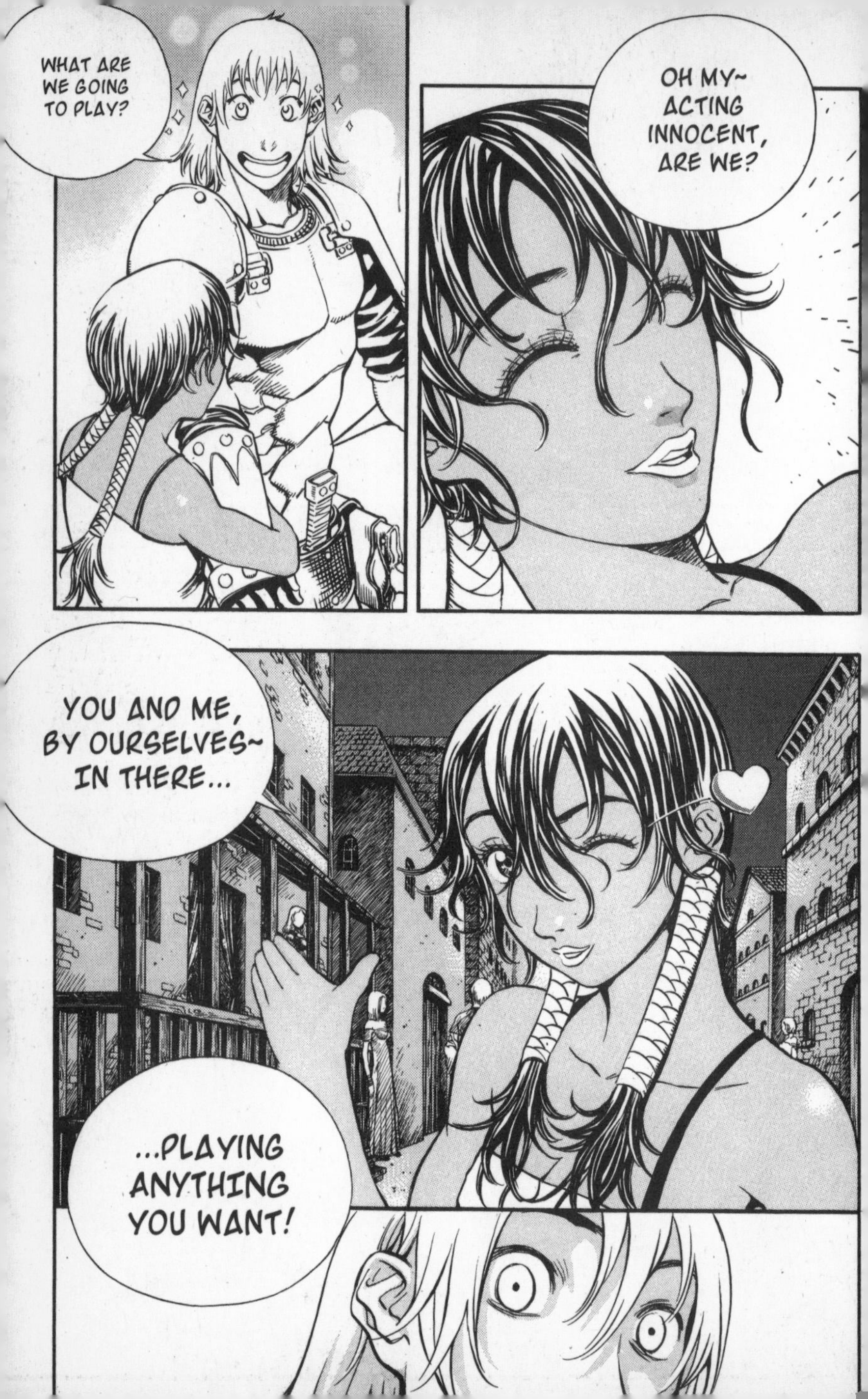
WHAT ARE WE GOING TO PLAY?
OH MY~ ACTING INNOCENT, ARE WE?
YOU AND ME, BY OURSELVES~ IN THERE...
...PLAYING ANYTHING YOU WANT!

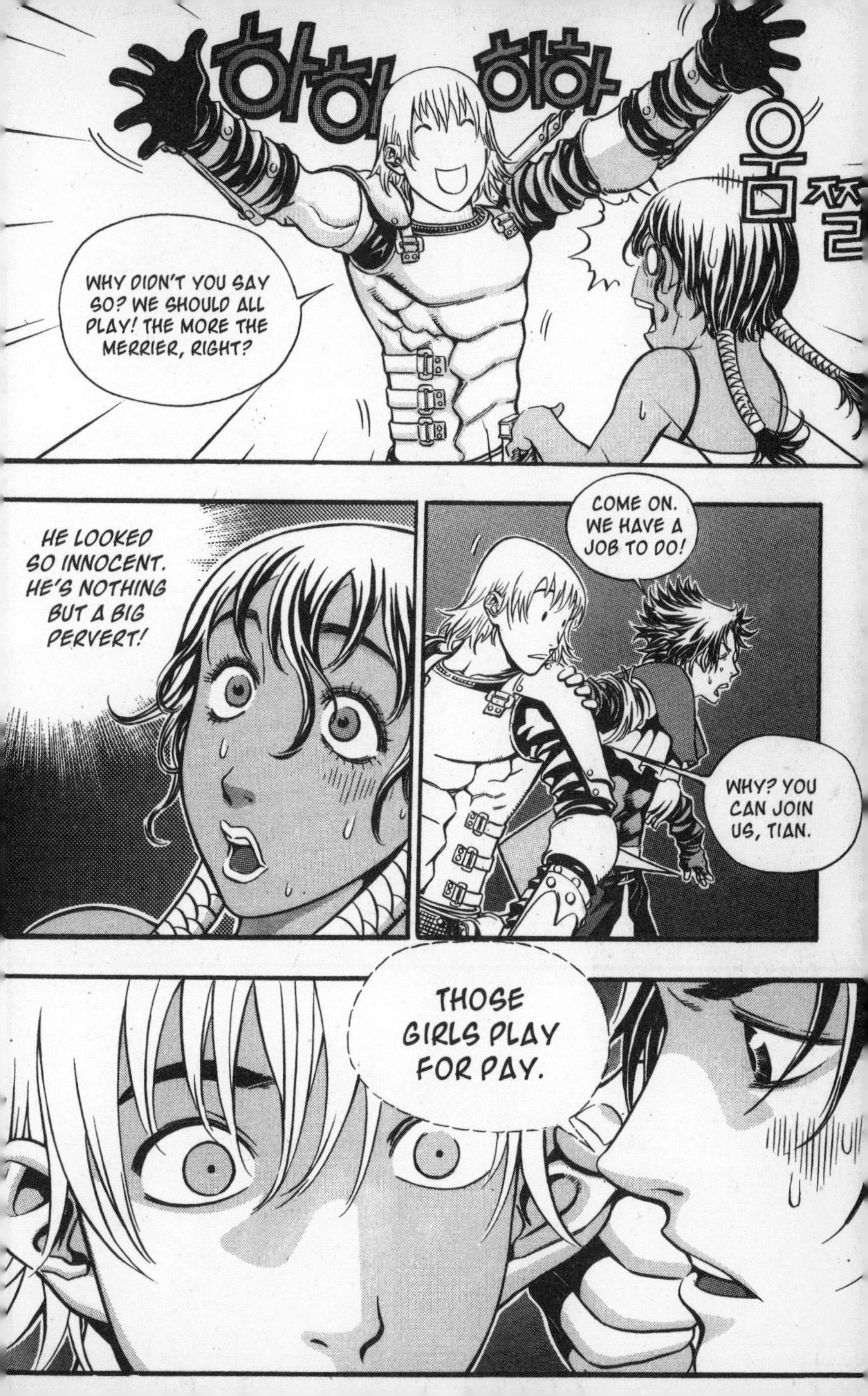
하하 하하
움찔
WHY DIDN'T YOU SAY SO? WE SHOULD ALL PLAY! THE MORE THE MERRIER, RIGHT?
HE LOOKED SO INNOCENT. HE'S NOTHING BUT A BIG PERVERT!
COME ON. WE HAVE A JOB TO DO!
WHY? YOU CAN JOIN US, TIAN.
THOSE GIRLS PLAY FOR PAY.

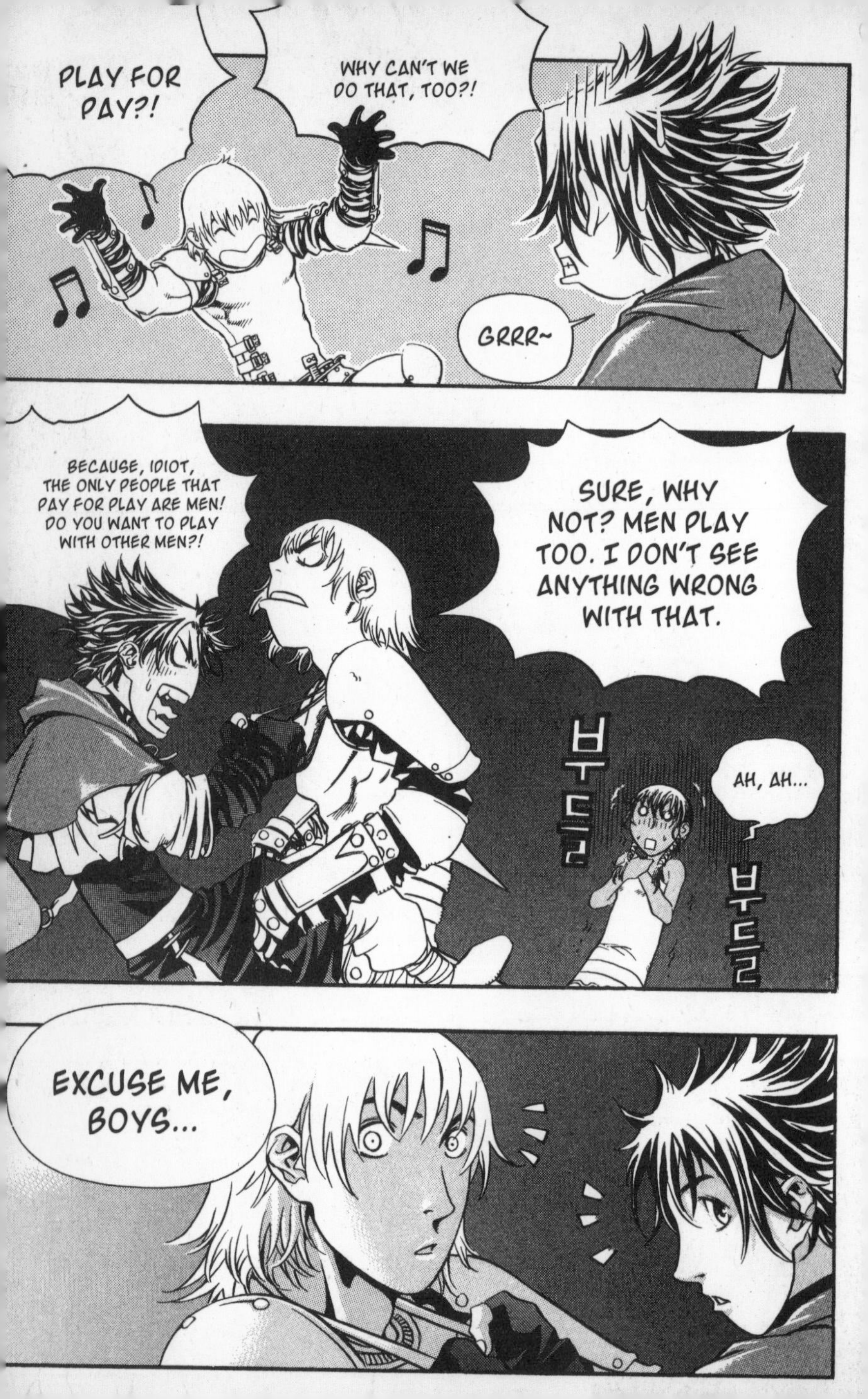
PLAY FOR PAY?!
WHY CAN'T WE DO THAT, TOO?!
GRRR~
BECAUSE, IDIOT, THE ONLY PEOPLE THAT PAY FOR PLAY ARE MEN! DO YOU WANT TO PLAY WITH OTHER MEN?!
SURE, WHY NOT? MEN PLAY TOO. I DON'T SEE ANYTHING WRONG WITH THAT.
AH, AH...
EXCUSE ME, BOYS...

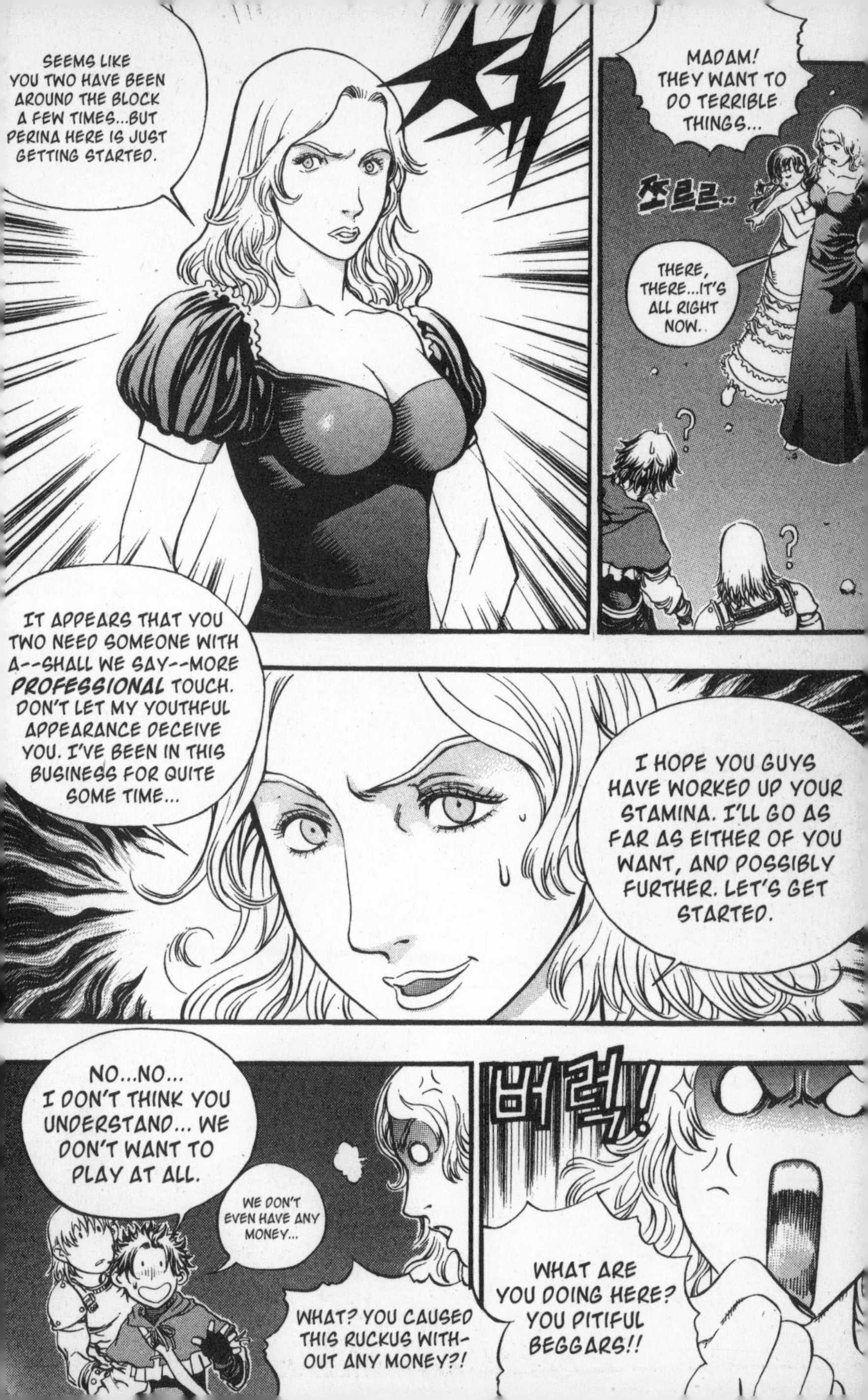
SEEMS LIKE YOU TWO HAVE BEEN AROUND THE BLOCK A FEW TIMES...BUT PERINA HERE IS JUST GETTING STARTED.
MADAM! THEY WANT TO DO TERRIBLE THINGS...
쪼르르..
THERE, THERE...IT'S ALL RIGHT NOW.
IT APPEARS THAT YOU TWO NEED SOMEONE WITH A--SHALL WE SAY--MORE **PROFESSIONAL** TOUCH. DON'T LET MY YOUTHFUL APPEARANCE DECEIVE YOU. I'VE BEEN IN THIS BUSINESS FOR QUITE SOME TIME...
I HOPE YOU GUYS HAVE WORKED UP YOUR STAMINA. I'LL GO AS FAR AS EITHER OF YOU WANT, AND POSSIBLY FURTHER. LET'S GET STARTED.
NO...NO... I DON'T THINK YOU UNDERSTAND... WE DON'T WANT TO PLAY AT ALL.
WE DON'T EVEN HAVE ANY MONEY...
WHAT? YOU CAUSED THIS RUCKUS WITH-OUT ANY MONEY?!
버럭!
WHAT ARE YOU DOING HERE? YOU PITIFUL BEGGARS!!

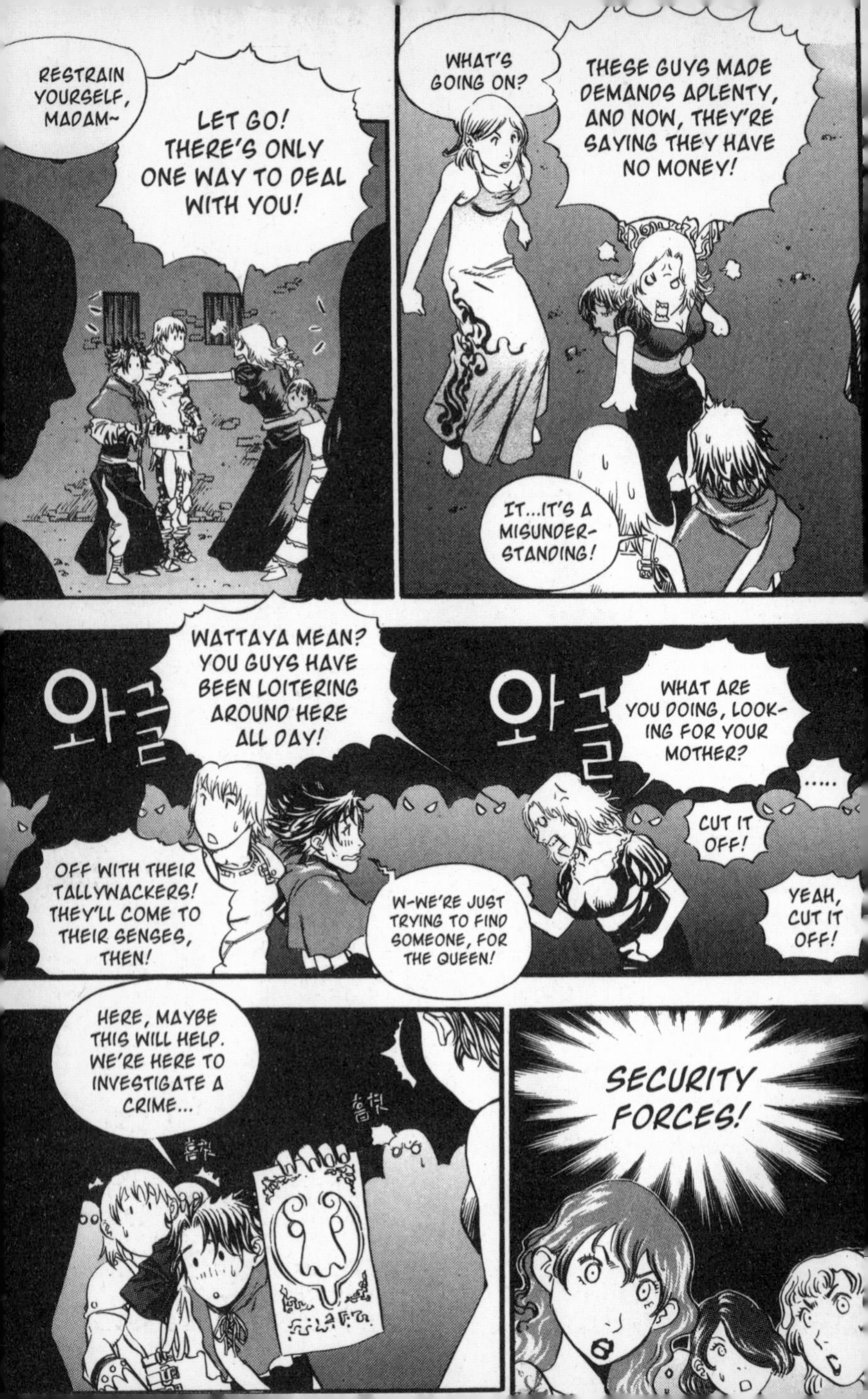
RESTRAIN YOURSELF, MADAM~
LET GO! THERE'S ONLY ONE WAY TO DEAL WITH YOU!
WHAT'S GOING ON?
THESE GUYS MADE DEMANDS APLENTY, AND NOW, THEY'RE SAYING THEY HAVE NO MONEY!
IT...IT'S A MISUNDER-STANDING!
WATTAYA MEAN? YOU GUYS HAVE BEEN LOITERING AROUND HERE ALL DAY!
와글
와글
WHAT ARE YOU DOING, LOOK-ING FOR YOUR MOTHER?
.....
CUT IT OFF!
OFF WITH THEIR TALLYWACKERS! THEY'LL COME TO THEIR SENSES, THEN!
W-WE'RE JUST TRYING TO FIND SOMEONE, FOR THE QUEEN!
YEAH, CUT IT OFF!
HERE, MAYBE THIS WILL HELP. WE'RE HERE TO INVESTIGATE A CRIME...
SECURITY FORCES!

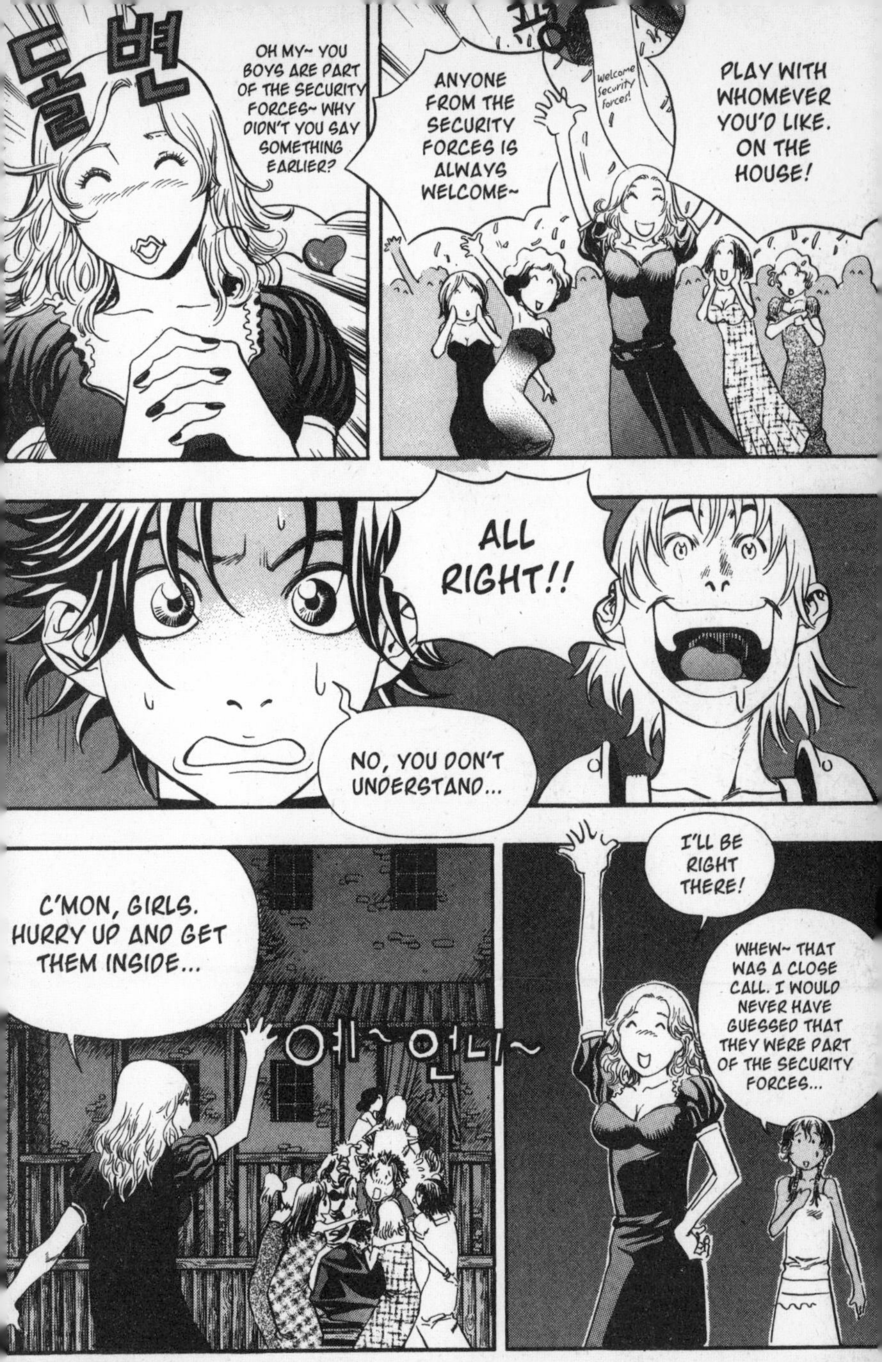

OH MY~ YOU BOYS ARE PART OF THE SECURITY FORCES~ WHY DIDN'T YOU SAY SOMETHING EARLIER?
ANYONE FROM THE SECURITY FORCES IS ALWAYS WELCOME~
Welcome Security Forces!
PLAY WITH WHOMEVER YOU'D LIKE. ON THE HOUSE!
ALL RIGHT!!
NO, YOU DON'T UNDERSTAND...
C'MON, GIRLS. HURRY UP AND GET THEM INSIDE...
예~ 언니~
I'LL BE RIGHT THERE!
WHEW~ THAT WAS A CLOSE CALL. I WOULD NEVER HAVE GUESSED THAT THEY WERE PART OF THE SECURITY FORCES...

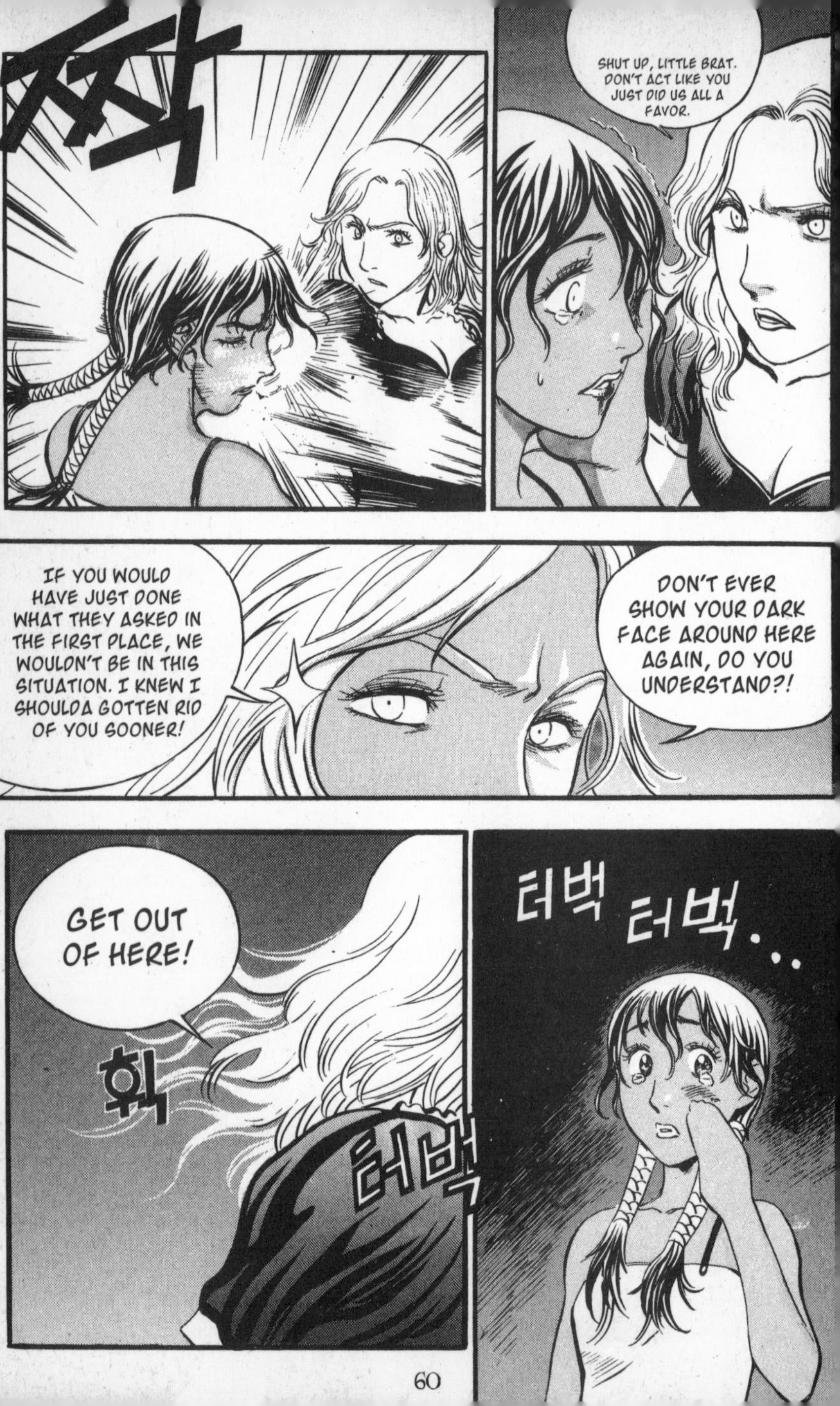

SHUT UP, LITTLE BRAT. DON'T ACT LIKE YOU JUST DID US ALL A FAVOR.
IF YOU WOULD HAVE JUST DONE WHAT THEY ASKED IN THE FIRST PLACE, WE WOULDN'T BE IN THIS SITUATION. I KNEW I SHOULDA GOTTEN RID OF YOU SOONER!
DON'T EVER SHOW YOUR DARK FACE AROUND HERE AGAIN, DO YOU UNDERSTAND?!
GET OUT OF HERE!
휙
터벅
터벅 터벅...

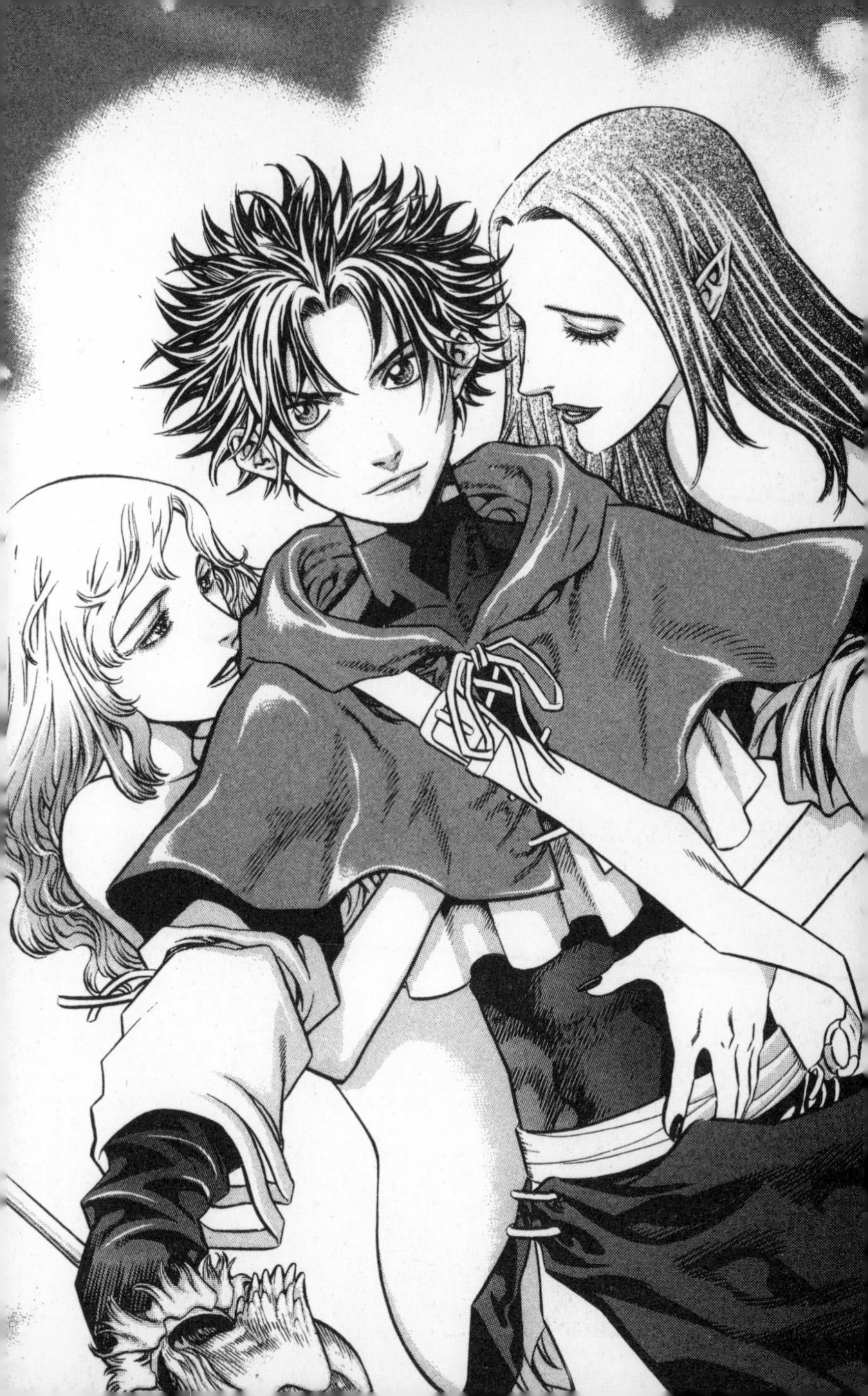

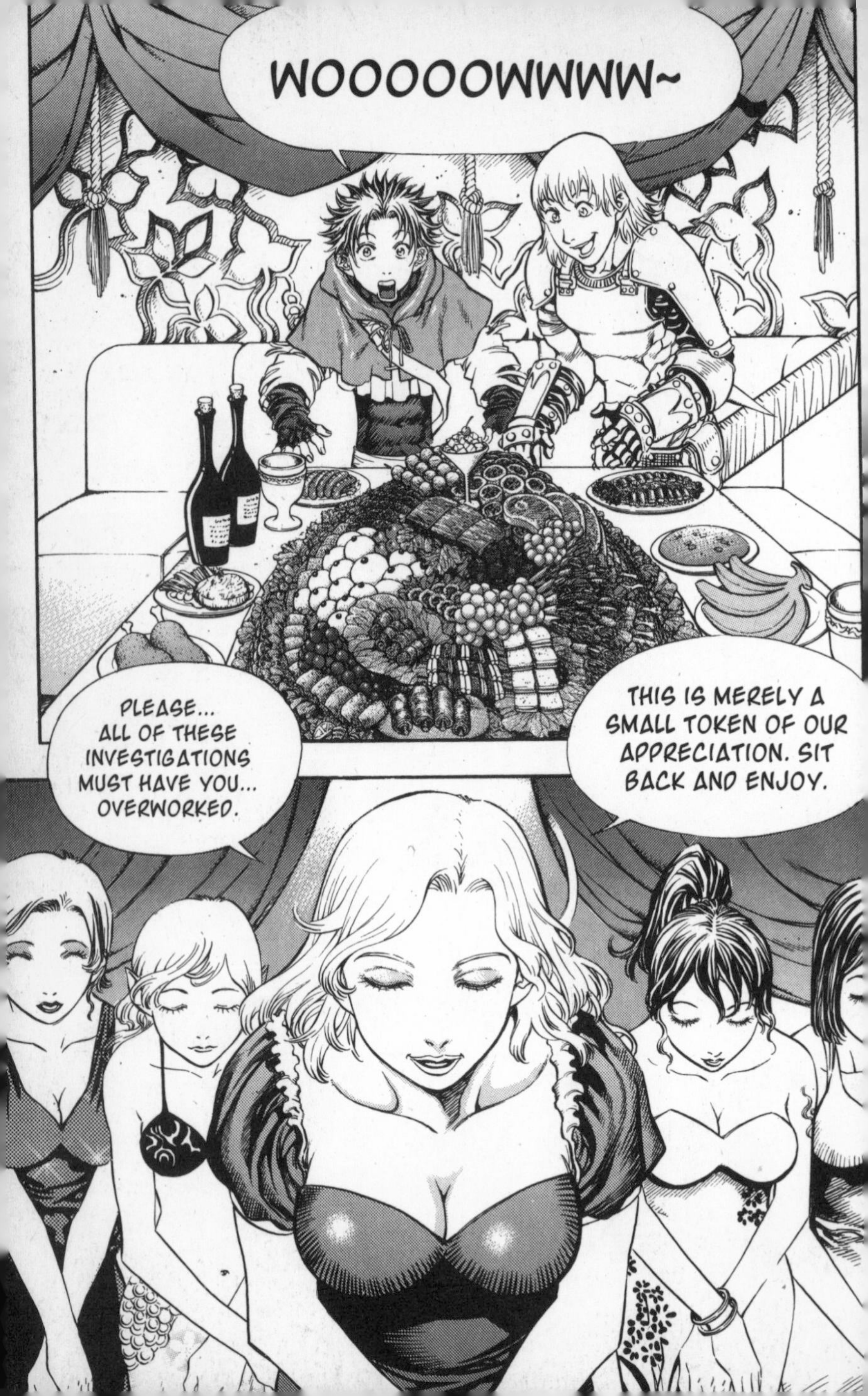
WOOOOOWWWW~
PLEASE... ALL OF THESE INVESTIGATIONS MUST HAVE YOU... OVERWORKED.
THIS IS MERELY A SMALL TOKEN OF OUR APPRECIATION. SIT BACK AND ENJOY.

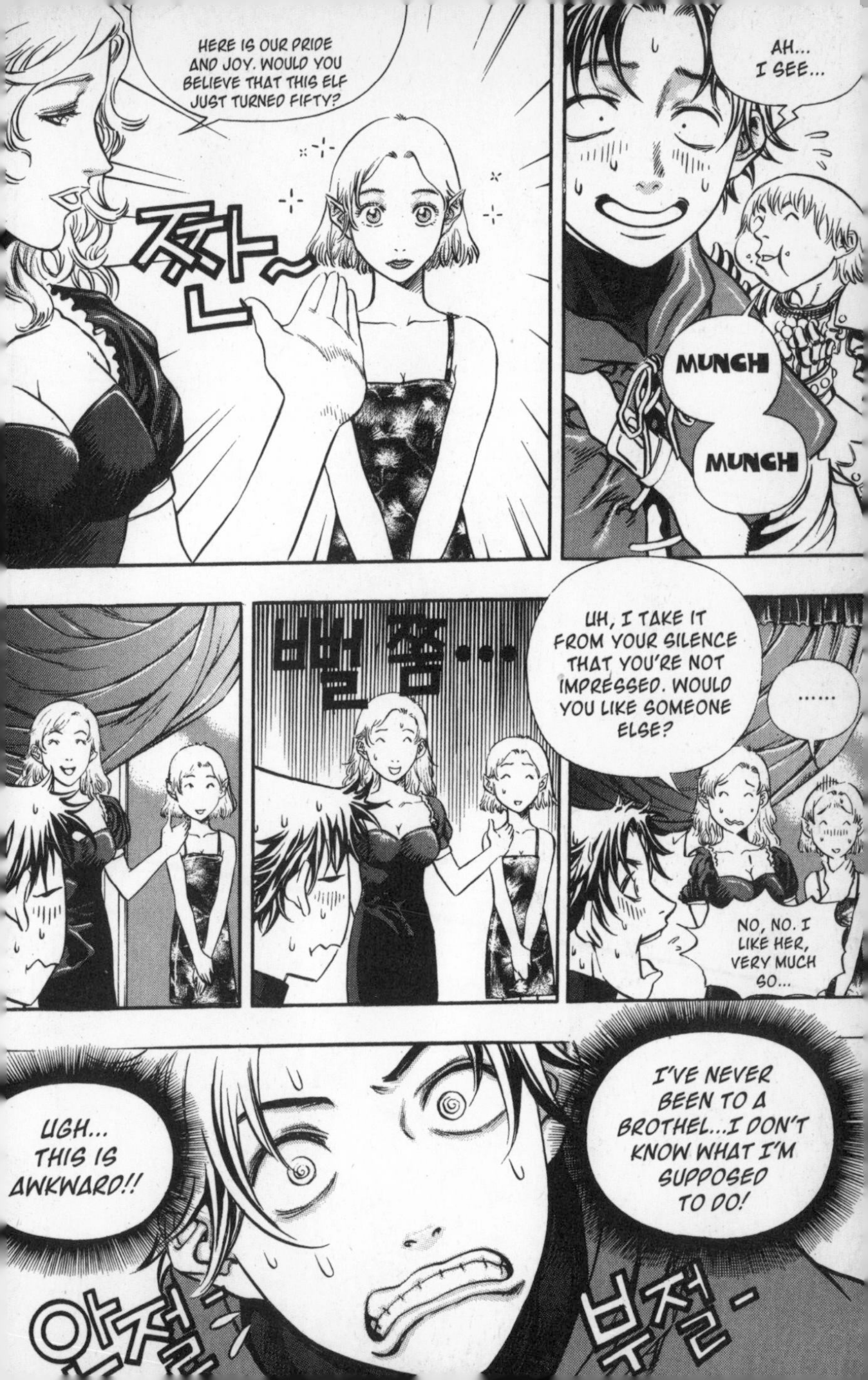

HERE IS OUR PRIDE AND JOY. WOULD YOU BELIEVE THAT THIS ELF JUST TURNED FIFTY?
AH... I SEE...
MUNCH
MUNCH
뻘쭘...
UH, I TAKE IT FROM YOUR SILENCE THAT YOU'RE NOT IMPRESSED. WOULD YOU LIKE SOMEONE ELSE?
......
NO, NO. I LIKE HER, VERY MUCH SO...
UGH... THIS IS AWKWARD!!
I'VE NEVER BEEN TO A BROTHEL...I DON'T KNOW WHAT I'M SUPPOSED TO DO!
안절
부절

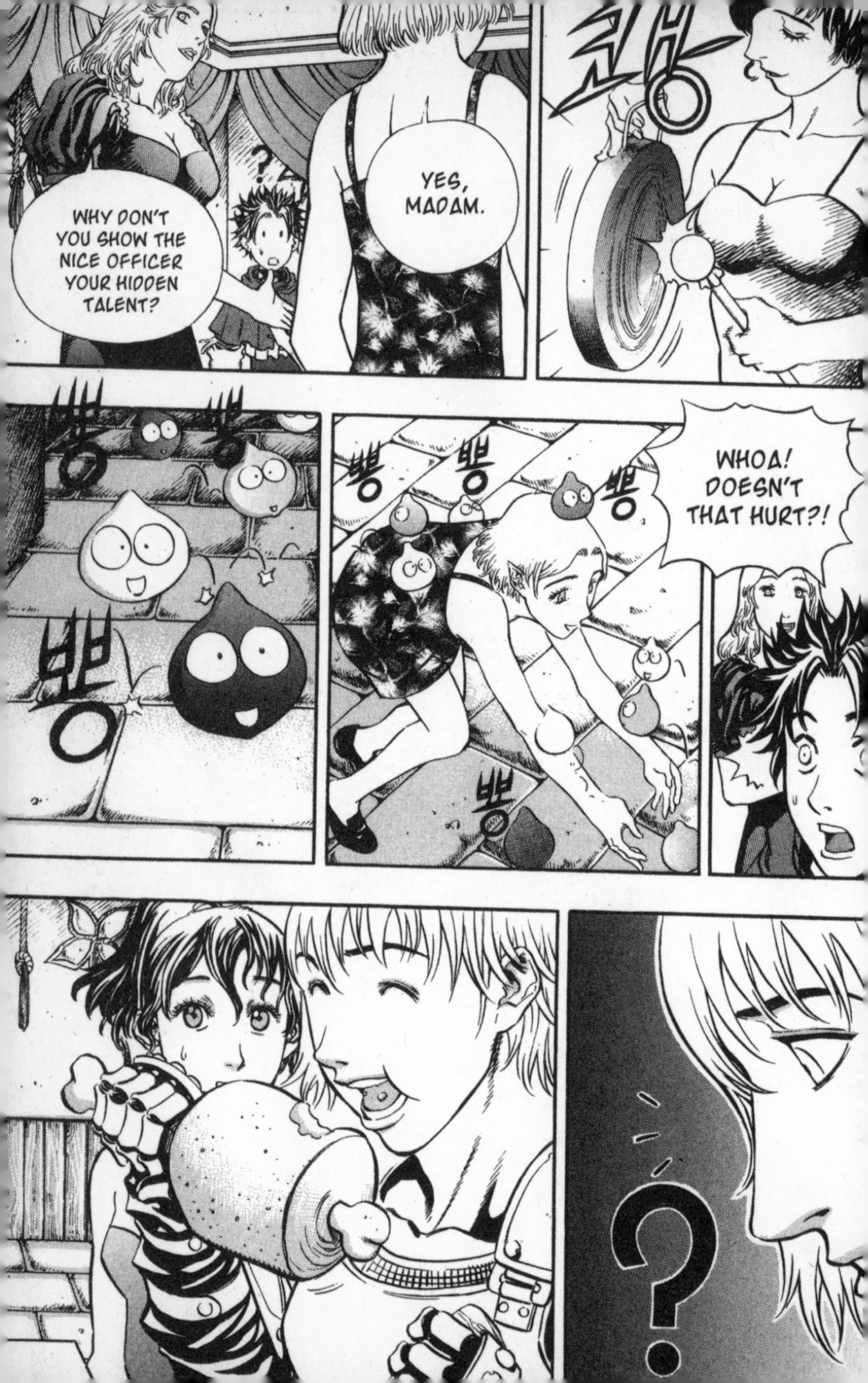
WHY DON'T YOU SHOW THE NICE OFFICER YOUR HIDDEN TALENT?
YES, MADAM.
뽕
뽕
뽕
뽕
뽕
뽕
뽕
WHOA! DOESN'T THAT HURT?!

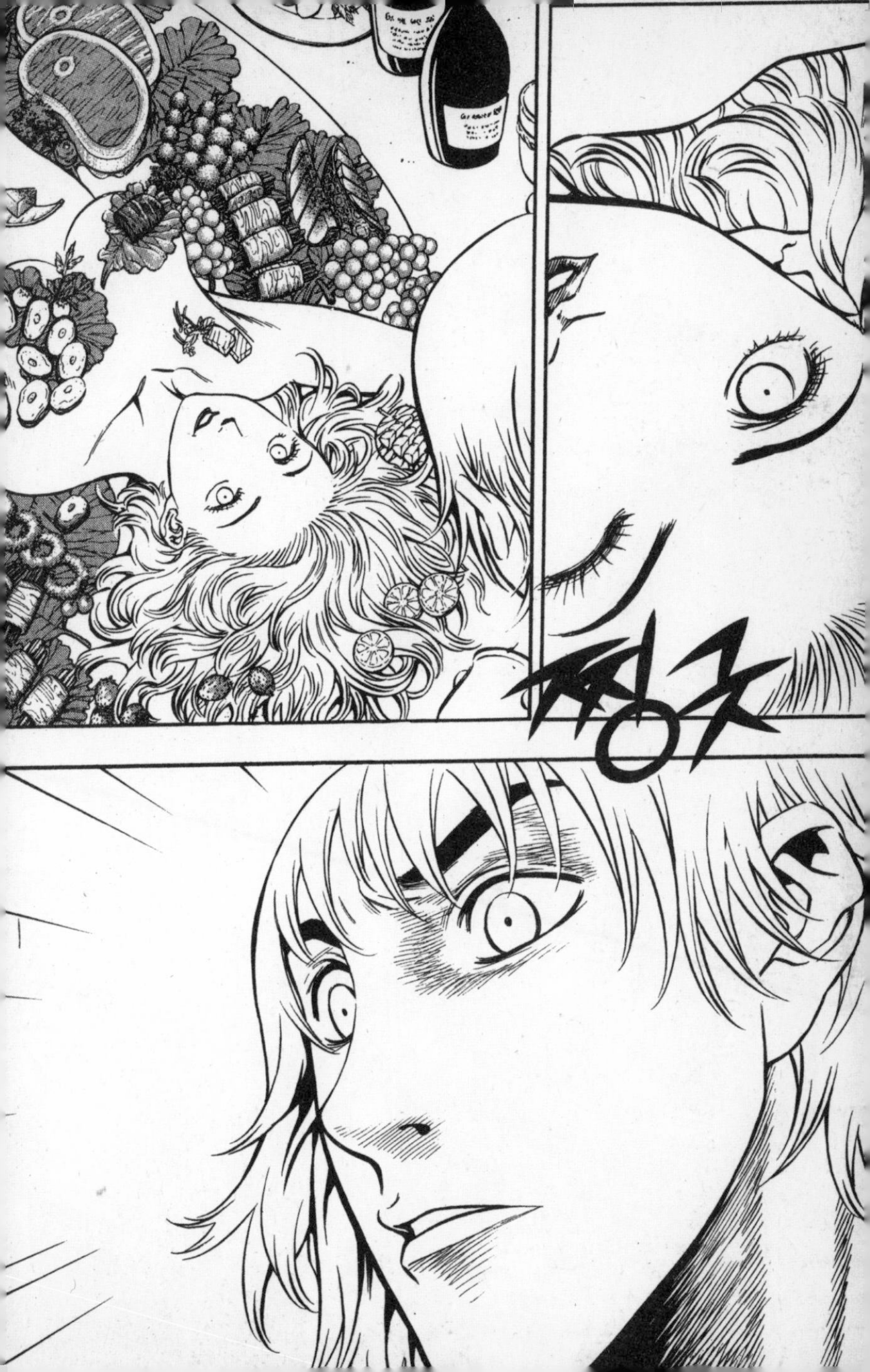

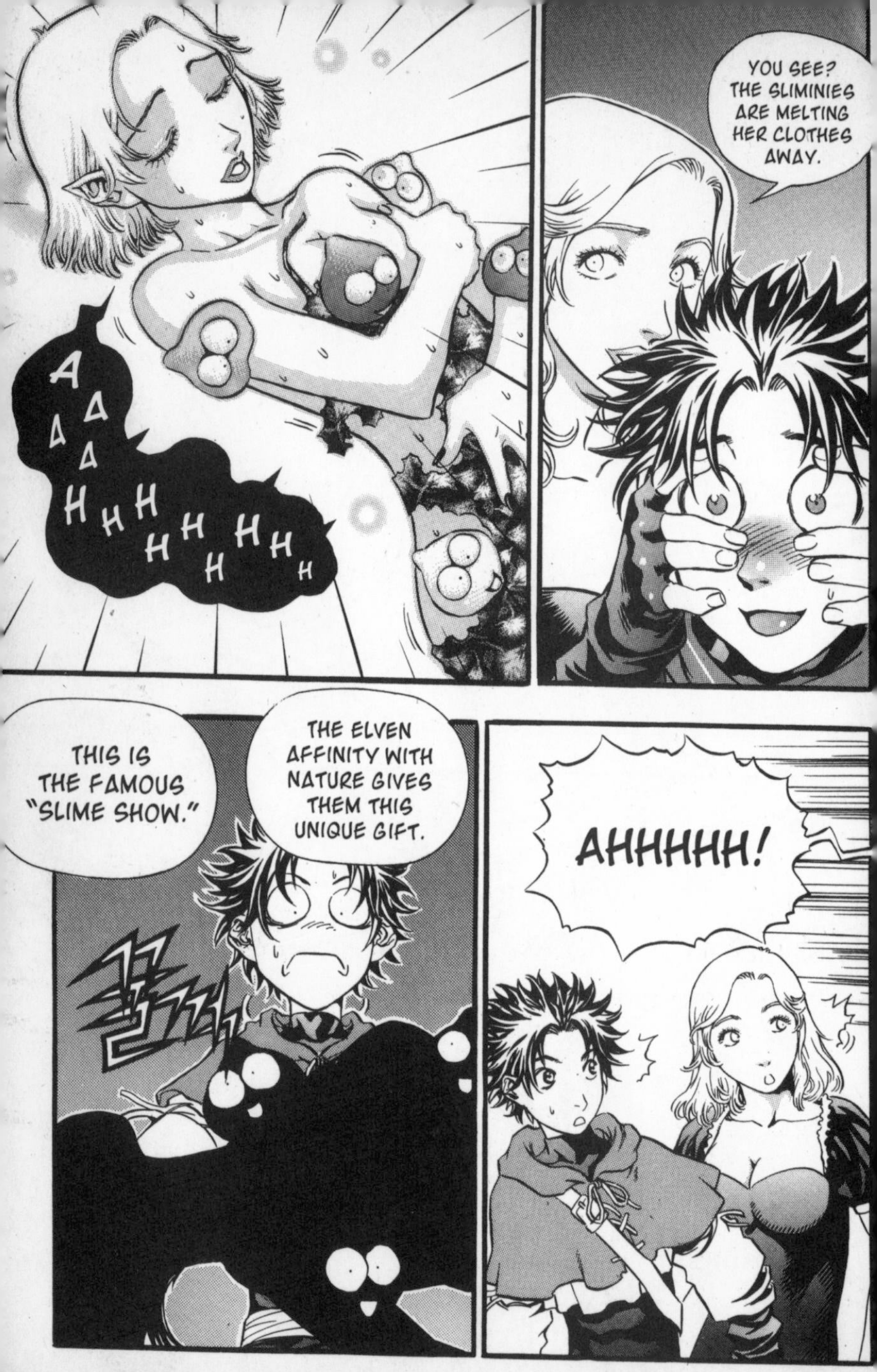
AAAAHHHHHHHHH
YOU SEE? THE SLIMINIES ARE MELTING HER CLOTHES AWAY.
THIS IS THE FAMOUS "SLIME SHOW."
THE ELVEN AFFINITY WITH NATURE GIVES THEM THIS UNIQUE GIFT.
AHHHHH!

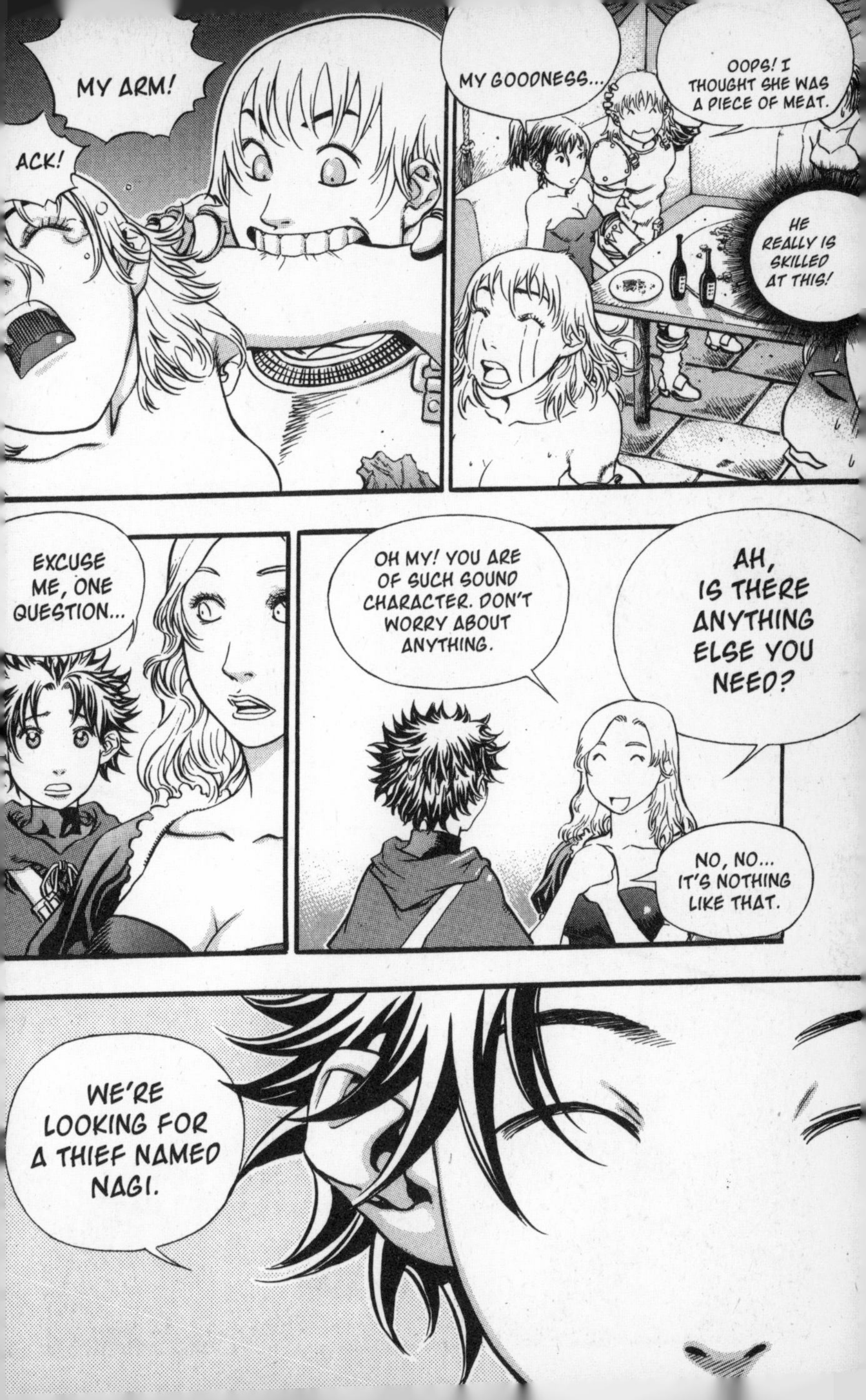
MY ARM!
ACK!
MY GOODNESS...
OOPS! I THOUGHT SHE WAS A PIECE OF MEAT.
HE REALLY IS SKILLED AT THIS!
EXCUSE ME, ONE QUESTION...
OH MY! YOU ARE OF SUCH SOUND CHARACTER. DON'T WORRY ABOUT ANYTHING.
AH, IS THERE ANYTHING ELSE YOU NEED?
NO, NO... IT'S NOTHING LIKE THAT.
WE'RE LOOKING FOR A THIEF NAMED NAGI.

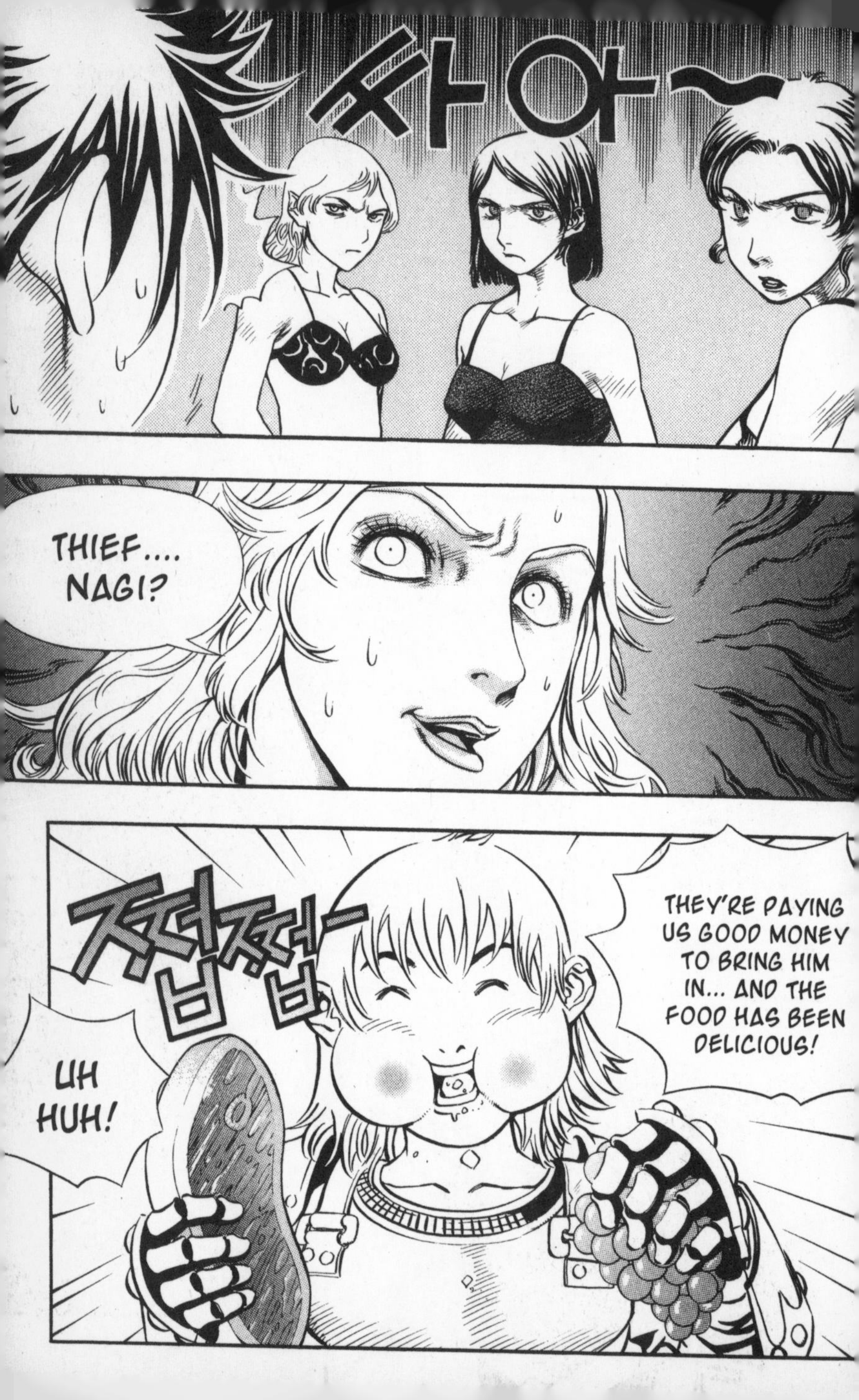
샤아~
THIEF.... NAGI?
UH HUH!
THEY'RE PAYING US GOOD MONEY TO BRING HIM IN... AND THE FOOD HAS BEEN DELICIOUS!

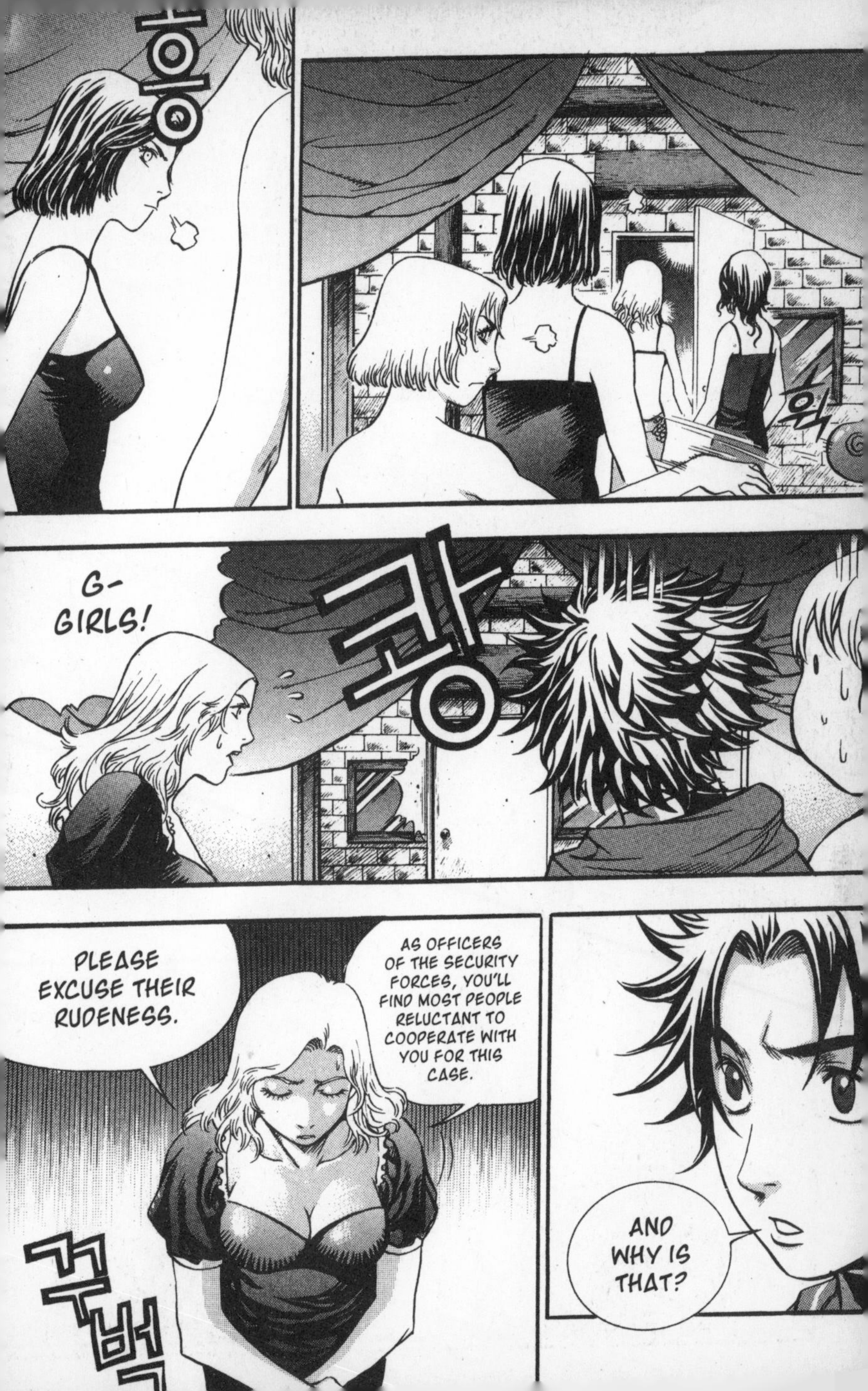
G-GIRLS!
PLEASE EXCUSE THEIR RUDENESS.
AS OFFICERS OF THE SECURITY FORCES, YOU'LL FIND MOST PEOPLE RELUCTANT TO COOPERATE WITH YOU FOR THIS CASE.
AND WHY IS THAT?

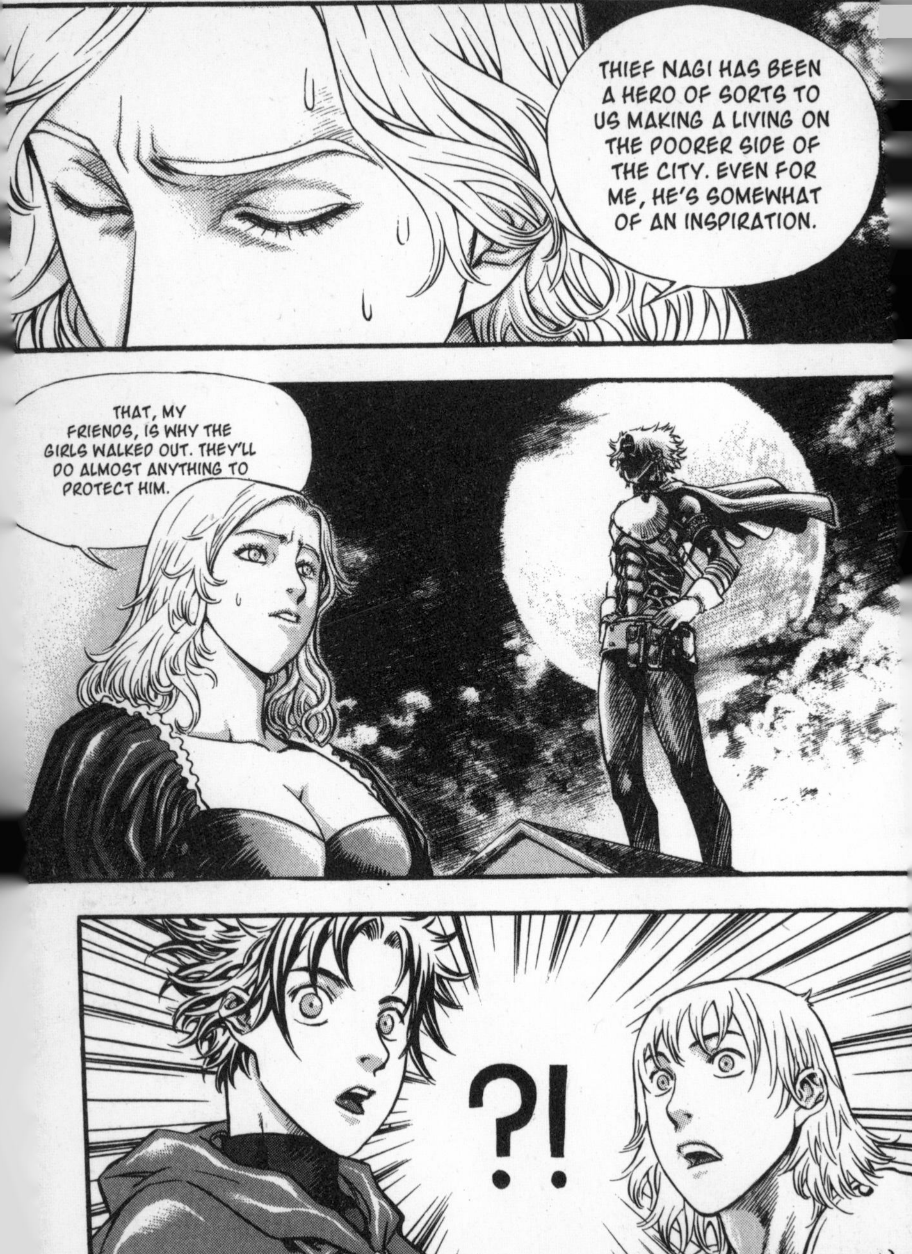
THIEF NAGI HAS BEEN A HERO OF SORTS TO US MAKING A LIVING ON THE POORER SIDE OF THE CITY. EVEN FOR ME, HE'S SOMEWHAT OF AN INSPIRATION.
THAT, MY FRIENDS, IS WHY THE GIRLS WALKED OUT. THEY'LL DO ALMOST ANYTHING TO PROTECT HIM.
?!

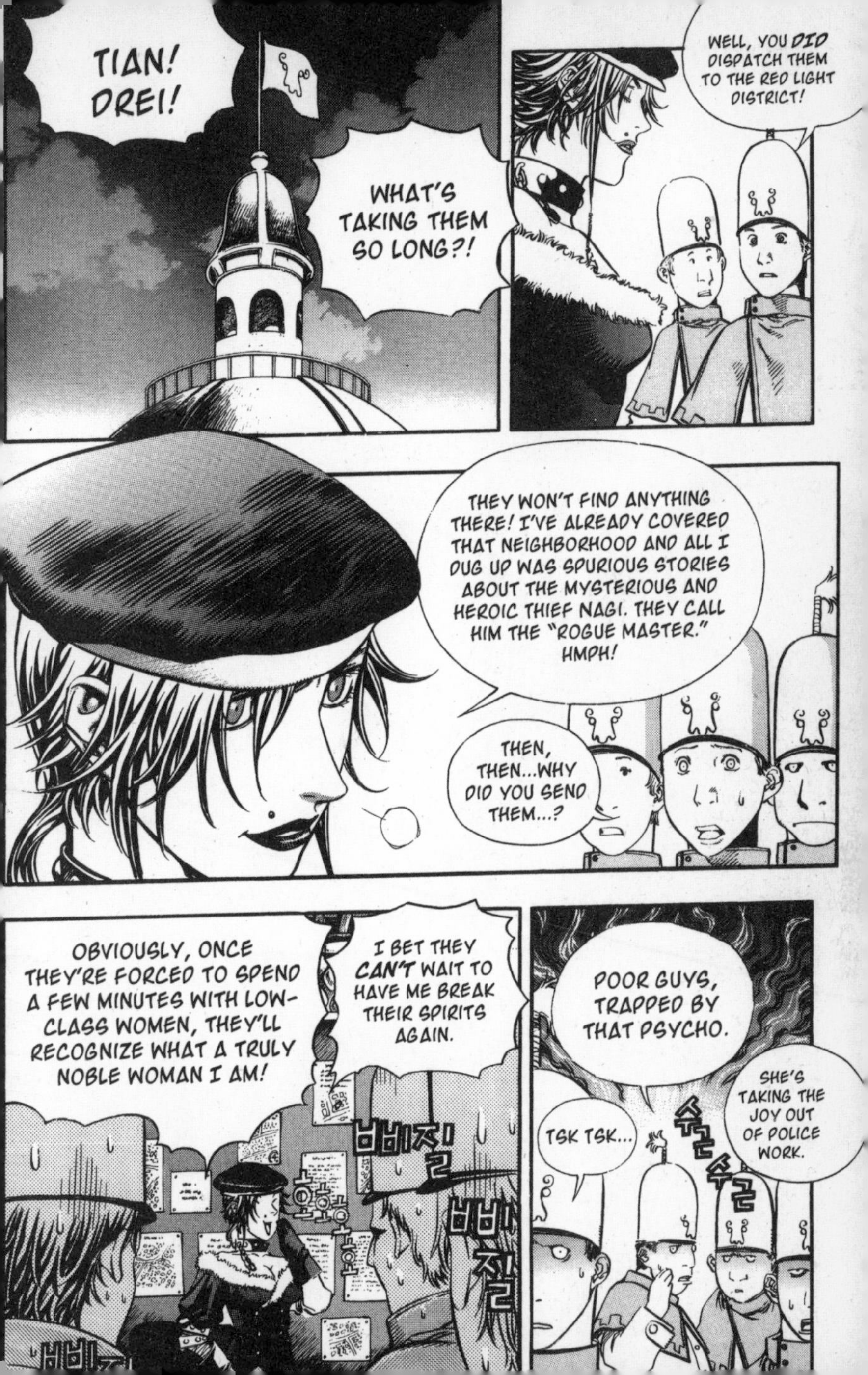
TIAN! DREI!
WHAT'S TAKING THEM SO LONG?!
WELL, YOU DID DISPATCH THEM TO THE RED LIGHT DISTRICT!
THEY WON'T FIND ANYTHING THERE! I'VE ALREADY COVERED THAT NEIGHBORHOOD AND ALL I DUG UP WAS SPURIOUS STORIES ABOUT THE MYSTERIOUS AND HEROIC THIEF NAGI. THEY CALL HIM THE "ROGUE MASTER." HMPH!
THEN, THEN...WHY DID YOU SEND THEM...?
OBVIOUSLY, ONCE THEY'RE FORCED TO SPEND A FEW MINUTES WITH LOW-CLASS WOMEN, THEY'LL RECOGNIZE WHAT A TRULY NOBLE WOMAN I AM!
I BET THEY CAN'T WAIT TO HAVE ME BREAK THEIR SPIRITS AGAIN.
삐질
POOR GUYS, TRAPPED BY THAT PSYCHO.
TSK TSK...
SHE'S TAKING THE JOY OUT OF POLICE WORK.
수군수군

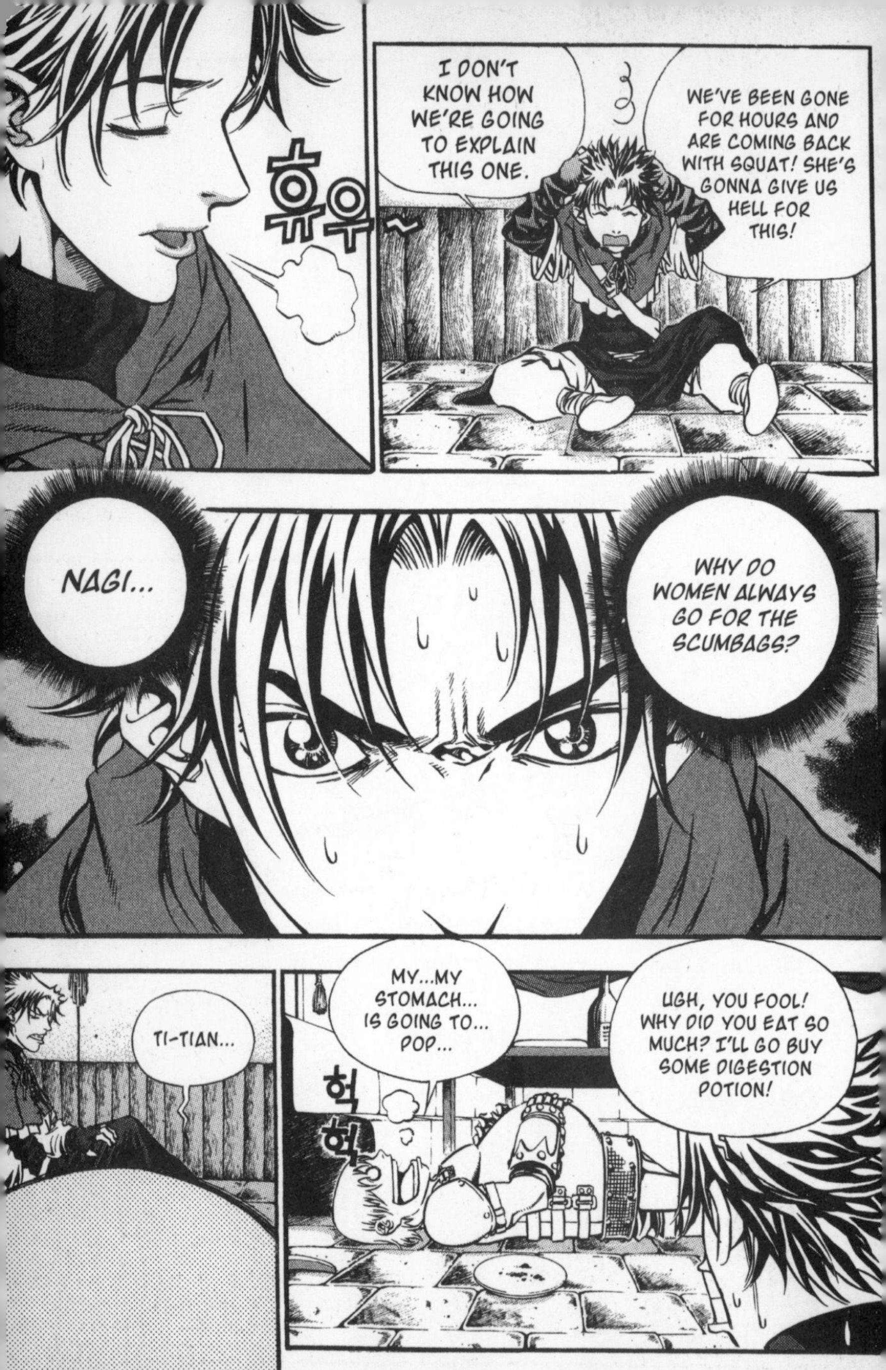
휴우~
I DON'T KNOW HOW WE'RE GOING TO EXPLAIN THIS ONE.
WE'VE BEEN GONE FOR HOURS AND ARE COMING BACK WITH SQUAT! SHE'S GONNA GIVE US HELL FOR THIS!
NAGI...
WHY DO WOMEN ALWAYS GO FOR THE SCUMBAGS?
TI-TIAN...
MY...MY STOMACH... IS GOING TO... POP...
헉헉
UGH, YOU FOOL! WHY DID YOU EAT SO MUCH? I'LL GO BUY SOME DIGESTION POTION!

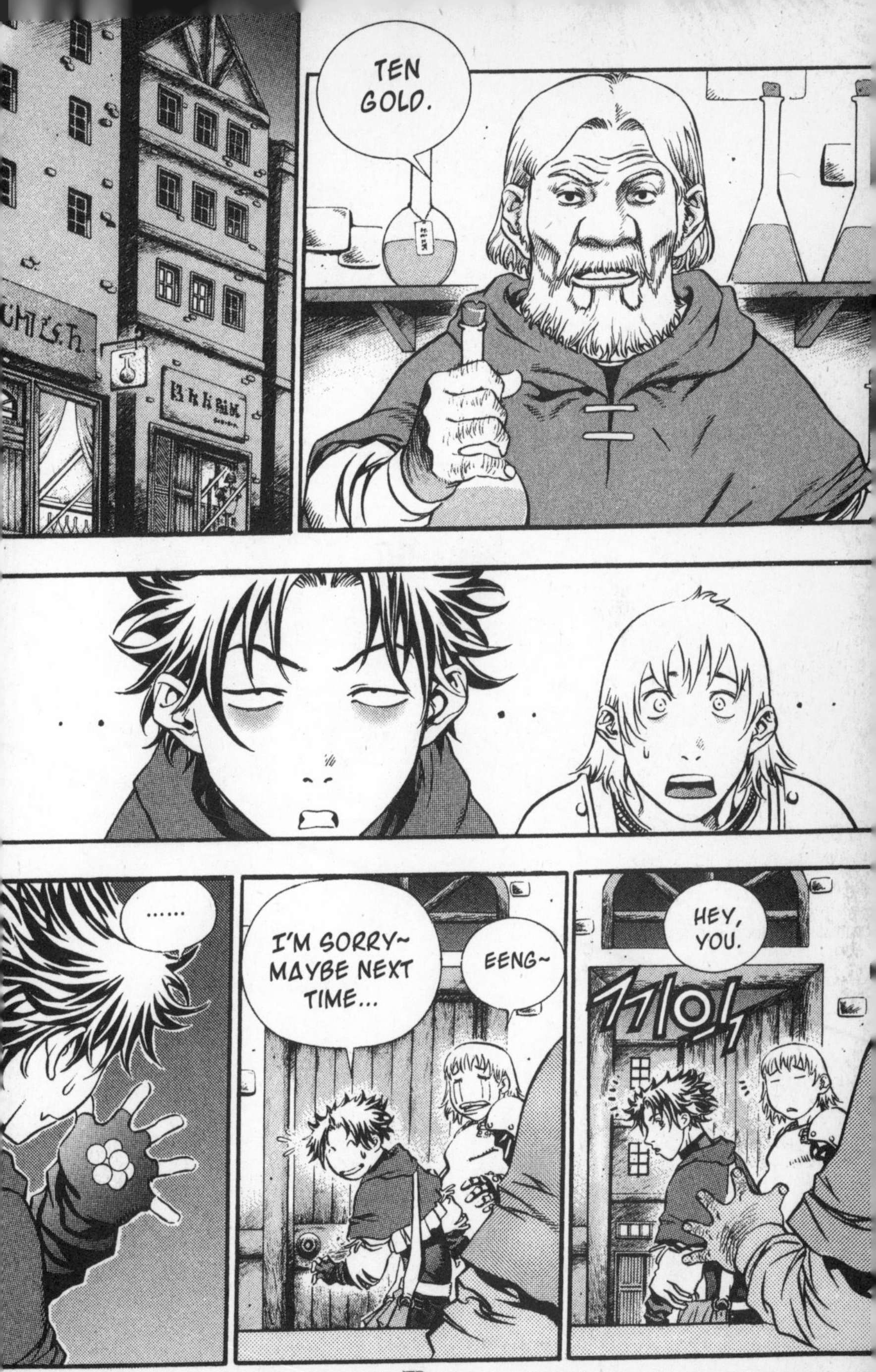
TEN GOLD.
......
I'M SORRY~ MAYBE NEXT TIME...
EENG~
HEY, YOU.

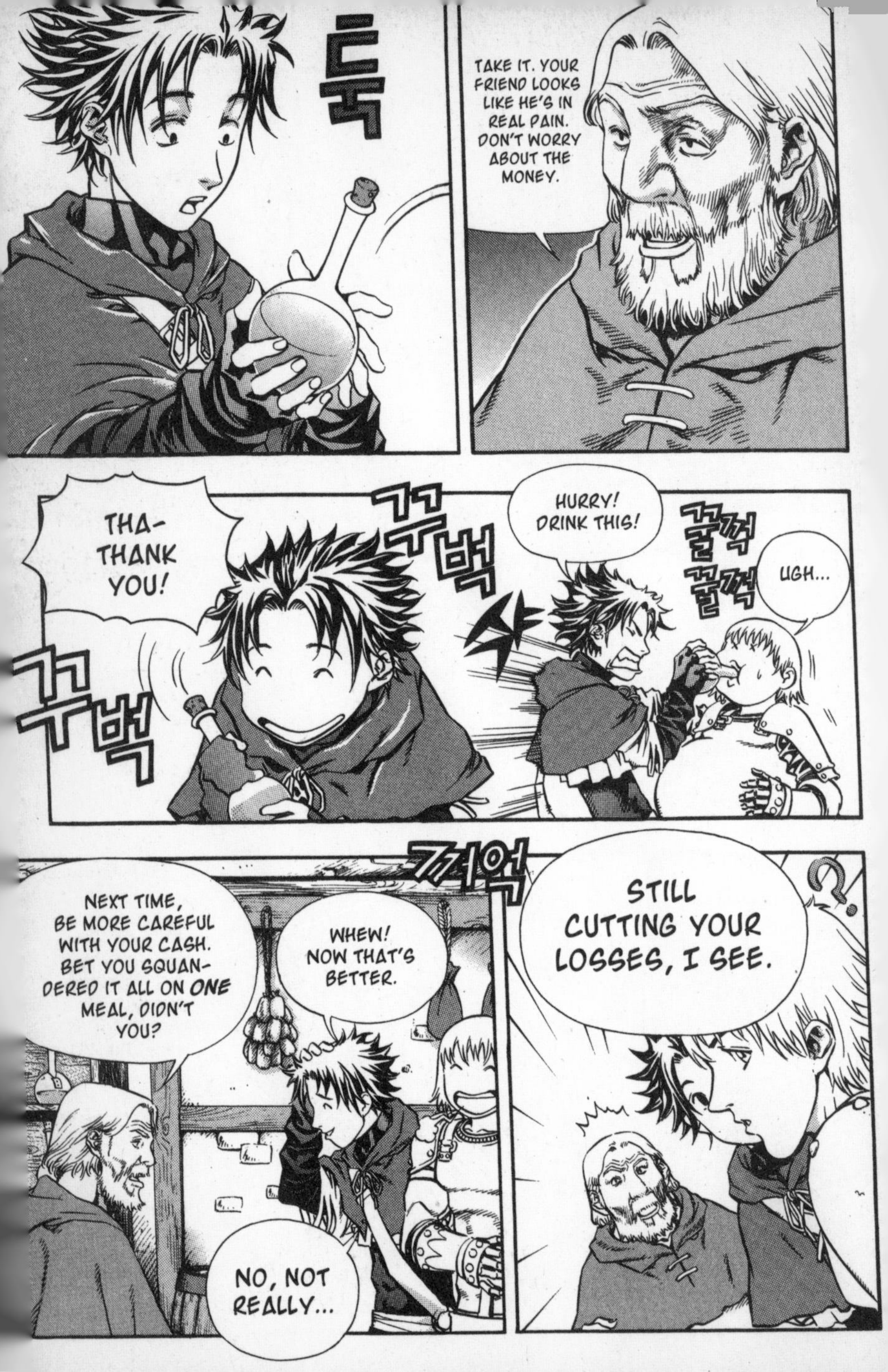

툭
TAKE IT. YOUR FRIEND LOOKS LIKE HE'S IN REAL PAIN. DON'T WORRY ABOUT THE MONEY.
THA- THANK YOU!
꾸벅
꾸벅
HURRY! DRINK THIS!
꿀꺽 꿀꺽
UGH...
꺼억
NEXT TIME, BE MORE CAREFUL WITH YOUR CASH. BET YOU SQUANDERED IT ALL ON *ONE* MEAL, DIDN'T YOU?
WHEW! NOW THAT'S BETTER.
NO, NOT REALLY...
STILL CUTTING YOUR LOSSES, I SEE.
?!

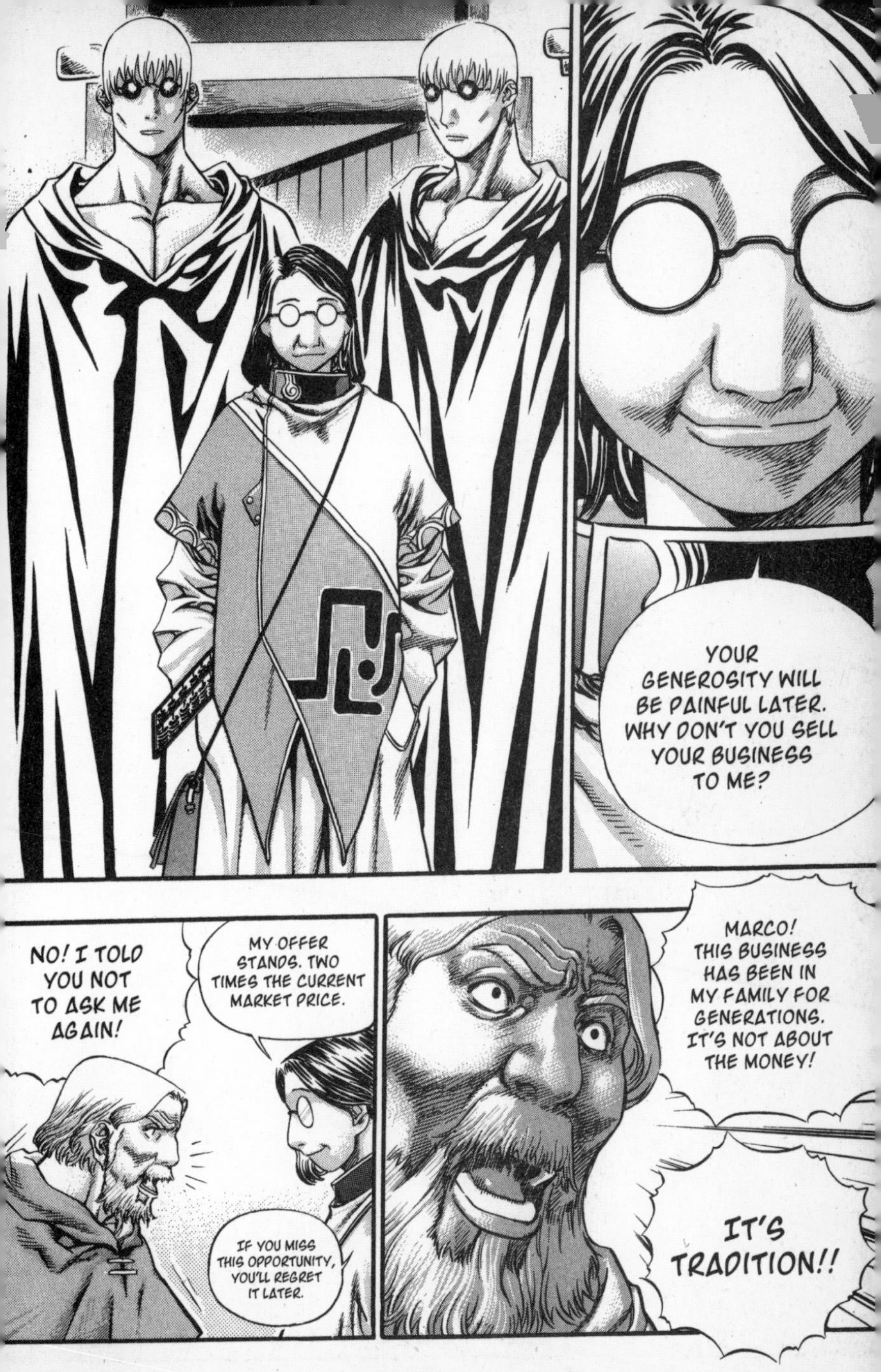
YOUR GENEROSITY WILL BE PAINFUL LATER. WHY DON'T YOU SELL YOUR BUSINESS TO ME?
NO! I TOLD YOU NOT TO ASK ME AGAIN!
MY OFFER STANDS. TWO TIMES THE CURRENT MARKET PRICE.
IF YOU MISS THIS OPPORTUNITY, YOU'LL REGRET IT LATER.
MARCO! THIS BUSINESS HAS BEEN IN MY FAMILY FOR GENERATIONS. IT'S NOT ABOUT THE MONEY!
IT'S TRADITION!!

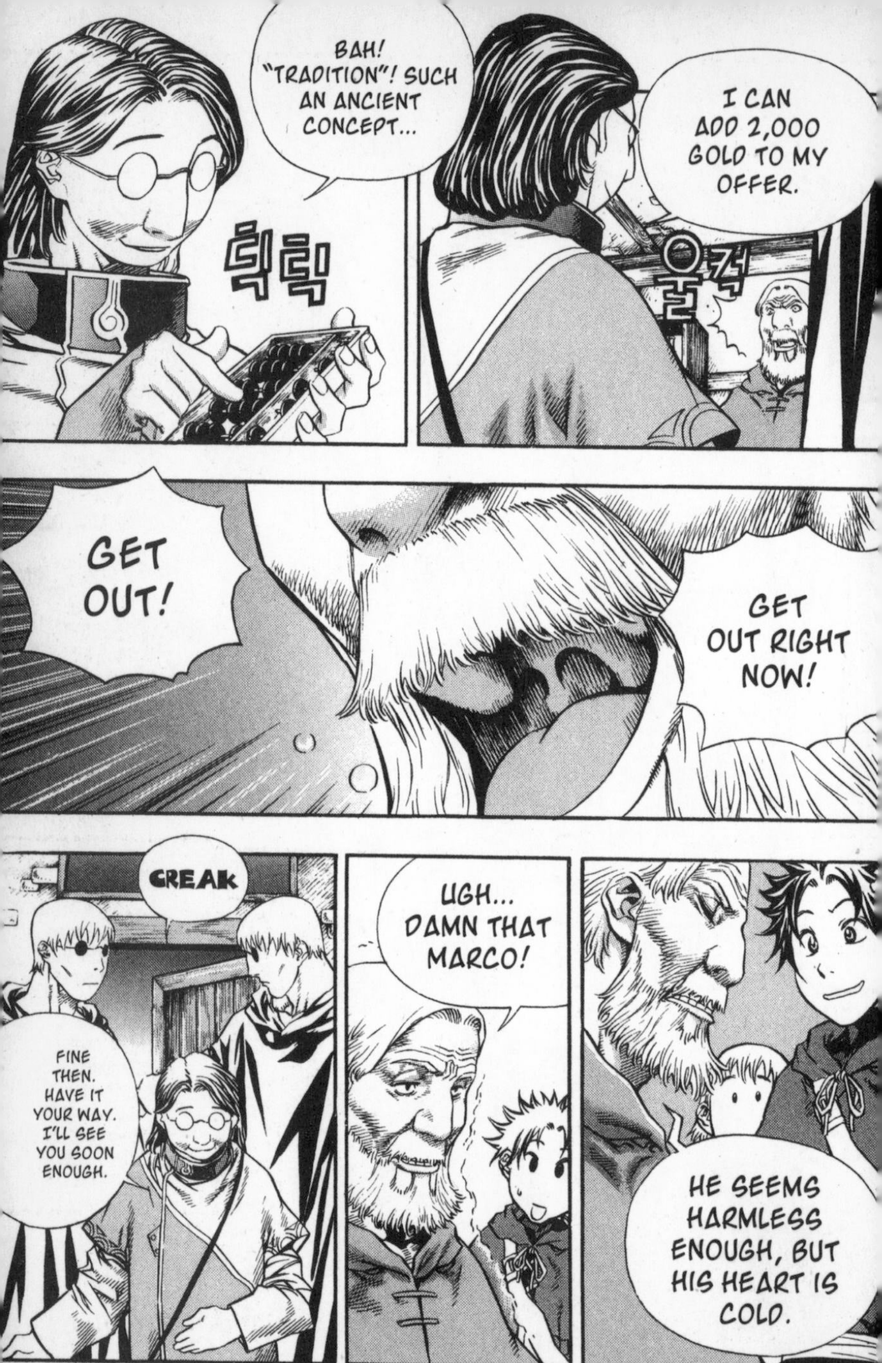

BAH! "TRADITION"! SUCH AN ANCIENT CONCEPT...
틱틱
I CAN ADD 2,000 GOLD TO MY OFFER.
울컥
GET OUT!
GET OUT RIGHT NOW!
CREAK
FINE THEN. HAVE IT YOUR WAY. I'LL SEE YOU SOON ENOUGH.
UGH... DAMN THAT MARCO!
HE SEEMS HARMLESS ENOUGH, BUT HIS HEART IS COLD.

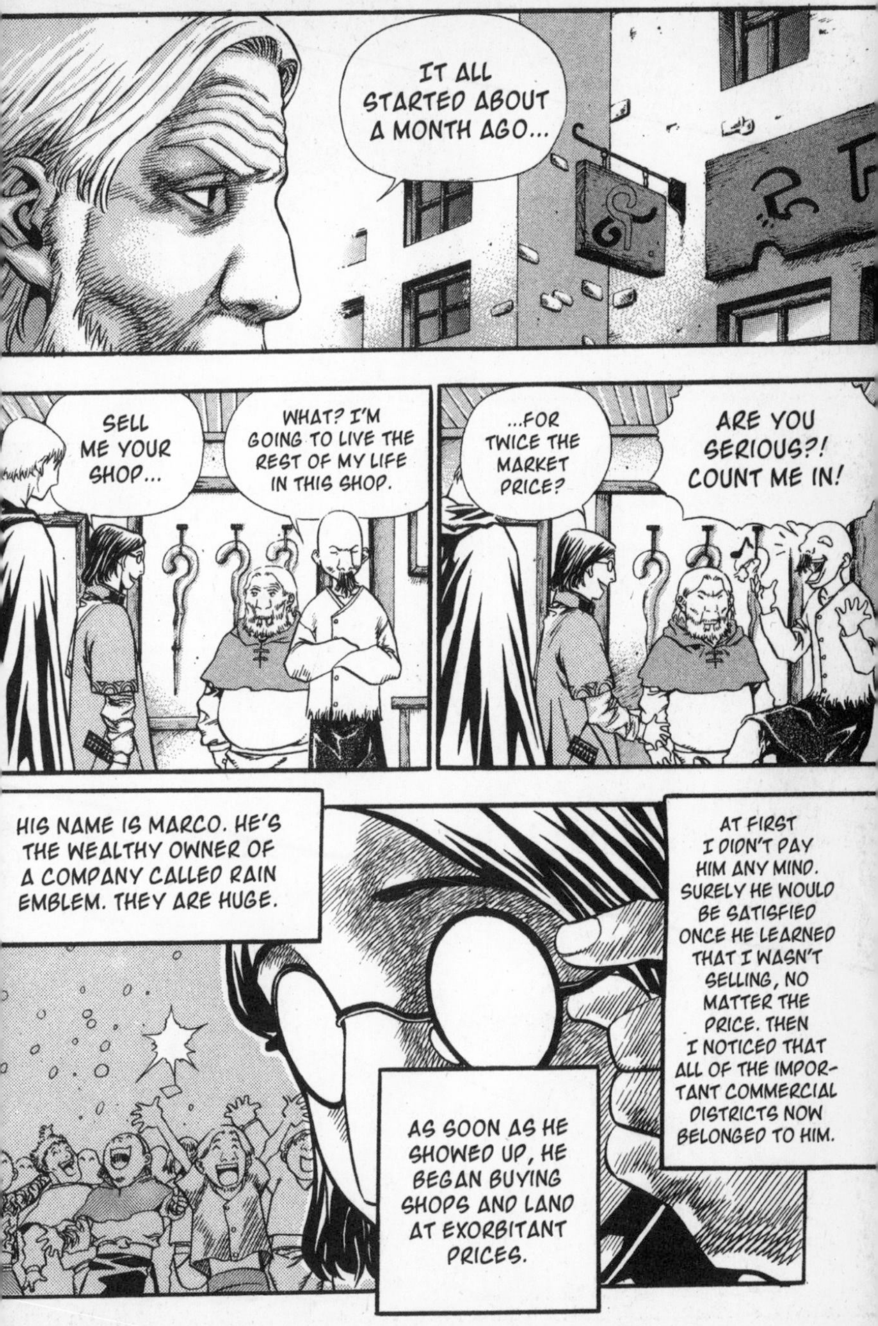
IT ALL STARTED ABOUT A MONTH AGO...
SELL ME YOUR SHOP...
WHAT? I'M GOING TO LIVE THE REST OF MY LIFE IN THIS SHOP.
...FOR TWICE THE MARKET PRICE?
ARE YOU SERIOUS?! COUNT ME IN!
HIS NAME IS MARCO. HE'S THE WEALTHY OWNER OF A COMPANY CALLED RAIN EMBLEM. THEY ARE HUGE.
AT FIRST I DIDN'T PAY HIM ANY MIND. SURELY HE WOULD BE SATISFIED ONCE HE LEARNED THAT I WASN'T SELLING, NO MATTER THE PRICE. THEN I NOTICED THAT ALL OF THE IMPORTANT COMMERCIAL DISTRICTS NOW BELONGED TO HIM.
AS SOON AS HE SHOWED UP, HE BEGAN BUYING SHOPS AND LAND AT EXORBITANT PRICES.

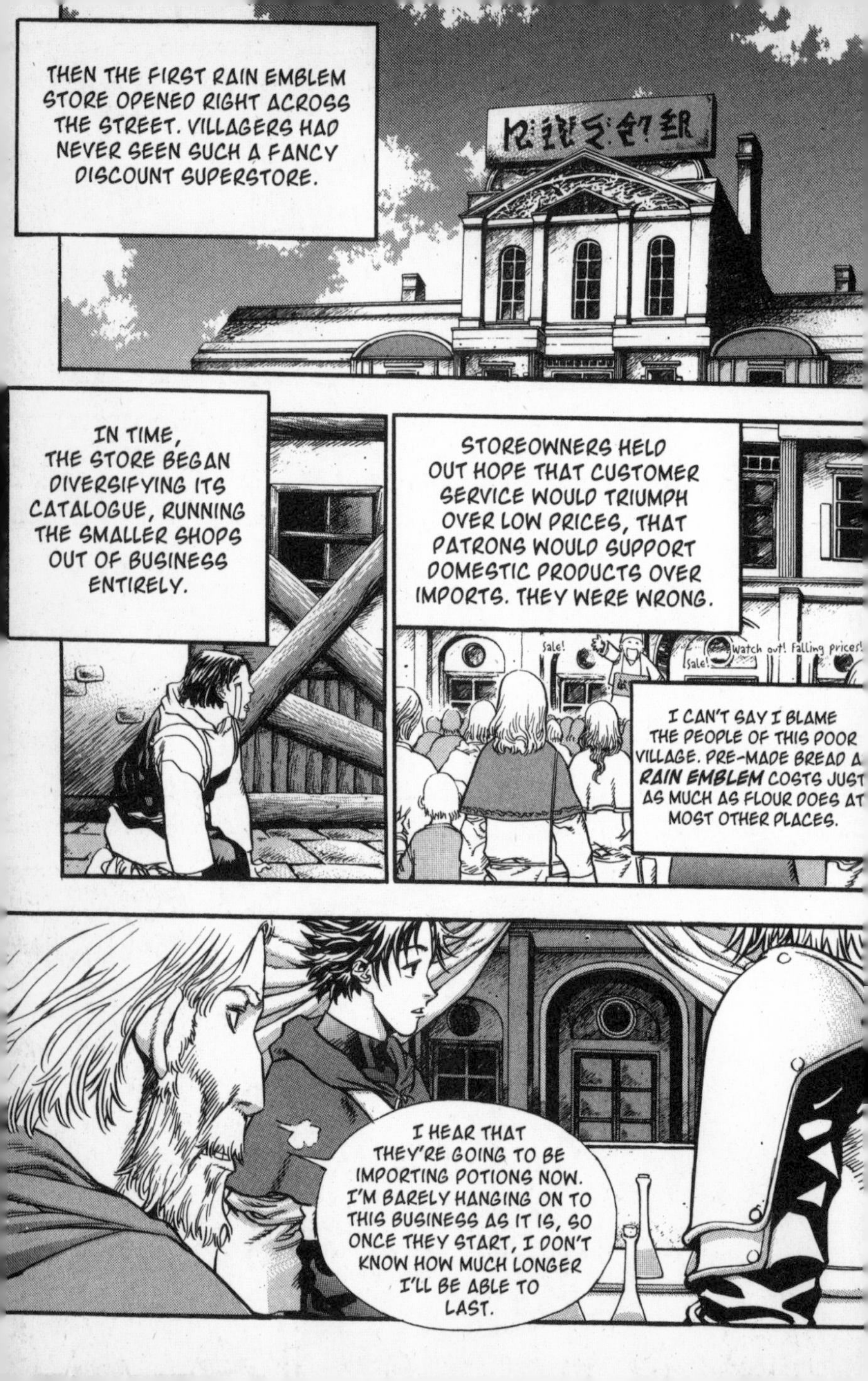
THEN THE FIRST RAIN EMBLEM STORE OPENED RIGHT ACROSS THE STREET. VILLAGERS HAD NEVER SEEN SUCH A FANCY DISCOUNT SUPERSTORE.
IN TIME, THE STORE BEGAN DIVERSIFYING ITS CATALOGUE, RUNNING THE SMALLER SHOPS OUT OF BUSINESS ENTIRELY.
STOREOWNERS HELD OUT HOPE THAT CUSTOMER SERVICE WOULD TRIUMPH OVER LOW PRICES, THAT PATRONS WOULD SUPPORT DOMESTIC PRODUCTS OVER IMPORTS. THEY WERE WRONG.
Sale!
Watch out! Falling prices!
Sale!
I CAN'T SAY I BLAME THE PEOPLE OF THIS POOR VILLAGE. PRE-MADE BREAD A RAIN EMBLEM COSTS JUST AS MUCH AS FLOUR DOES AT MOST OTHER PLACES.
I HEAR THAT THEY'RE GOING TO BE IMPORTING POTIONS NOW. I'M BARELY HANGING ON TO THIS BUSINESS AS IT IS, SO ONCE THEY START, I DON'T KNOW HOW MUCH LONGER I'LL BE ABLE TO LAST.

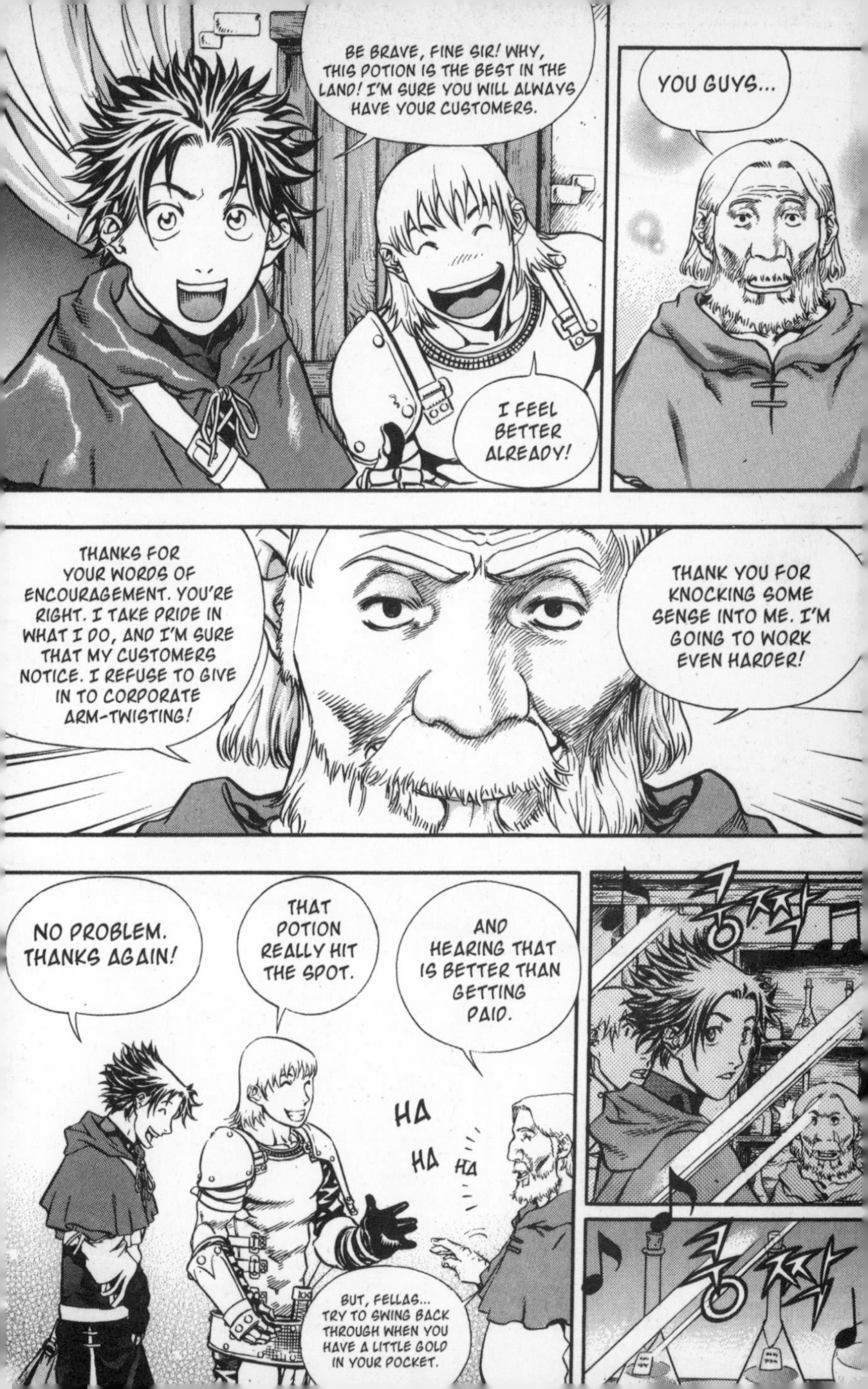

BE BRAVE, FINE SIR! WHY, THIS POTION IS THE BEST IN THE LAND! I'M SURE YOU WILL ALWAYS HAVE YOUR CUSTOMERS.
I FEEL BETTER ALREADY!
YOU GUYS...
THANKS FOR YOUR WORDS OF ENCOURAGEMENT. YOU'RE RIGHT. I TAKE PRIDE IN WHAT I DO, AND I'M SURE THAT MY CUSTOMERS NOTICE. I REFUSE TO GIVE IN TO CORPORATE ARM-TWISTING!
THANK YOU FOR KNOCKING SOME SENSE INTO ME. I'M GOING TO WORK EVEN HARDER!
NO PROBLEM. THANKS AGAIN!
THAT POTION REALLY HIT THE SPOT.
AND HEARING THAT IS BETTER THAN GETTING PAID.
HA
HA
HA
BUT, FELLAS... TRY TO SWING BACK THROUGH WHEN YOU HAVE A LITTLE GOLD IN YOUR POCKET.

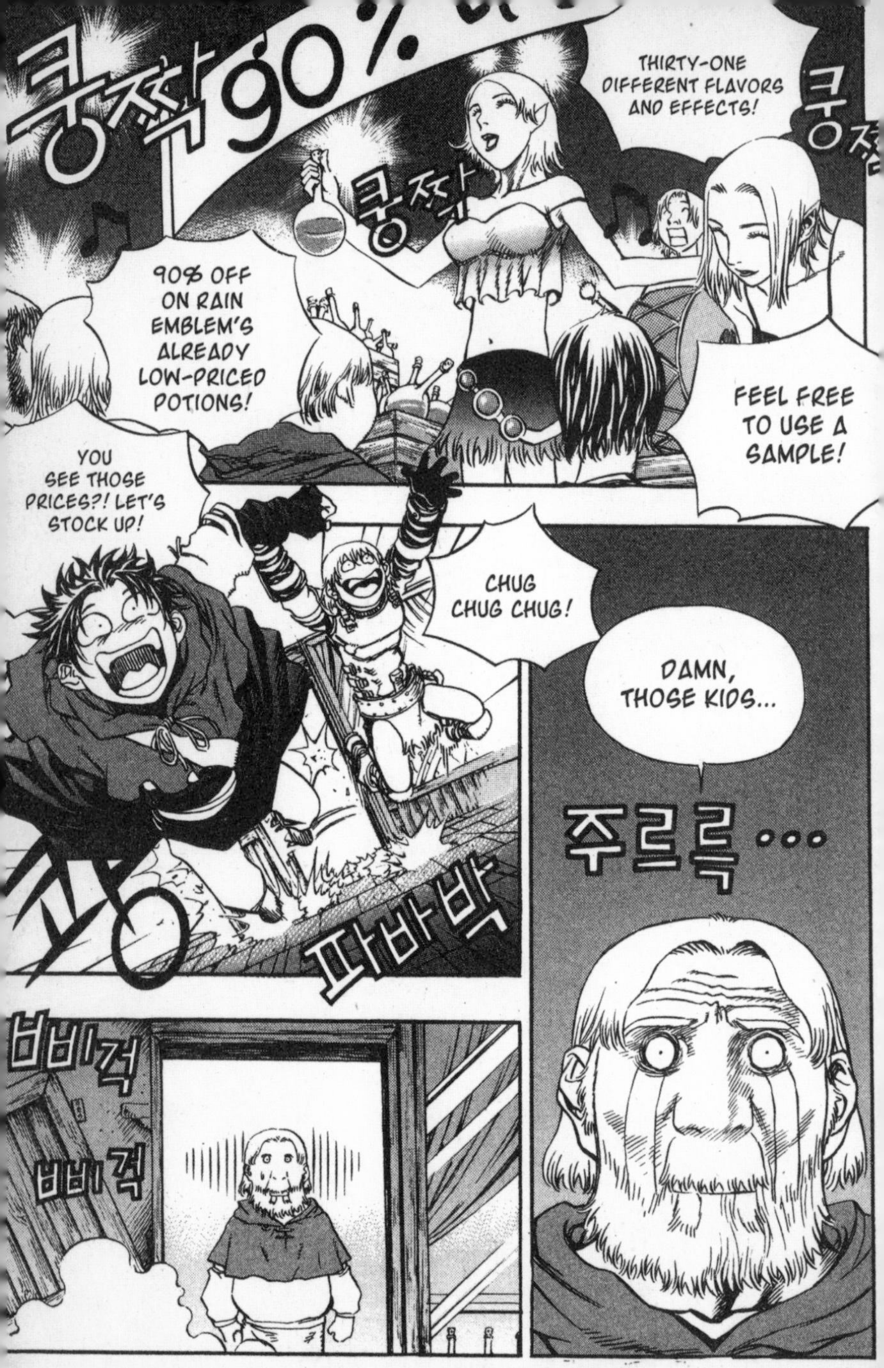

콩짝 90%
THIRTY-ONE DIFFERENT FLAVORS AND EFFECTS!
콩짝
콩짝
90% OFF ON RAIN EMBLEM'S ALREADY LOW-PRICED POTIONS!
FEEL FREE TO USE A SAMPLE!
YOU SEE THOSE PRICES?! LET'S STOCK UP!
CHUG CHUG CHUG!
DAMN, THOSE KIDS...
주르륵...
파바박
비비적
비비적

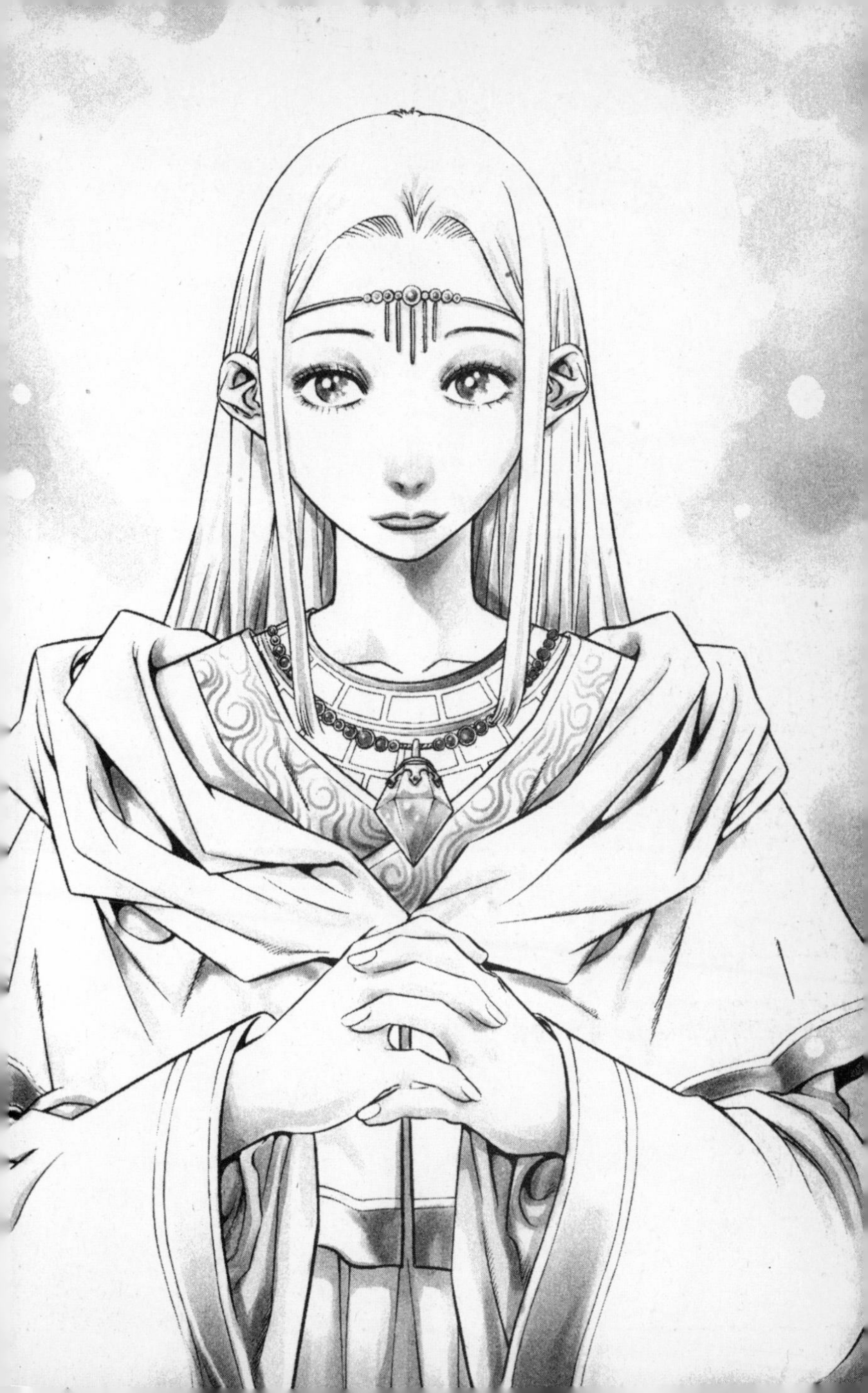

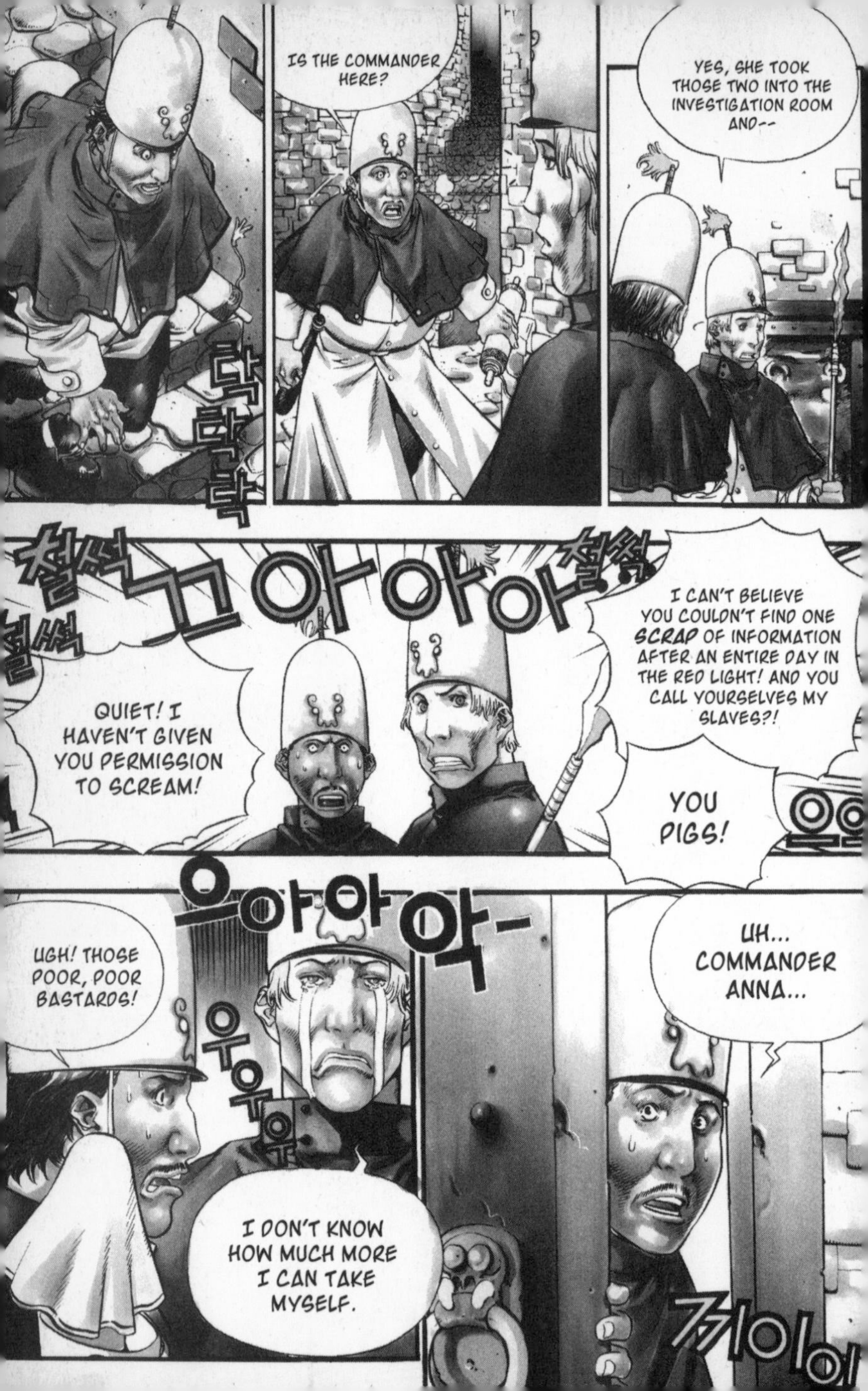
IS THE COMMANDER HERE?
YES, SHE TOOK THOSE TWO INTO THE INVESTIGATION ROOM AND--
I CAN'T BELIEVE YOU COULDN'T FIND ONE SCRAP OF INFORMATION AFTER AN ENTIRE DAY IN THE RED LIGHT! AND YOU CALL YOURSELVES MY SLAVES?!
QUIET! I HAVEN'T GIVEN YOU PERMISSION TO SCREAM!
YOU PIGS!
UH... COMMANDER ANNA...
UGH! THOSE POOR, POOR BASTARDS!
I DON'T KNOW HOW MUCH MORE I CAN TAKE MYSELF.

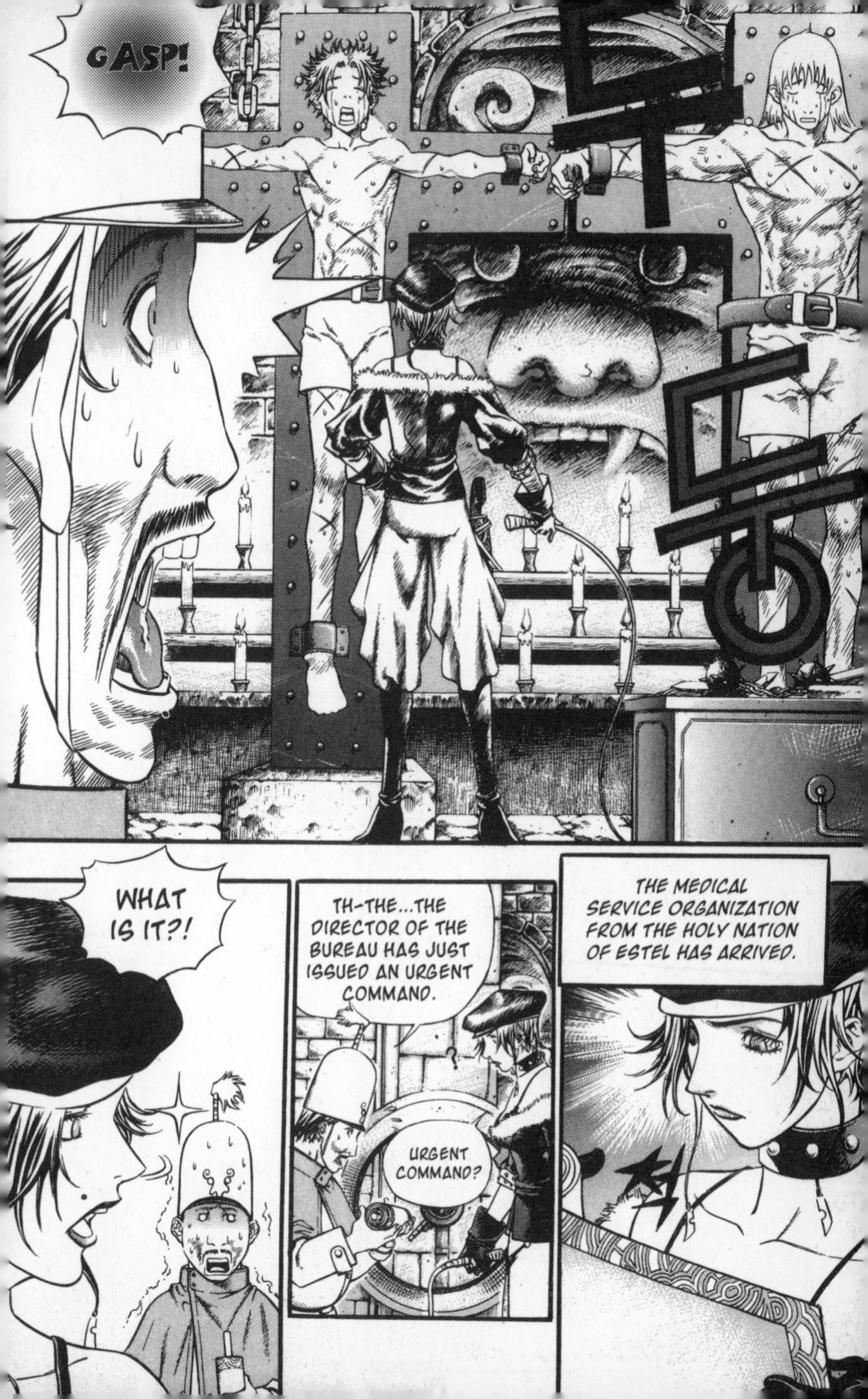
GASP!
WHAT IS IT?!
TH-THE...THE DIRECTOR OF THE BUREAU HAS JUST ISSUED AN URGENT COMMAND.
URGENT COMMAND?
THE MEDICAL SERVICE ORGANIZATION FROM THE HOLY NATION OF ESTEL HAS ARRIVED.

THE ECCLESIASTICAL NATION OF ESTEL CONSIDERS ITSELF AN INDEPENDENT RELIGIOUS NATION, BUT AS YOU ARE WELL AWARE, IT IS BUT A COLONY OF AMERIA.

WHATEVER THE CASE, I'VE JUST RECEIVED ORDERS FROM THE TOP, SAYING THAT WE SHOULD TAKE ADVANTAGE OF THEM AS LONG AS THEY ADVOCATE MEDICAL SERVICES, THEN QUIETLY SEND THEM ON THEIR WAY.

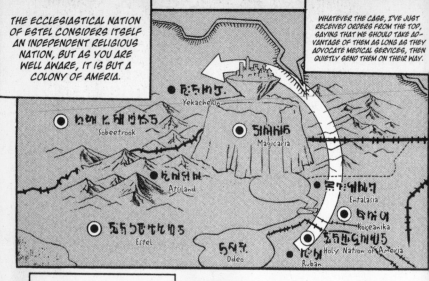

Yekachekin

Sobeetrook

Magicaria

Atuland

Estel

Entalasia

Koreanika

Ddeo

Ruban

Holy Nation of Ameria

THEY ARE LED BY A WOMAN BY THE NAME OF MARIEL. MANY IN ESTEL SEE HER AS THE SANCTIFIED WOMAN WHO WILL BIRTH THE MESSIAH, HE WHO SHALL BRING SALVATION TO THE WORLD.

ALSO, THE NECKLACE THAT SHE WEARS AROUND HER NECK IS CALLED "TEARS OF THE HOLY LADY" AND IS CONSIDERED PRICELESS. TAKE ALL PRECAUTIONS NECESSARY TO SAFEGUARD HER FROM ANY SORT OF ATTEMPTED THEFT. IF WE MAKE ONE MISTAKE, THIS CAN ESCALATE INTO A FULL-BLOWN DIPLOMATIC PROBLEM.

YOU MUST TAKE GREAT CARE AS HER ESCORT. WE SUSPECT THAT THERE MIGHT BE SPIES OPERATING RIGHT IN HER ENTOURAGE.

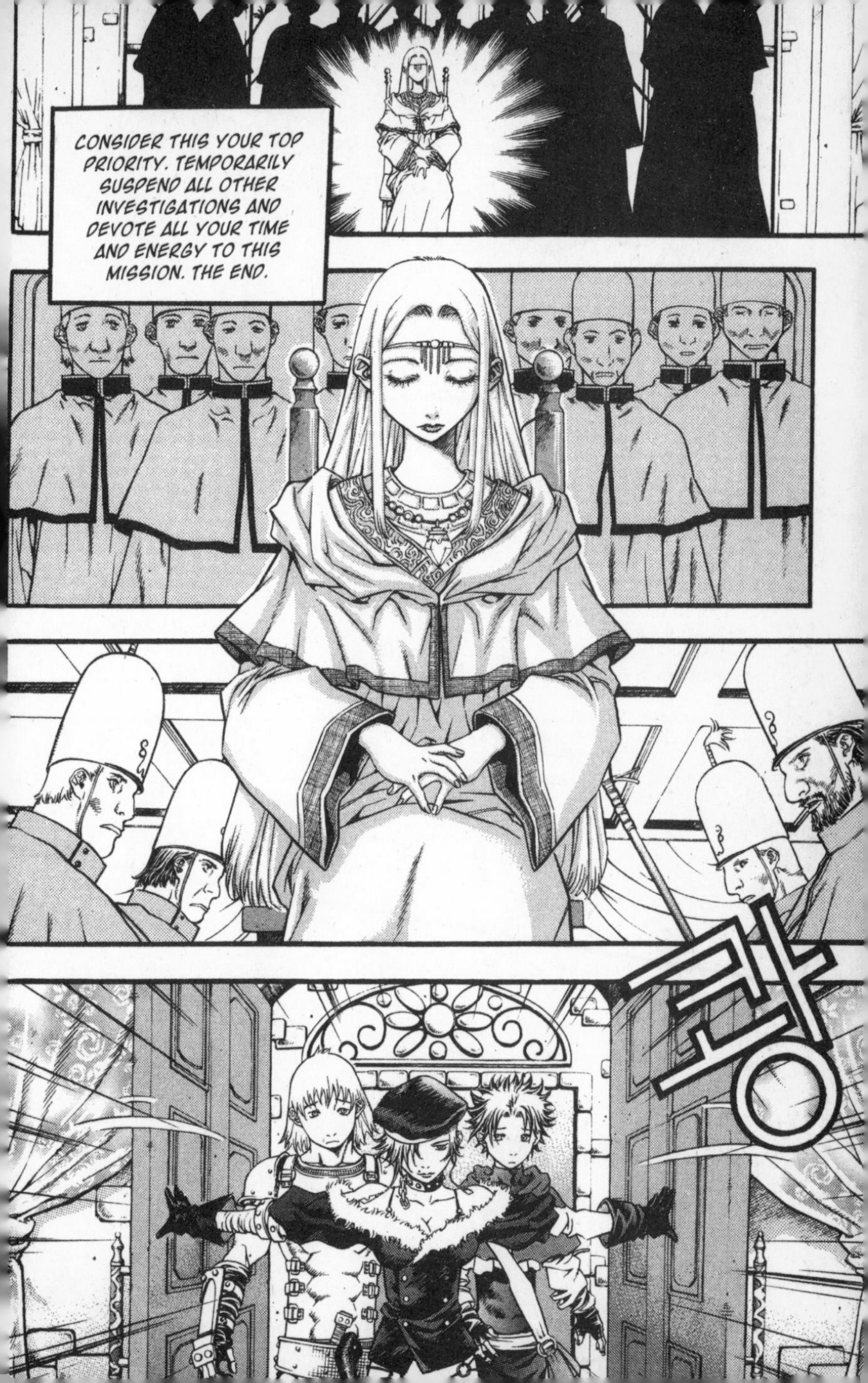
CONSIDER THIS YOUR TOP PRIORITY. TEMPORARILY SUSPEND ALL OTHER INVESTIGATIONS AND DEVOTE ALL YOUR TIME AND ENERGY TO THIS MISSION. THE END.

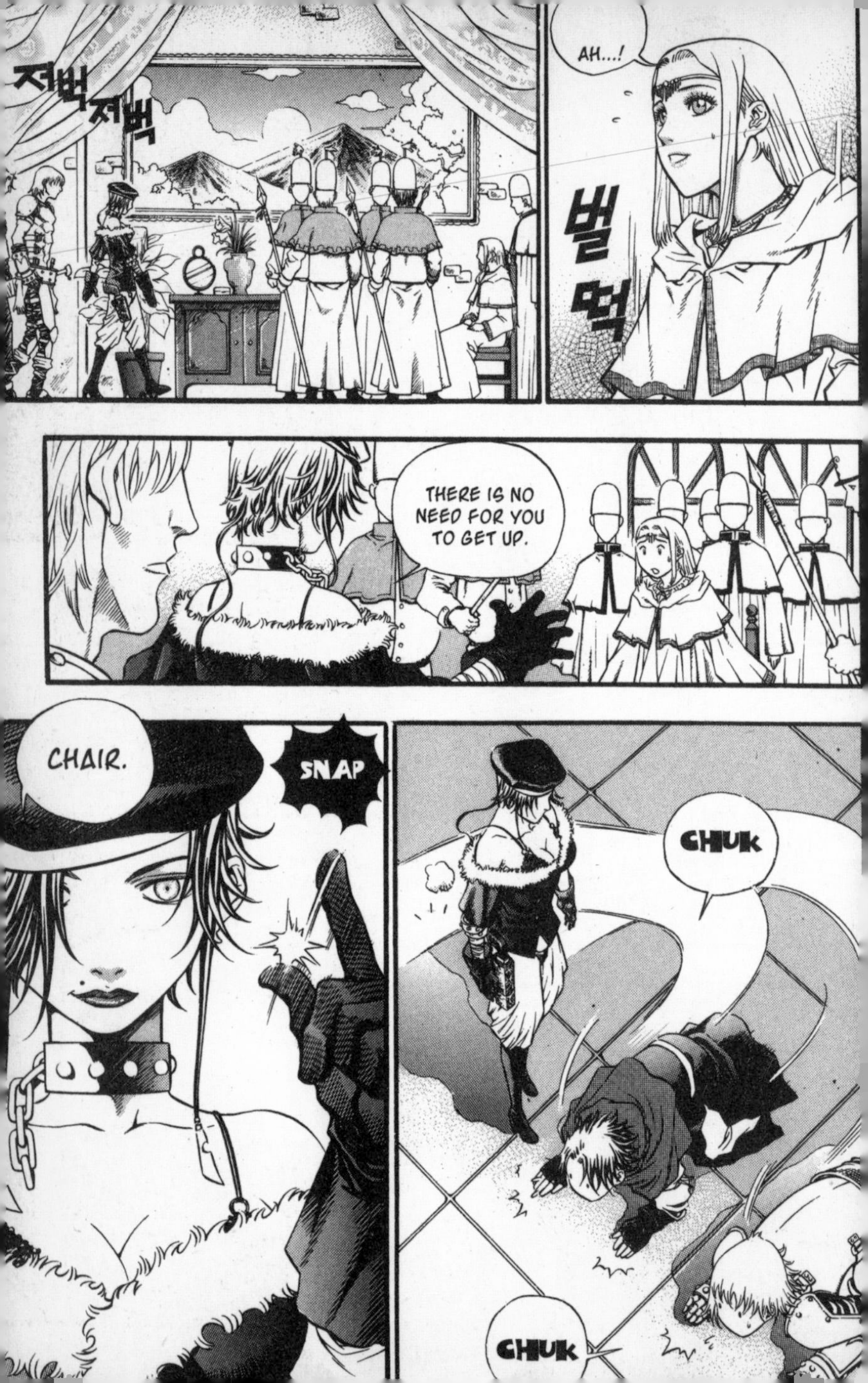
저벅저벅
AH...!
벌떡
THERE IS NO NEED FOR YOU TO GET UP.
CHAIR.
SNAP
CHUK
CHUK

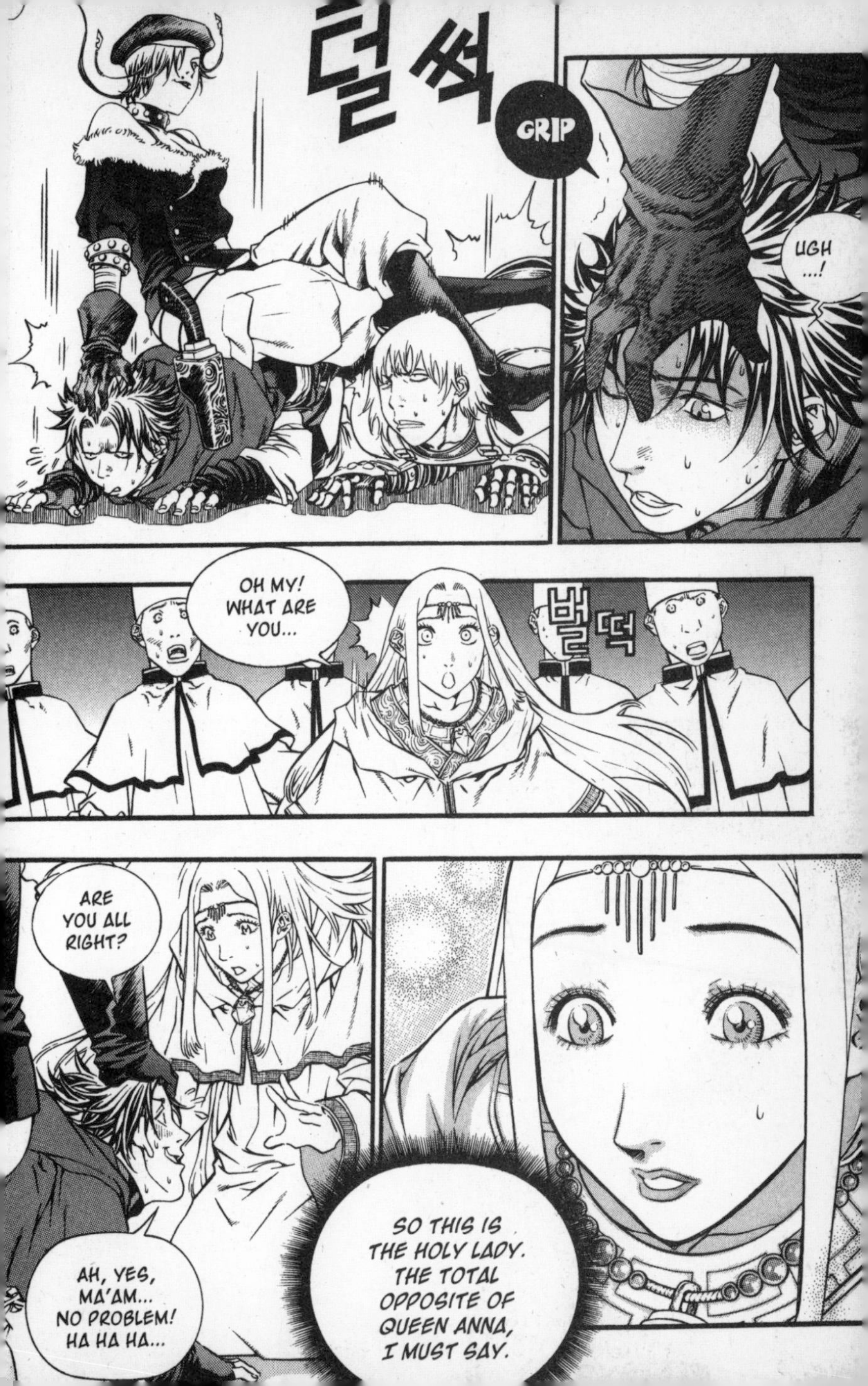
덜썩
GRIP
UGH ...!
OH MY! WHAT ARE YOU...
벌떡
ARE YOU ALL RIGHT?
AH, YES, MA'AM... NO PROBLEM! HA HA HA...
SO THIS IS THE HOLY LADY. THE TOTAL OPPOSITE OF QUEEN ANNA, I MUST SAY.

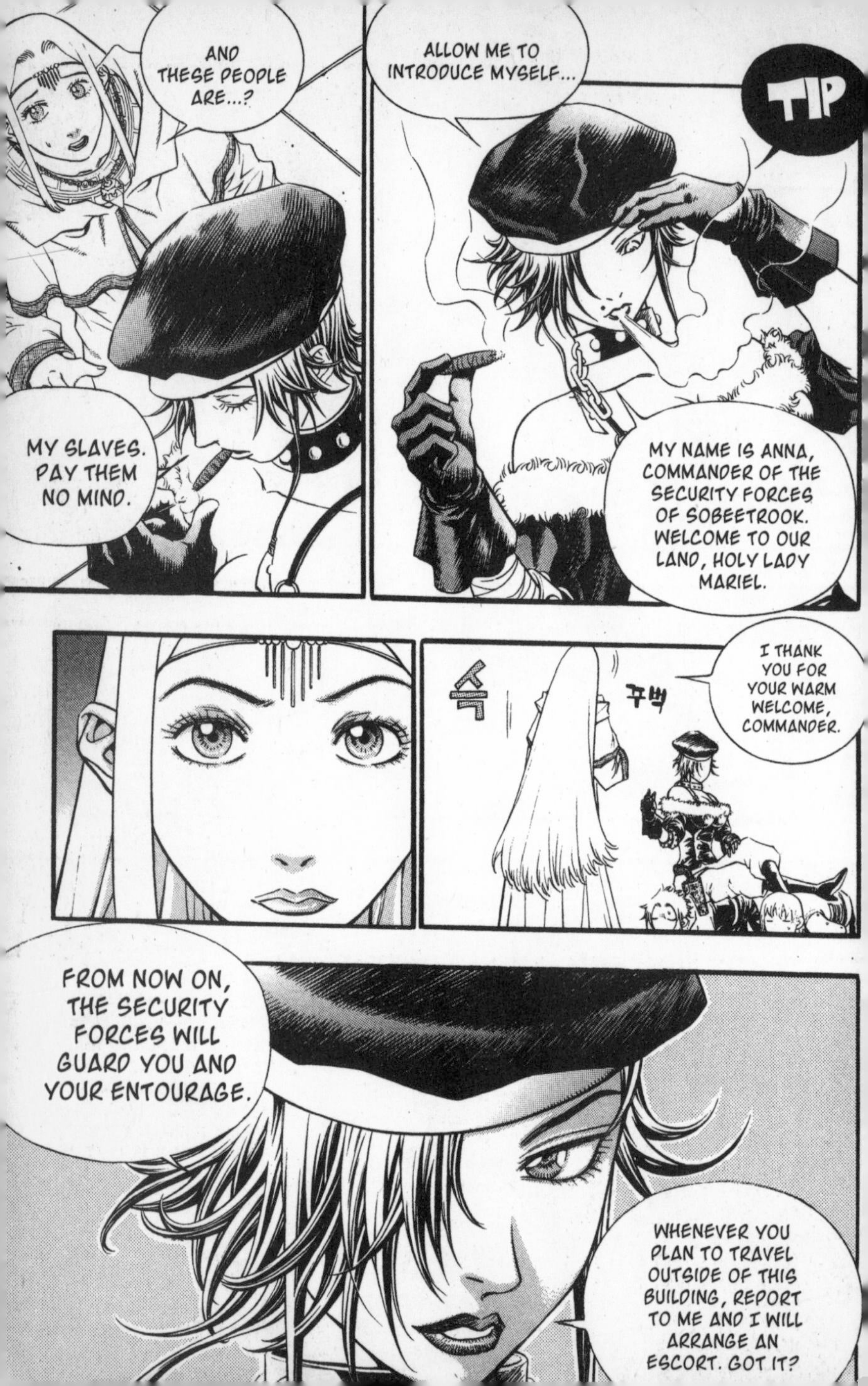
AND THESE PEOPLE ARE...?
MY SLAVES. PAY THEM NO MIND.
ALLOW ME TO INTRODUCE MYSELF...
TIP
MY NAME IS ANNA, COMMANDER OF THE SECURITY FORCES OF SOBEETROOK. WELCOME TO OUR LAND, HOLY LADY MARIEL.
I THANK YOU FOR YOUR WARM WELCOME, COMMANDER.
FROM NOW ON, THE SECURITY FORCES WILL GUARD YOU AND YOUR ENTOURAGE.
WHENEVER YOU PLAN TO TRAVEL OUTSIDE OF THIS BUILDING, REPORT TO ME AND I WILL ARRANGE AN ESCORT. GOT IT?

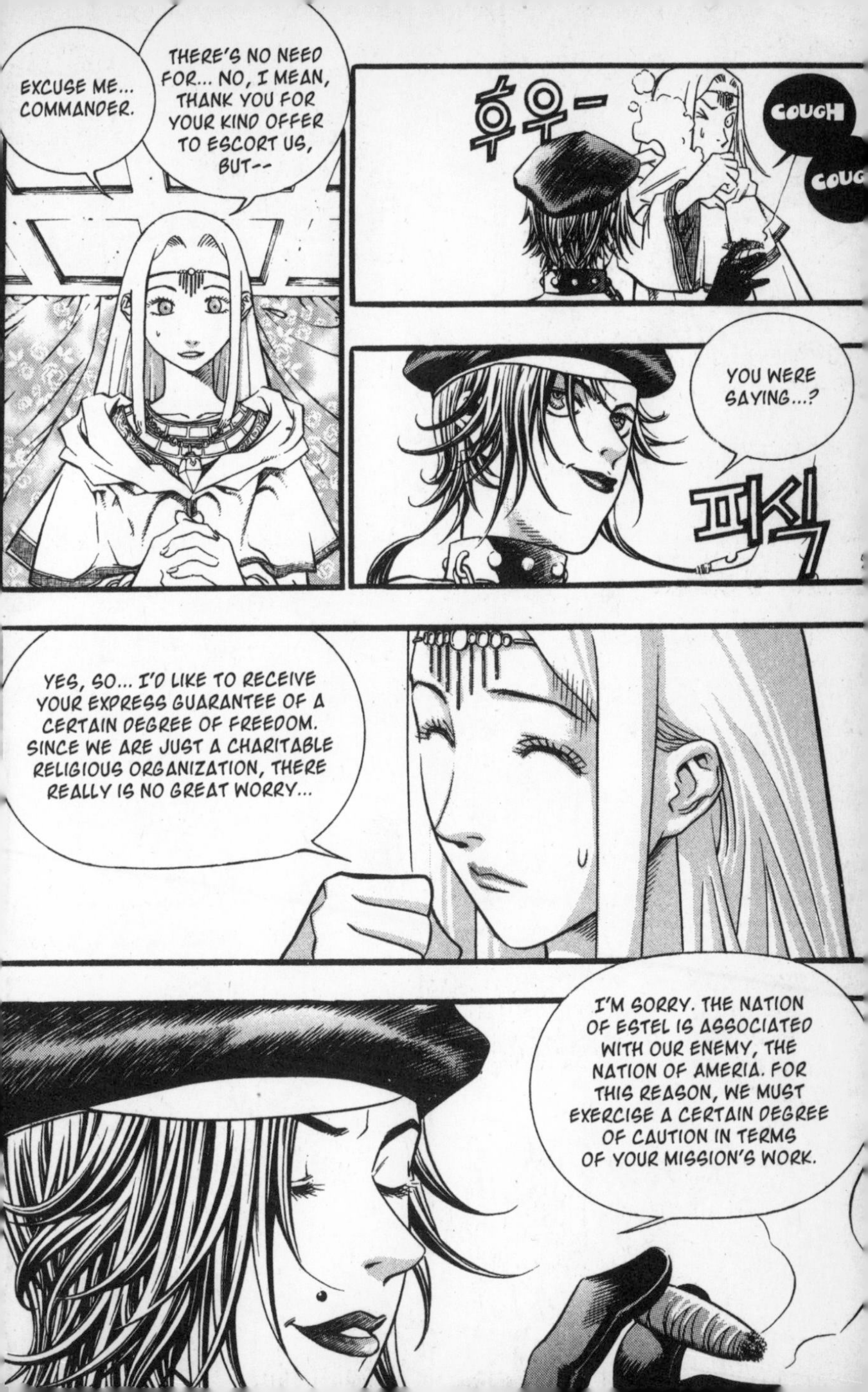
EXCUSE ME... COMMANDER.
THERE'S NO NEED FOR... NO, I MEAN, THANK YOU FOR YOUR KIND OFFER TO ESCORT US, BUT--
후우-
COUGH
COUG
YOU WERE SAYING...?
피식
YES, SO... I'D LIKE TO RECEIVE YOUR EXPRESS GUARANTEE OF A CERTAIN DEGREE OF FREEDOM. SINCE WE ARE JUST A CHARITABLE RELIGIOUS ORGANIZATION, THERE REALLY IS NO GREAT WORRY...
I'M SORRY. THE NATION OF ESTEL IS ASSOCIATED WITH OUR ENEMY, THE NATION OF AMERIA. FOR THIS REASON, WE MUST EXERCISE A CERTAIN DEGREE OF CAUTION IN TERMS OF YOUR MISSION'S WORK.

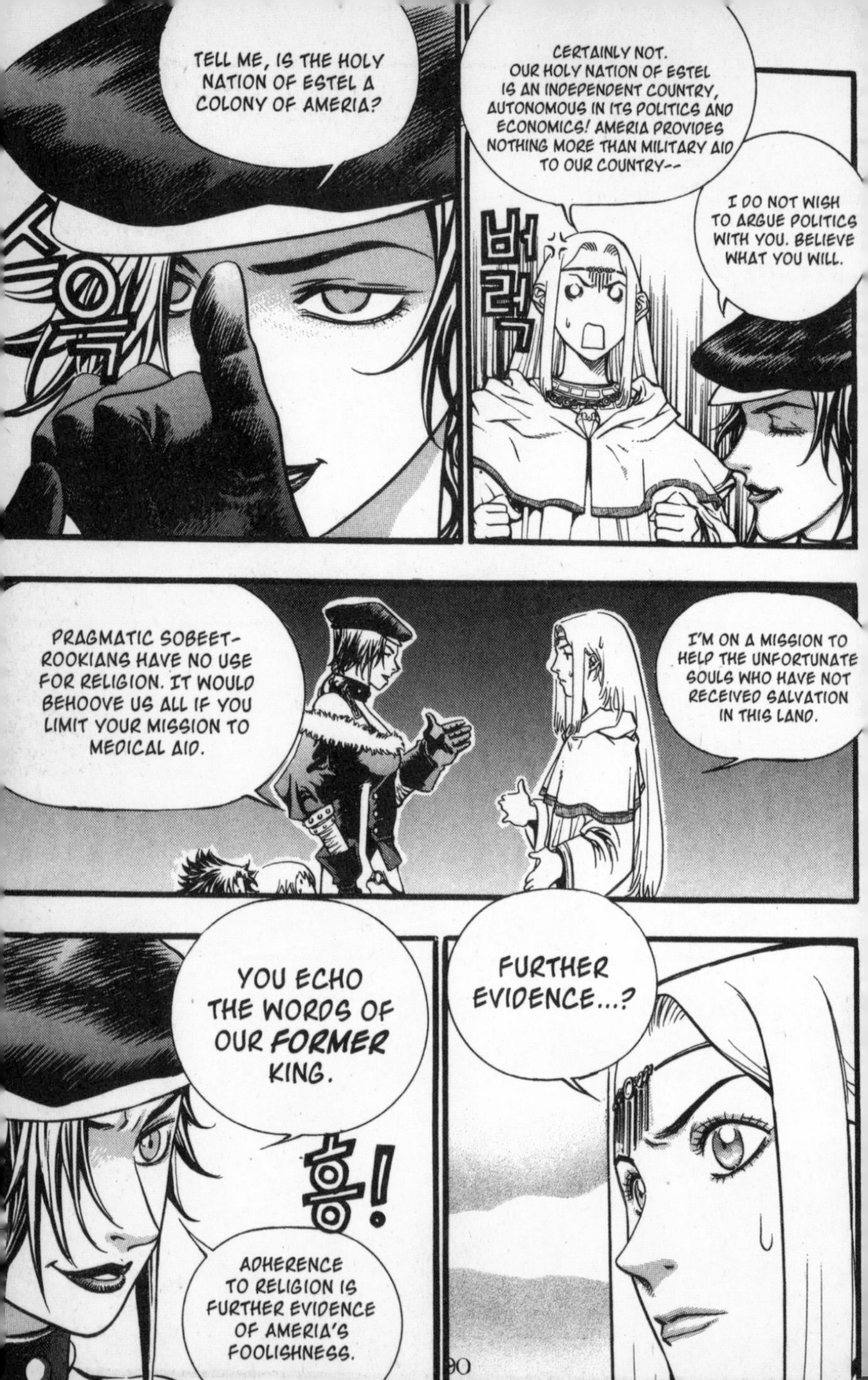

TELL ME, IS THE HOLY NATION OF ESTEL A COLONY OF AMERIA?
CERTAINLY NOT. OUR HOLY NATION OF ESTEL IS AN INDEPENDENT COUNTRY, AUTONOMOUS IN ITS POLITICS AND ECONOMICS! AMERIA PROVIDES NOTHING MORE THAN MILITARY AID TO OUR COUNTRY--
I DO NOT WISH TO ARGUE POLITICS WITH YOU. BELIEVE WHAT YOU WILL.
PRAGMATIC SOBEET-ROOKIANS HAVE NO USE FOR RELIGION. IT WOULD BEHOOVE US ALL IF YOU LIMIT YOUR MISSION TO MEDICAL AID.
I'M ON A MISSION TO HELP THE UNFORTUNATE SOULS WHO HAVE NOT RECEIVED SALVATION IN THIS LAND.
YOU ECHO THE WORDS OF OUR *FORMER* KING.
흥!
ADHERENCE TO RELIGION IS FURTHER EVIDENCE OF AMERIA'S FOOLISHNESS.
FURTHER EVIDENCE...?

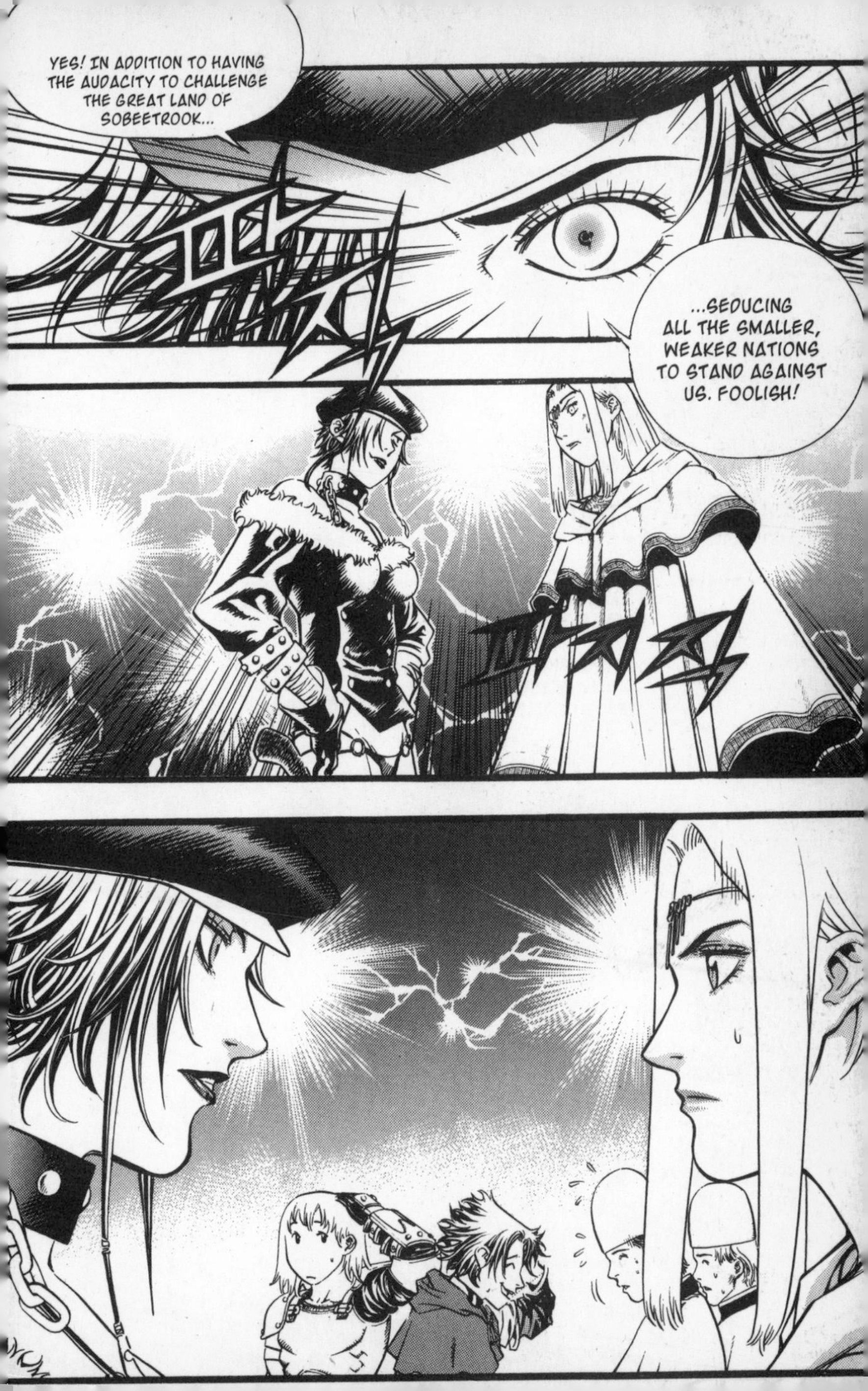
YES! IN ADDITION TO HAVING THE AUDACITY TO CHALLENGE THE GREAT LAND OF SOBEETROOK...
...SEDUCING ALL THE SMALLER, WEAKER NATIONS TO STAND AGAINST US. FOOLISH!

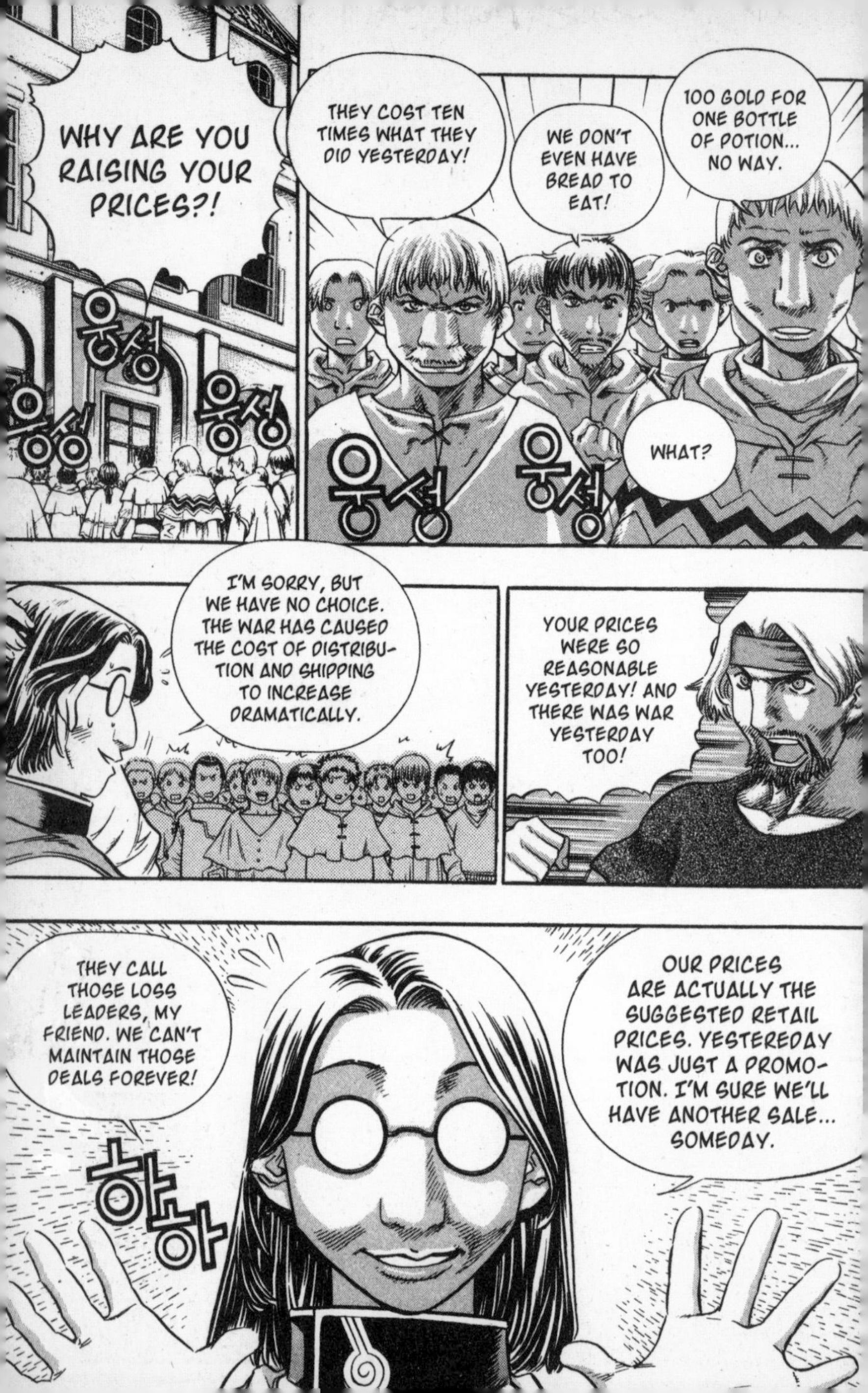
WHY ARE YOU RAISING YOUR PRICES?!
웅성
웅성
웅성
THEY COST TEN TIMES WHAT THEY DID YESTERDAY!
WE DON'T EVEN HAVE BREAD TO EAT!
100 GOLD FOR ONE BOTTLE OF POTION... NO WAY.
WHAT?
웅성
웅성
I'M SORRY, BUT WE HAVE NO CHOICE. THE WAR HAS CAUSED THE COST OF DISTRIBUTION AND SHIPPING TO INCREASE DRAMATICALLY.
YOUR PRICES WERE SO REASONABLE YESTERDAY! AND THERE WAS WAR YESTERDAY TOO!
THEY CALL THOSE LOSS LEADERS, MY FRIEND. WE CAN'T MAINTAIN THOSE DEALS FOREVER!
OUR PRICES ARE ACTUALLY THE SUGGESTED RETAIL PRICES. YESTEREDAY WAS JUST A PROMOTION. I'M SURE WE'LL HAVE ANOTHER SALE... SOMEDAY.
하하

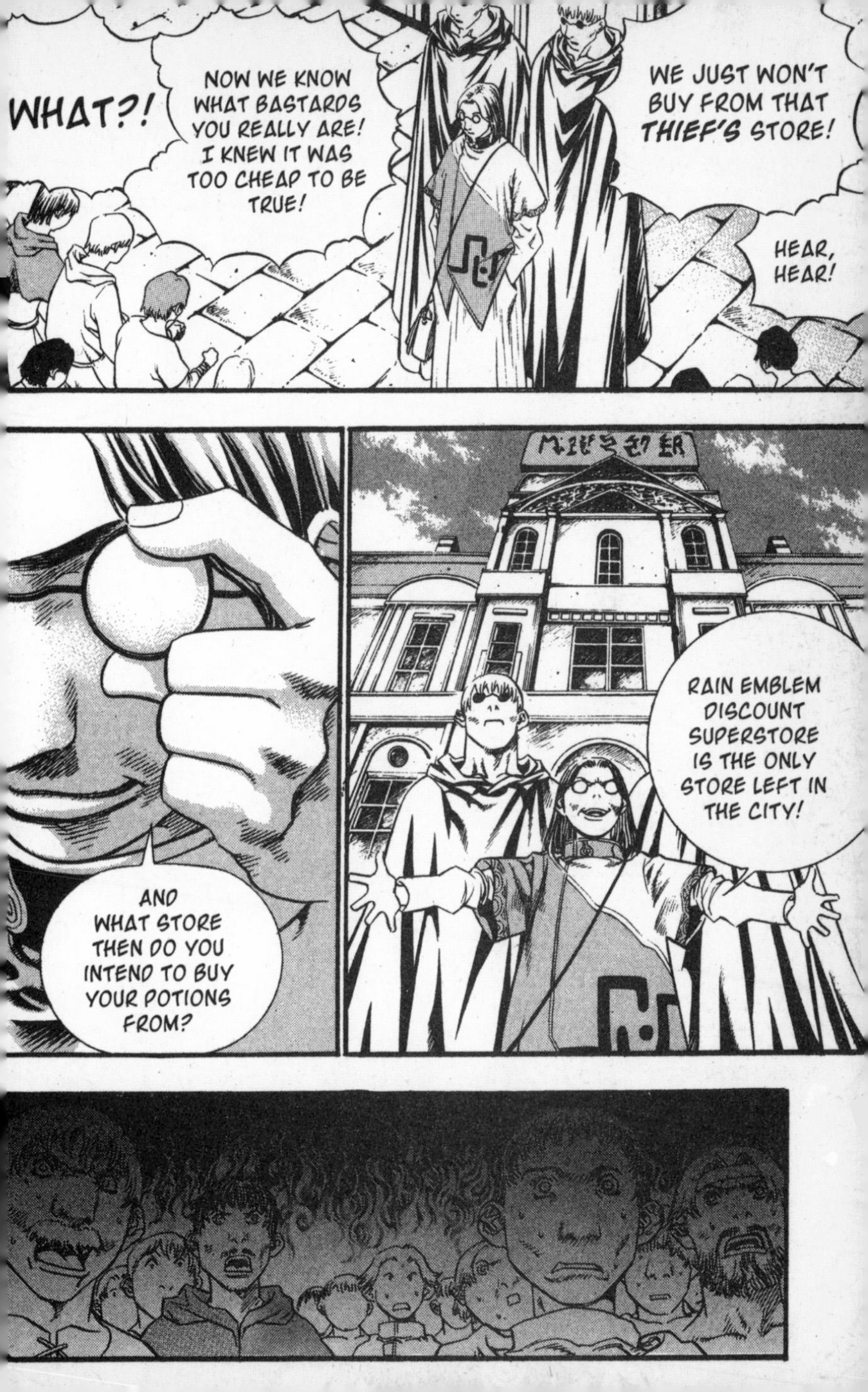
WHAT?!
NOW WE KNOW WHAT BASTARDS YOU REALLY ARE! I KNEW IT WAS TOO CHEAP TO BE TRUE!
WE JUST WON'T BUY FROM THAT THIEF'S STORE!
HEAR, HEAR!
AND WHAT STORE THEN DO YOU INTEND TO BUY YOUR POTIONS FROM?
RAIN EMBLEM DISCOUNT SUPERSTORE IS THE ONLY STORE LEFT IN THE CITY!

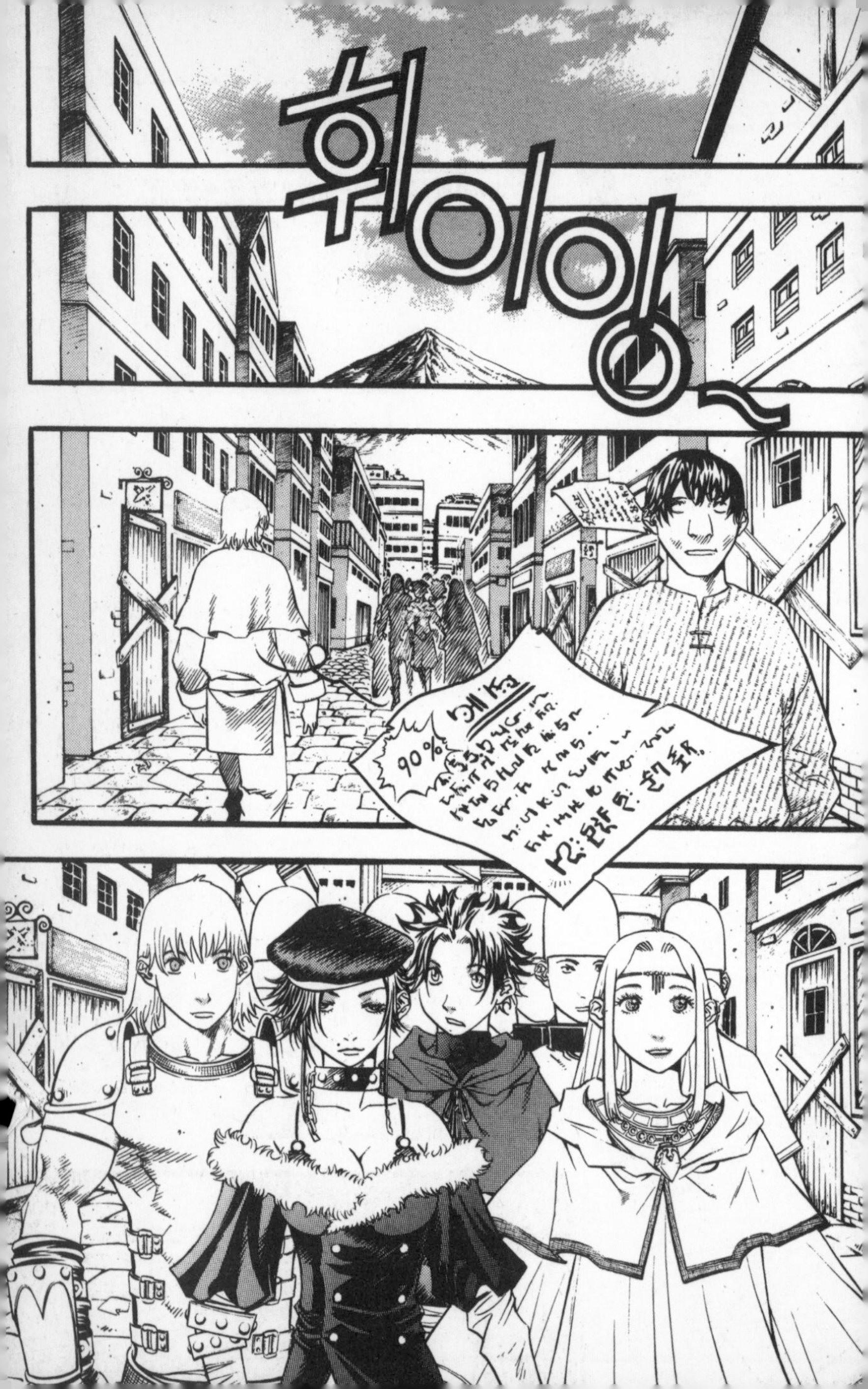
휘이이잉~
90%

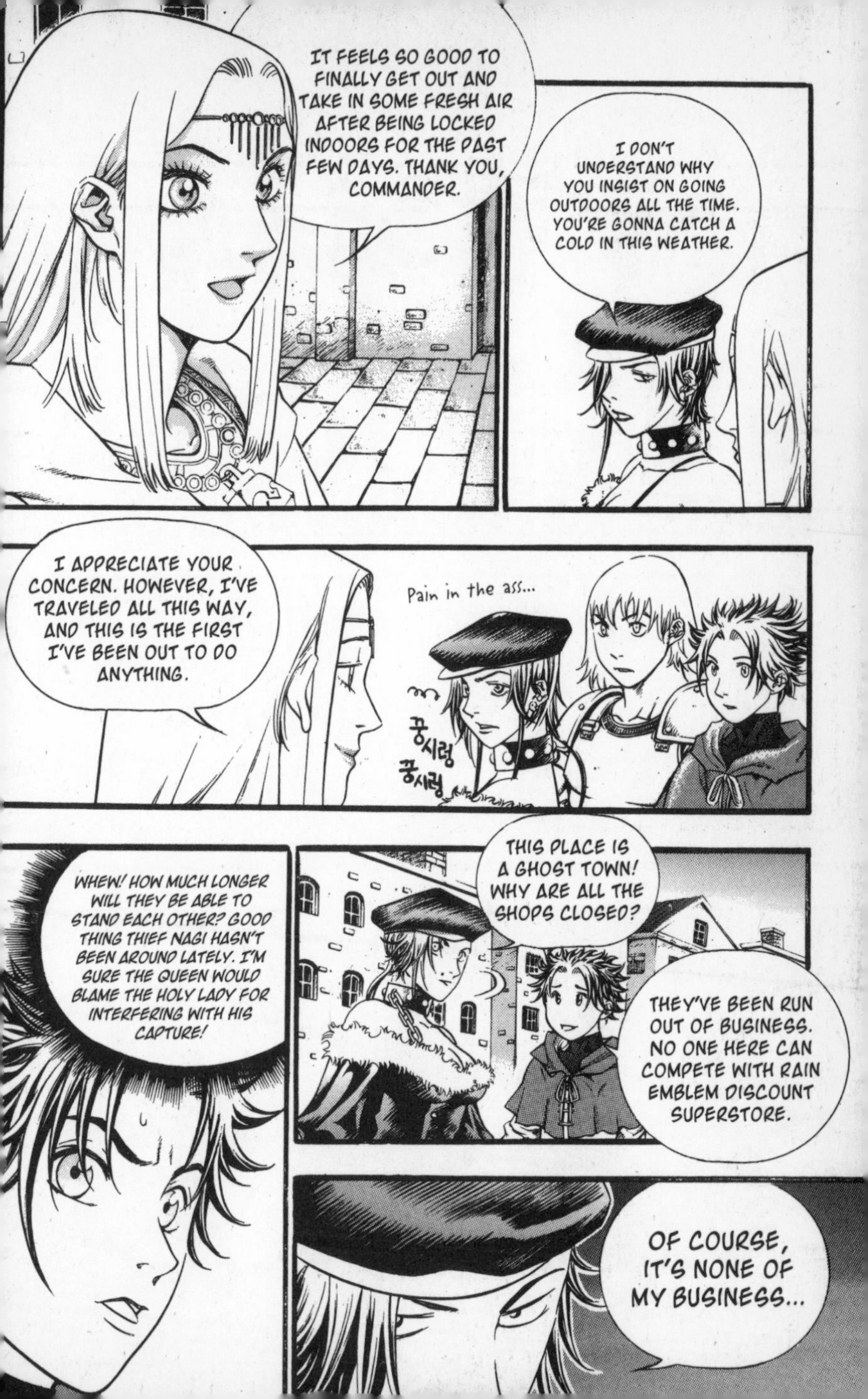
IT FEELS SO GOOD TO FINALLY GET OUT AND TAKE IN SOME FRESH AIR AFTER BEING LOCKED INDOORS FOR THE PAST FEW DAYS. THANK YOU, COMMANDER.
I DON'T UNDERSTAND WHY YOU INSIST ON GOING OUTDOORS ALL THE TIME. YOU'RE GONNA CATCH A COLD IN THIS WEATHER.
I APPRECIATE YOUR CONCERN. HOWEVER, I'VE TRAVELED ALL THIS WAY, AND THIS IS THE FIRST I'VE BEEN OUT TO DO ANYTHING.
Pain in the ass...
궁시렁
궁시렁
WHEW! HOW MUCH LONGER WILL THEY BE ABLE TO STAND EACH OTHER? GOOD THING THIEF NAGI HASN'T BEEN AROUND LATELY. I'M SURE THE QUEEN WOULD BLAME THE HOLY LADY FOR INTERFERING WITH HIS CAPTURE!
THIS PLACE IS A GHOST TOWN! WHY ARE ALL THE SHOPS CLOSED?
THEY'VE BEEN RUN OUT OF BUSINESS. NO ONE HERE CAN COMPETE WITH RAIN EMBLEM DISCOUNT SUPERSTORE.
OF COURSE, IT'S NONE OF MY BUSINESS...

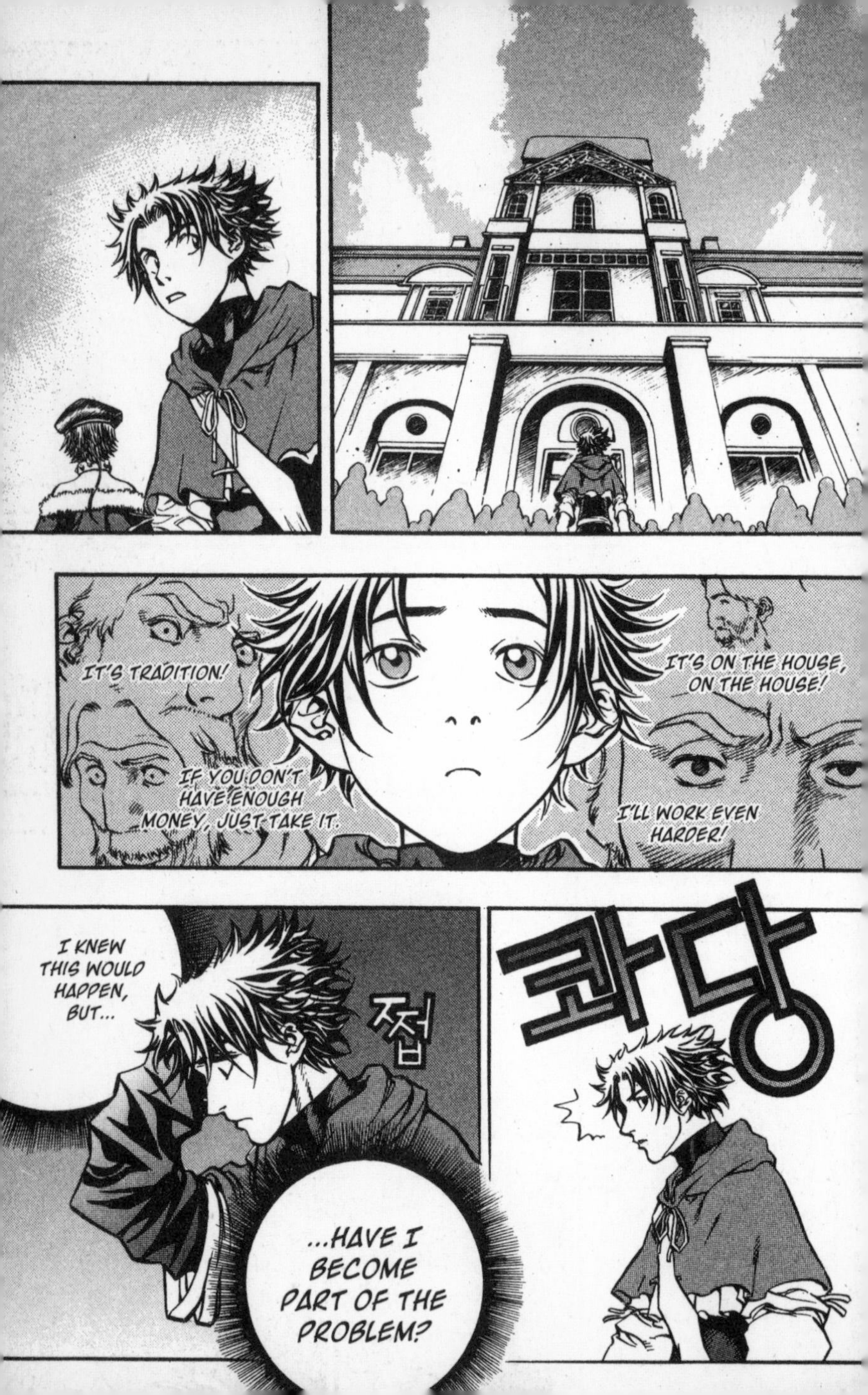

IT'S TRADITION!
IF YOU DON'T HAVE ENOUGH MONEY, JUST TAKE IT.
IT'S ON THE HOUSE, ON THE HOUSE!
I'LL WORK EVEN HARDER!
I KNEW THIS WOULD HAPPEN, BUT...
접
...HAVE I BECOME PART OF THE PROBLEM?
콰당

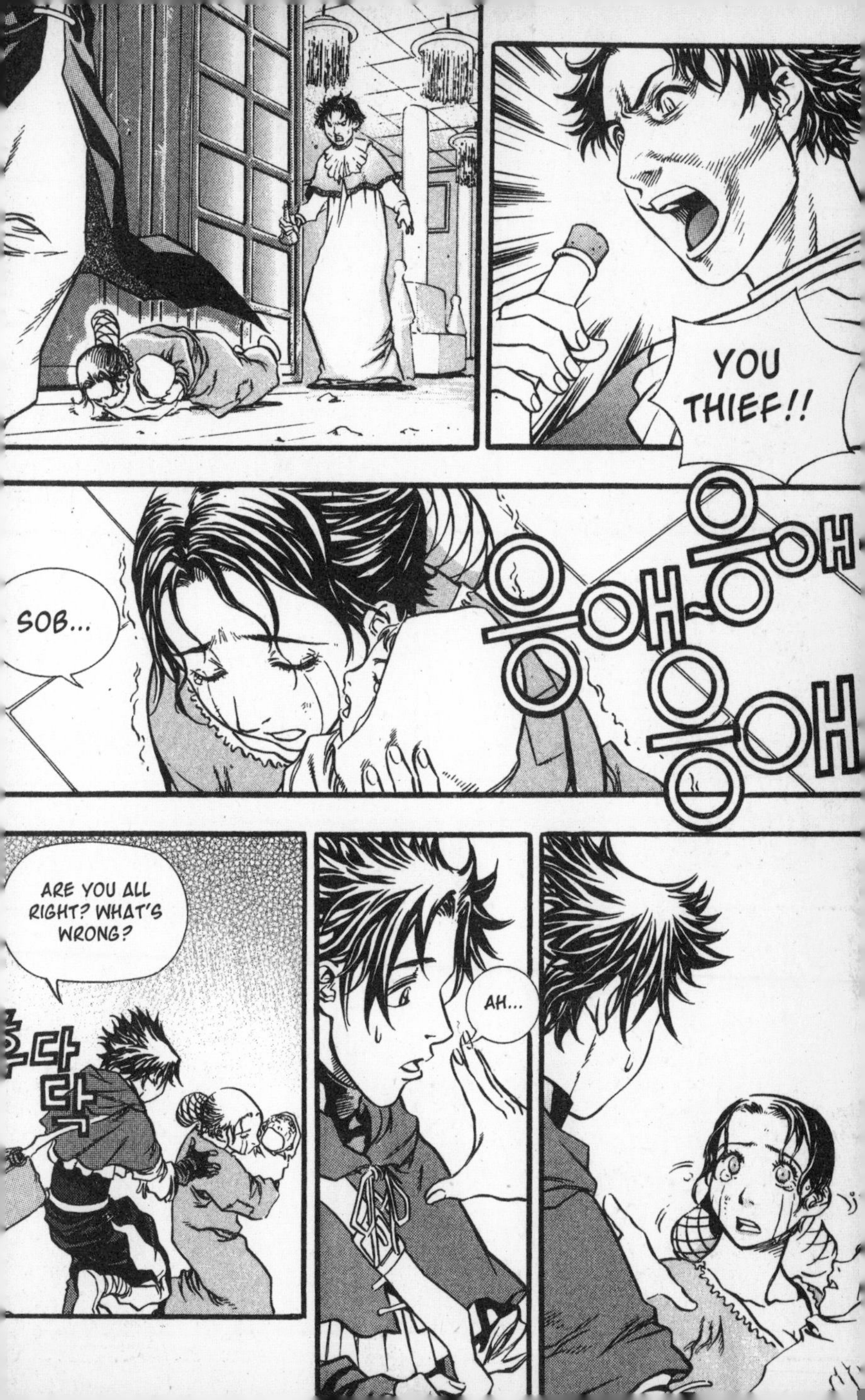
YOU THIEF!!
SOB...
ARE YOU ALL RIGHT? WHAT'S WRONG?
AH...

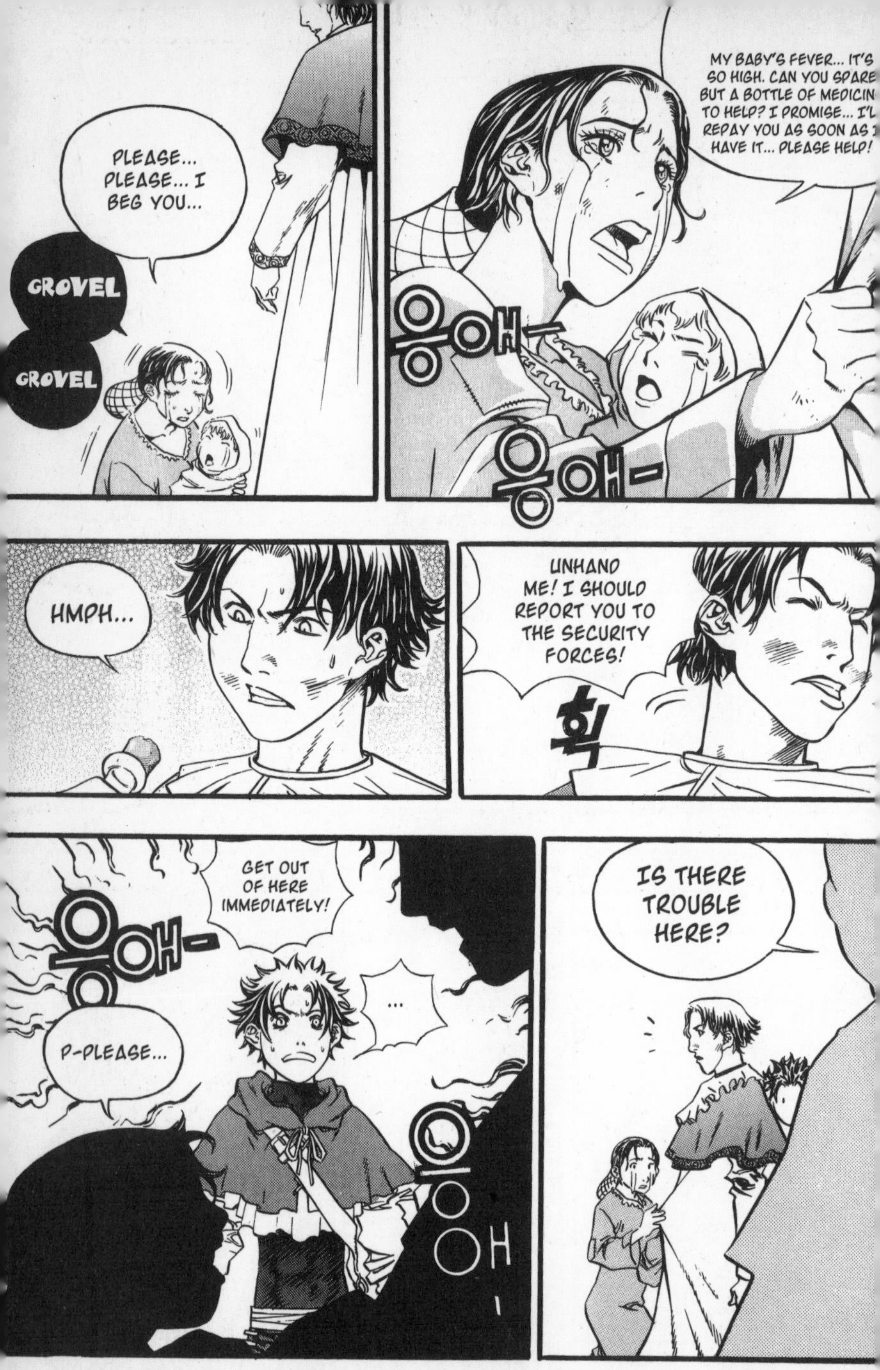
PLEASE... PLEASE... I BEG YOU...
GROVEL
GROVEL
MY BABY'S FEVER... IT'S SO HIGH. CAN YOU SPARE BUT A BOTTLE OF MEDICIN TO HELP? I PROMISE... I'L REPAY YOU AS SOON AS I HAVE IT... PLEASE HELP!
OOH-
OOH-
HMPH...
UNHAND ME! I SHOULD REPORT YOU TO THE SECURITY FORCES!
GET OUT OF HERE IMMEDIATELY!
OOH-
P-PLEASE...
...
OOH-
IS THERE TROUBLE HERE?

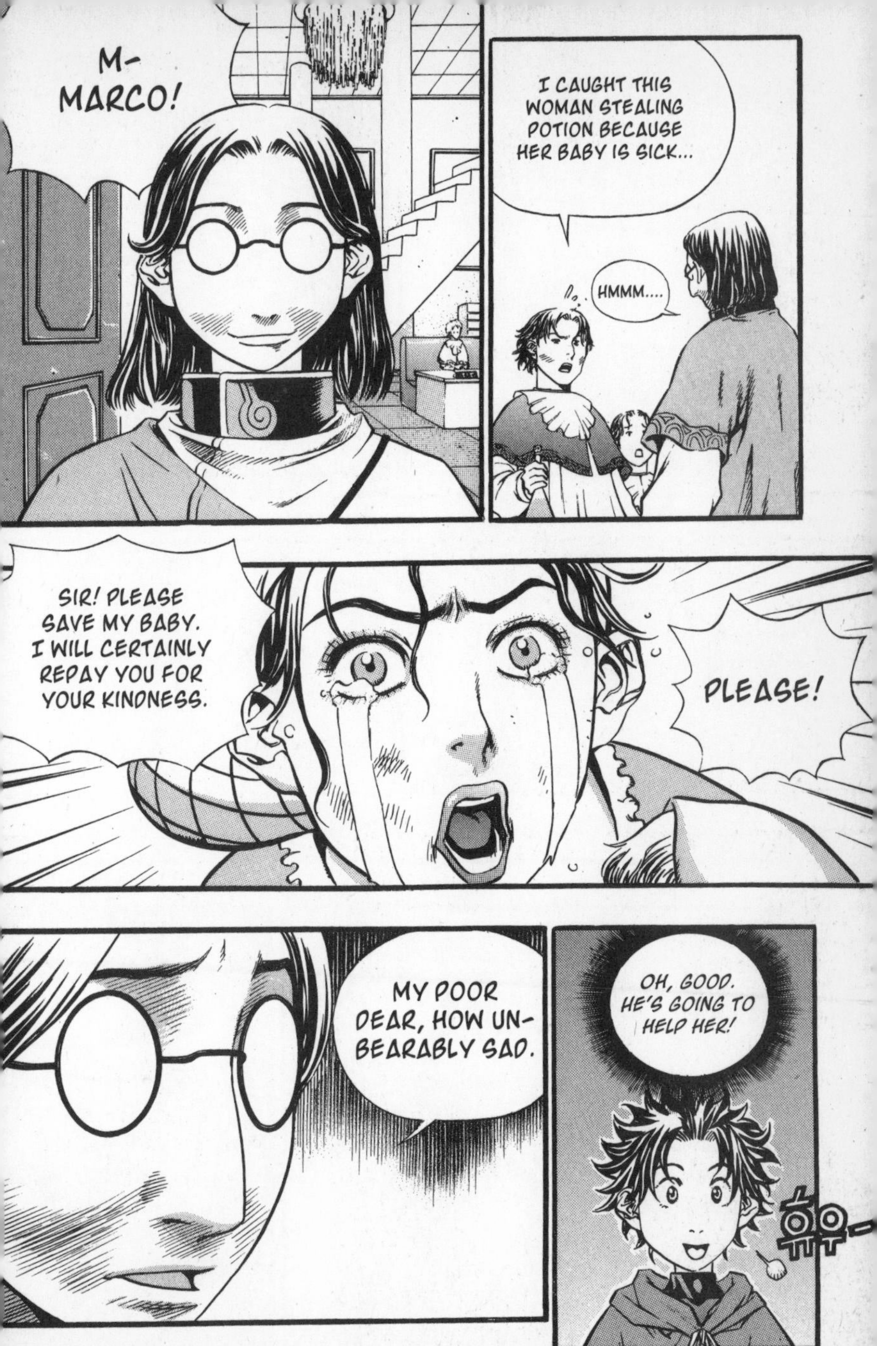
M-
MARCO!
I CAUGHT THIS WOMAN STEALING POTION BECAUSE HER BABY IS SICK...
HMMM....
SIR! PLEASE SAVE MY BABY. I WILL CERTAINLY REPAY YOU FOR YOUR KINDNESS.
PLEASE!
MY POOR DEAR, HOW UN-BEARABLY SAD.
OH, GOOD. HE'S GOING TO HELP HER!
후우-

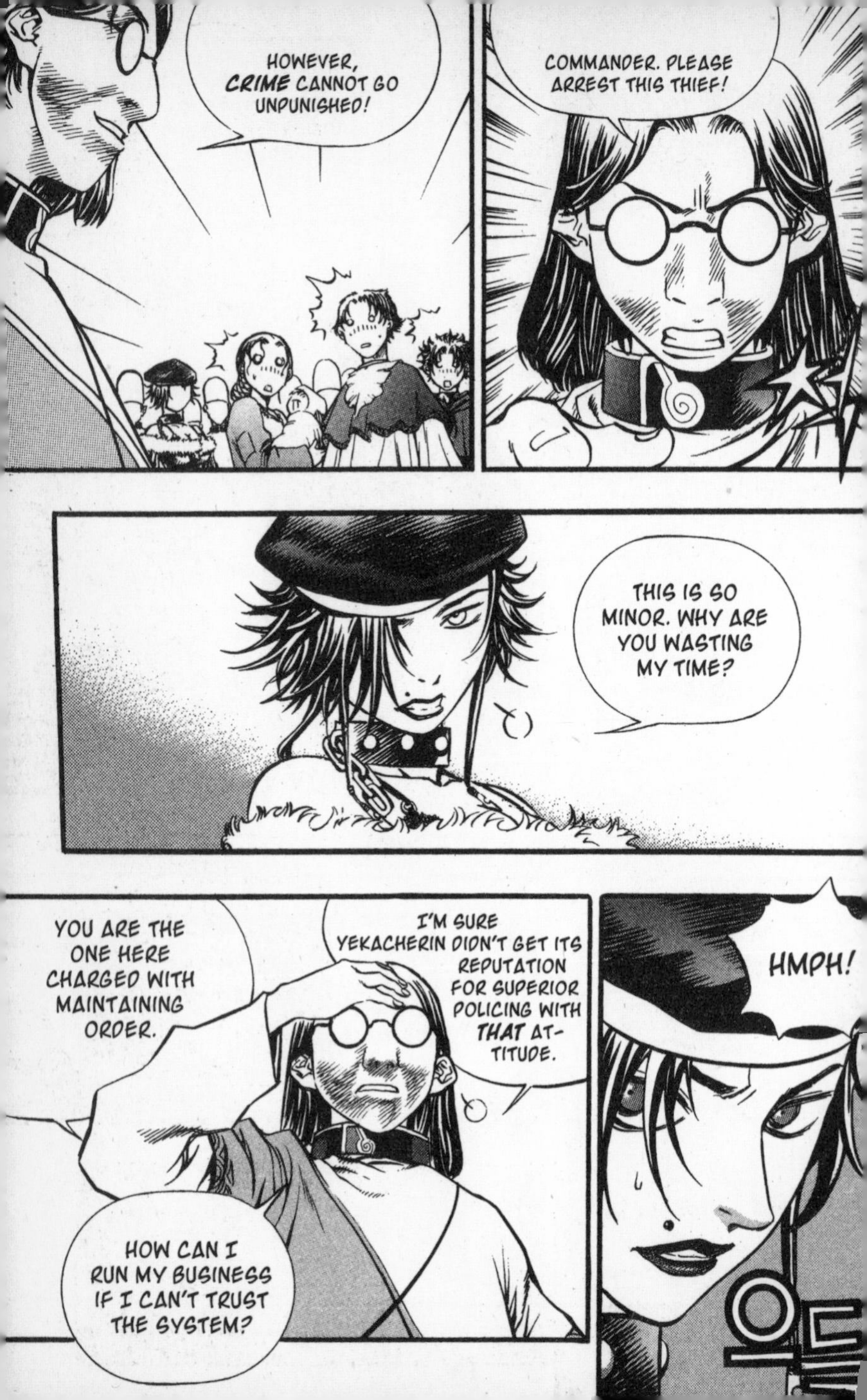
HOWEVER, CRIME CANNOT GO UNPUNISHED!
COMMANDER. PLEASE ARREST THIS THIEF!
THIS IS SO MINOR. WHY ARE YOU WASTING MY TIME?
YOU ARE THE ONE HERE CHARGED WITH MAINTAINING ORDER.
I'M SURE YEKACHERIN DIDN'T GET ITS REPUTATION FOR SUPERIOR POLICING WITH THAT AT-TITUDE.
HOW CAN I RUN MY BUSINESS IF I CAN'T TRUST THE SYSTEM?
HMPH!

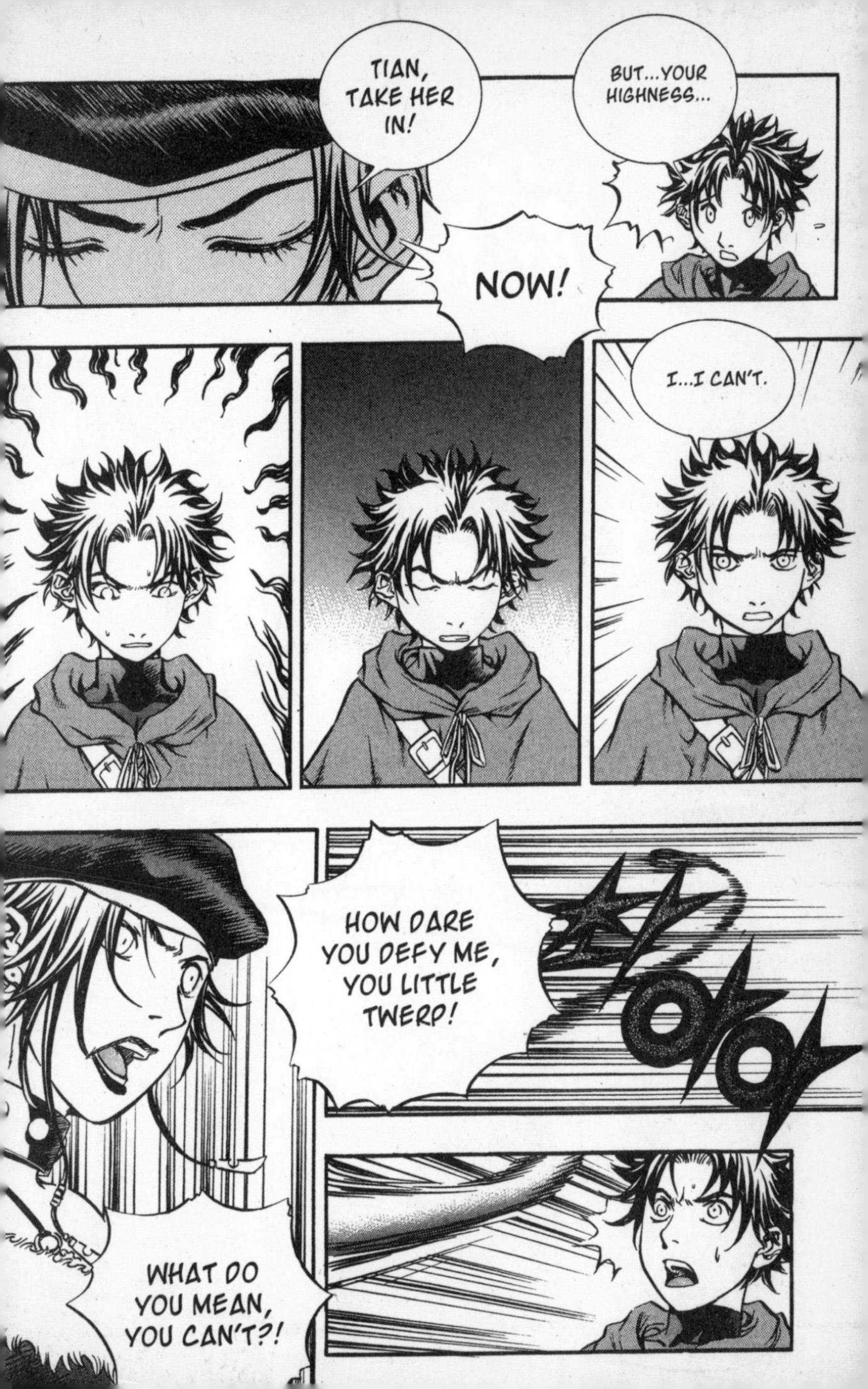
TIAN, TAKE HER IN!
BUT...YOUR HIGHNESS...
NOW!
I...I CAN'T.
WHAT DO YOU MEAN, YOU CAN'T?!
HOW DARE YOU DEFY ME, YOU LITTLE TWERP!

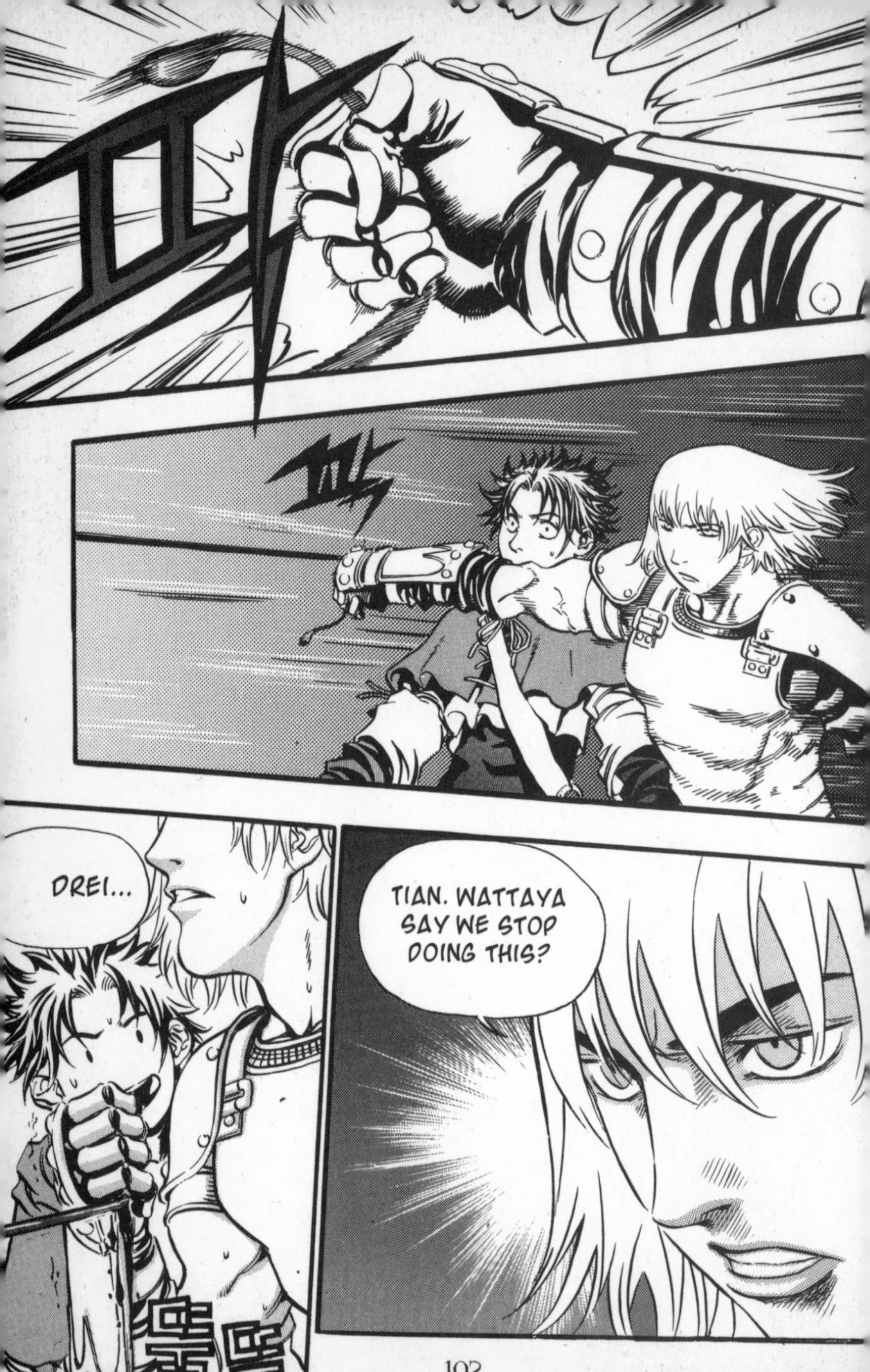
DREI...
TIAN. WATTAYA SAY WE STOP DOING THIS?

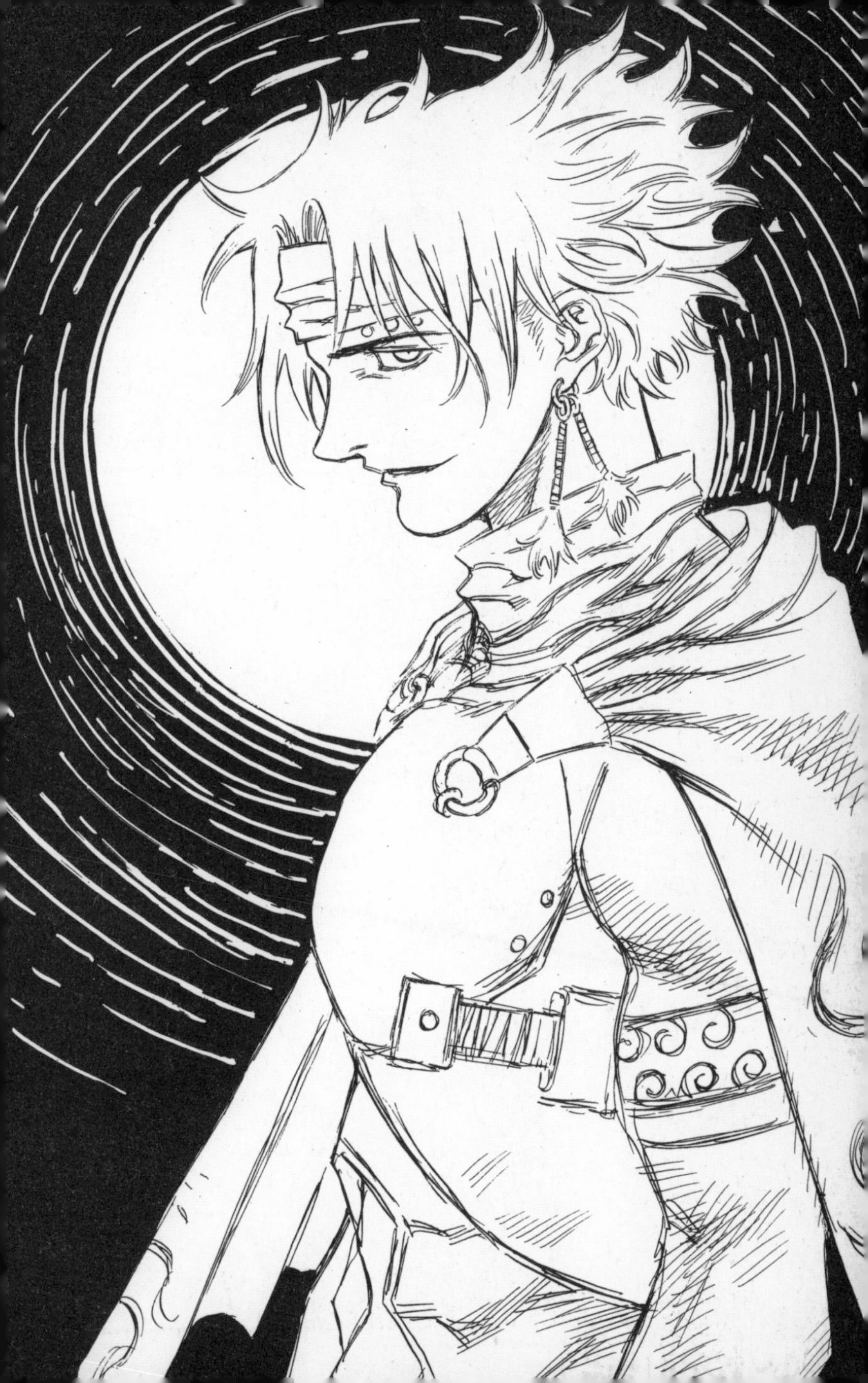

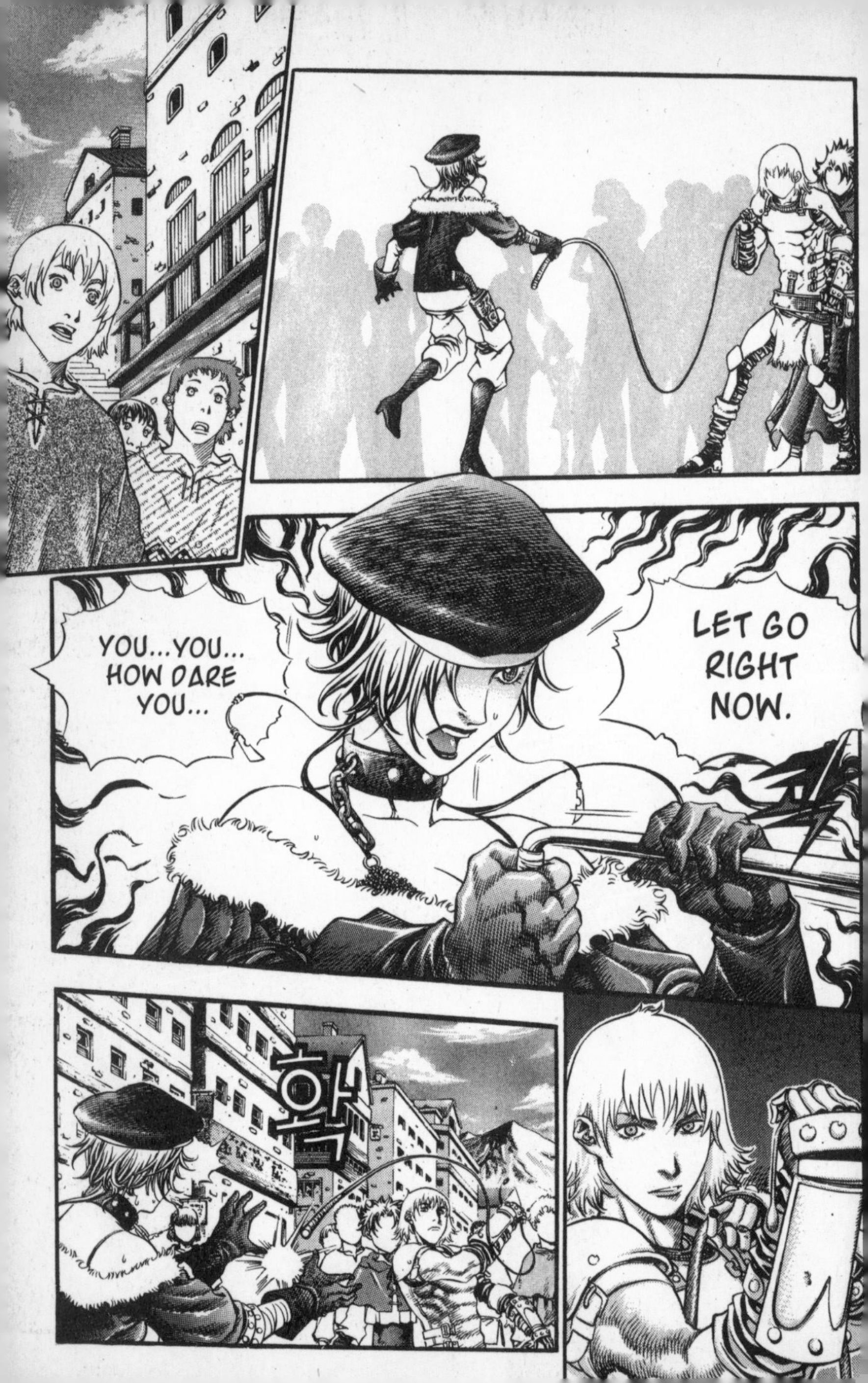
YOU...YOU... HOW DARE YOU...
LET GO RIGHT NOW.
확

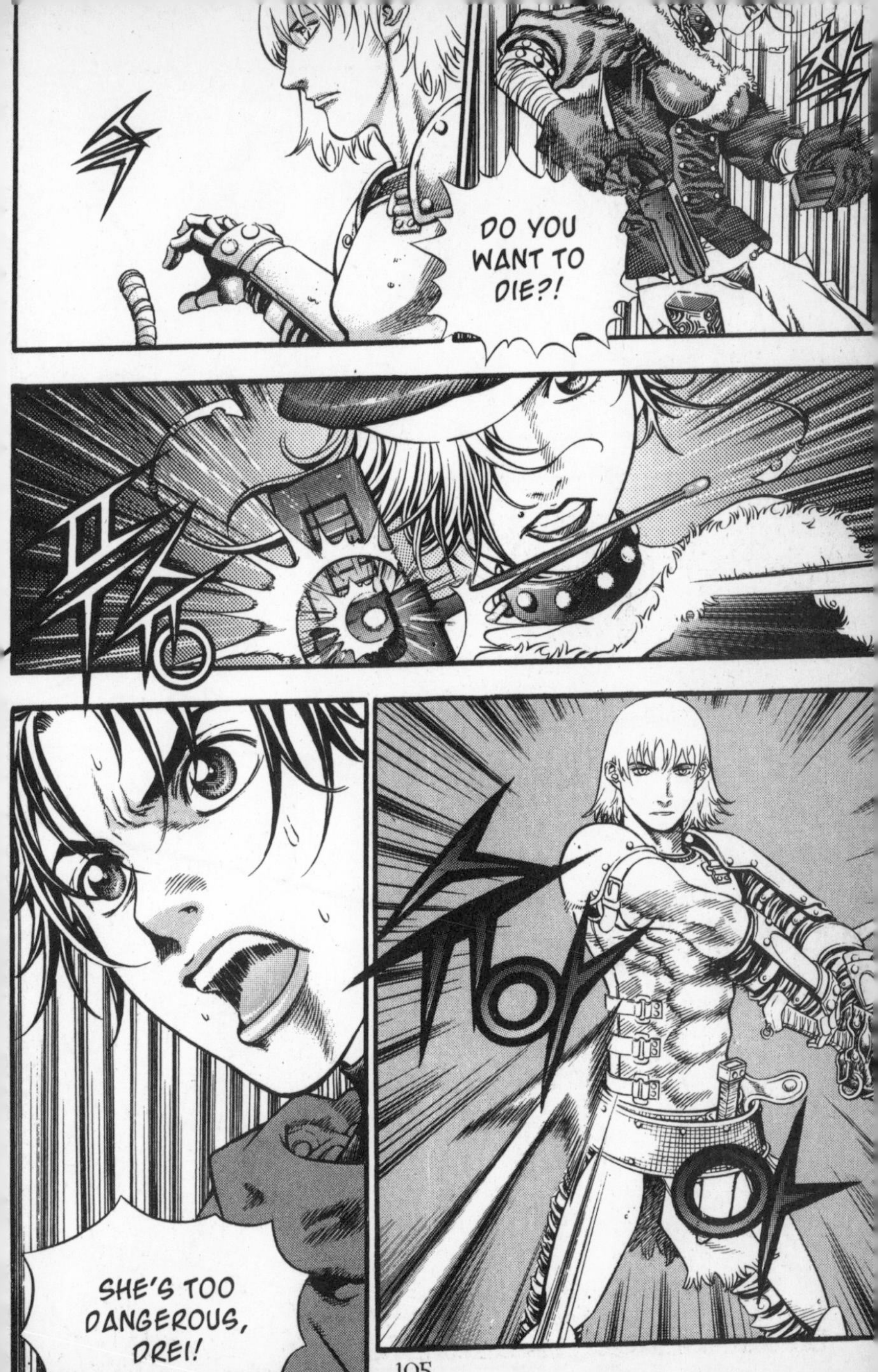
DO YOU WANT TO DIE?!
SHE'S TOO DANGEROUS, DREI!

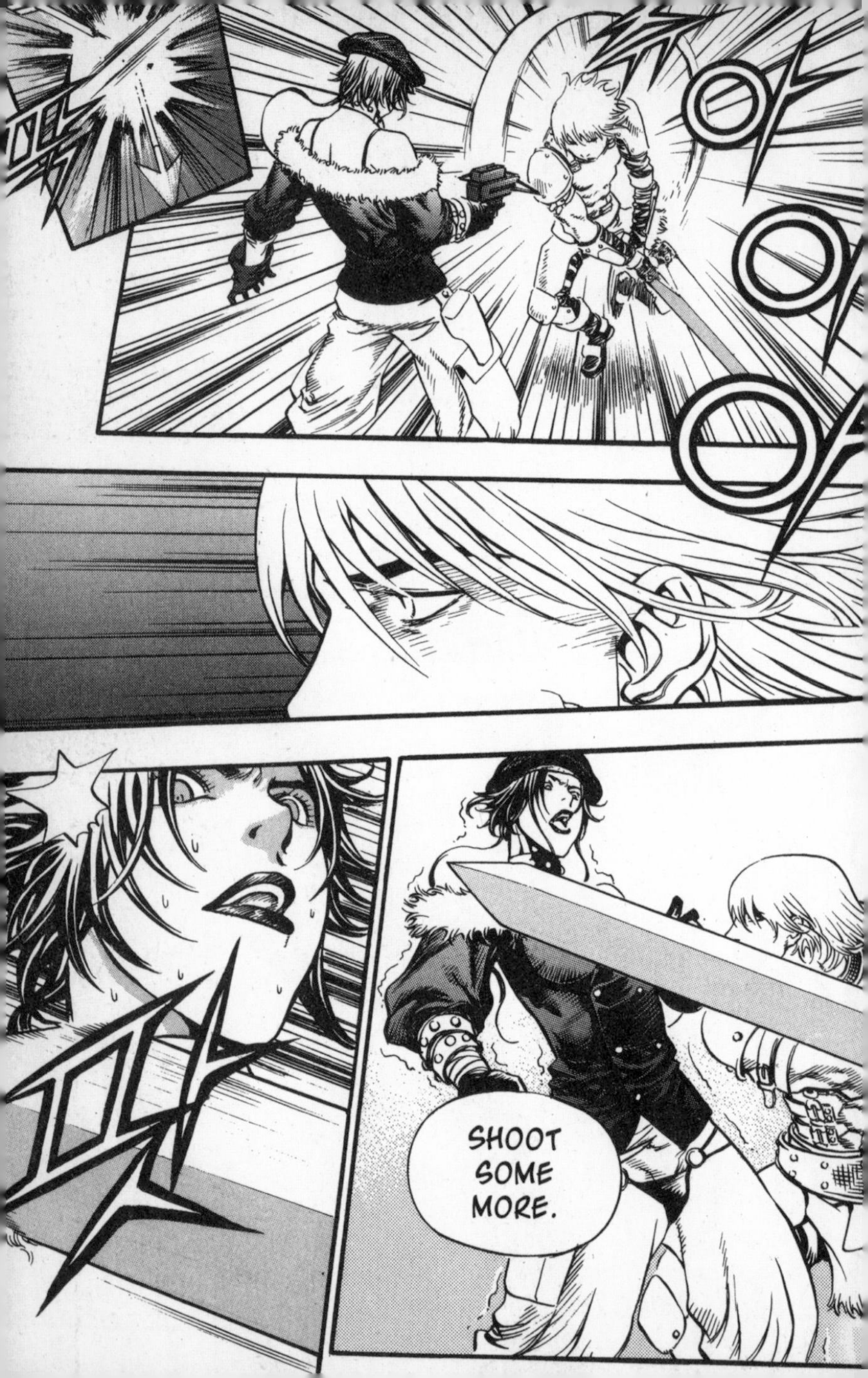
SHOOT SOME MORE.

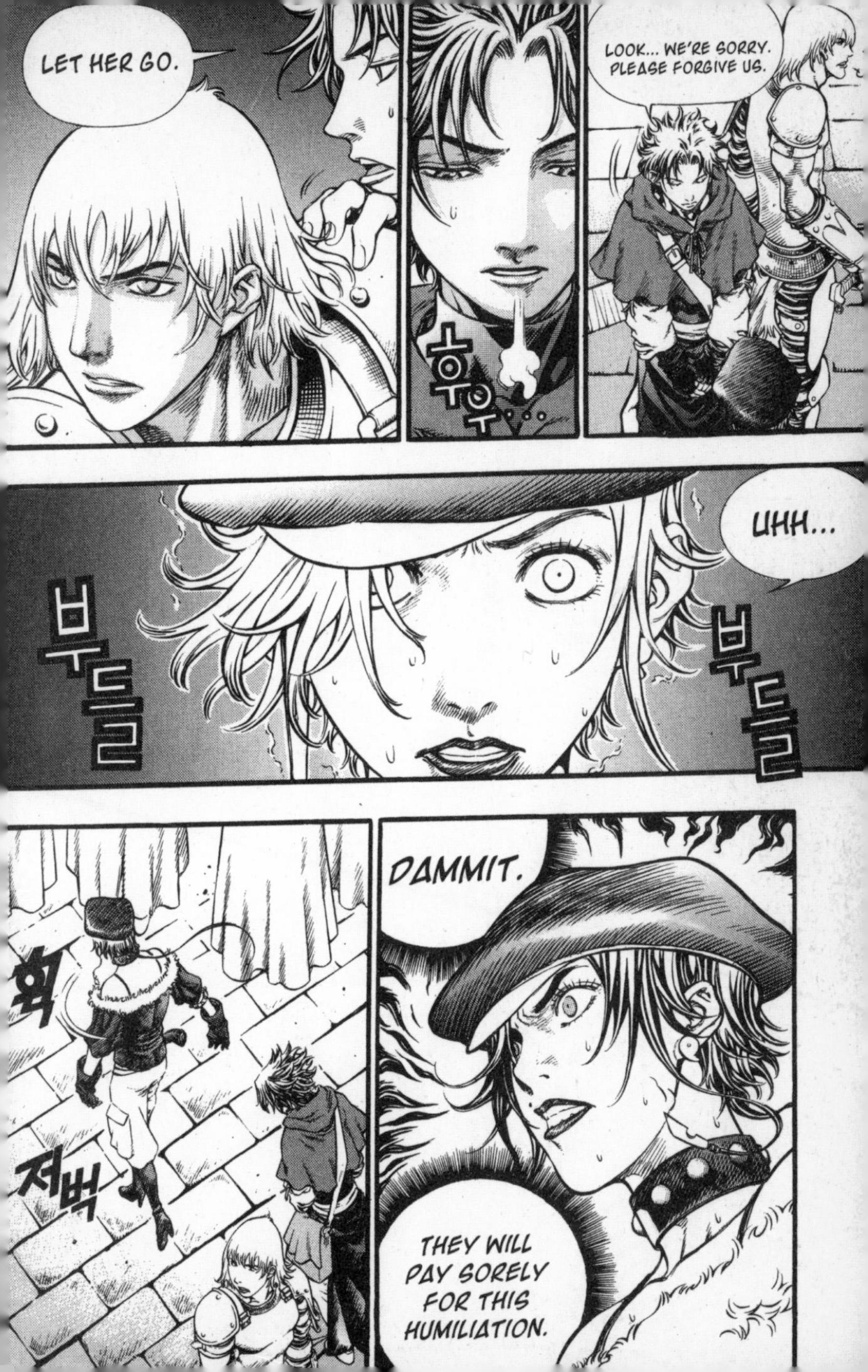
LET HER GO.
후우...
LOOK... WE'RE SORRY. PLEASE FORGIVE US.
부들
UHH...
부들
획
저벅
DAMMIT.
THEY WILL PAY SORELY FOR THIS HUMILIATION.

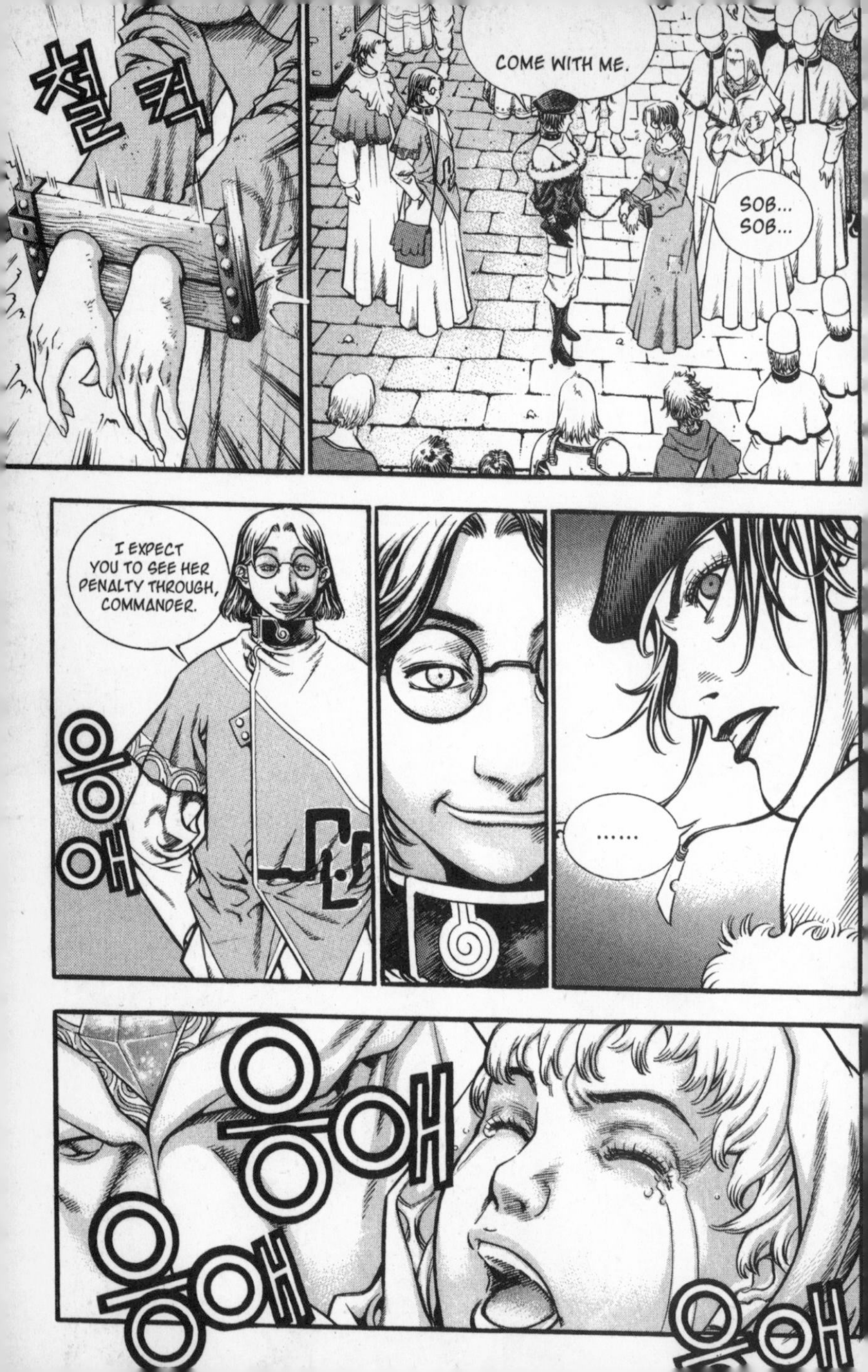

철컥
COME WITH ME.
SOB... SOB...
I EXPECT YOU TO SEE HER PENALTY THROUGH, COMMANDER.
흐응
......
흐으으
흐으으
흐으

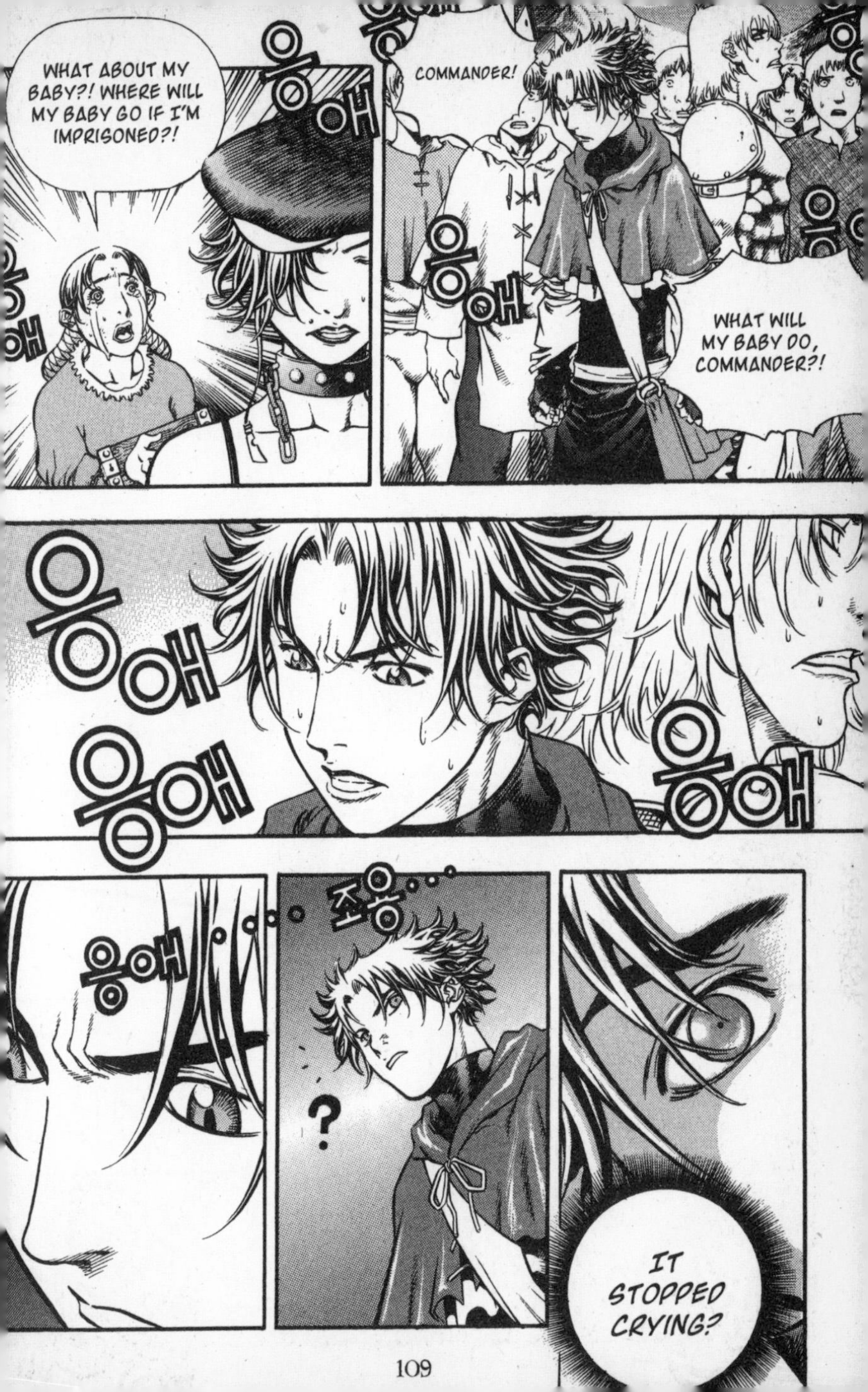
WHAT ABOUT MY BABY?! WHERE WILL MY BABY GO IF I'M IMPRISONED?!
COMMANDER!
WHAT WILL MY BABY DO, COMMANDER?!
?
IT STOPPED CRYING?

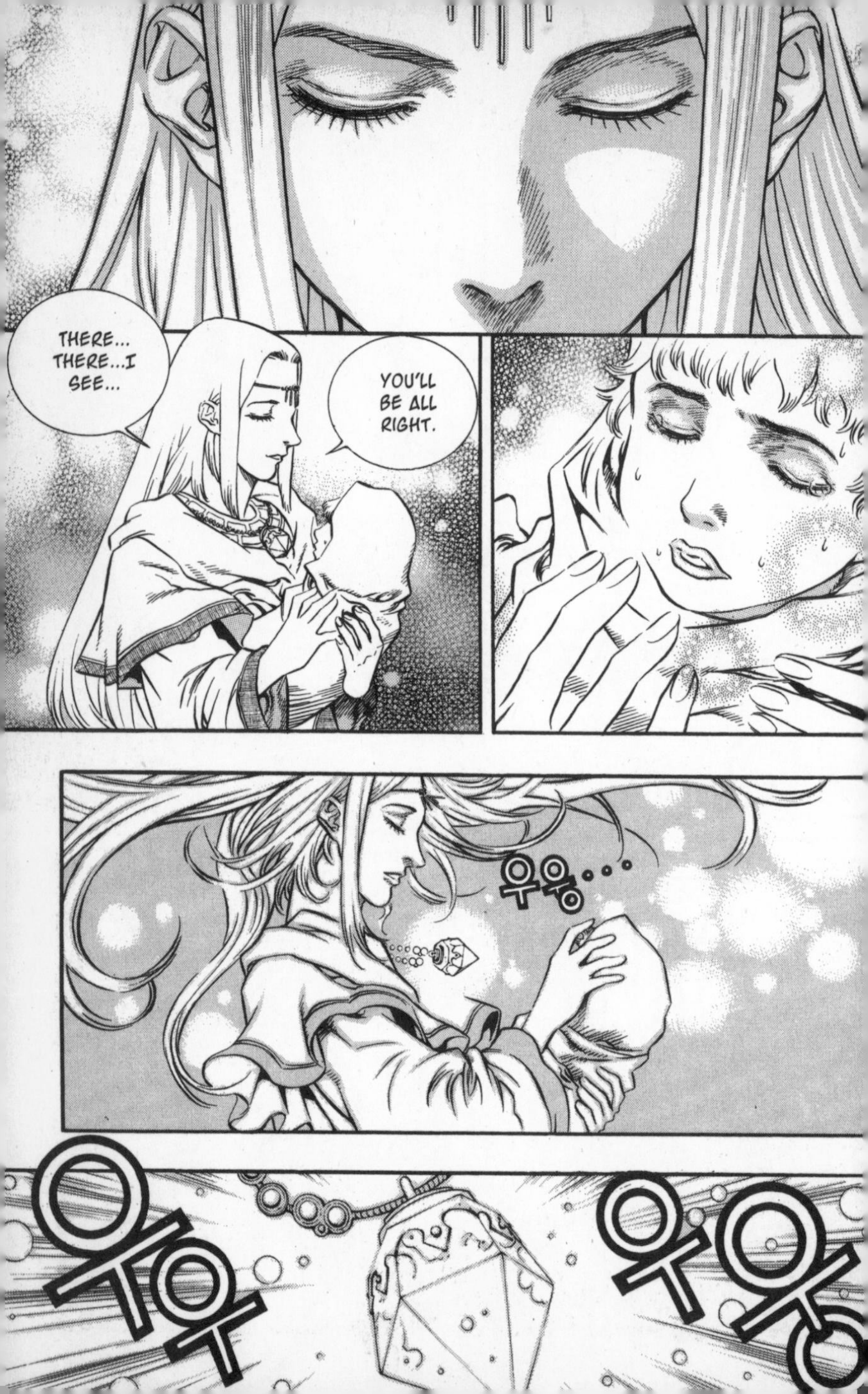
THERE... THERE...I SEE...
YOU'LL BE ALL RIGHT.

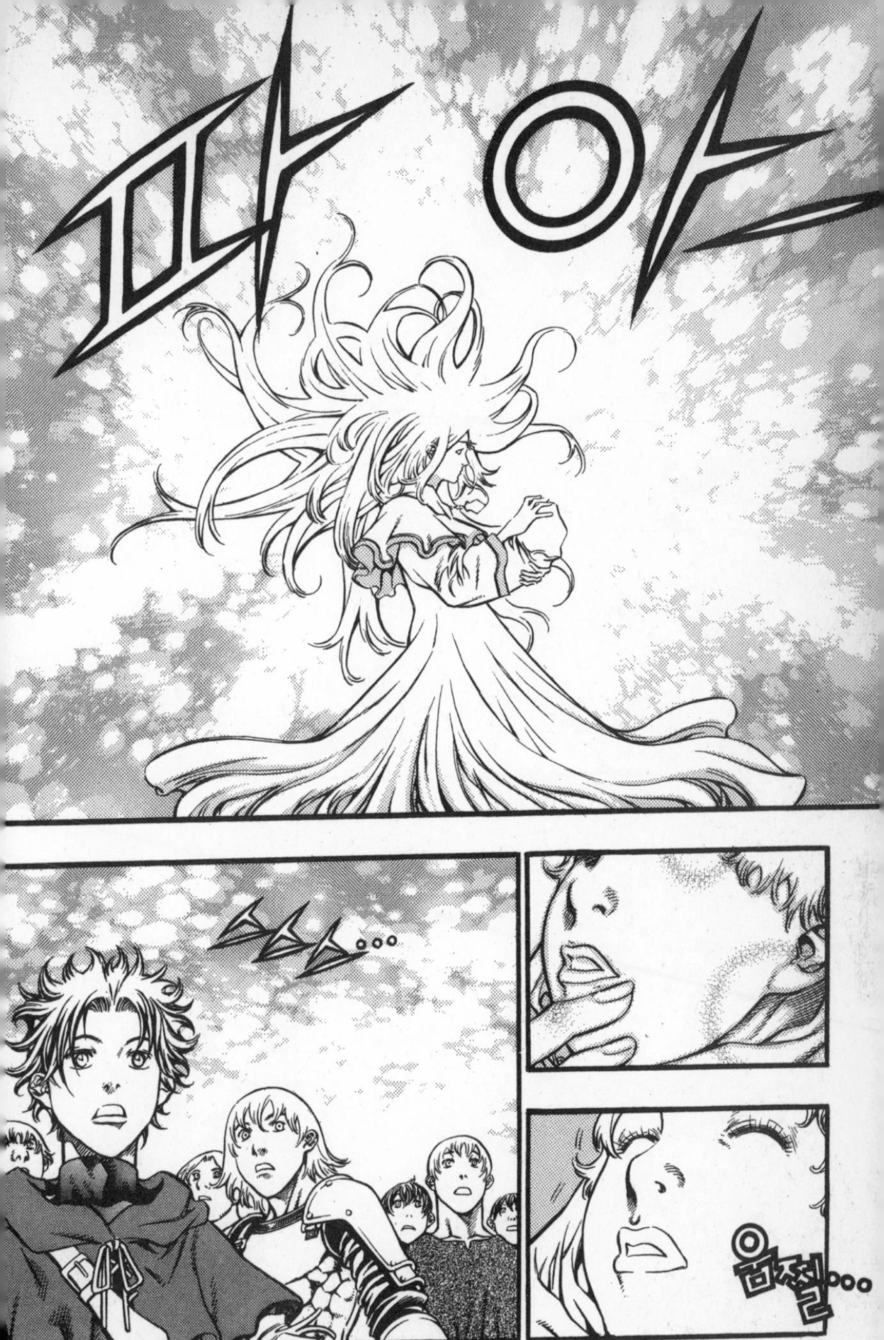
파아
스스스...
움찔...

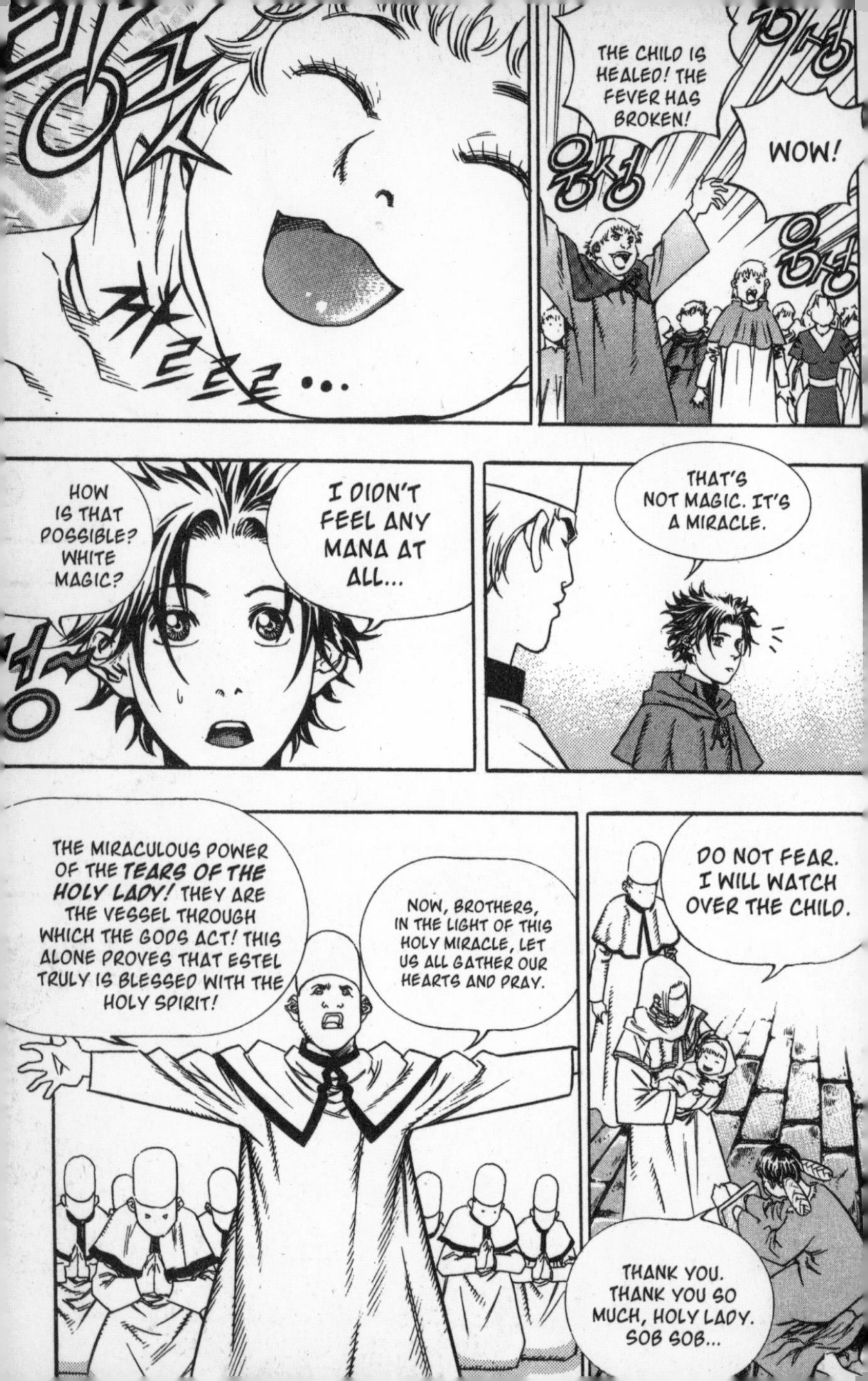

THE CHILD IS HEALED! THE FEVER HAS BROKEN!
WOW!
HOW IS THAT POSSIBLE? WHITE MAGIC?
I DIDN'T FEEL ANY MANA AT ALL...
THAT'S NOT MAGIC. IT'S A MIRACLE.
THE MIRACULOUS POWER OF THE TEARS OF THE HOLY LADY! THEY ARE THE VESSEL THROUGH WHICH THE GODS ACT! THIS ALONE PROVES THAT ESTEL TRULY IS BLESSED WITH THE HOLY SPIRIT!
NOW, BROTHERS, IN THE LIGHT OF THIS HOLY MIRACLE, LET US ALL GATHER OUR HEARTS AND PRAY.
DO NOT FEAR. I WILL WATCH OVER THE CHILD.
THANK YOU. THANK YOU SO MUCH, HOLY LADY. SOB SOB...

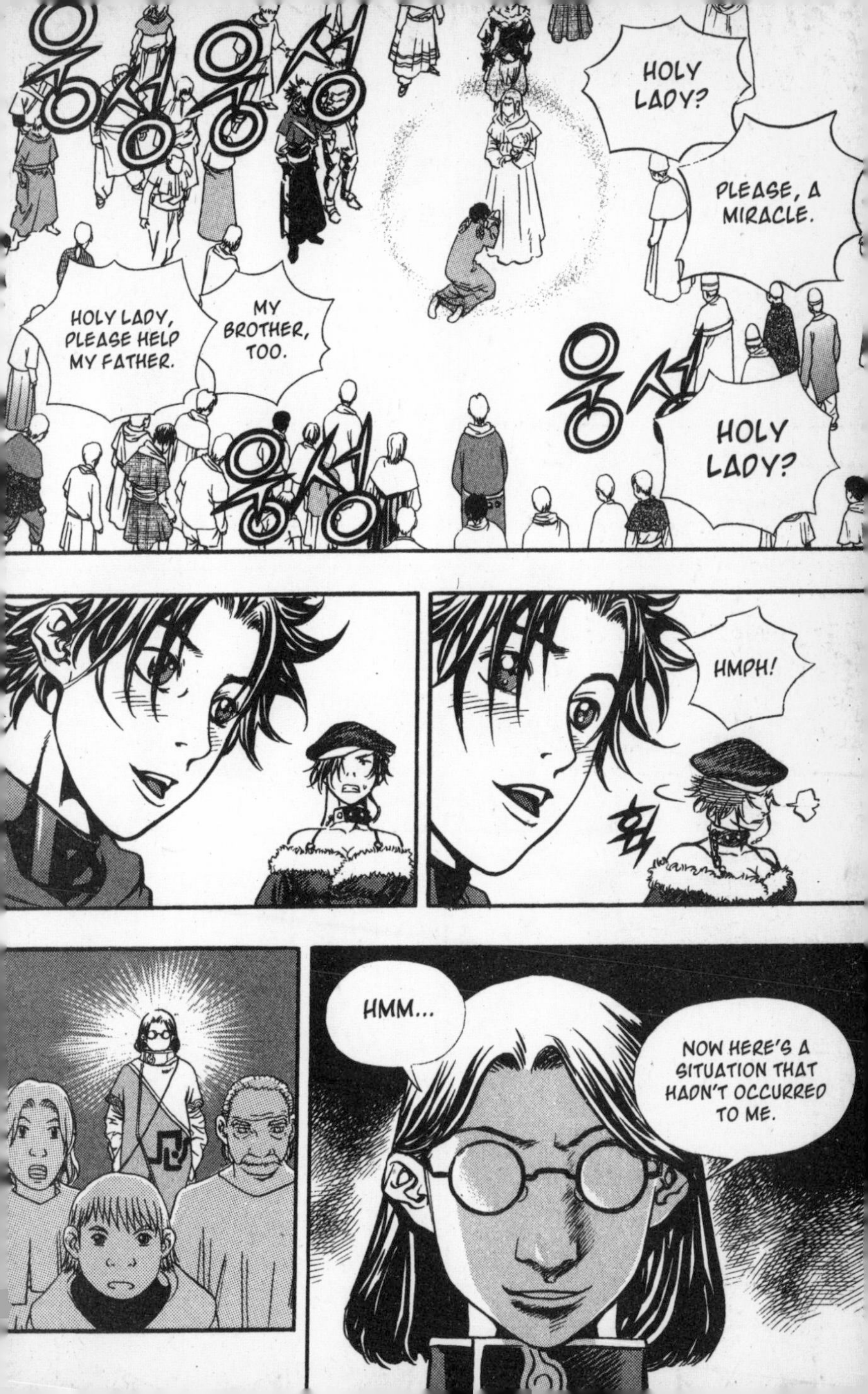
HOLY LADY?
PLEASE, A MIRACLE.
HOLY LADY, PLEASE HELP MY FATHER.
MY BROTHER, TOO.
HOLY LADY?
HMPH!
HMM...
NOW HERE'S A SITUATION THAT HADN'T OCCURRED TO ME.

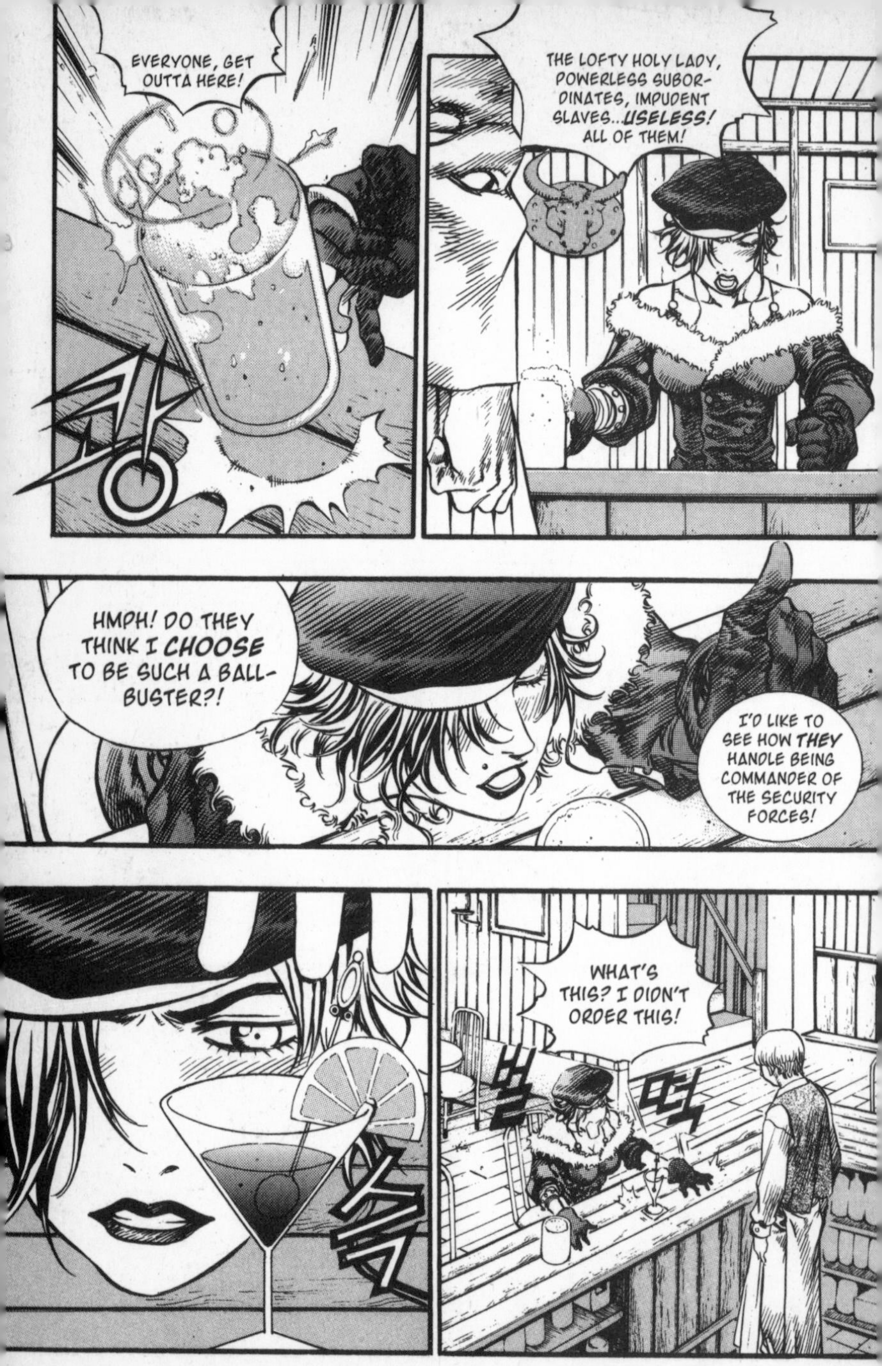
EVERYONE, GET OUTTA HERE!
THE LOFTY HOLY LADY, POWERLESS SUBOR-DINATES, IMPUDENT SLAVES... USELESS! ALL OF THEM!
HMPH! DO THEY THINK I CHOOSE TO BE SUCH A BALL-BUSTER?!
I'D LIKE TO SEE HOW THEY HANDLE BEING COMMANDER OF THE SECURITY FORCES!
WHAT'S THIS? I DIDN'T ORDER THIS!

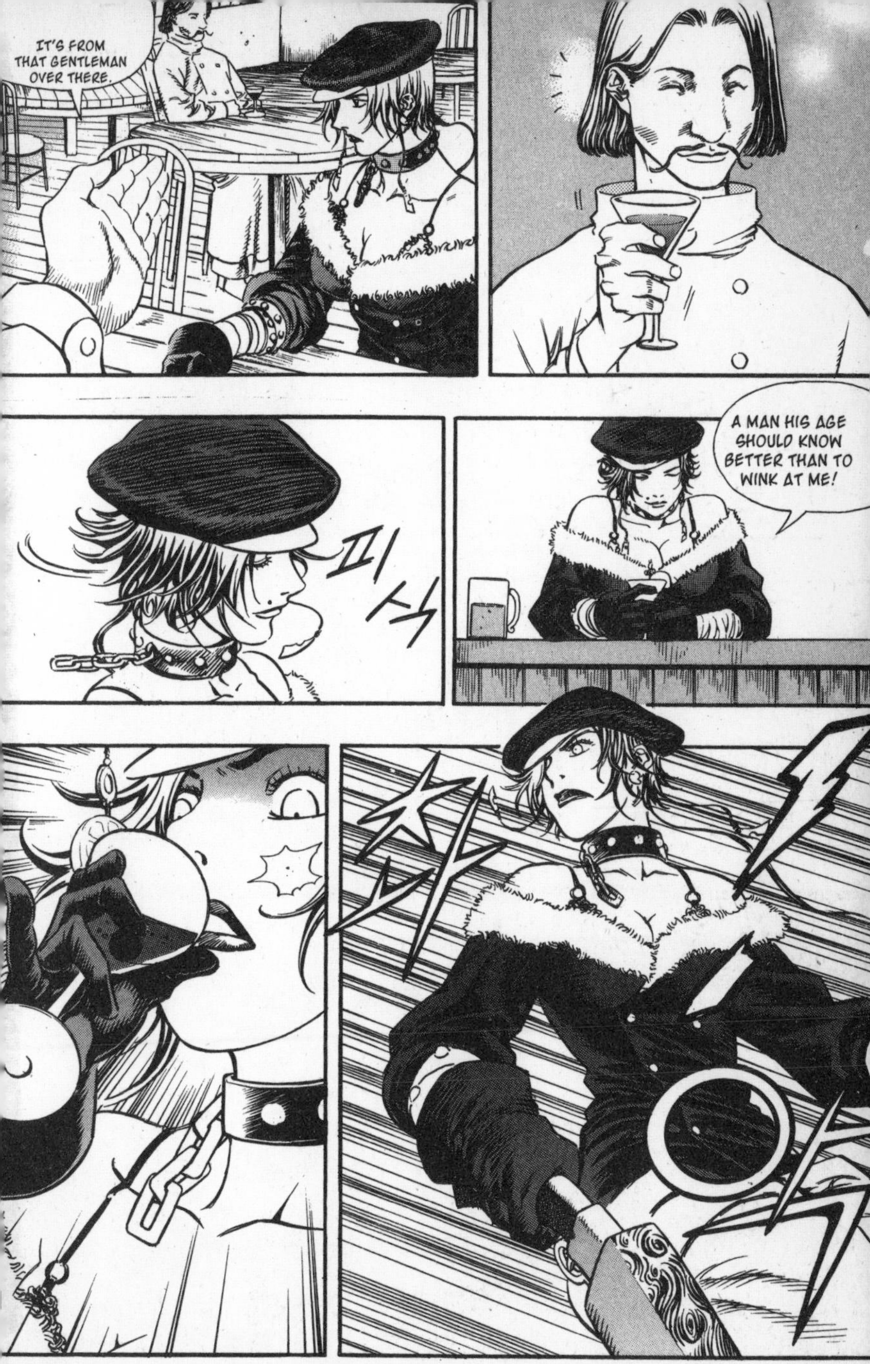
IT'S FROM THAT GENTLEMAN OVER THERE.
A MAN HIS AGE SHOULD KNOW BETTER THAN TO WINK AT ME!

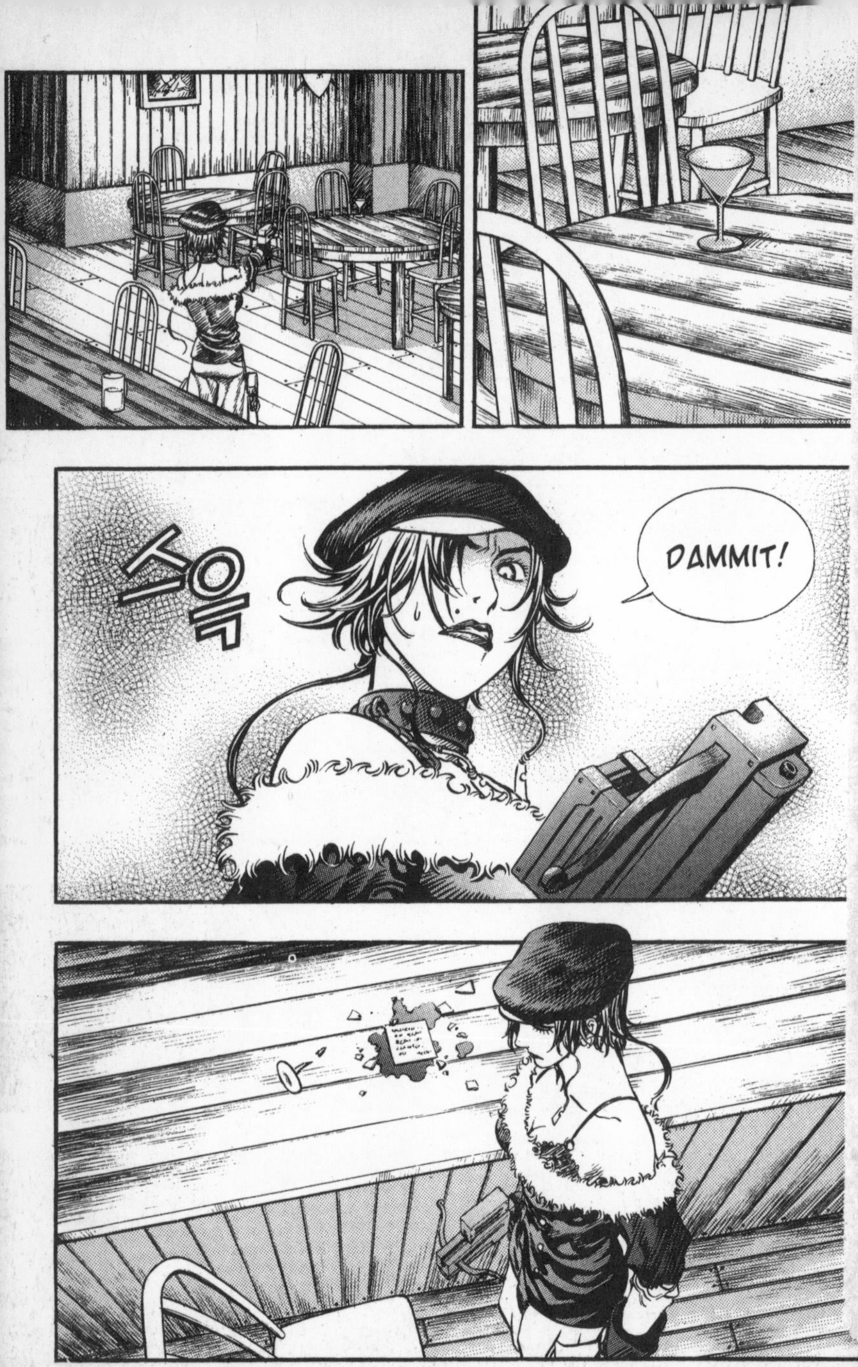
DAMMIT!

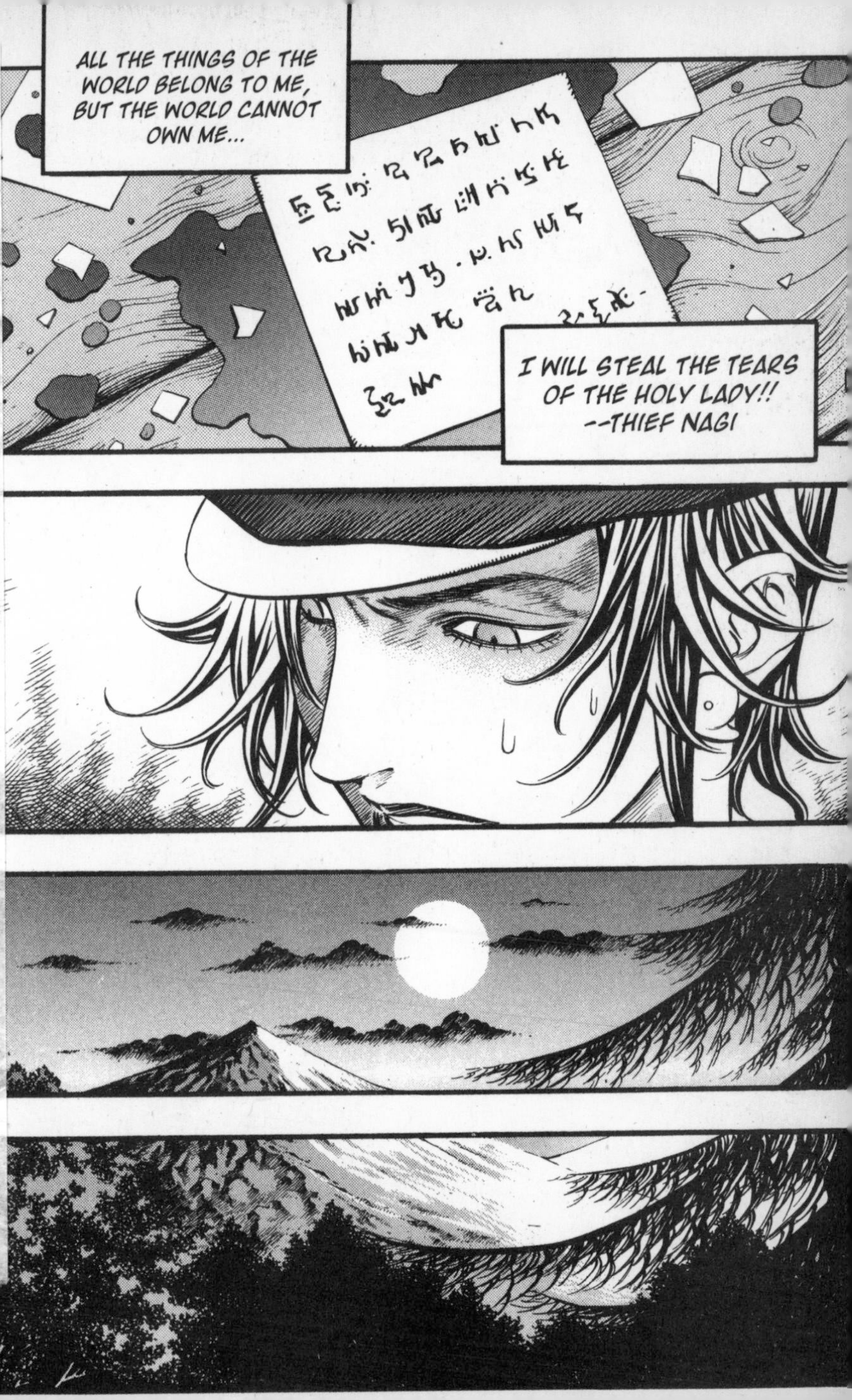

ALL THE THINGS OF THE WORLD BELONG TO ME, BUT THE WORLD CANNOT OWN ME...
I WILL STEAL THE TEARS OF THE HOLY LADY!! --THIEF NAGI

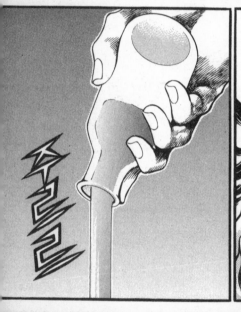

THAT
SHOULD BE
SUFFICIENT.

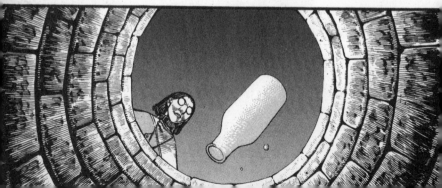

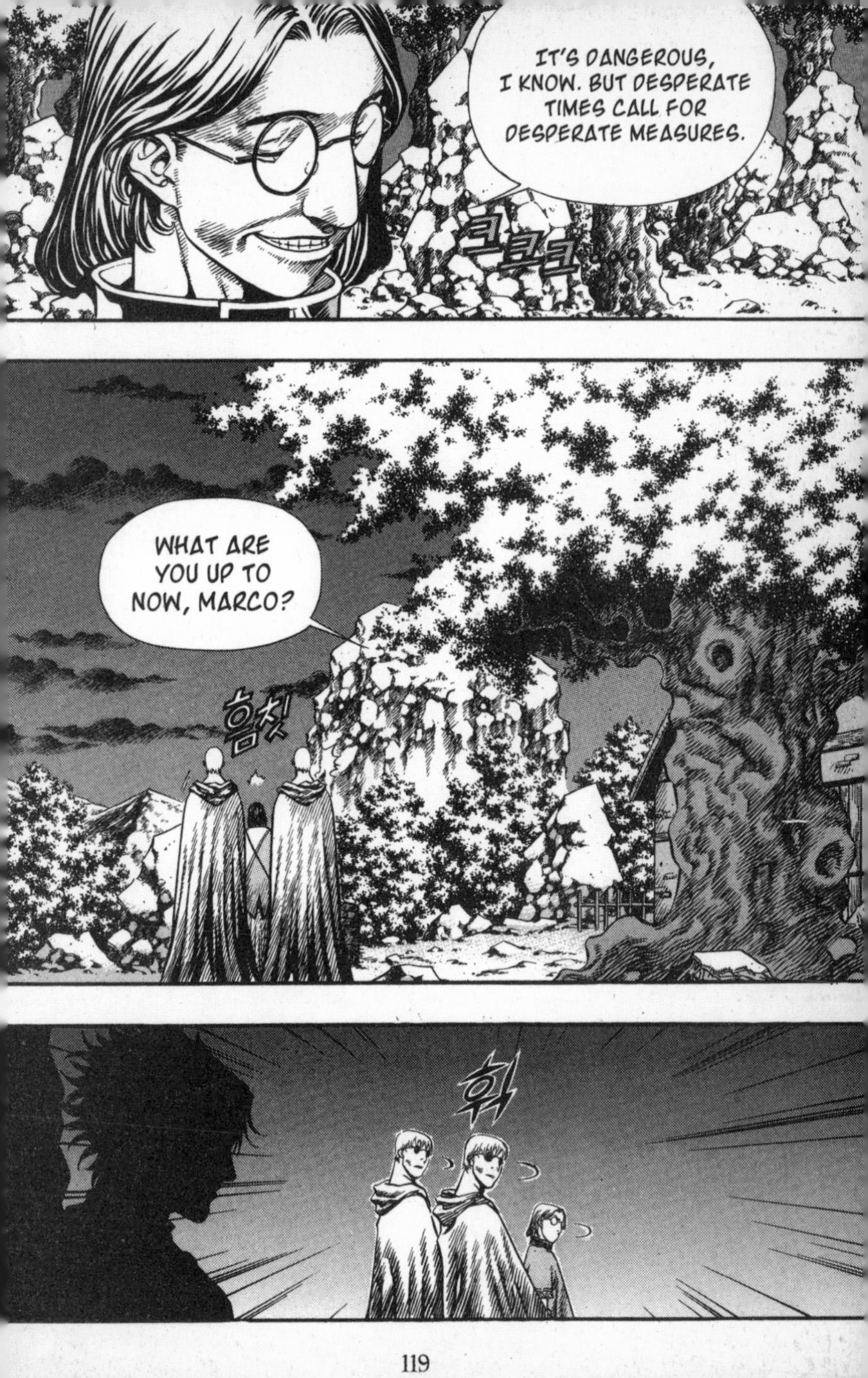
IT'S DANGEROUS, I KNOW. BUT DESPERATE TIMES CALL FOR DESPERATE MEASURES.
크크크...
WHAT ARE YOU UP TO NOW, MARCO?
흠칫!
홱

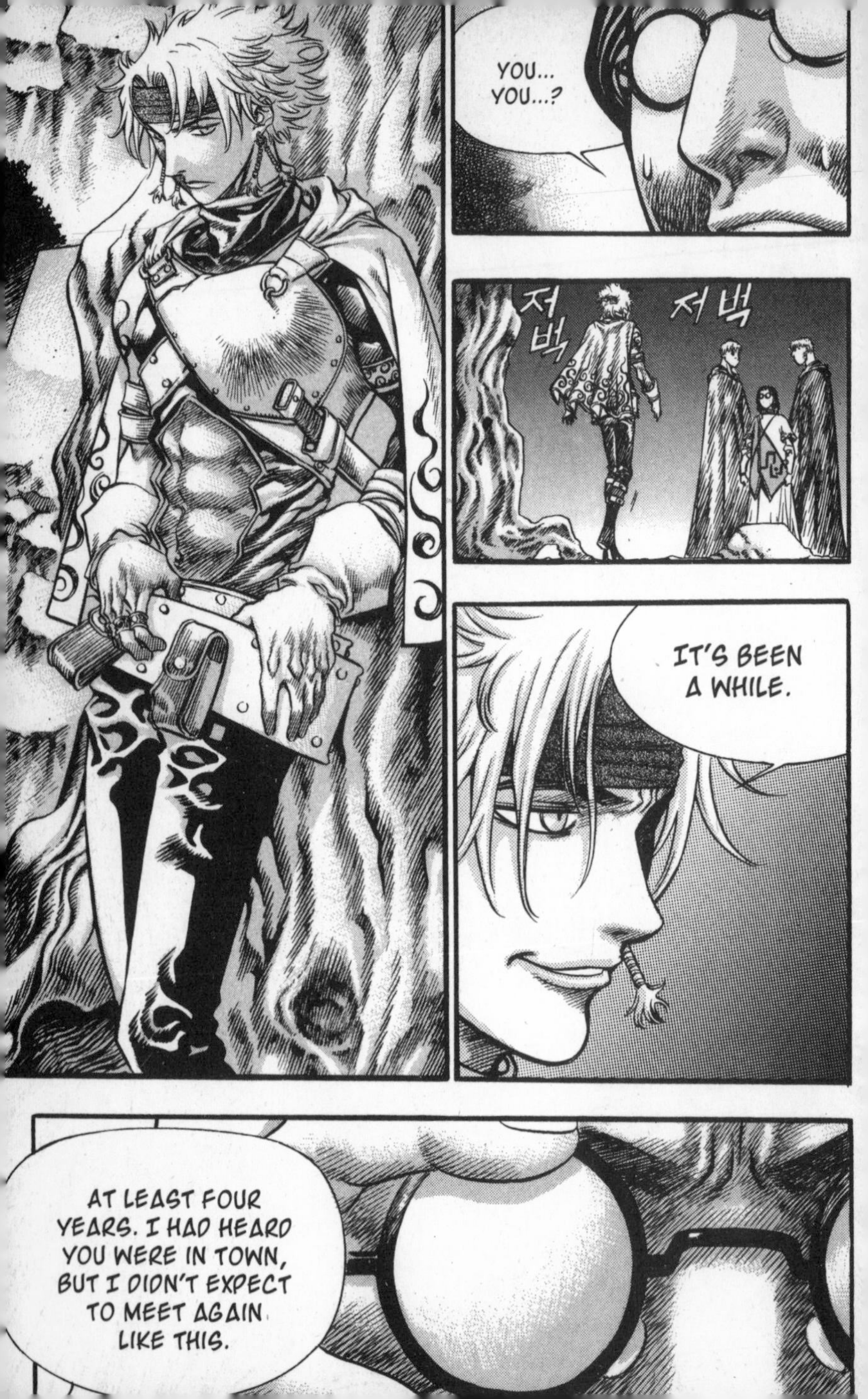
YOU...
YOU...?
저벅 저벅
IT'S BEEN A WHILE.
AT LEAST FOUR YEARS. I HAD HEARD YOU WERE IN TOWN, BUT I DIDN'T EXPECT TO MEET AGAIN LIKE THIS.

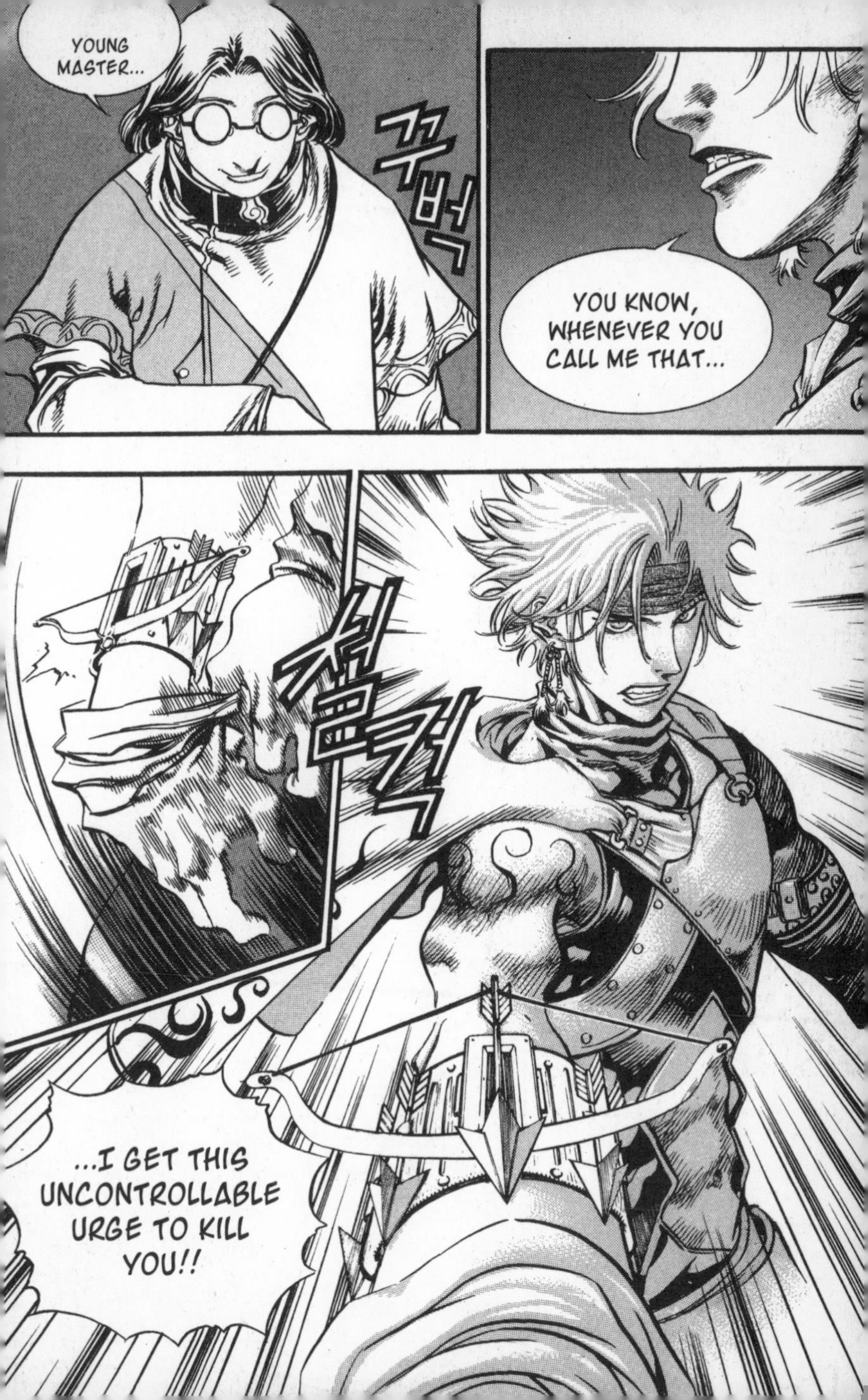
YOUNG MASTER...
YOU KNOW, WHENEVER YOU CALL ME THAT...
...I GET THIS UNCONTROLLABLE URGE TO KILL YOU!!

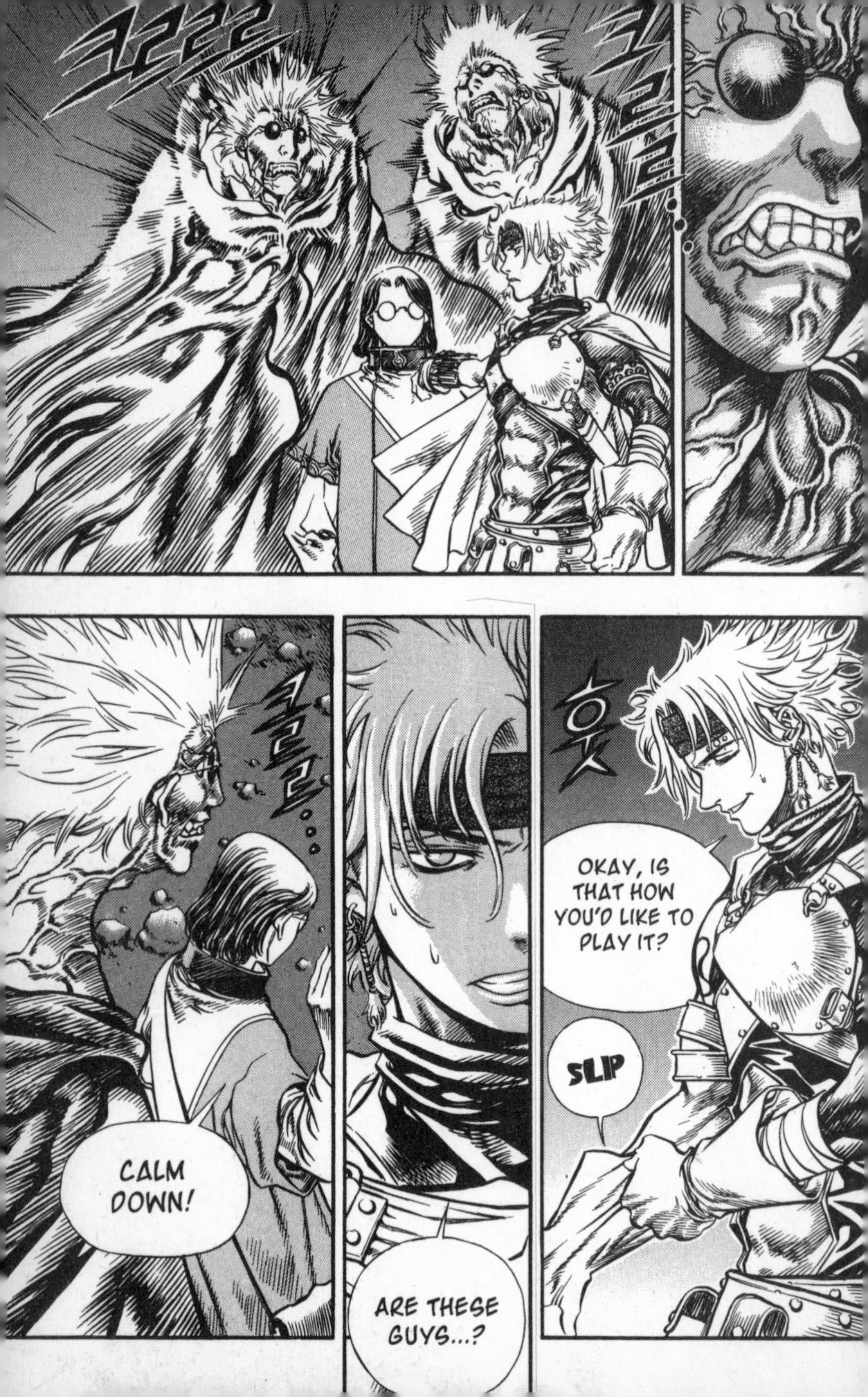
CALM DOWN!
ARE THESE GUYS...?
OKAY, IS THAT HOW YOU'D LIKE TO PLAY IT?
SLIP

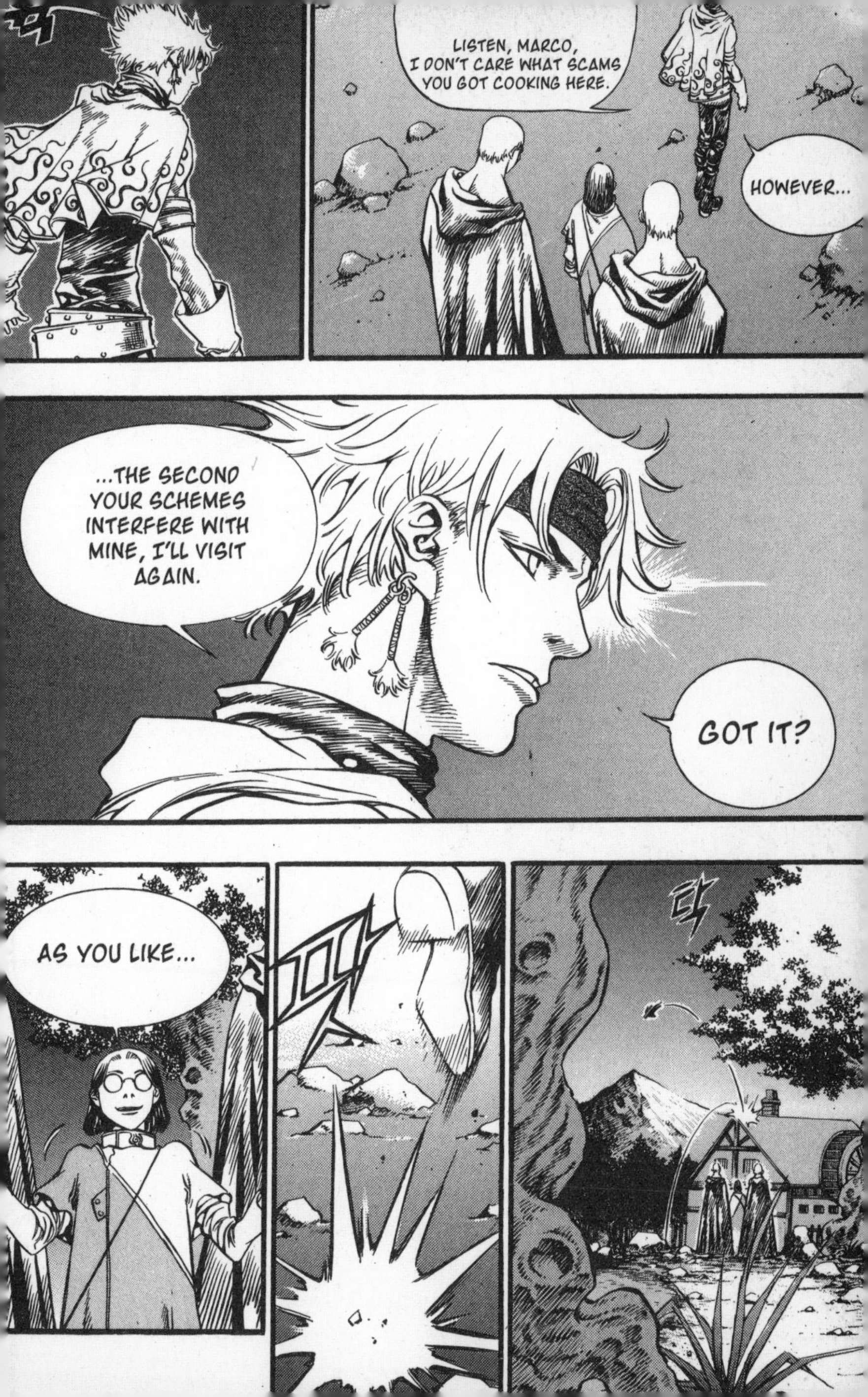
LISTEN, MARCO, I DON'T CARE WHAT SCAMS YOU GOT COOKING HERE.
HOWEVER...
...THE SECOND YOUR SCHEMES INTERFERE WITH MINE, I'LL VISIT AGAIN.
GOT IT?
AS YOU LIKE...

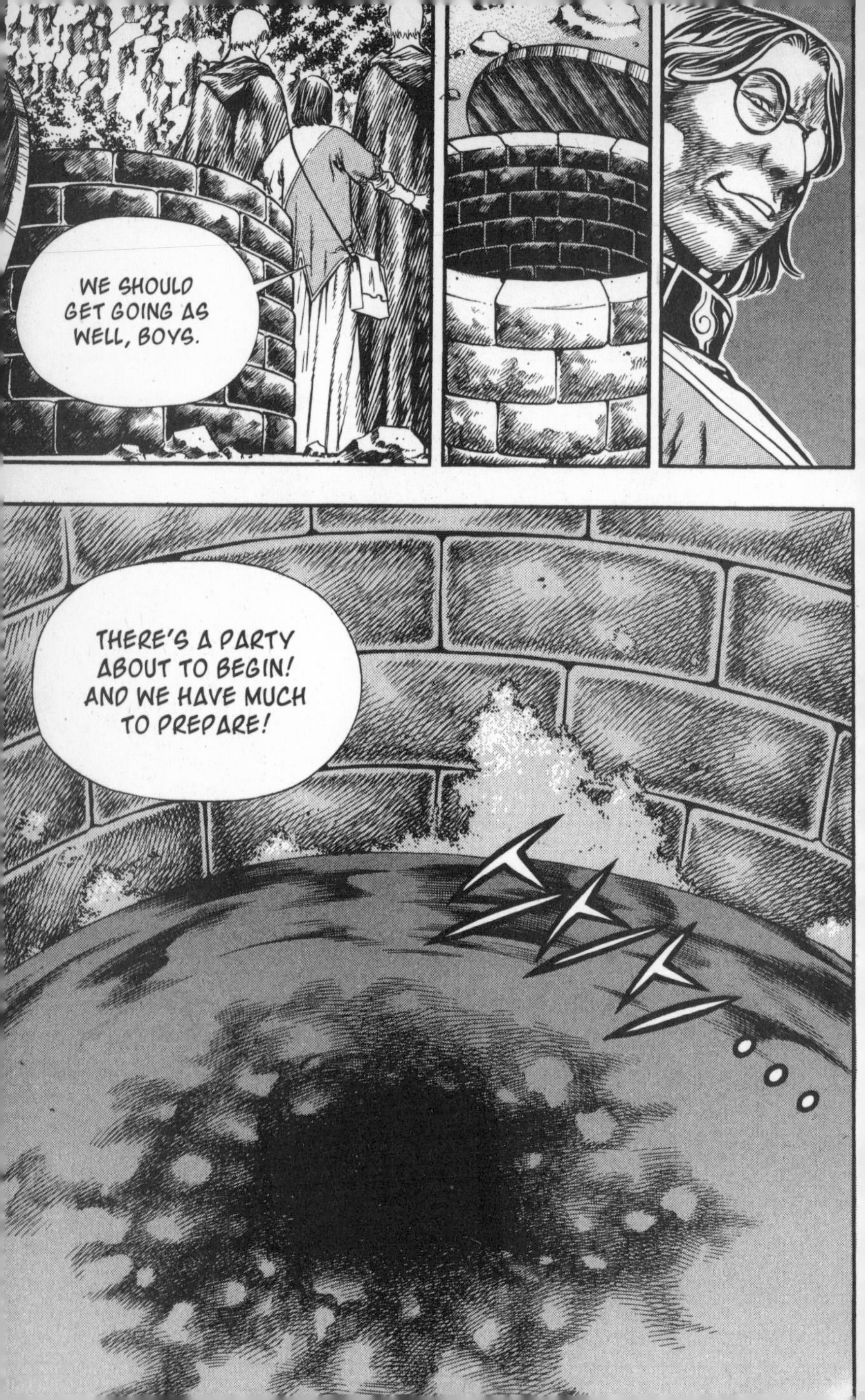
WE SHOULD GET GOING AS WELL, BOYS.
THERE'S A PARTY ABOUT TO BEGIN! AND WE HAVE MUCH TO PREPARE!

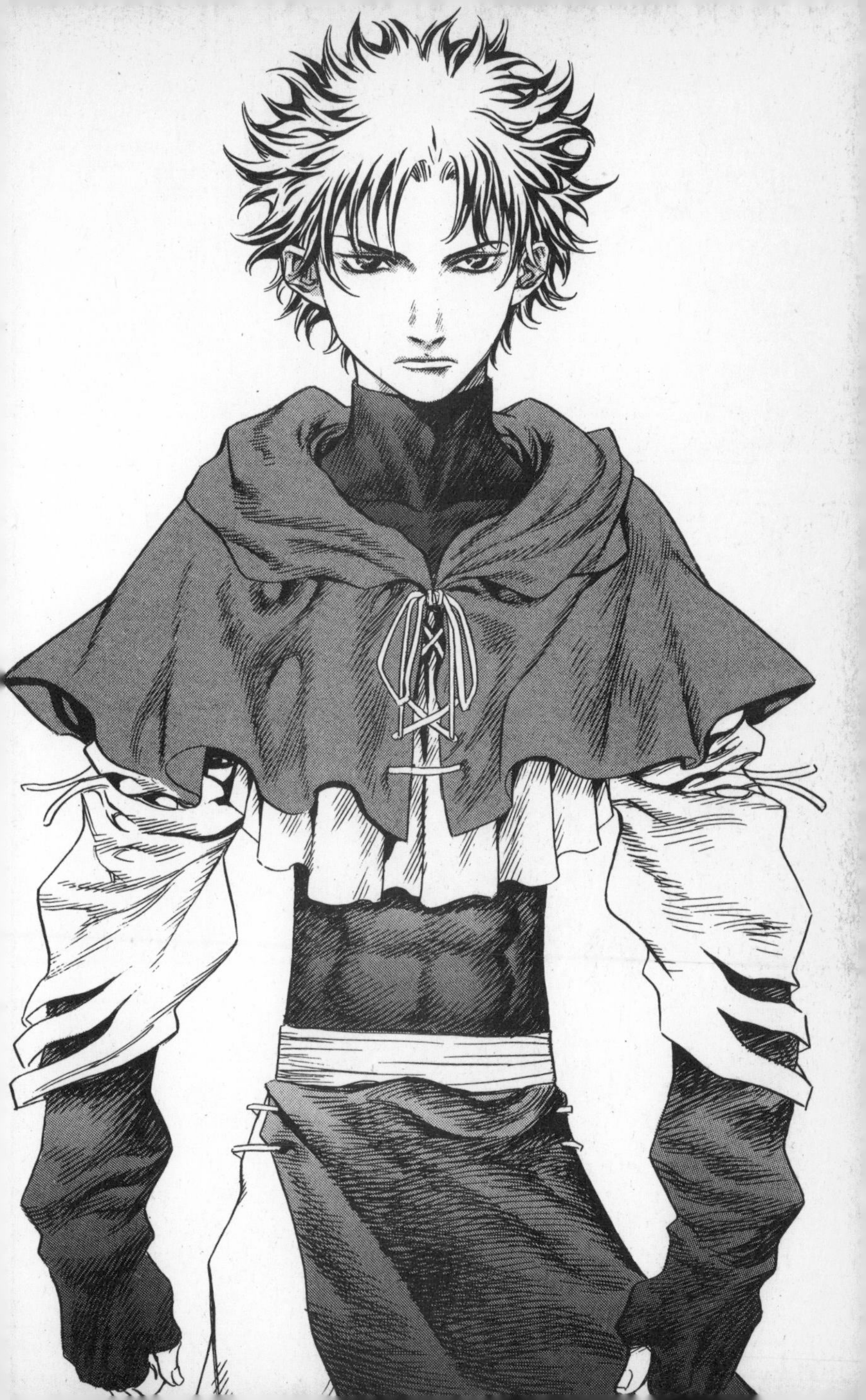

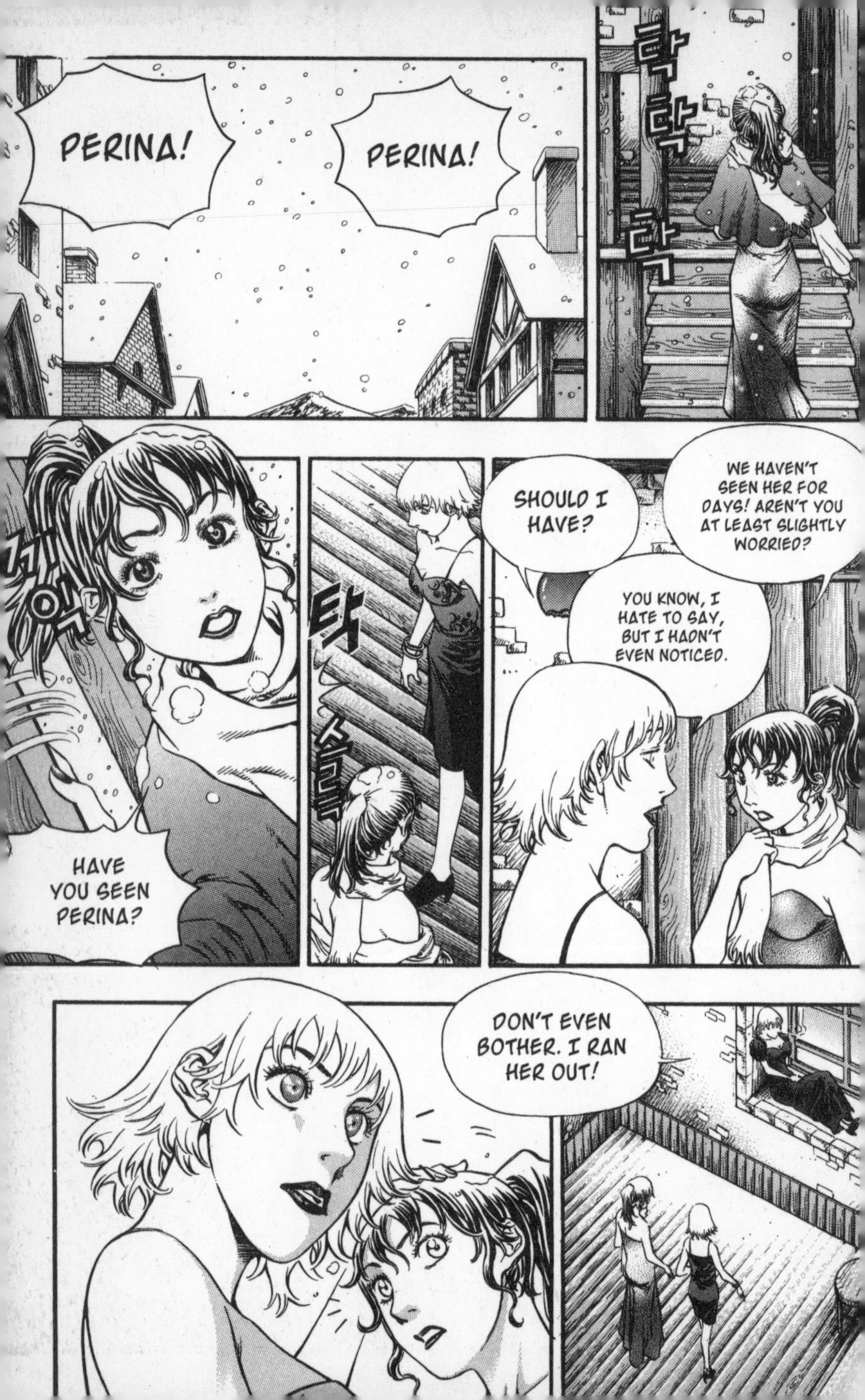

PERINA!
PERINA!
Have you seen Perina?
Should I have?
We haven't seen her for days! Aren't you at least slightly worried?
You know, I hate to say, but I hadn't even noticed.
...
Don't even bother. I ran her out!

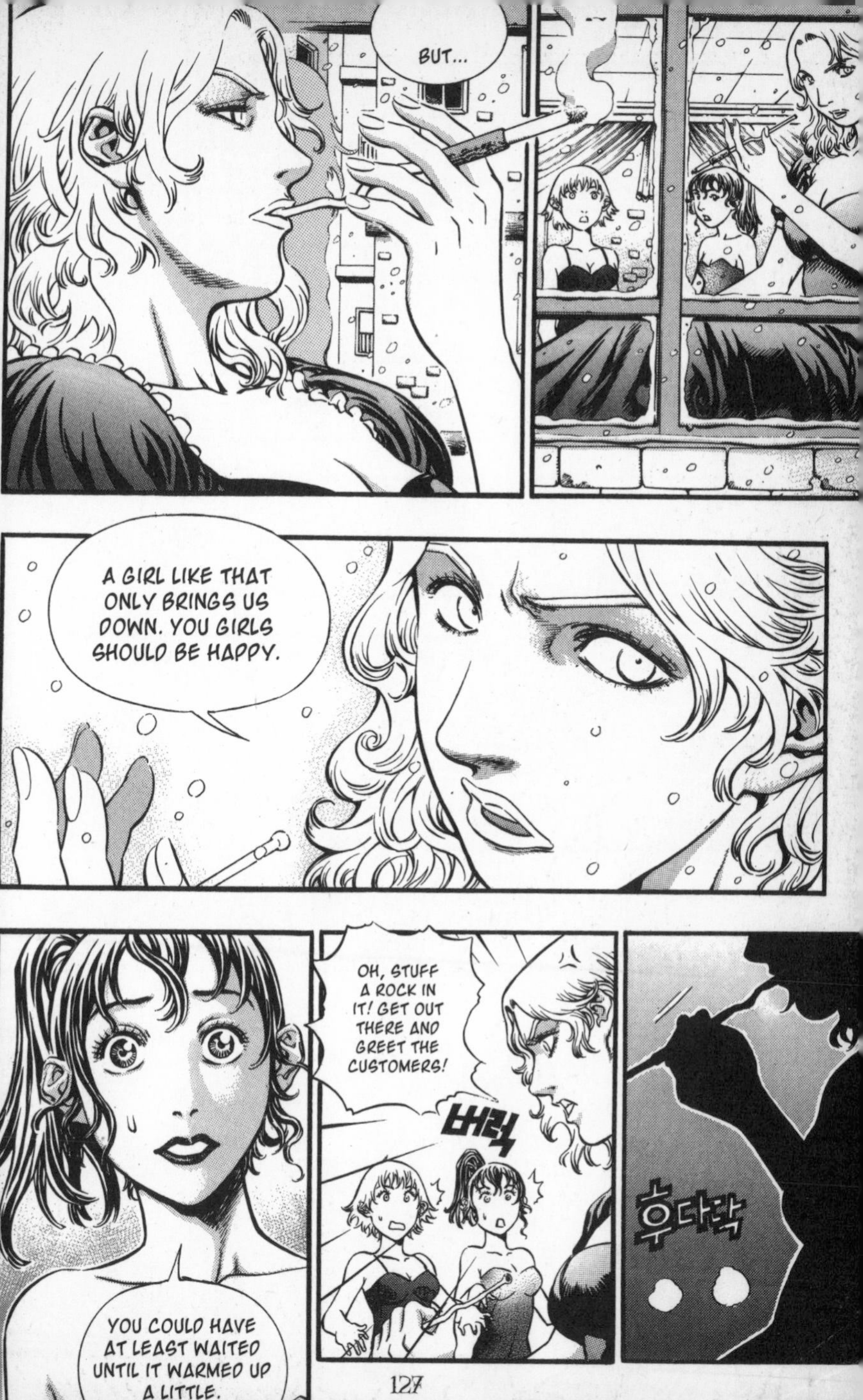

BUT...
A GIRL LIKE THAT ONLY BRINGS US DOWN. YOU GIRLS SHOULD BE HAPPY.
YOU COULD HAVE AT LEAST WAITED UNTIL IT WARMED UP A LITTLE.
OH, STUFF A ROCK IN IT! GET OUT THERE AND GREET THE CUSTOMERS!
버럭
후다닥

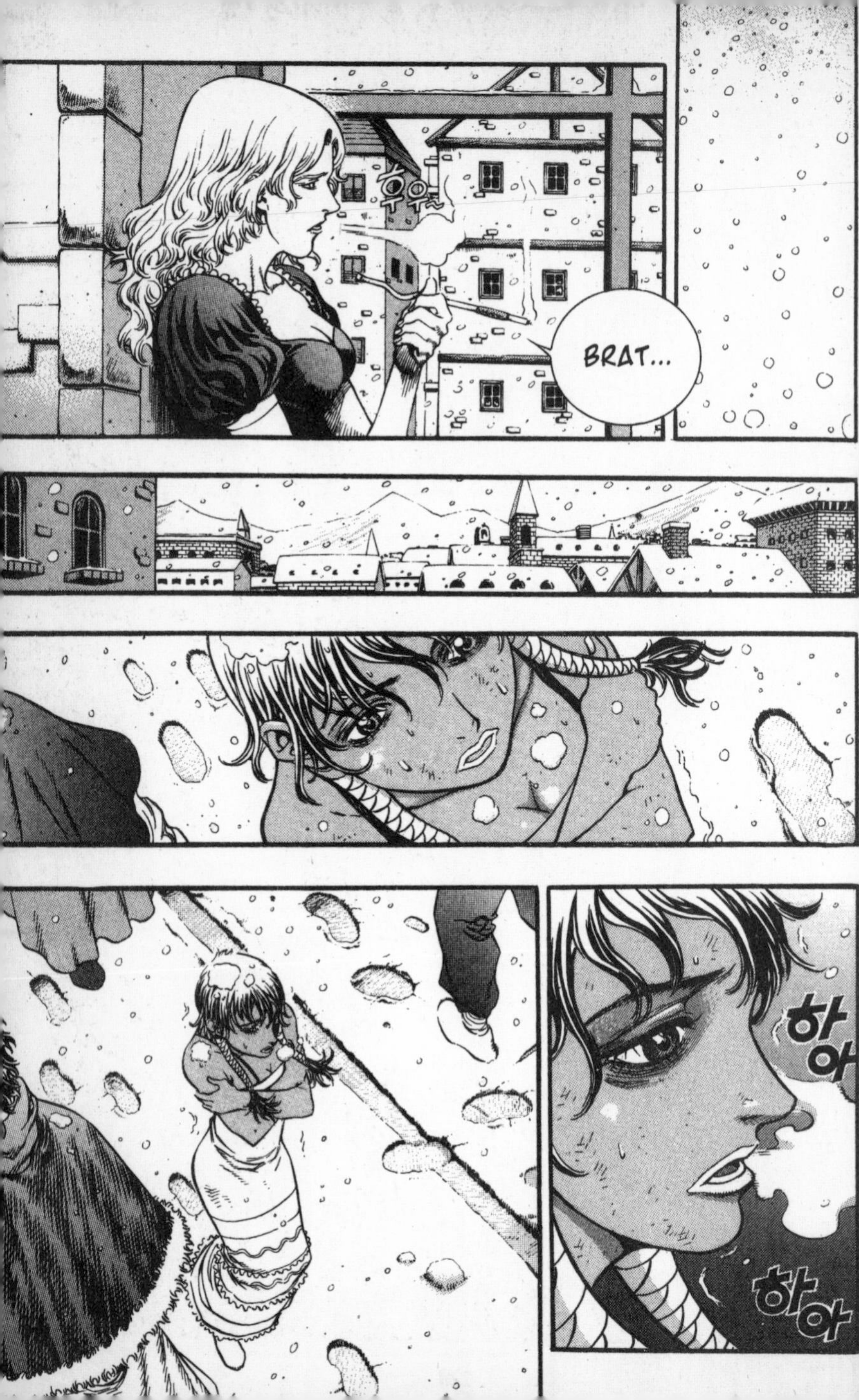
후우~
BRAT...
하아
하아

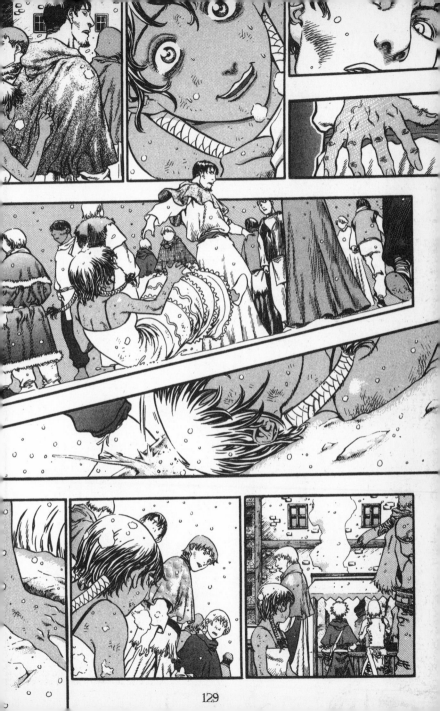

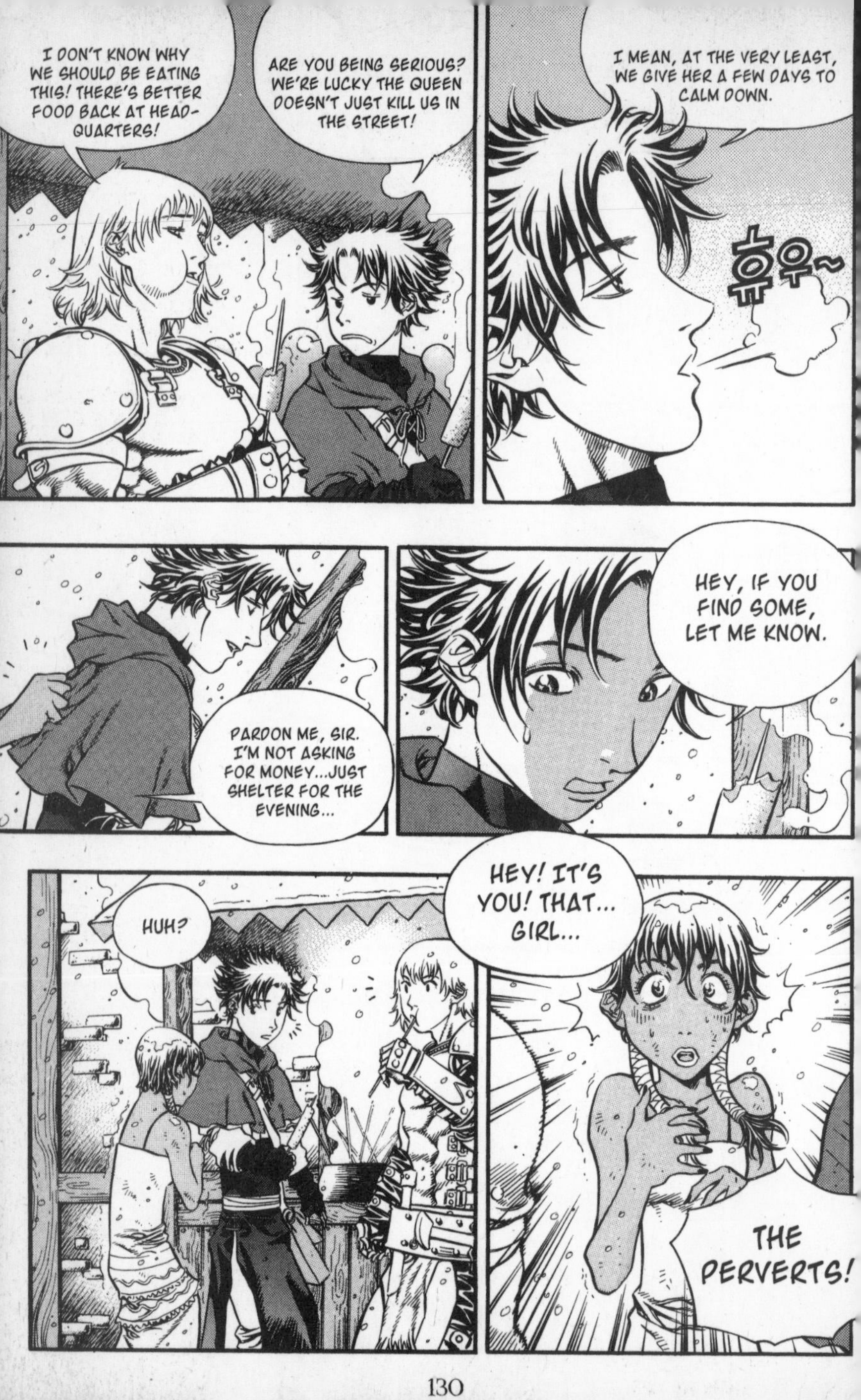

I DON'T KNOW WHY WE SHOULD BE EATING THIS! THERE'S BETTER FOOD BACK AT HEAD-QUARTERS!
ARE YOU BEING SERIOUS? WE'RE LUCKY THE QUEEN DOESN'T JUST KILL US IN THE STREET!
I MEAN, AT THE VERY LEAST, WE GIVE HER A FEW DAYS TO CALM DOWN.
후우~
PARDON ME, SIR. I'M NOT ASKING FOR MONEY...JUST SHELTER FOR THE EVENING...
HEY, IF YOU FIND SOME, LET ME KNOW.
HUH?
HEY! IT'S YOU! THAT... GIRL...
THE PERVERTS!

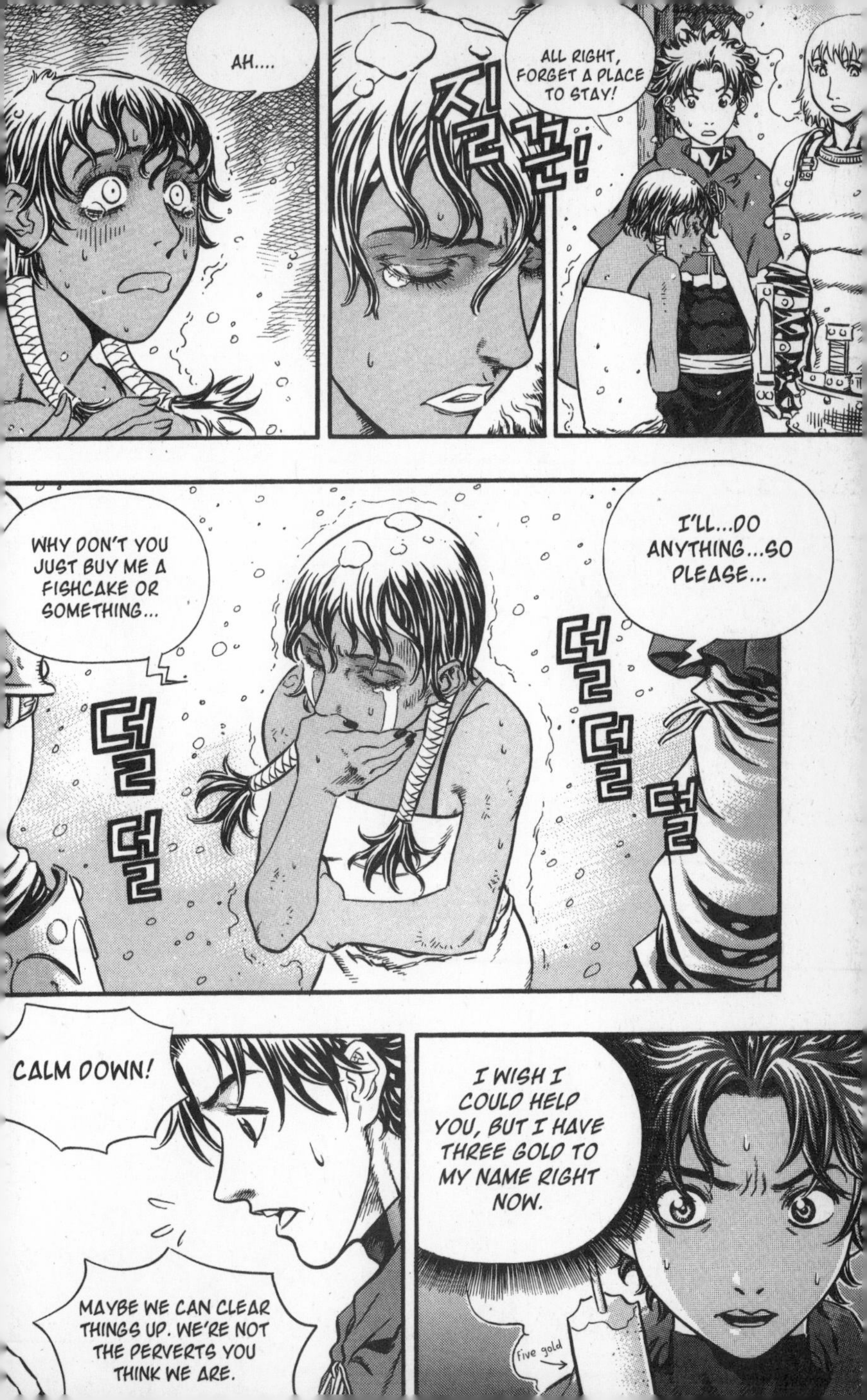
AH....
질끈!
ALL RIGHT, FORGET A PLACE TO STAY!
WHY DON'T YOU JUST BUY ME A FISHCAKE OR SOMETHING...
덜 덜
I'LL...DO ANYTHING...SO PLEASE...
덜 덜 덜
CALM DOWN!
MAYBE WE CAN CLEAR THINGS UP. WE'RE NOT THE PERVERTS YOU THINK WE ARE.
I WISH I COULD HELP YOU, BUT I HAVE THREE GOLD TO MY NAME RIGHT NOW.
Five gold

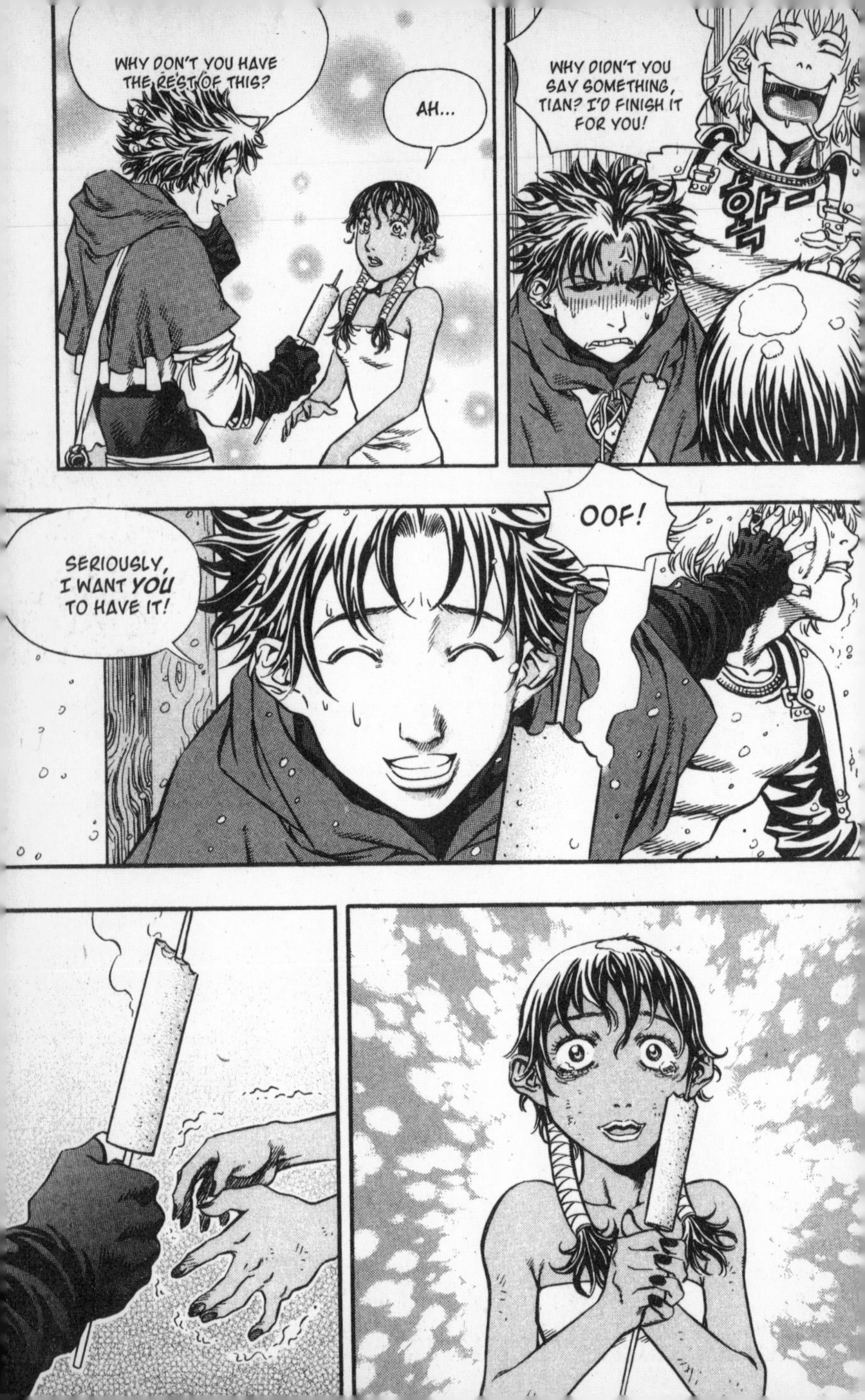
WHY DON'T YOU HAVE THE REST OF THIS?
AH...
WHY DIDN'T YOU SAY SOMETHING, TIAN? I'D FINISH IT FOR YOU!
SERIOUSLY, I WANT YOU TO HAVE IT!
OOF!

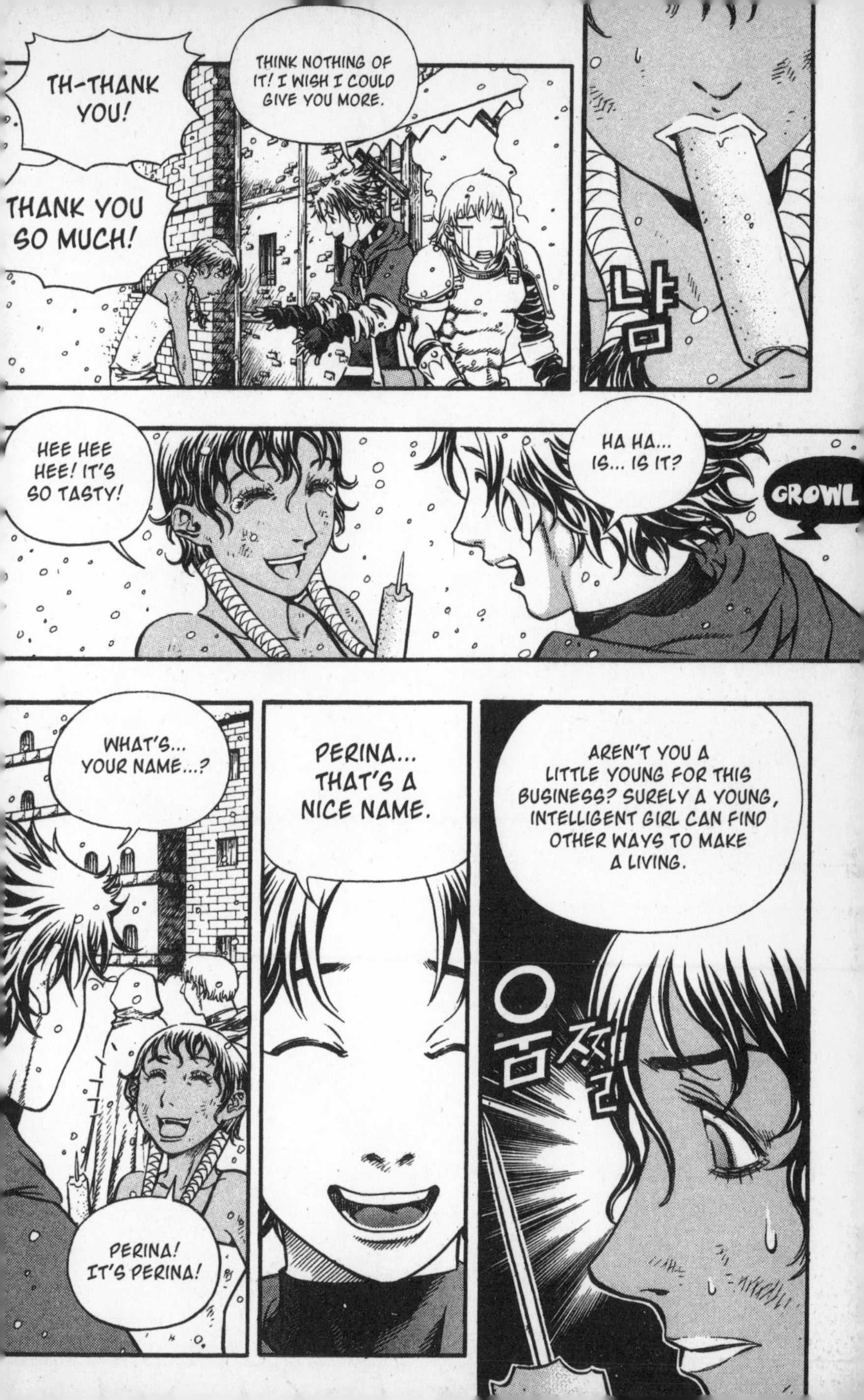

TH-THANK YOU!
THANK YOU SO MUCH!
THINK NOTHING OF IT! I WISH I COULD GIVE YOU MORE.
냠
HEE HEE HEE! IT'S SO TASTY!
HA HA... IS... IS IT?
GROWL
WHAT'S... YOUR NAME...?
PERINA! IT'S PERINA!
PERINA... THAT'S A NICE NAME.
AREN'T YOU A LITTLE YOUNG FOR THIS BUSINESS? SURELY A YOUNG, INTELLIGENT GIRL CAN FIND OTHER WAYS TO MAKE A LIVING.
움찔

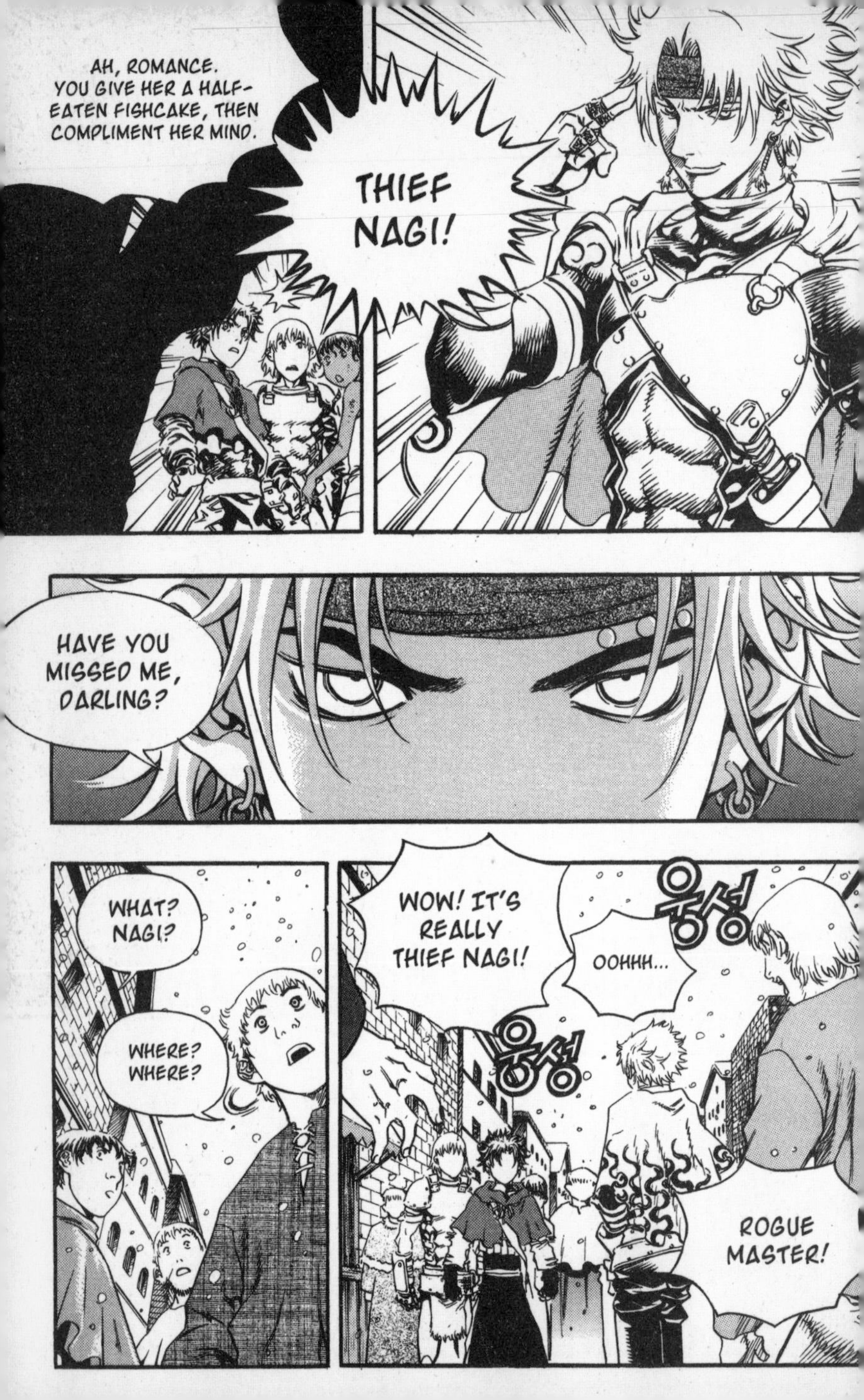
AH, ROMANCE. YOU GIVE HER A HALF-EATEN FISHCAKE, THEN COMPLIMENT HER MIND.
THIEF NAGI!
HAVE YOU MISSED ME, DARLING?
WHAT? NAGI?
WHERE? WHERE?
WOW! IT'S REALLY THIEF NAGI!
OOHHH...
ROGUE MASTER!

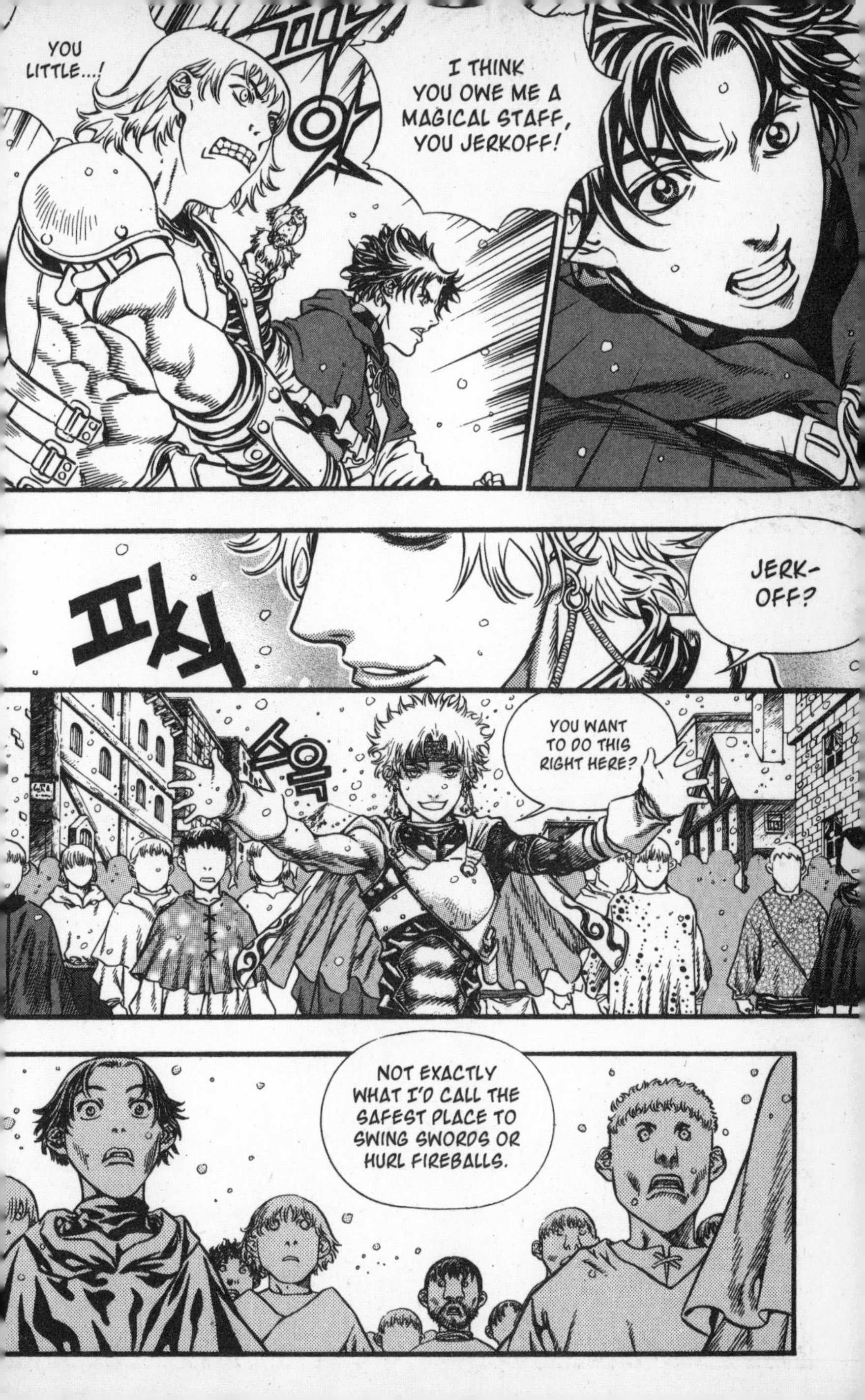
YOU LITTLE...!
I THINK YOU OWE ME A MAGICAL STAFF, YOU JERKOFF!
JERK-OFF?
YOU WANT TO DO THIS RIGHT HERE?
NOT EXACTLY WHAT I'D CALL THE SAFEST PLACE TO SWING SWORDS OR HURL FIREBALLS.

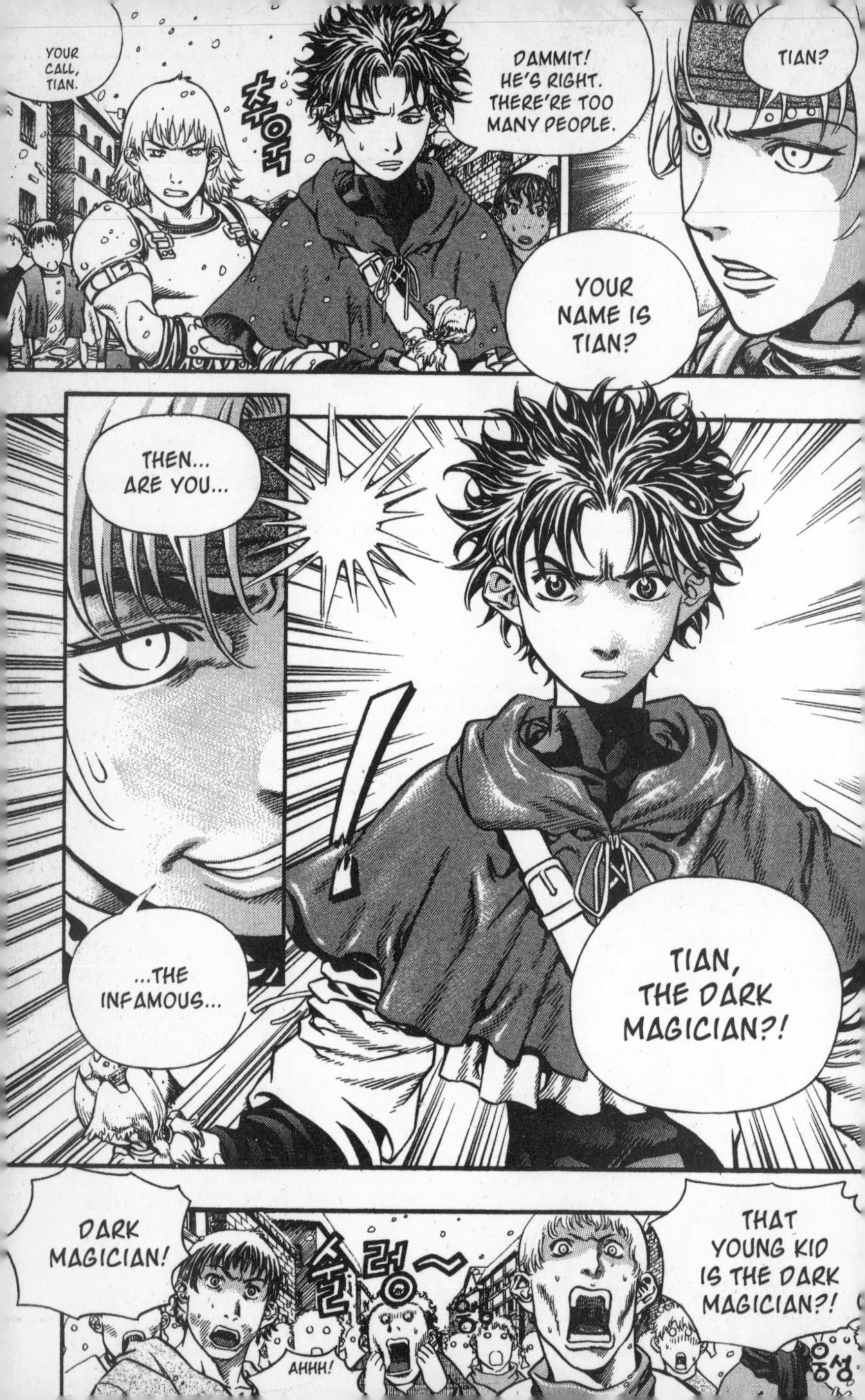
YOUR CALL, TIAN.
DAMMIT! HE'S RIGHT. THERE'RE TOO MANY PEOPLE.
TIAN?
YOUR NAME IS TIAN?
THEN... ARE YOU...
...THE INFAMOUS...
TIAN, THE DARK MAGICIAN?!
DARK MAGICIAN!
술렁~
AHHH!
THAT YOUNG KID IS THE DARK MAGICIAN?!
웅성

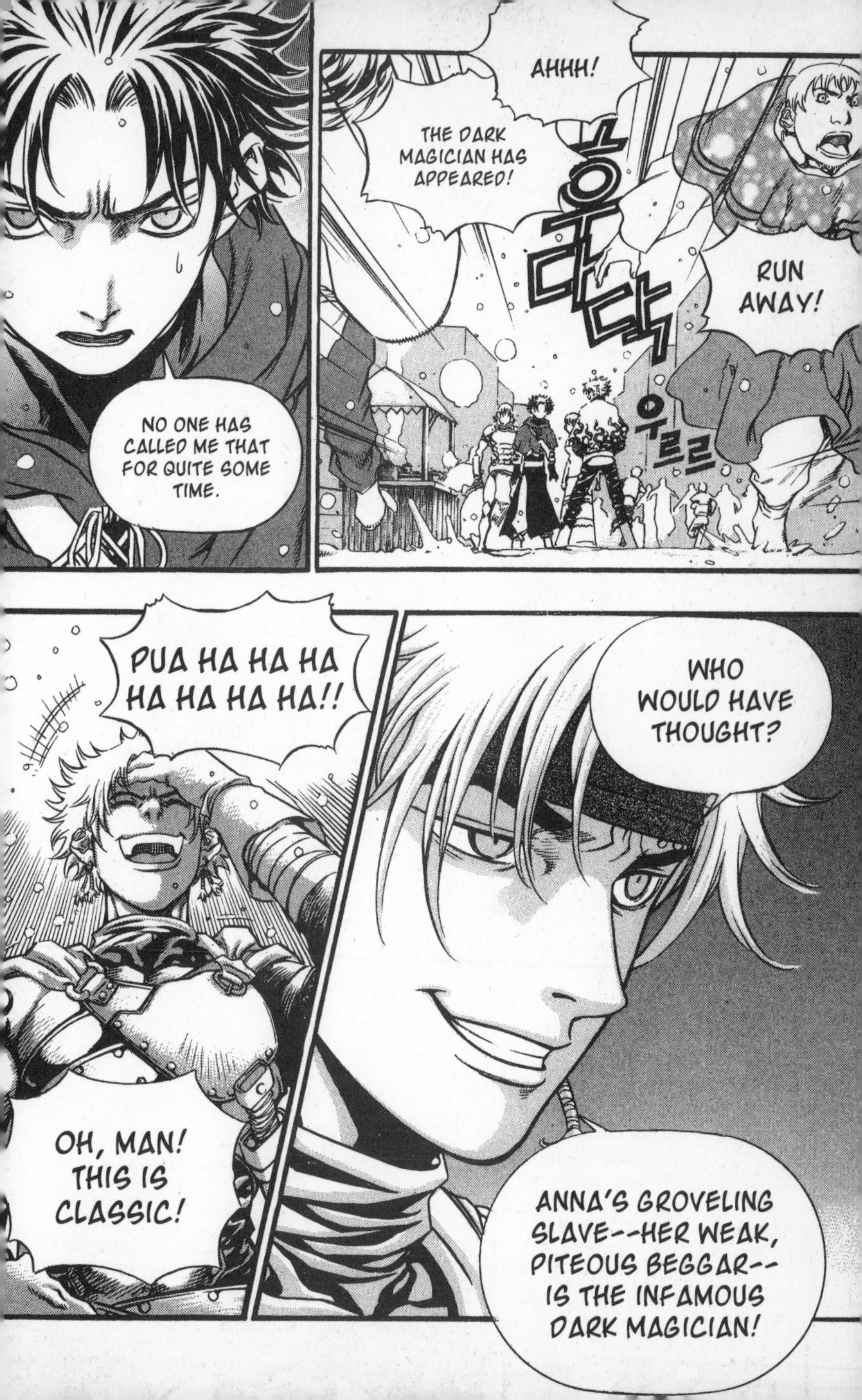

NO ONE HAS CALLED ME THAT FOR QUITE SOME TIME.
AHHH!
THE DARK MAGICIAN HAS APPEARED!
후다닥
RUN AWAY!
우르르
PUA HA HA HA HA HA HA HA!!
OH, MAN! THIS IS CLASSIC!
WHO WOULD HAVE THOUGHT?
ANNA'S GROVELING SLAVE--HER WEAK, PITEOUS BEGGAR--IS THE INFAMOUS DARK MAGICIAN!

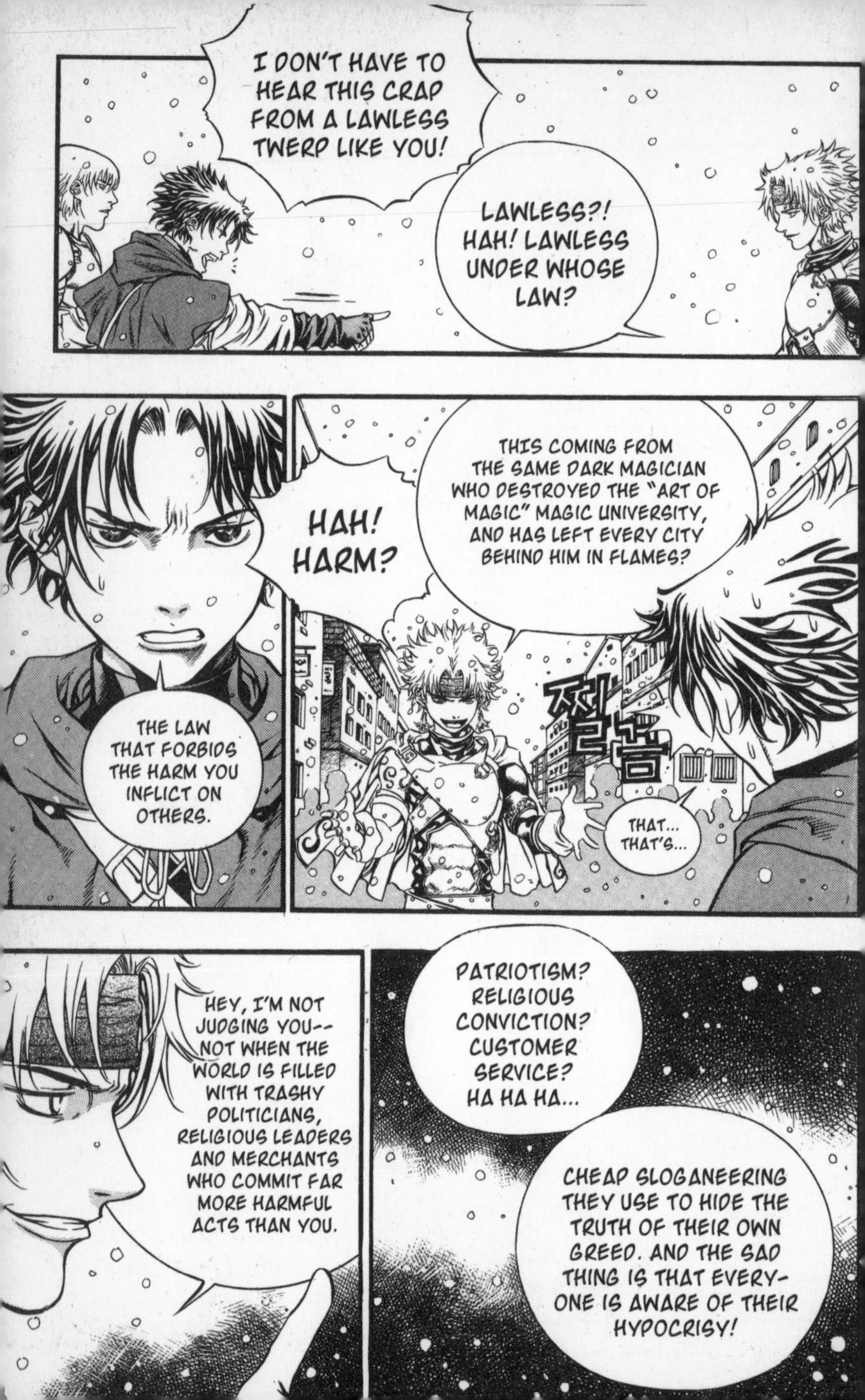
I DON'T HAVE TO HEAR THIS CRAP FROM A LAWLESS TWERP LIKE YOU!
LAWLESS?! HAH! LAWLESS UNDER WHOSE LAW?
THE LAW THAT FORBIDS THE HARM YOU INFLICT ON OTHERS.
HAH! HARM?
THIS COMING FROM THE SAME DARK MAGICIAN WHO DESTROYED THE "ART OF MAGIC" MAGIC UNIVERSITY, AND HAS LEFT EVERY CITY BEHIND HIM IN FLAMES?
THAT... THAT'S...
HEY, I'M NOT JUDGING YOU-- NOT WHEN THE WORLD IS FILLED WITH TRASHY POLITICIANS, RELIGIOUS LEADERS AND MERCHANTS WHO COMMIT FAR MORE HARMFUL ACTS THAN YOU.
PATRIOTISM? RELIGIOUS CONVICTION? CUSTOMER SERVICE? HA HA HA...
CHEAP SLOGANEERING THEY USE TO HIDE THE TRUTH OF THEIR OWN GREED. AND THE SAD THING IS THAT EVERY-ONE IS AWARE OF THEIR HYPOCRISY!

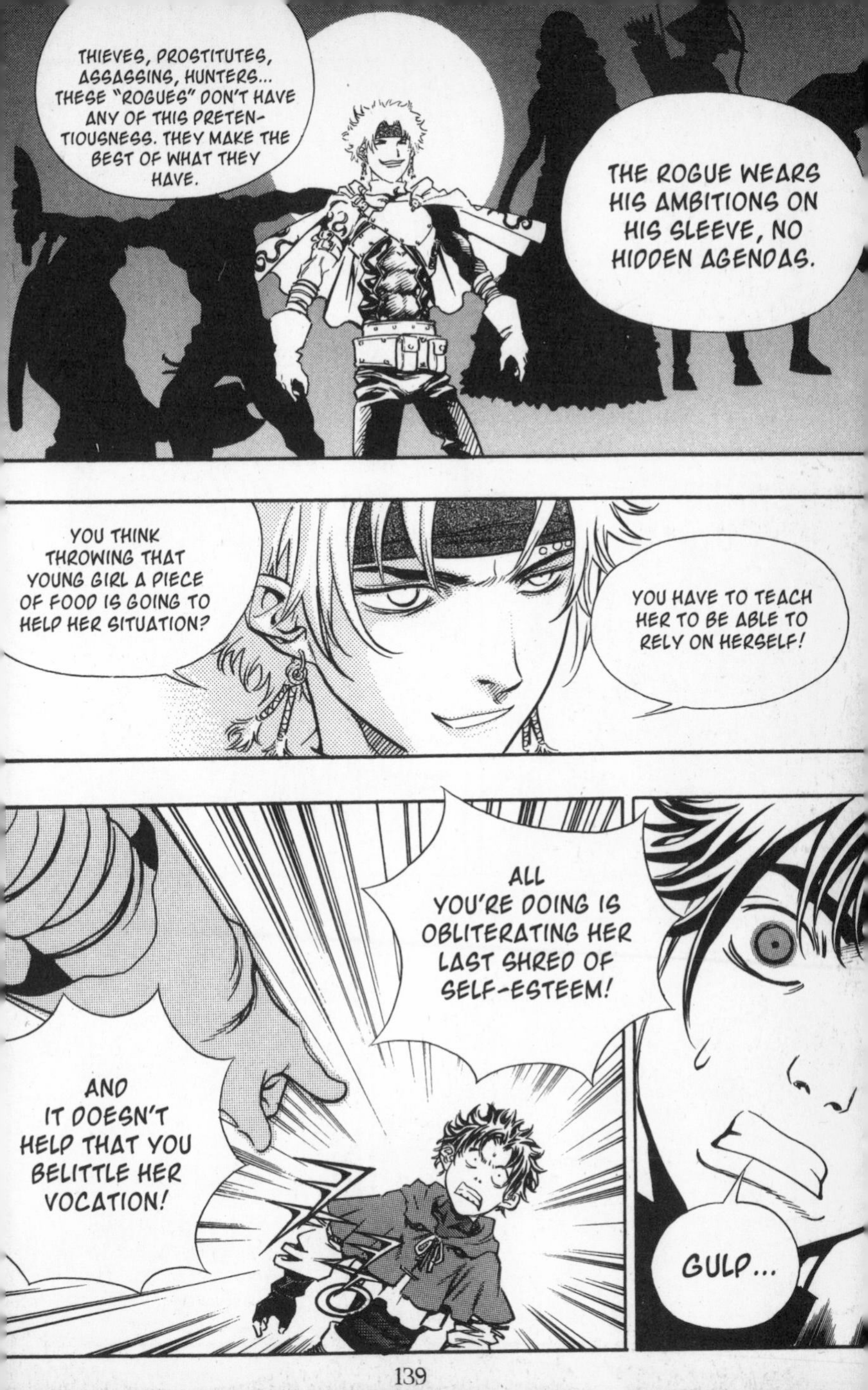
THIEVES, PROSTITUTES, ASSASSINS, HUNTERS... THESE "ROGUES" DON'T HAVE ANY OF THIS PRETENTIOUSNESS. THEY MAKE THE BEST OF WHAT THEY HAVE.
THE ROGUE WEARS HIS AMBITIONS ON HIS SLEEVE, NO HIDDEN AGENDAS.
YOU THINK THROWING THAT YOUNG GIRL A PIECE OF FOOD IS GOING TO HELP HER SITUATION?
YOU HAVE TO TEACH HER TO BE ABLE TO RELY ON HERSELF!
ALL YOU'RE DOING IS OBLITERATING HER LAST SHRED OF SELF-ESTEEM!
AND IT DOESN'T HELP THAT YOU BELITTLE HER VOCATION!
GULP...

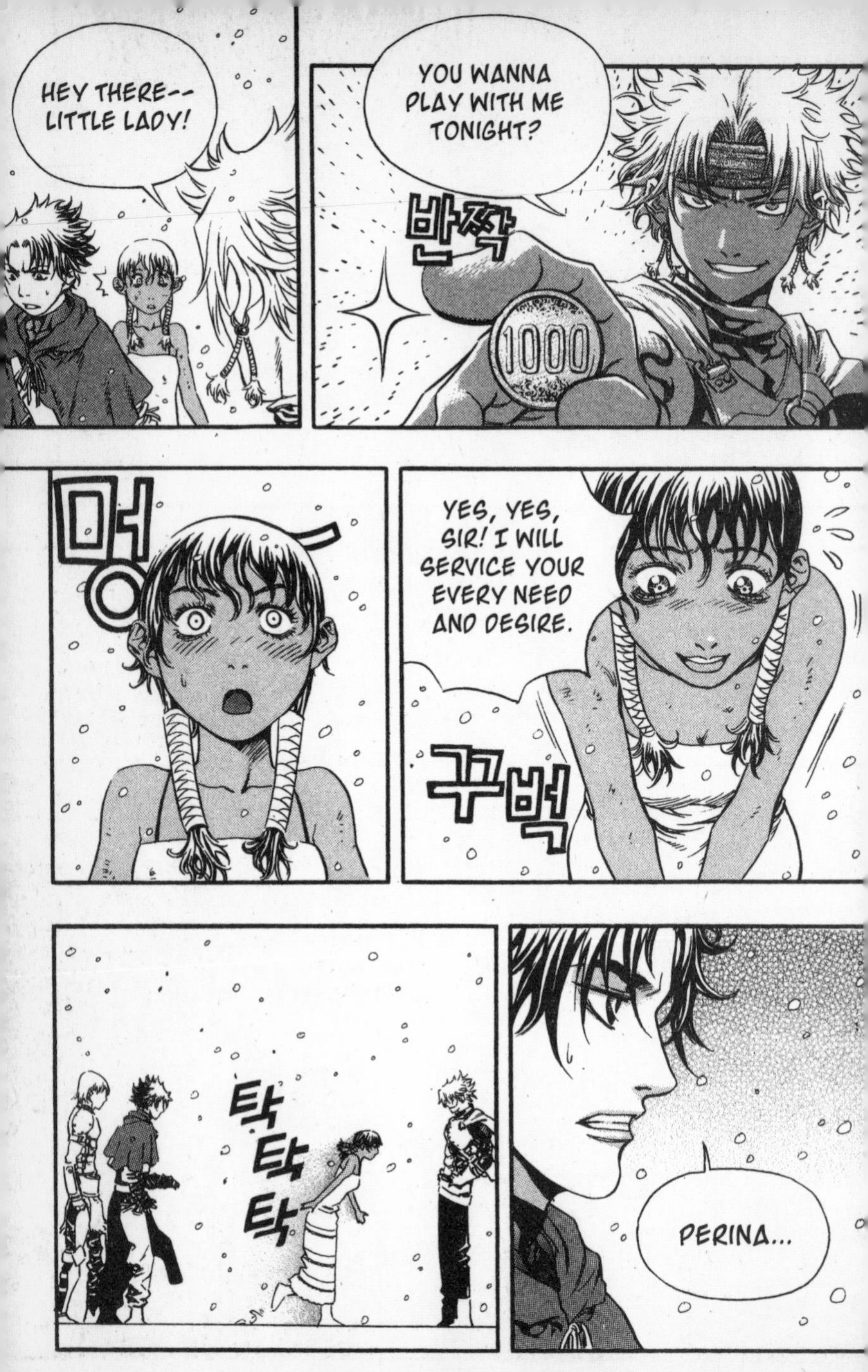
HEY THERE--
LITTLE LADY!
YOU WANNA PLAY WITH ME TONIGHT?
반짝
1000
멍~
YES, YES, SIR! I WILL SERVICE YOUR EVERY NEED AND DESIRE.
꾸벅
탁
탁
탁
PERINA...

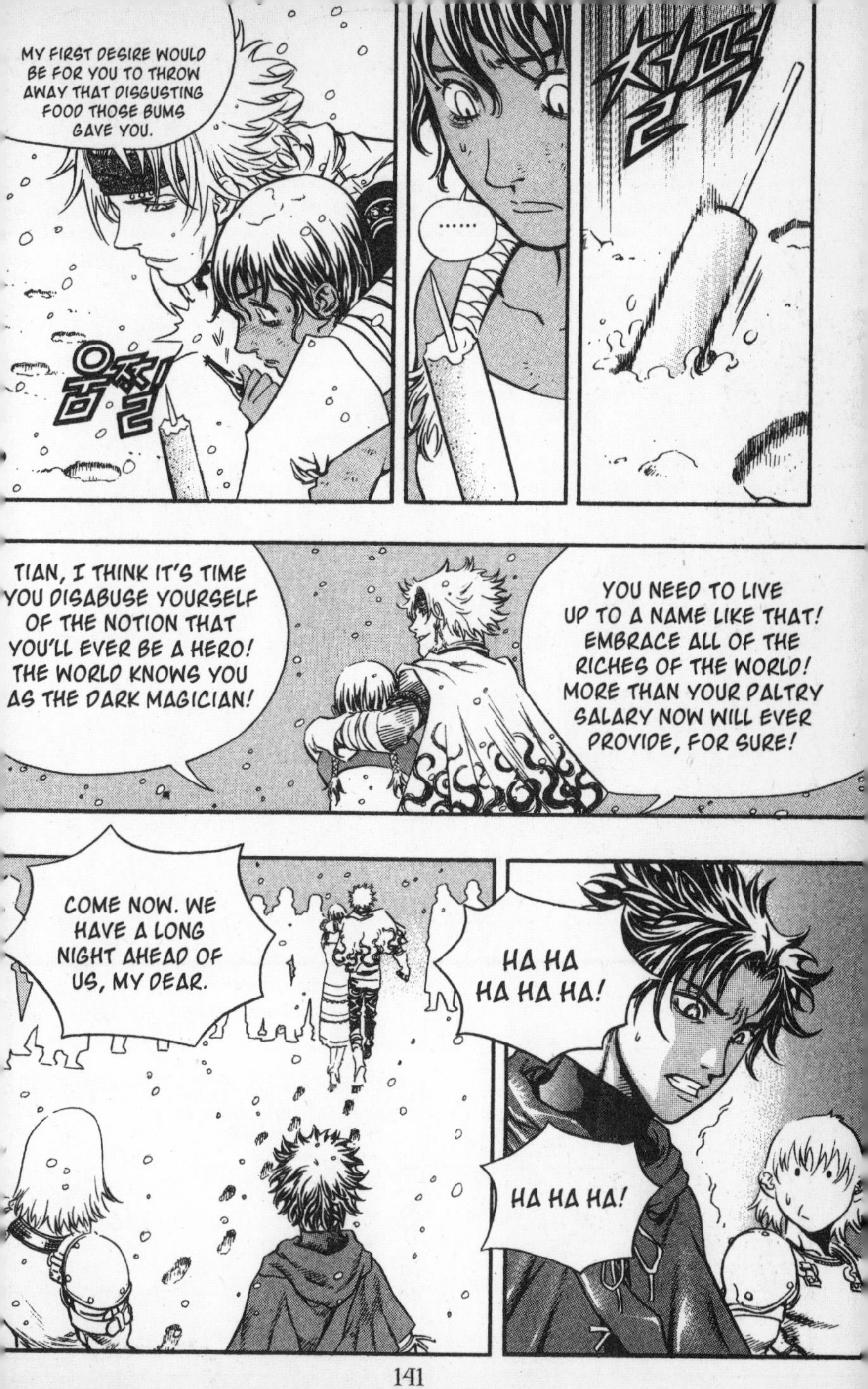
MY FIRST DESIRE WOULD BE FOR YOU TO THROW AWAY THAT DISGUSTING FOOD THOSE BUMS GAVE YOU.
......
TIAN, I THINK IT'S TIME YOU DISABUSE YOURSELF OF THE NOTION THAT YOU'LL EVER BE A HERO! THE WORLD KNOWS YOU AS THE DARK MAGICIAN!
YOU NEED TO LIVE UP TO A NAME LIKE THAT! EMBRACE ALL OF THE RICHES OF THE WORLD! MORE THAN YOUR PALTRY SALARY NOW WILL EVER PROVIDE, FOR SURE!
COME NOW. WE HAVE A LONG NIGHT AHEAD OF US, MY DEAR.
HA HA HA HA HA!
HA HA HA!

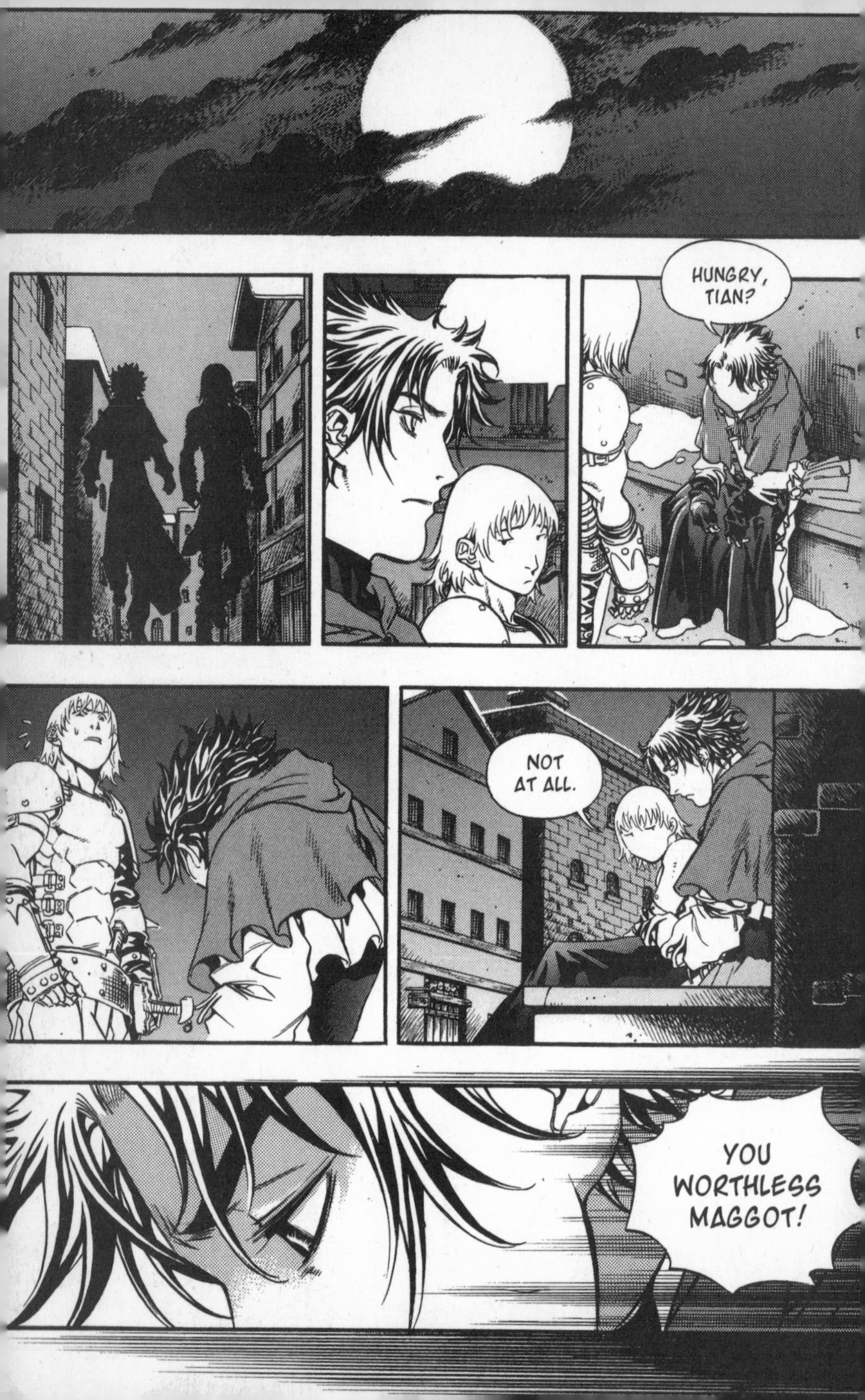
HUNGRY, TIAN?
NOT AT ALL.
YOU WORTHLESS MAGGOT!

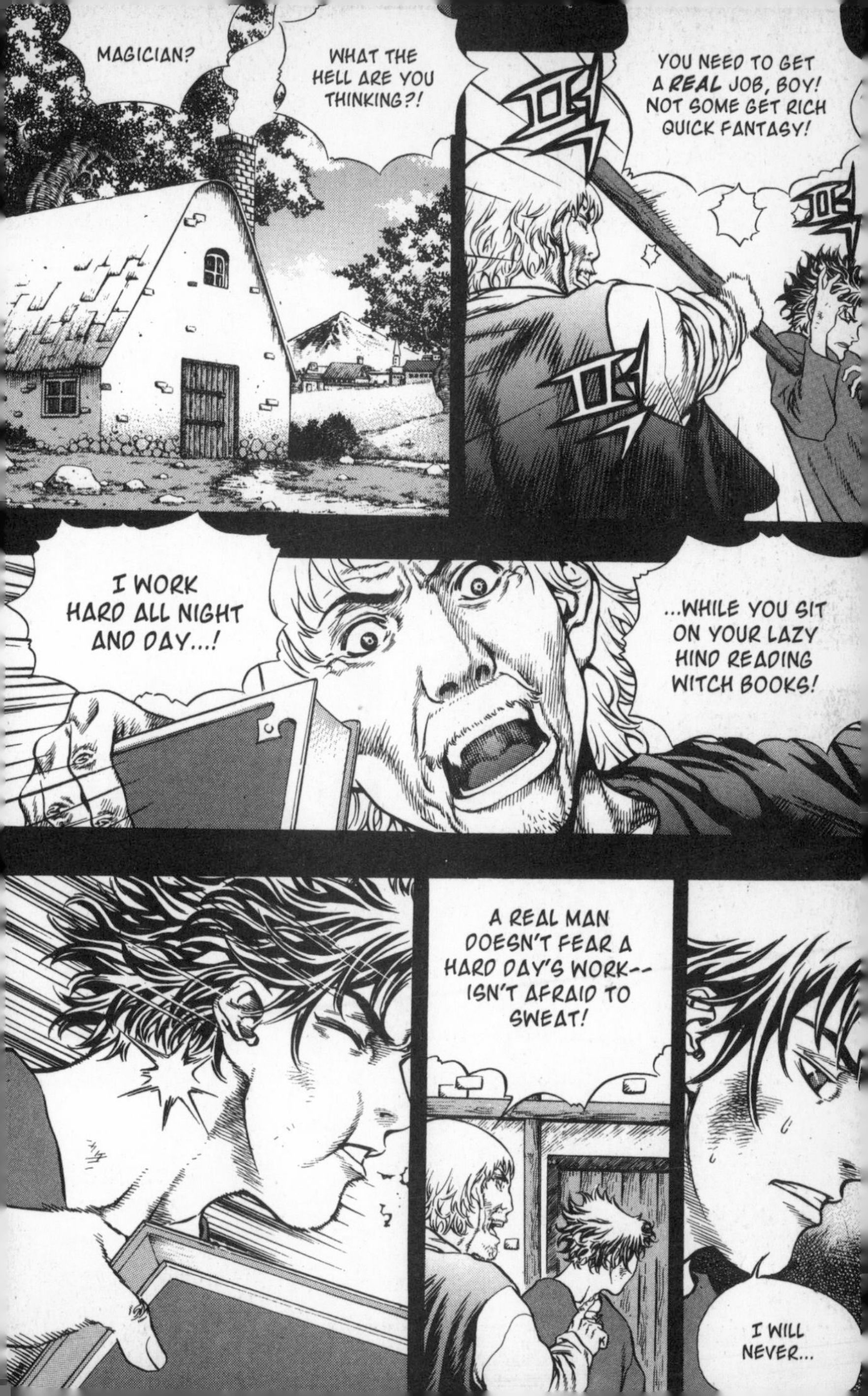

MAGICIAN?
WHAT THE HELL ARE YOU THINKING?!
YOU NEED TO GET A REAL JOB, BOY! NOT SOME GET RICH QUICK FANTASY!
I WORK HARD ALL NIGHT AND DAY...!
...WHILE YOU SIT ON YOUR LAZY HIND READING WITCH BOOKS!
A REAL MAN DOESN'T FEAR A HARD DAY'S WORK--ISN'T AFRAID TO SWEAT!
I WILL NEVER...

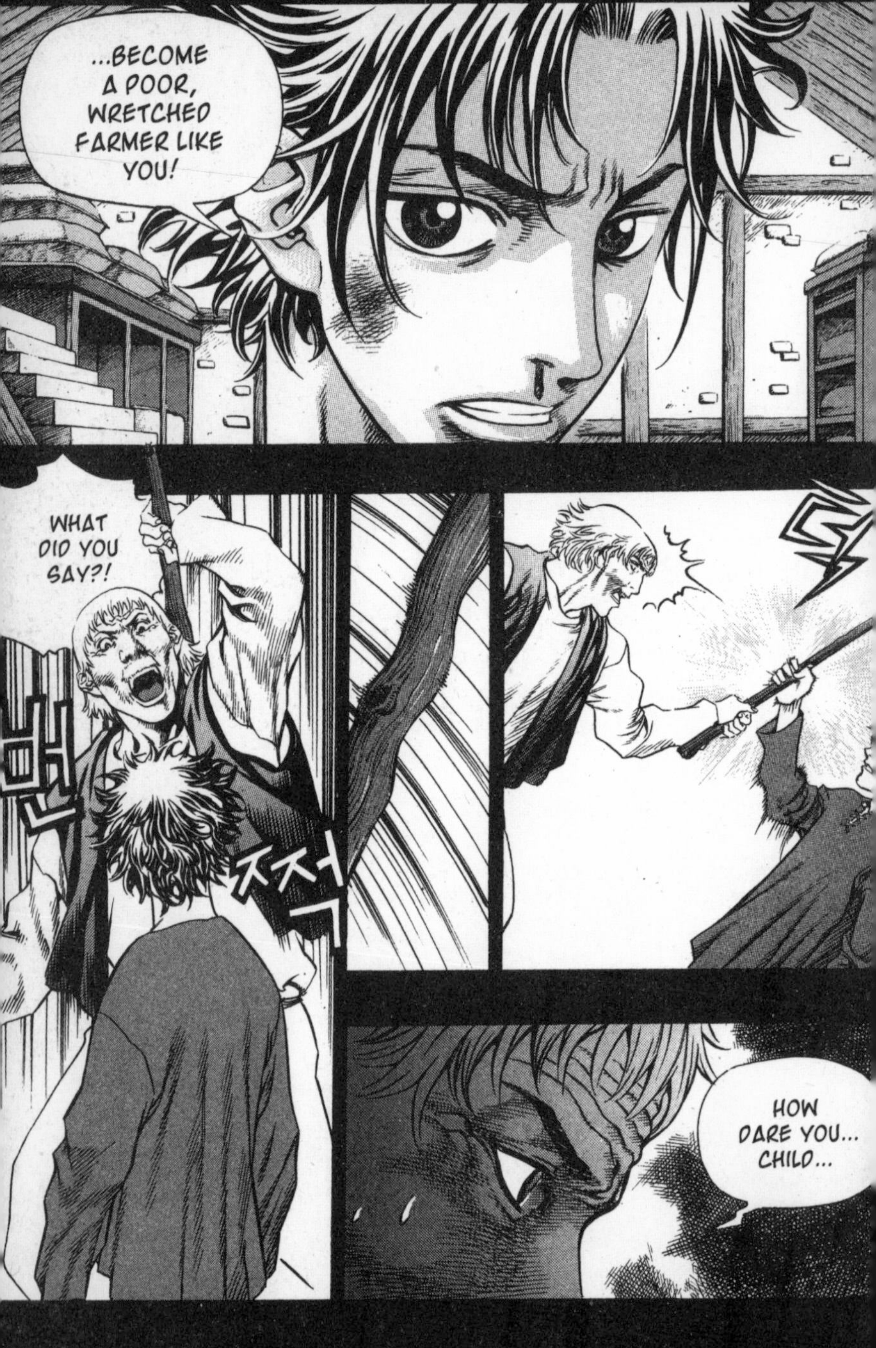
...BECOME A POOR, WRETCHED FARMER LIKE YOU!
WHAT DID YOU SAY?!
HOW DARE YOU... CHILD...

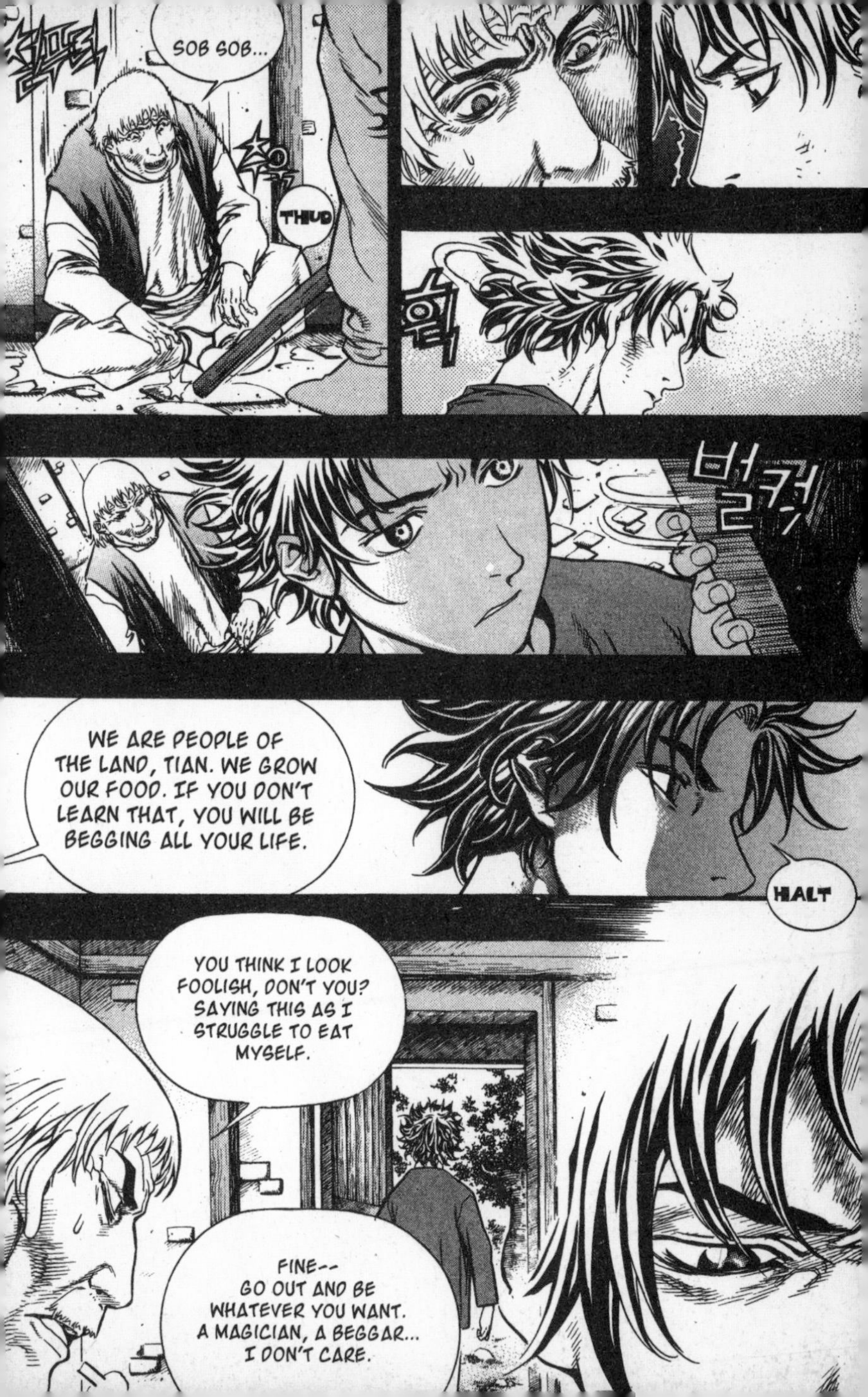
SOB SOB...
THUD
WE ARE PEOPLE OF THE LAND, TIAN. WE GROW OUR FOOD. IF YOU DON'T LEARN THAT, YOU WILL BE BEGGING ALL YOUR LIFE.
HALT
YOU THINK I LOOK FOOLISH, DON'T YOU? SAYING THIS AS I STRUGGLE TO EAT MYSELF.
FINE-- GO OUT AND BE WHATEVER YOU WANT. A MAGICIAN, A BEGGAR... I DON'T CARE.

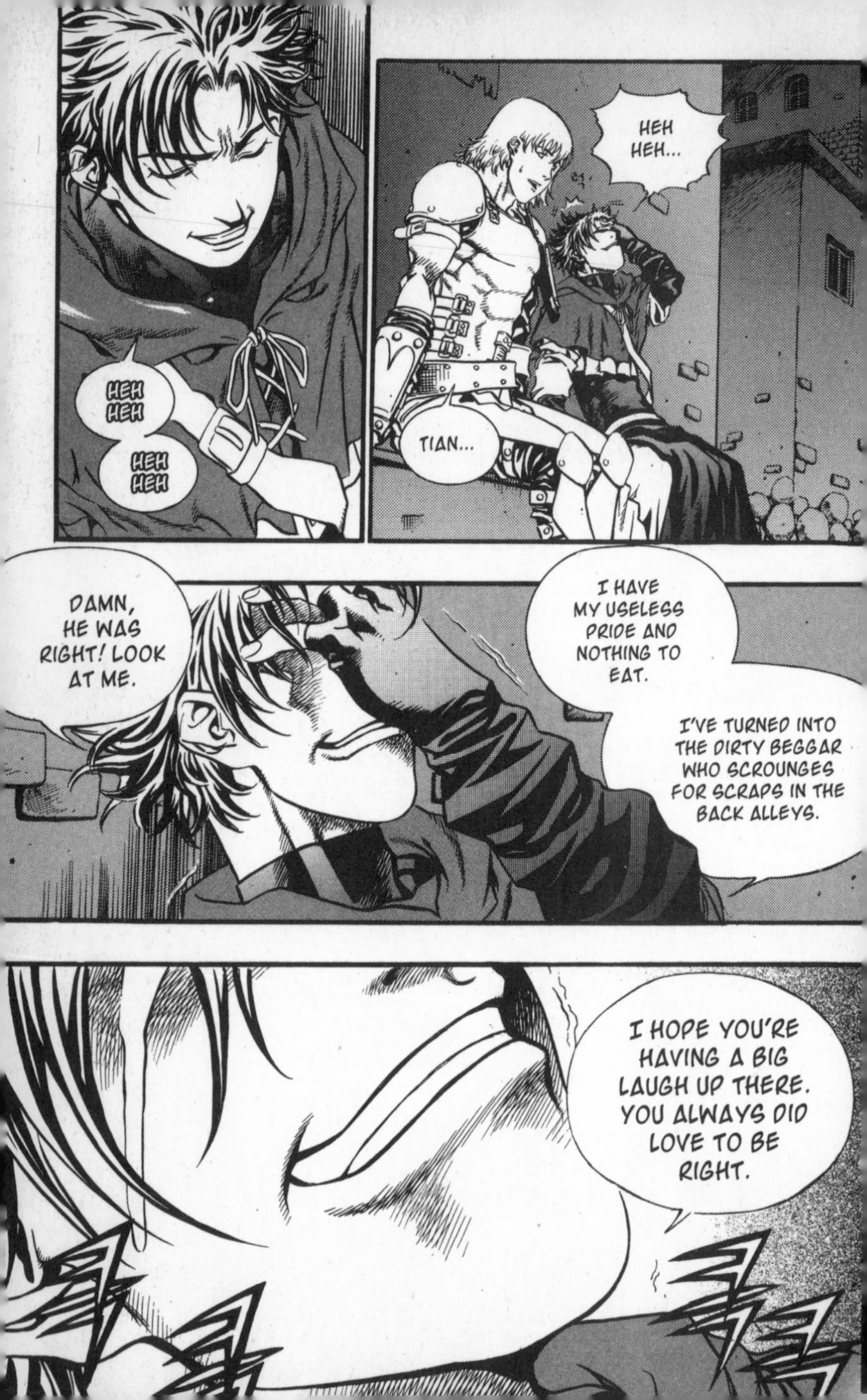
HEH HEH
HEH HEH
HEH HEH...
TIAN...
DAMN, HE WAS RIGHT! LOOK AT ME.
I HAVE MY USELESS PRIDE AND NOTHING TO EAT.
I'VE TURNED INTO THE DIRTY BEGGAR WHO SCROUNGES FOR SCRAPS IN THE BACK ALLEYS.
I HOPE YOU'RE HAVING A BIG LAUGH UP THERE. YOU ALWAYS DID LOVE TO BE RIGHT.

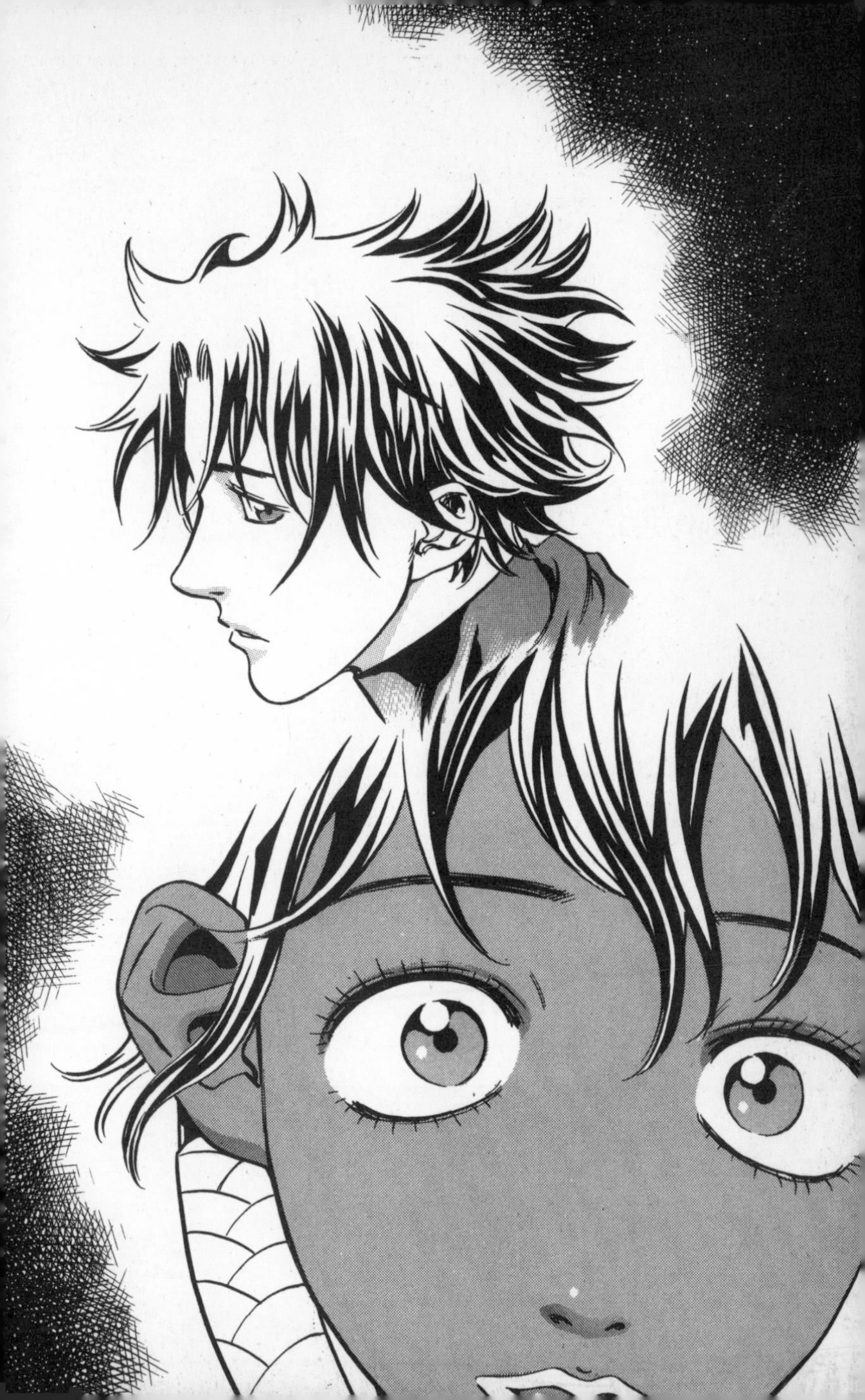

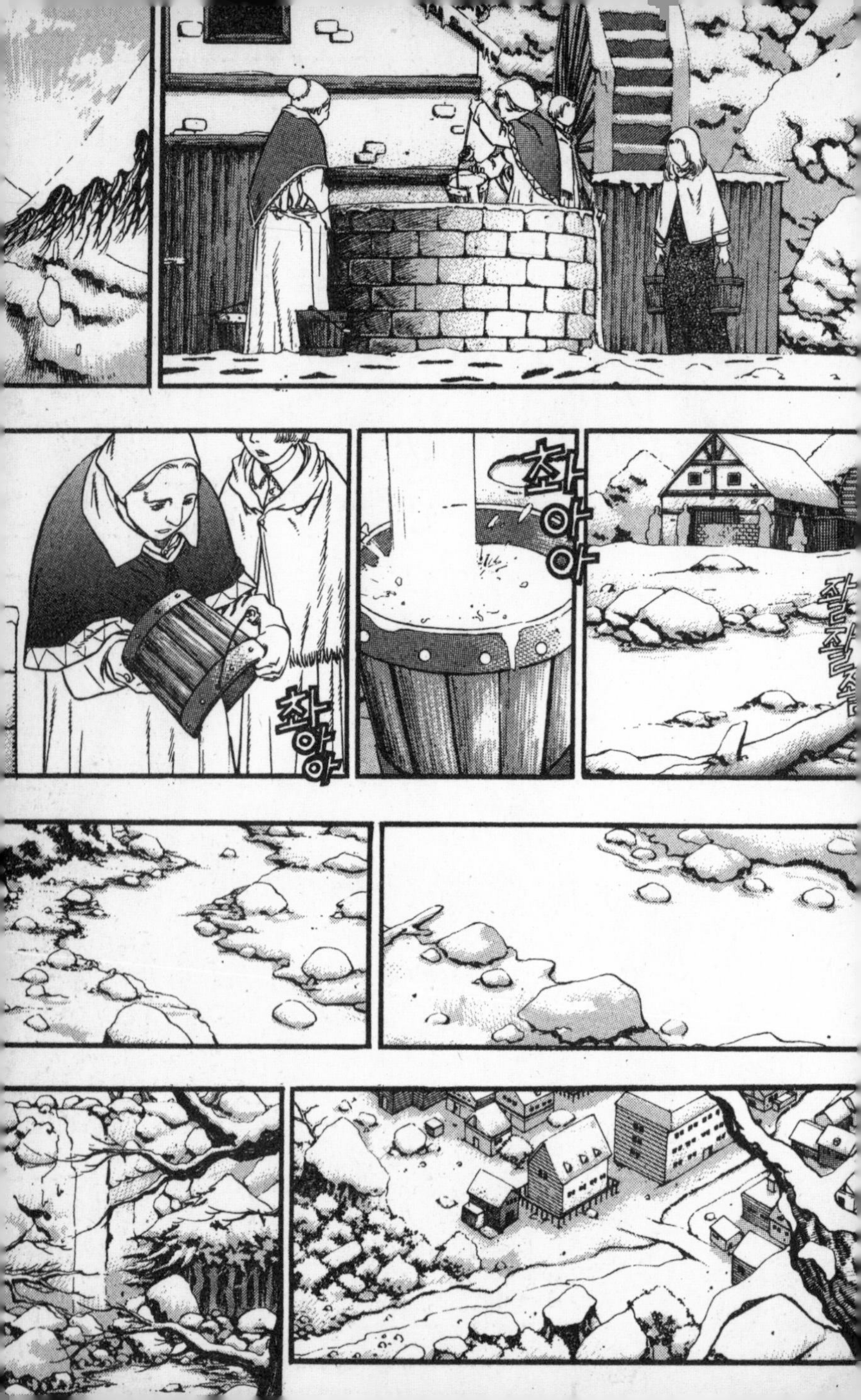
촤아아
촤아아

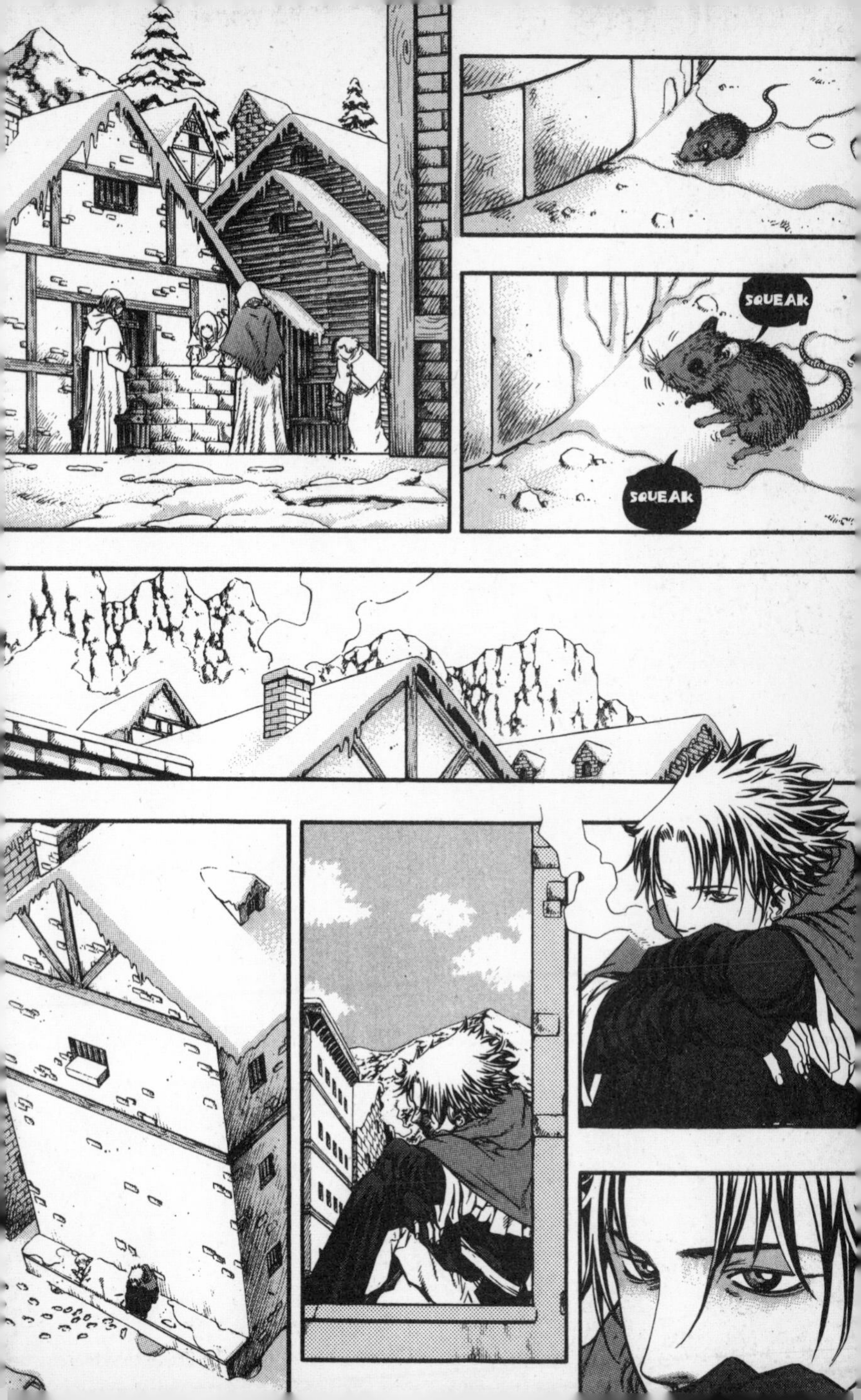
SQUEAK
SQUEAK

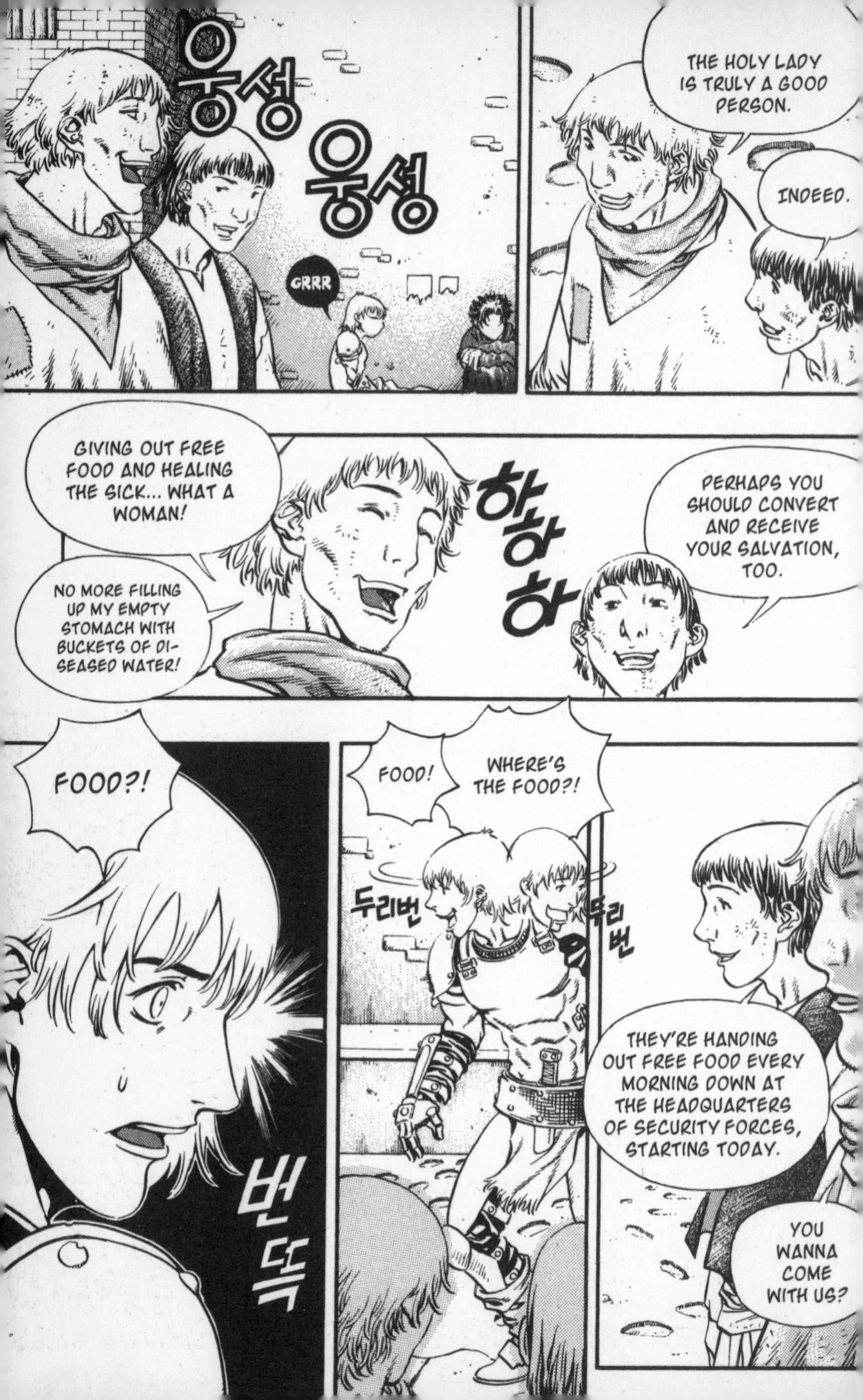

웅성 웅성
GRRR
THE HOLY LADY IS TRULY A GOOD PERSON.
INDEED.
GIVING OUT FREE FOOD AND HEALING THE SICK... WHAT A WOMAN!
NO MORE FILLING UP MY EMPTY STOMACH WITH BUCKETS OF DI-SEASED WATER!
하하하
PERHAPS YOU SHOULD CONVERT AND RECEIVE YOUR SALVATION, TOO.
FOOD?!
번뜩
FOOD!
WHERE'S THE FOOD?!
두리번
두리번
THEY'RE HANDING OUT FREE FOOD EVERY MORNING DOWN AT THE HEADQUARTERS OF SECURITY FORCES, STARTING TODAY.
YOU WANNA COME WITH US?

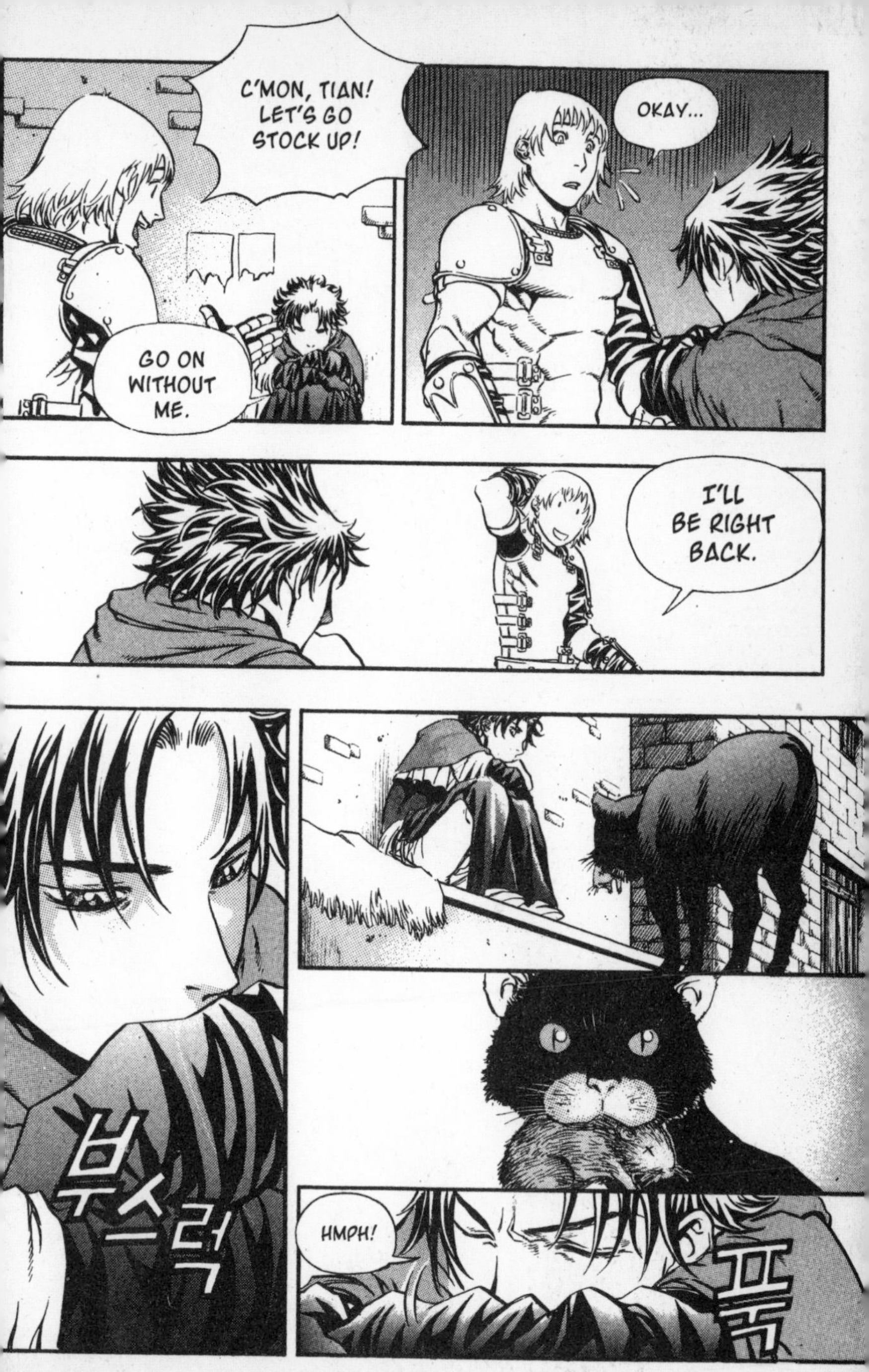
C'MON, TIAN! LET'S GO STOCK UP!
GO ON WITHOUT ME.
OKAY...
I'LL BE RIGHT BACK.
부스럭
HMPH!
프쿡

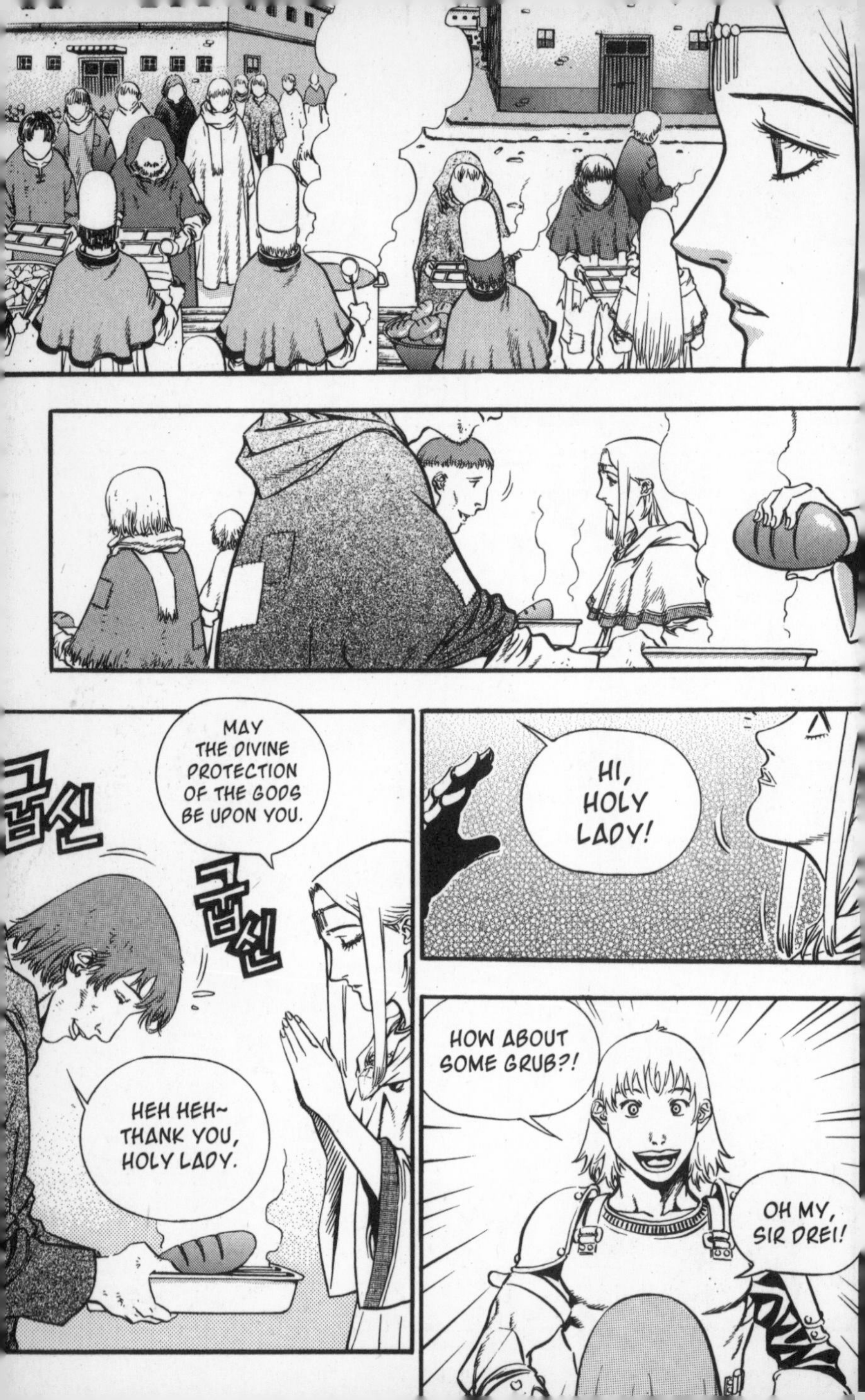
MAY THE DIVINE PROTECTION OF THE GODS BE UPON YOU.
굽신
굽신
HEH HEH~ THANK YOU, HOLY LADY.
HI, HOLY LADY!
HOW ABOUT SOME GRUB?!
OH MY, SIR DREI!

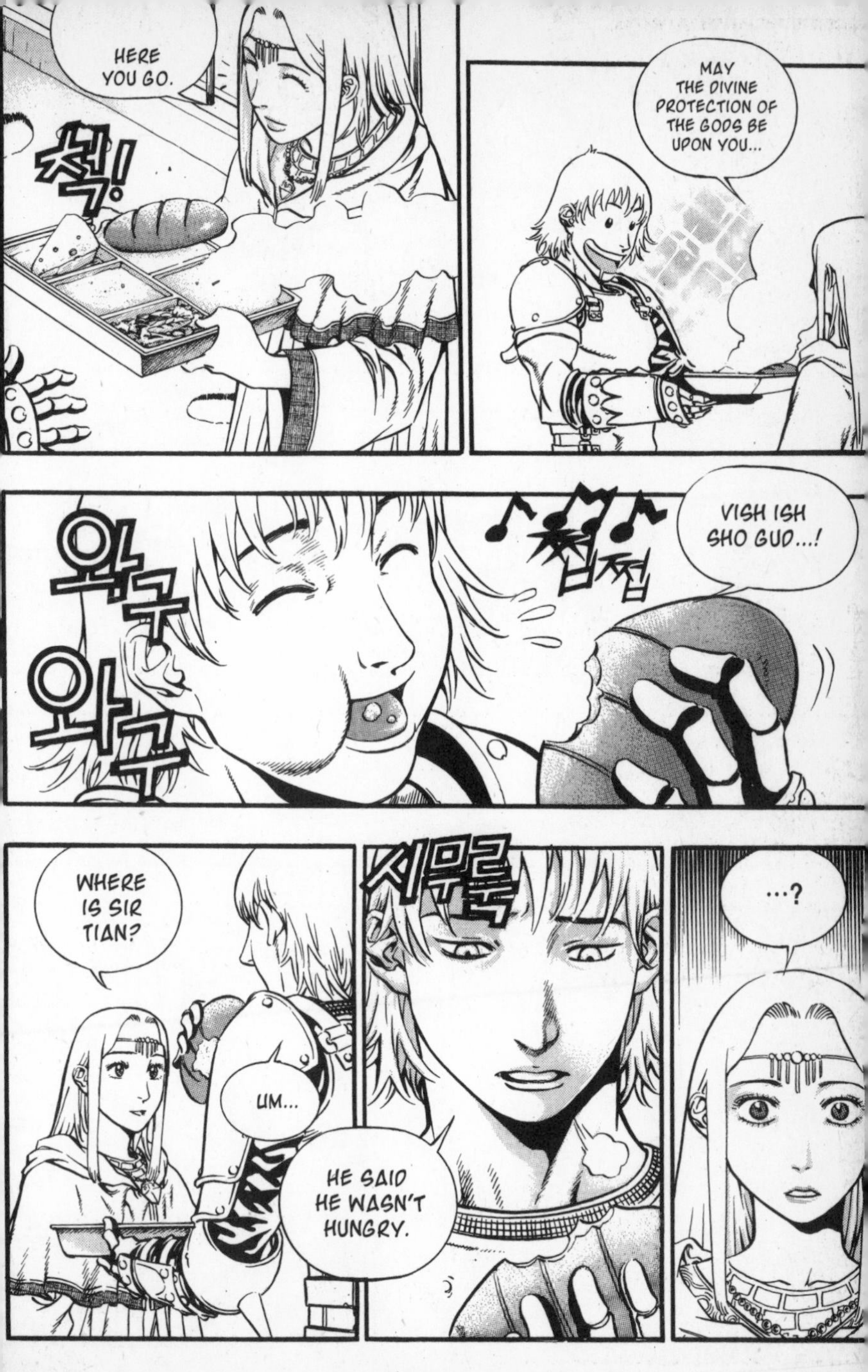
HERE YOU GO.
척!
MAY THE DIVINE PROTECTION OF THE GODS BE UPON YOU...
와구 와구
VISH ISH SHO GUD...!
WHERE IS SIR TIAN?
UM...
HE SAID HE WASN'T HUNGRY.
시무룩
...?

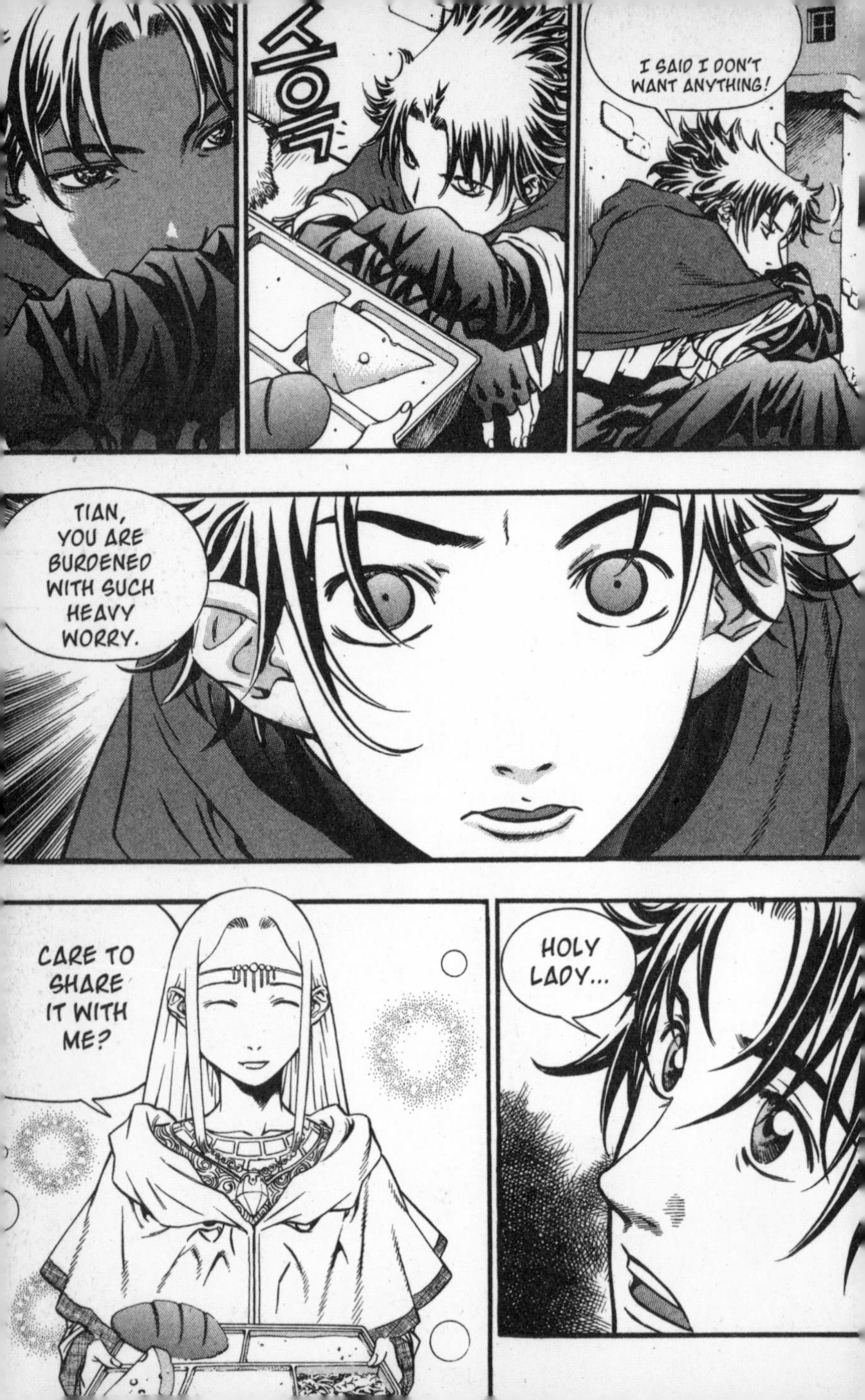

I SAID I DON'T WANT ANYTHING!
TIAN, YOU ARE BURDENED WITH SUCH HEAVY WORRY.
CARE TO SHARE IT WITH ME?
HOLY LADY...

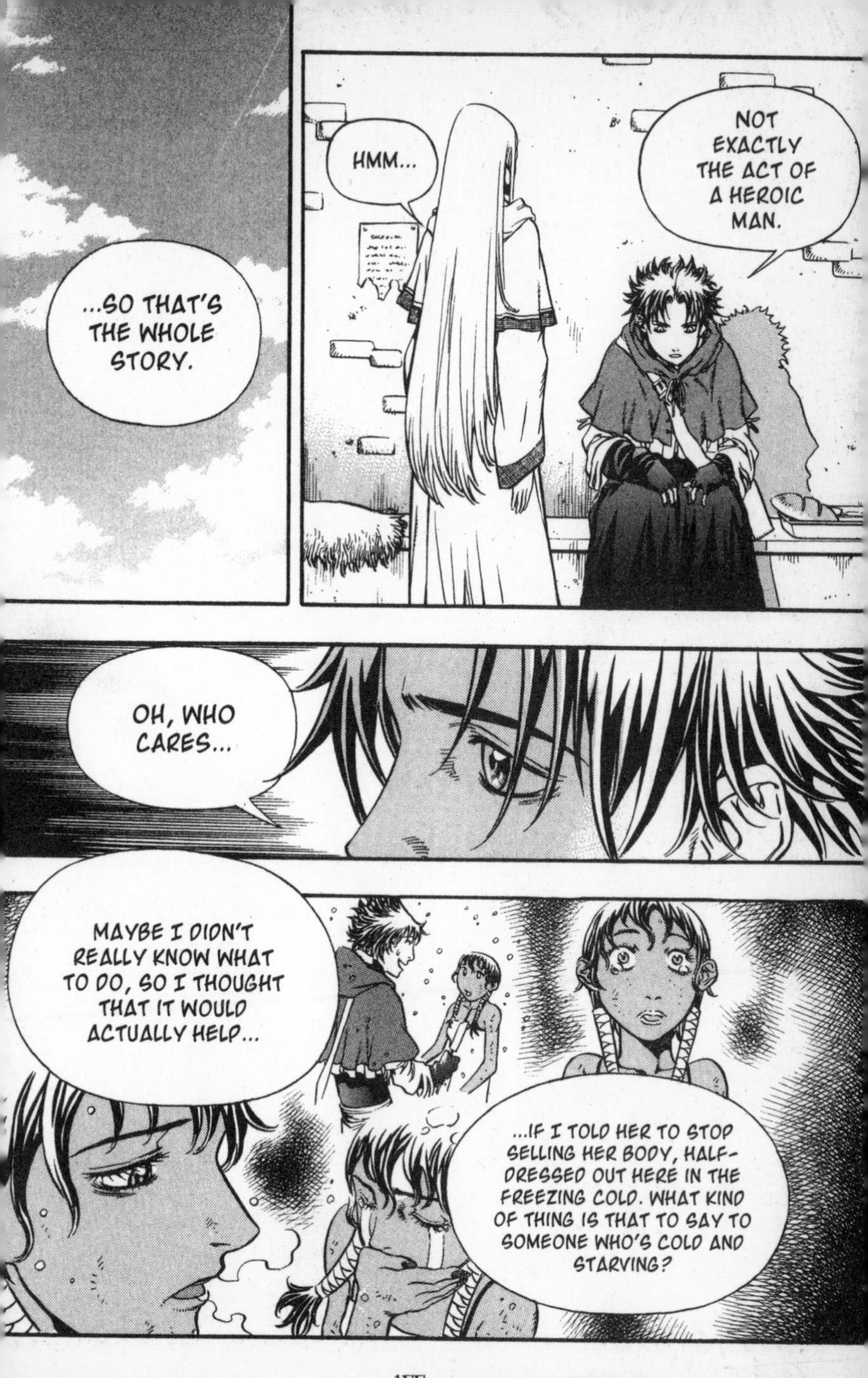
NOT EXACTLY THE ACT OF A HEROIC MAN.
HMM...
...SO THAT'S THE WHOLE STORY.
OH, WHO CARES...
MAYBE I DIDN'T REALLY KNOW WHAT TO DO, SO I THOUGHT THAT IT WOULD ACTUALLY HELP...
...IF I TOLD HER TO STOP SELLING HER BODY, HALF-DRESSED OUT HERE IN THE FREEZING COLD. WHAT KIND OF THING IS THAT TO SAY TO SOMEONE WHO'S COLD AND STARVING?

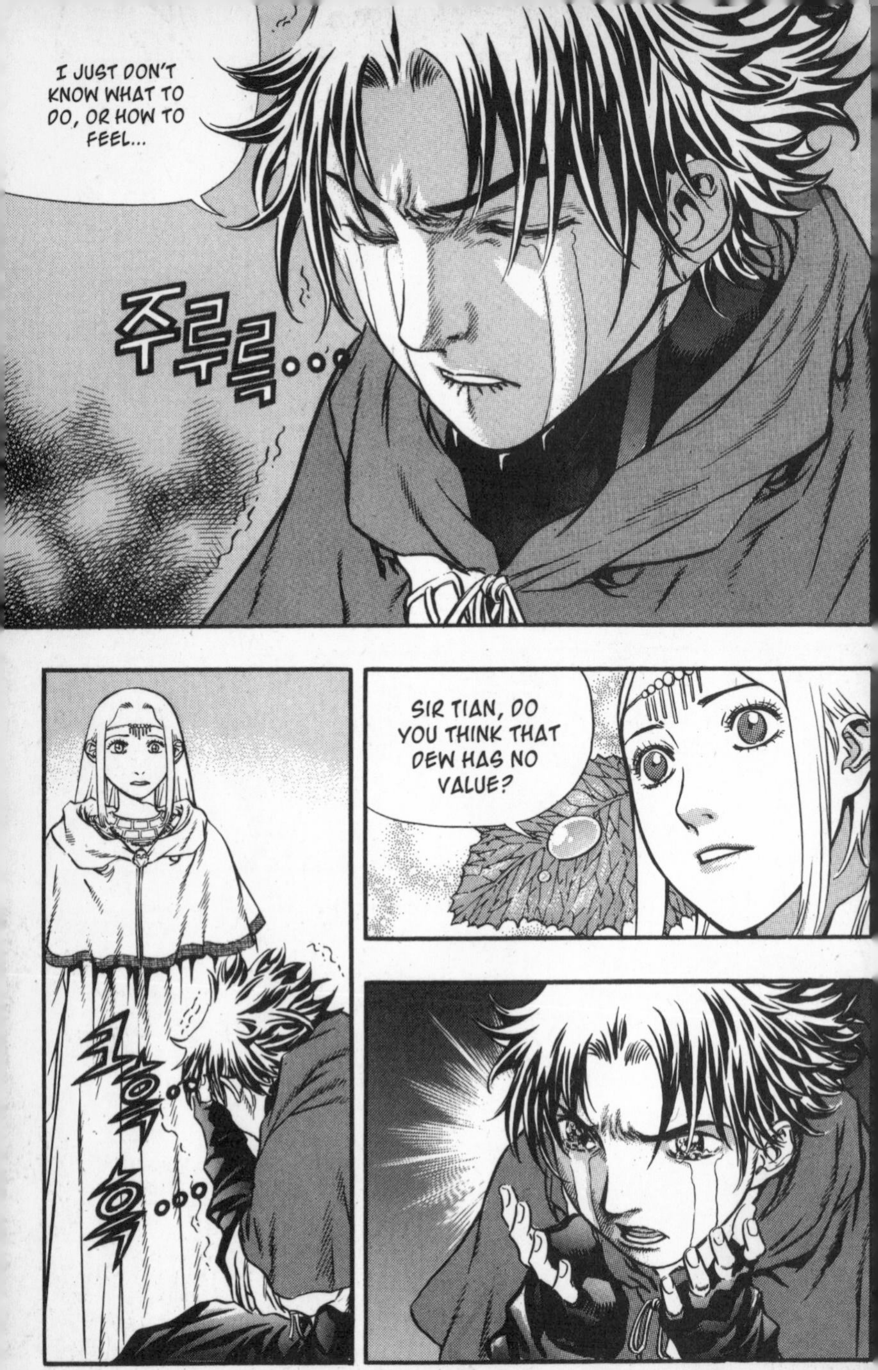
I JUST DON'T KNOW WHAT TO DO, OR HOW TO FEEL...
주루륵...
SIR TIAN, DO YOU THINK THAT DEW HAS NO VALUE?
크흑...
흑...

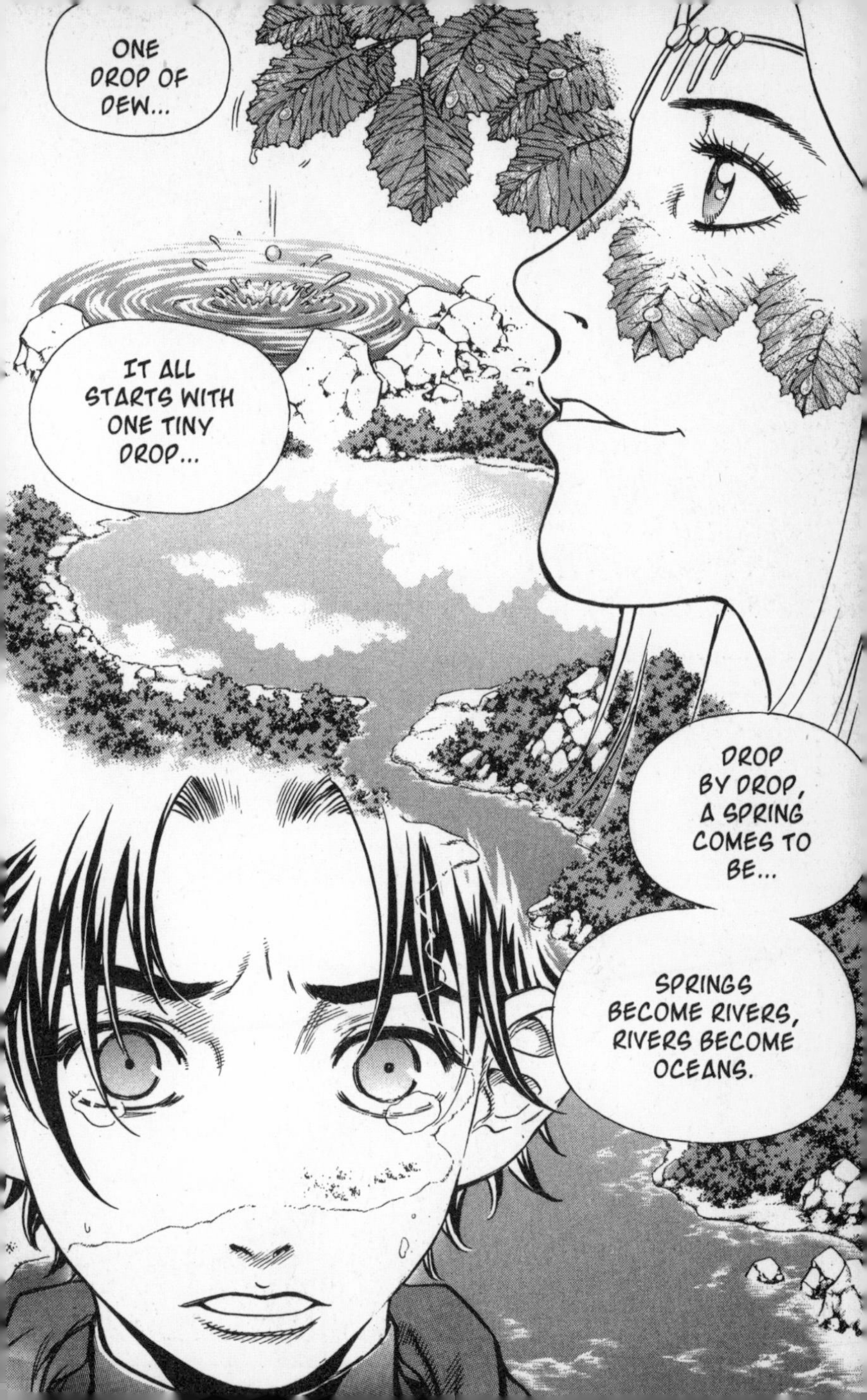
ONE DROP OF DEW...
IT ALL STARTS WITH ONE TINY DROP...
DROP BY DROP, A SPRING COMES TO BE...
SPRINGS BECOME RIVERS, RIVERS BECOME OCEANS.

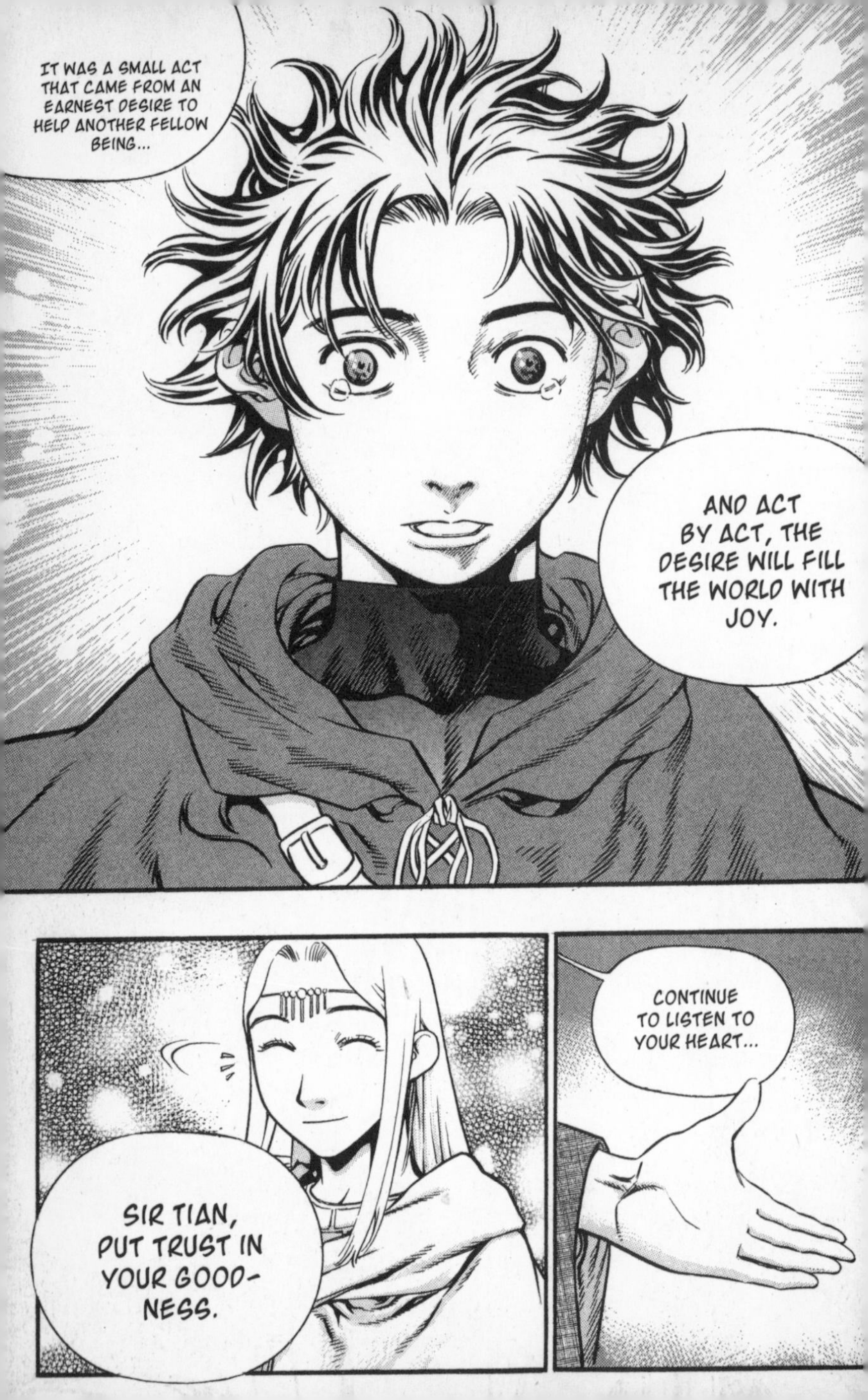
IT WAS A SMALL ACT THAT CAME FROM AN EARNEST DESIRE TO HELP ANOTHER FELLOW BEING...
AND ACT BY ACT, THE DESIRE WILL FILL THE WORLD WITH JOY.
CONTINUE TO LISTEN TO YOUR HEART...
SIR TIAN, PUT TRUST IN YOUR GOOD-NESS.

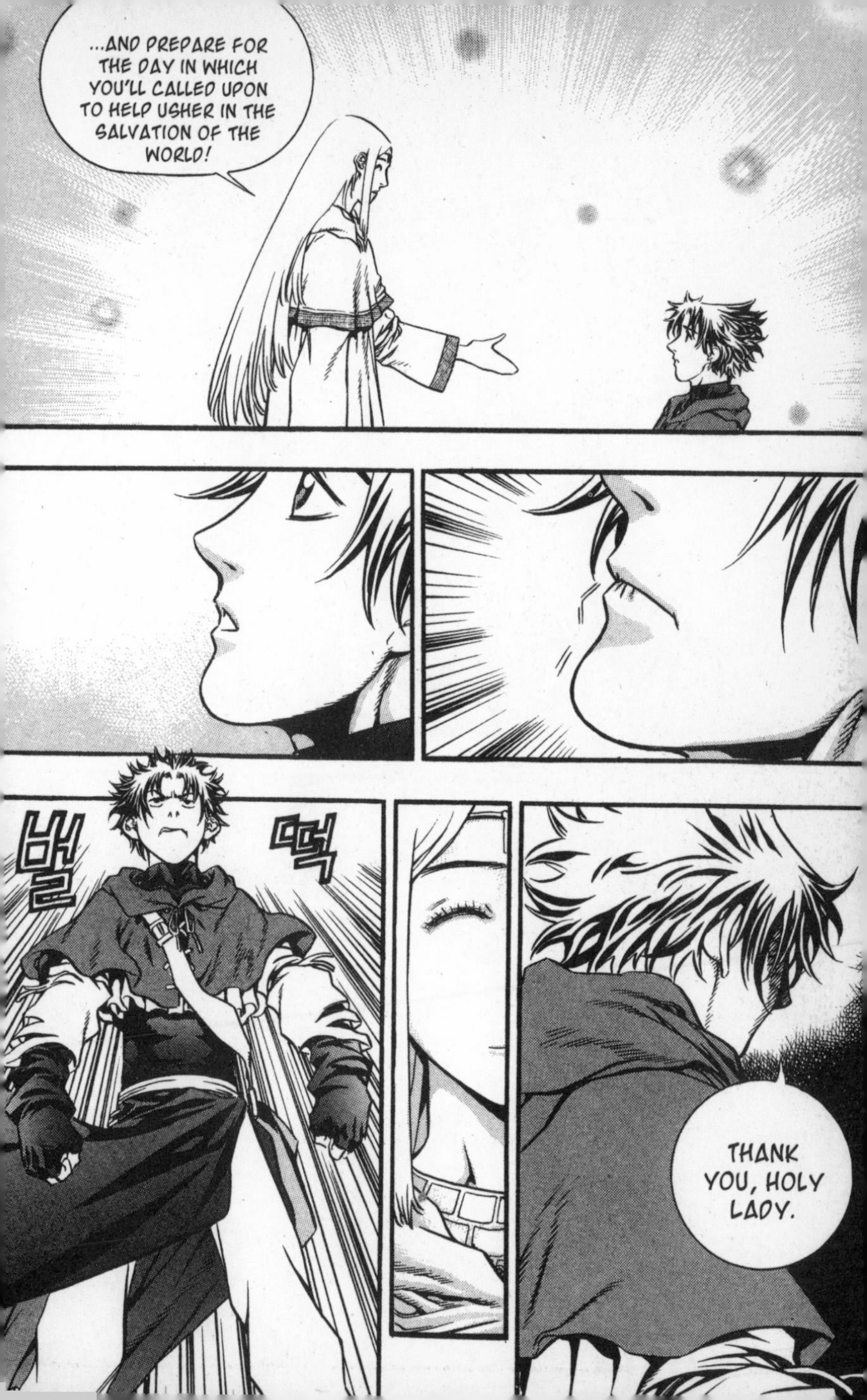
...AND PREPARE FOR THE DAY IN WHICH YOU'LL CALLED UPON TO HELP USHER IN THE SALVATION OF THE WORLD!
THANK YOU, HOLY LADY.

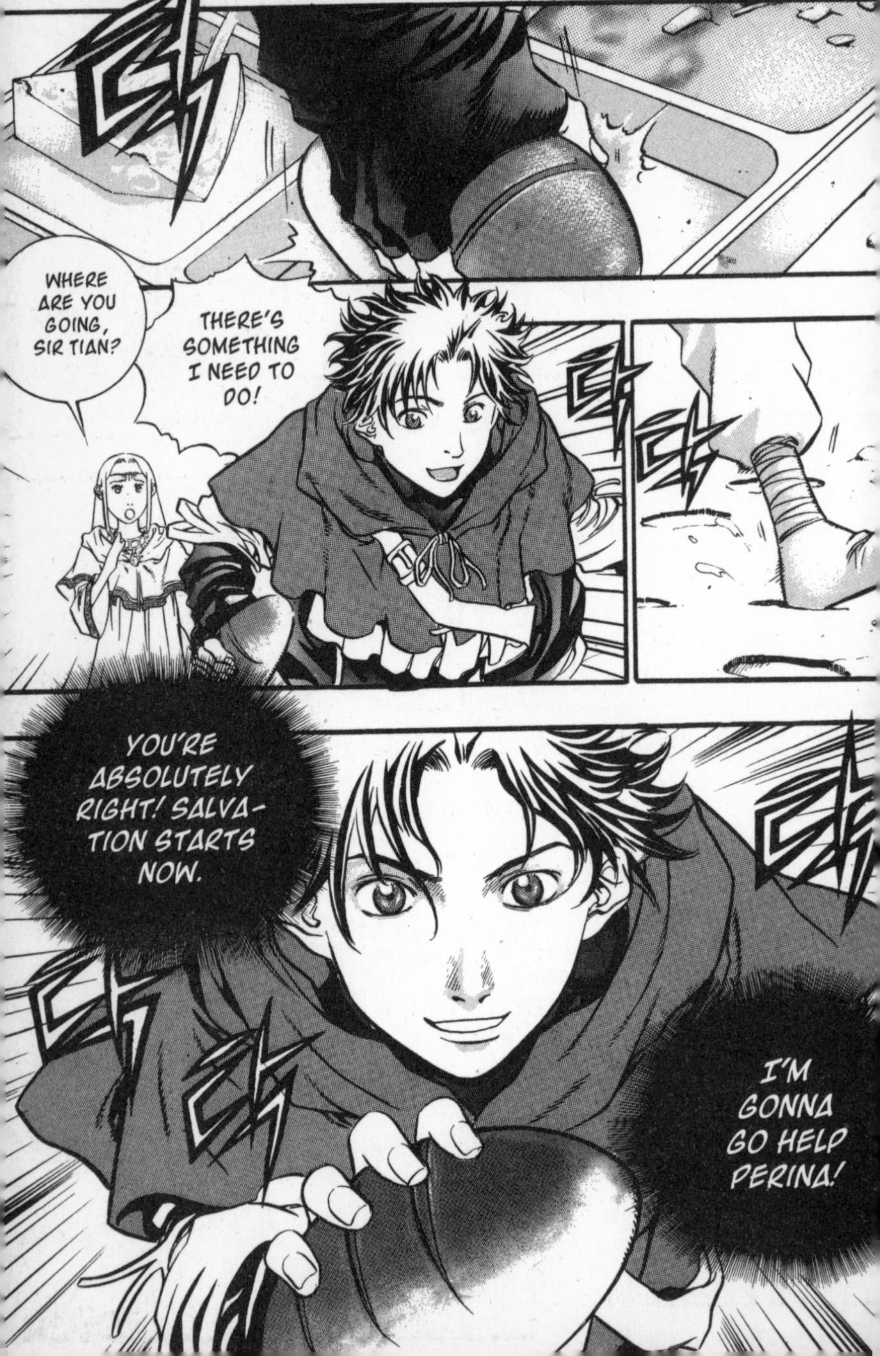
THERE'S SOMETHING I NEED TO DO!
WHERE ARE YOU GOING, SIR TIAN?
YOU'RE ABSOLUTELY RIGHT! SALVATION STARTS NOW.
I'M GONNA GO HELP PERINA!

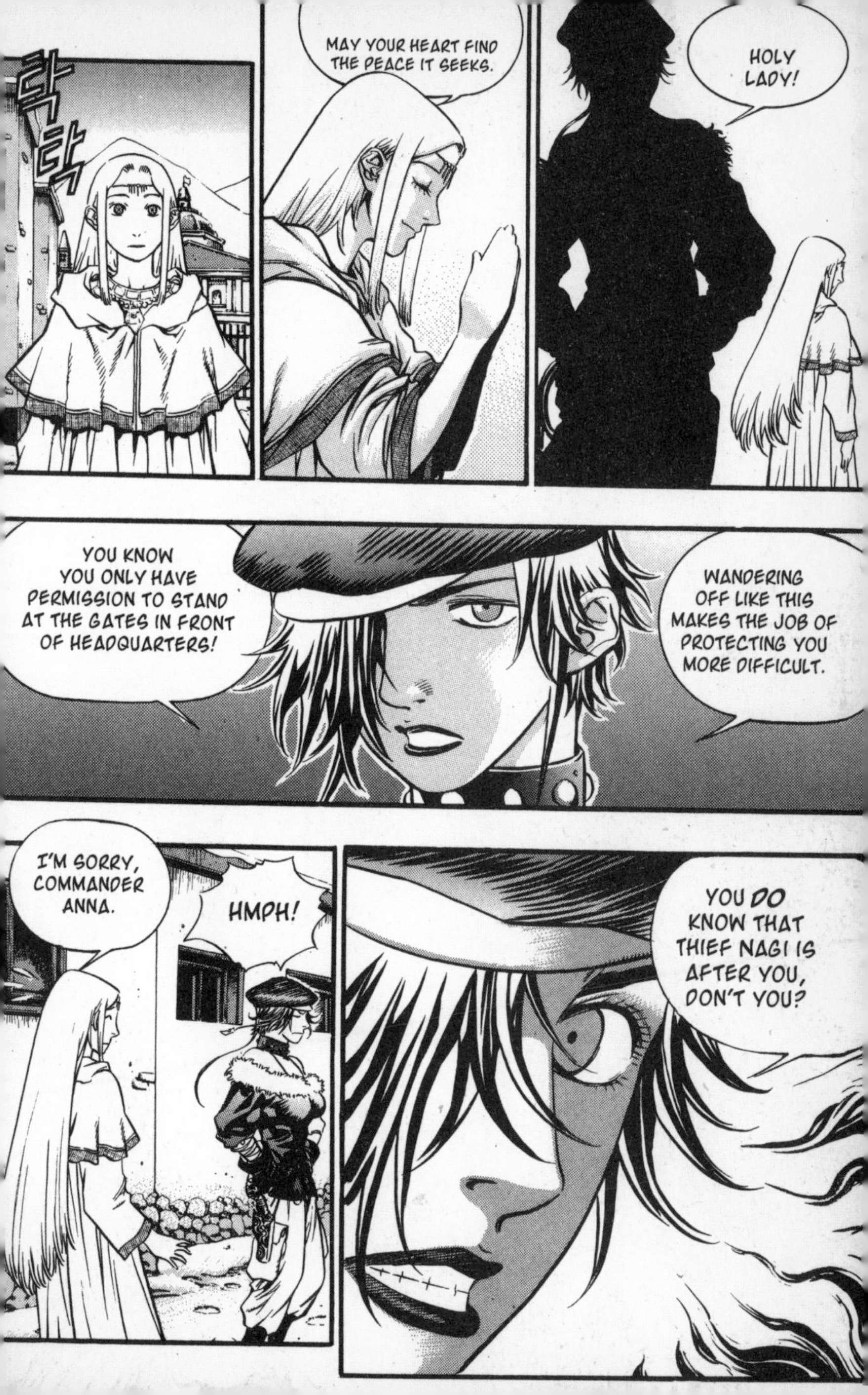
MAY YOUR HEART FIND THE PEACE IT SEEKS.
HOLY LADY!
YOU KNOW YOU ONLY HAVE PERMISSION TO STAND AT THE GATES IN FRONT OF HEADQUARTERS!
WANDERING OFF LIKE THIS MAKES THE JOB OF PROTECTING YOU MORE DIFFICULT.
I'M SORRY, COMMANDER ANNA.
HMPH!
YOU *DO* KNOW THAT THIEF NAGI IS AFTER YOU, DON'T YOU?

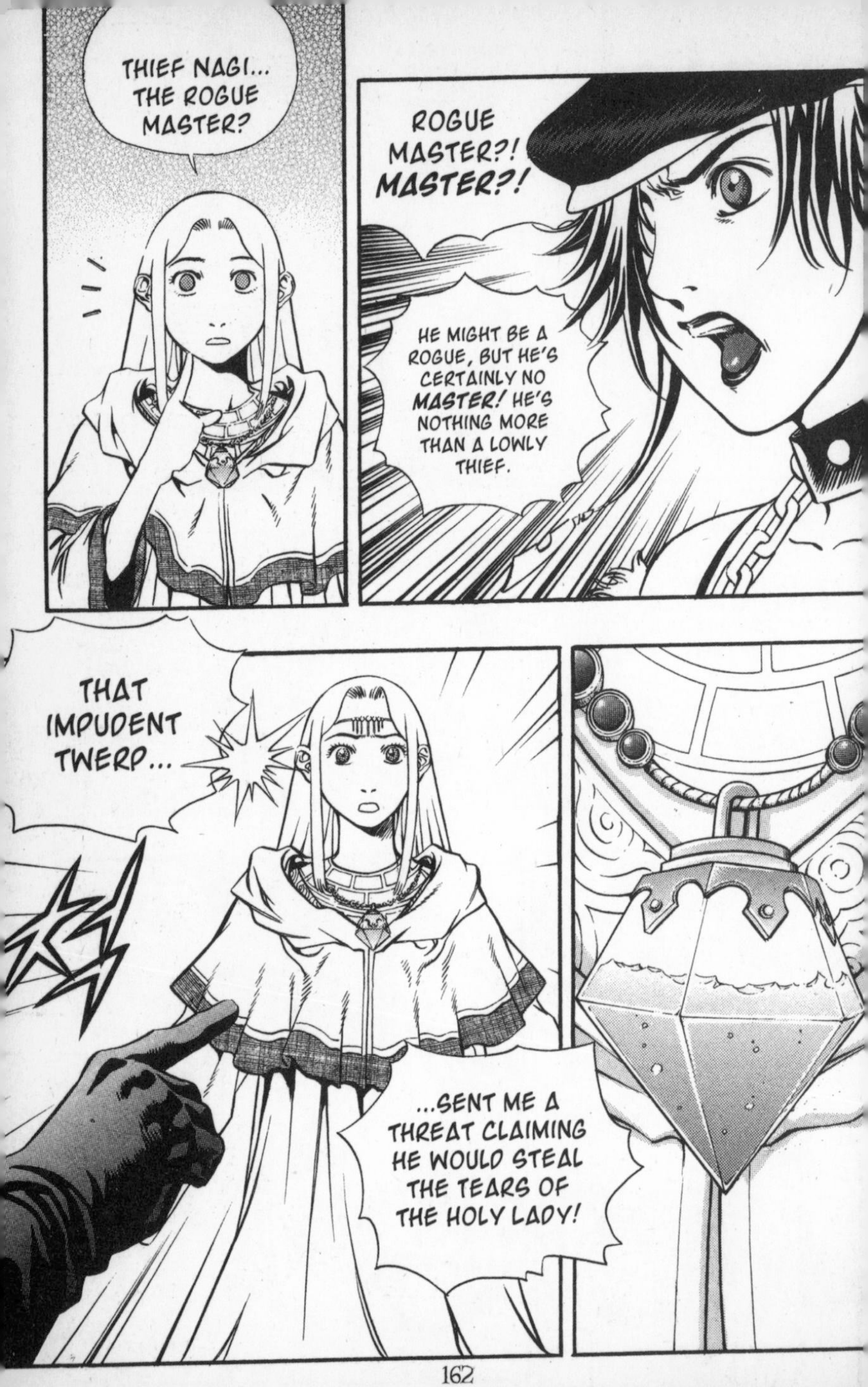
THIEF NAGI... THE ROGUE MASTER?
ROGUE MASTER?! MASTER?!
HE MIGHT BE A ROGUE, BUT HE'S CERTAINLY NO MASTER! HE'S NOTHING MORE THAN A LOWLY THIEF.
THAT IMPUDENT TWERP...
...SENT ME A THREAT CLAIMING HE WOULD STEAL THE TEARS OF THE HOLY LADY!

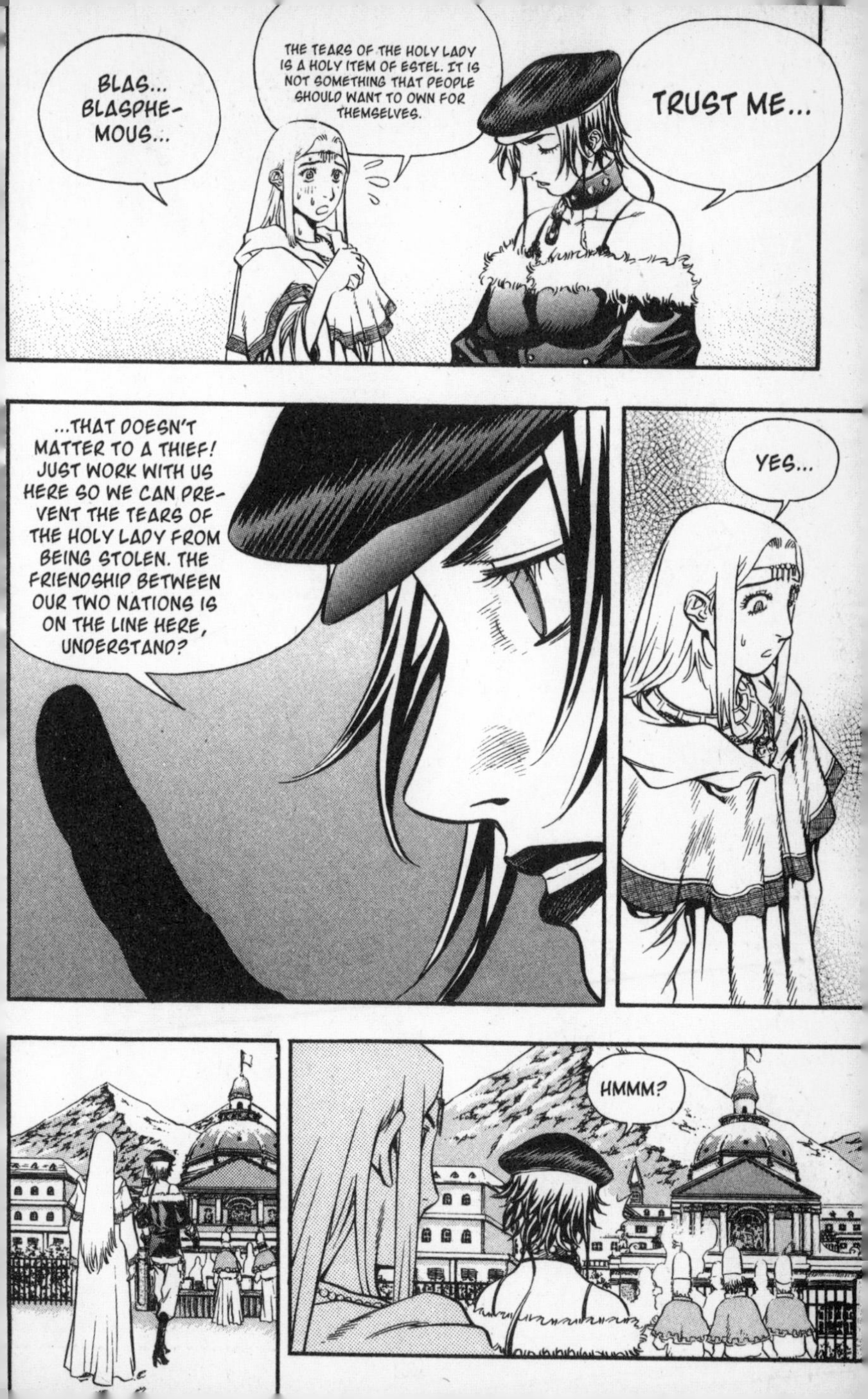

BLAS... BLASPHEMOUS...
THE TEARS OF THE HOLY LADY IS A HOLY ITEM OF ESTEL. IT IS NOT SOMETHING THAT PEOPLE SHOULD WANT TO OWN FOR THEMSELVES.
TRUST ME...
...THAT DOESN'T MATTER TO A THIEF! JUST WORK WITH US HERE SO WE CAN PREVENT THE TEARS OF THE HOLY LADY FROM BEING STOLEN. THE FRIENDSHIP BETWEEN OUR TWO NATIONS IS ON THE LINE HERE, UNDERSTAND?
YES...
HMMM?

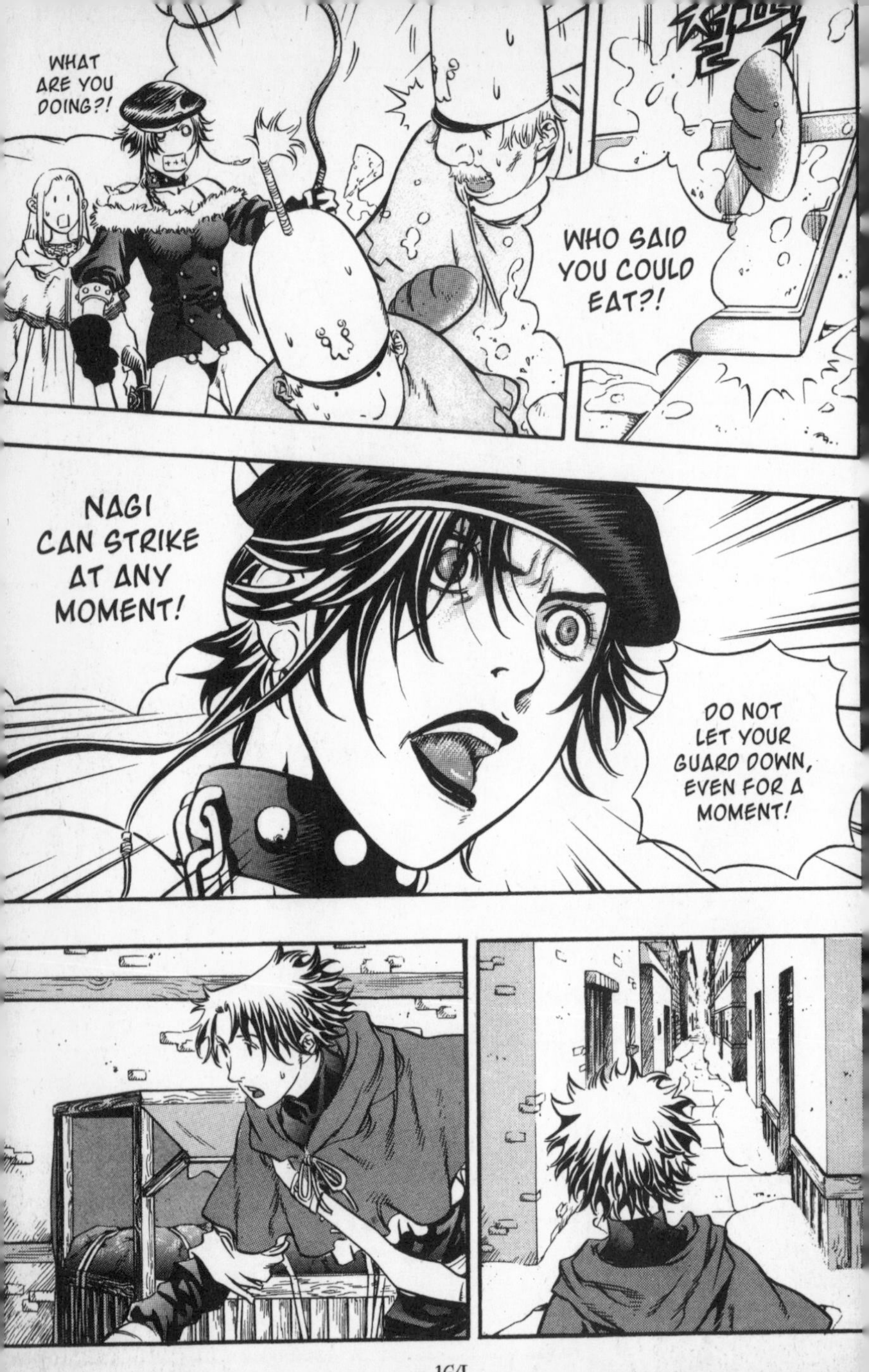
WHO SAID YOU COULD EAT?!
WHAT ARE YOU DOING?!
DO NOT LET YOUR GUARD DOWN, EVEN FOR A MOMENT!
NAGI CAN STRIKE AT ANY MOMENT!

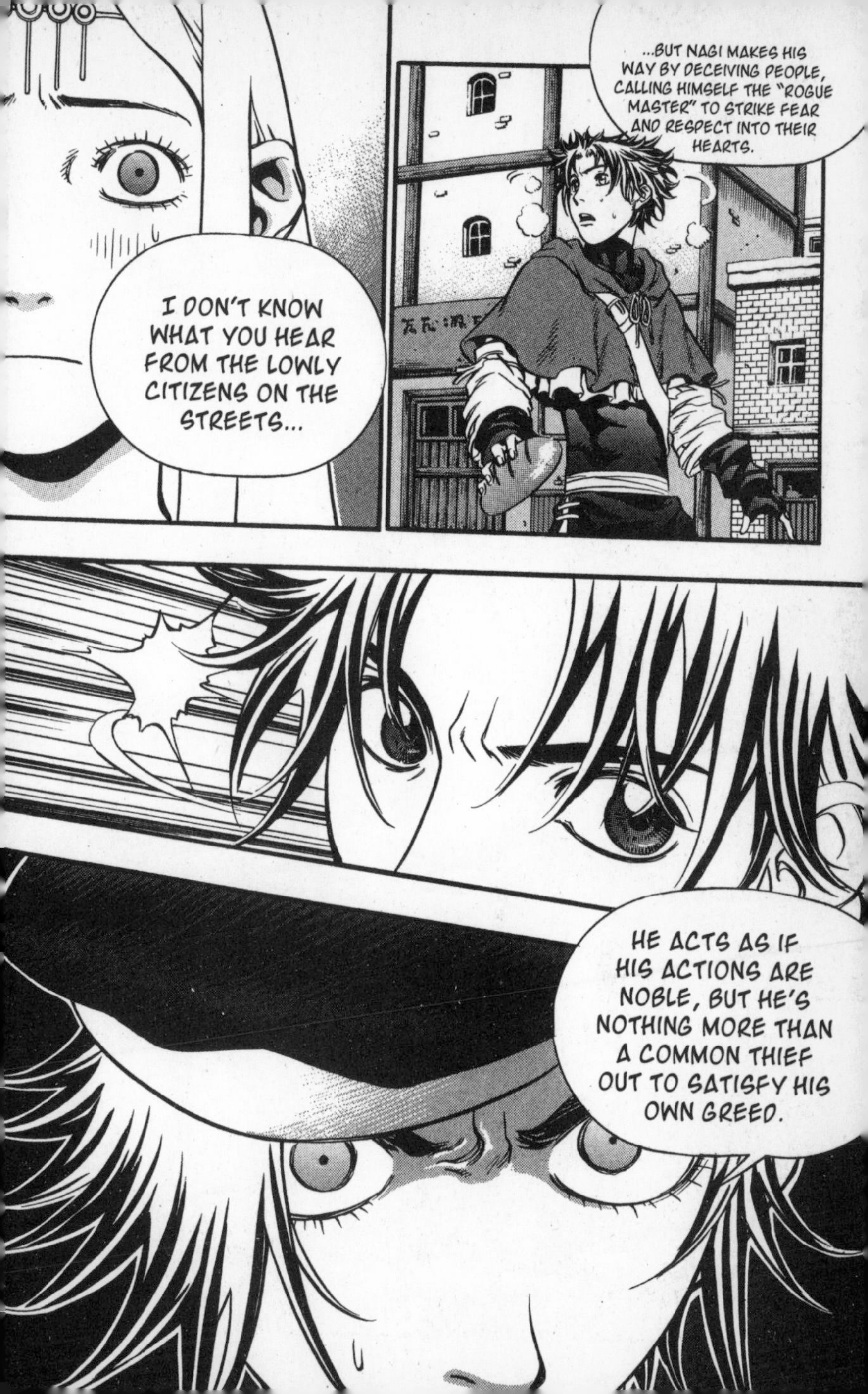

...BUT NAGI MAKES HIS WAY BY DECEIVING PEOPLE, CALLING HIMSELF THE "ROGUE MASTER" TO STRIKE FEAR AND RESPECT INTO THEIR HEARTS.
I DON'T KNOW WHAT YOU HEAR FROM THE LOWLY CITIZENS ON THE STREETS...
HE ACTS AS IF HIS ACTIONS ARE NOBLE, BUT HE'S NOTHING MORE THAN A COMMON THIEF OUT TO SATISFY HIS OWN GREED.

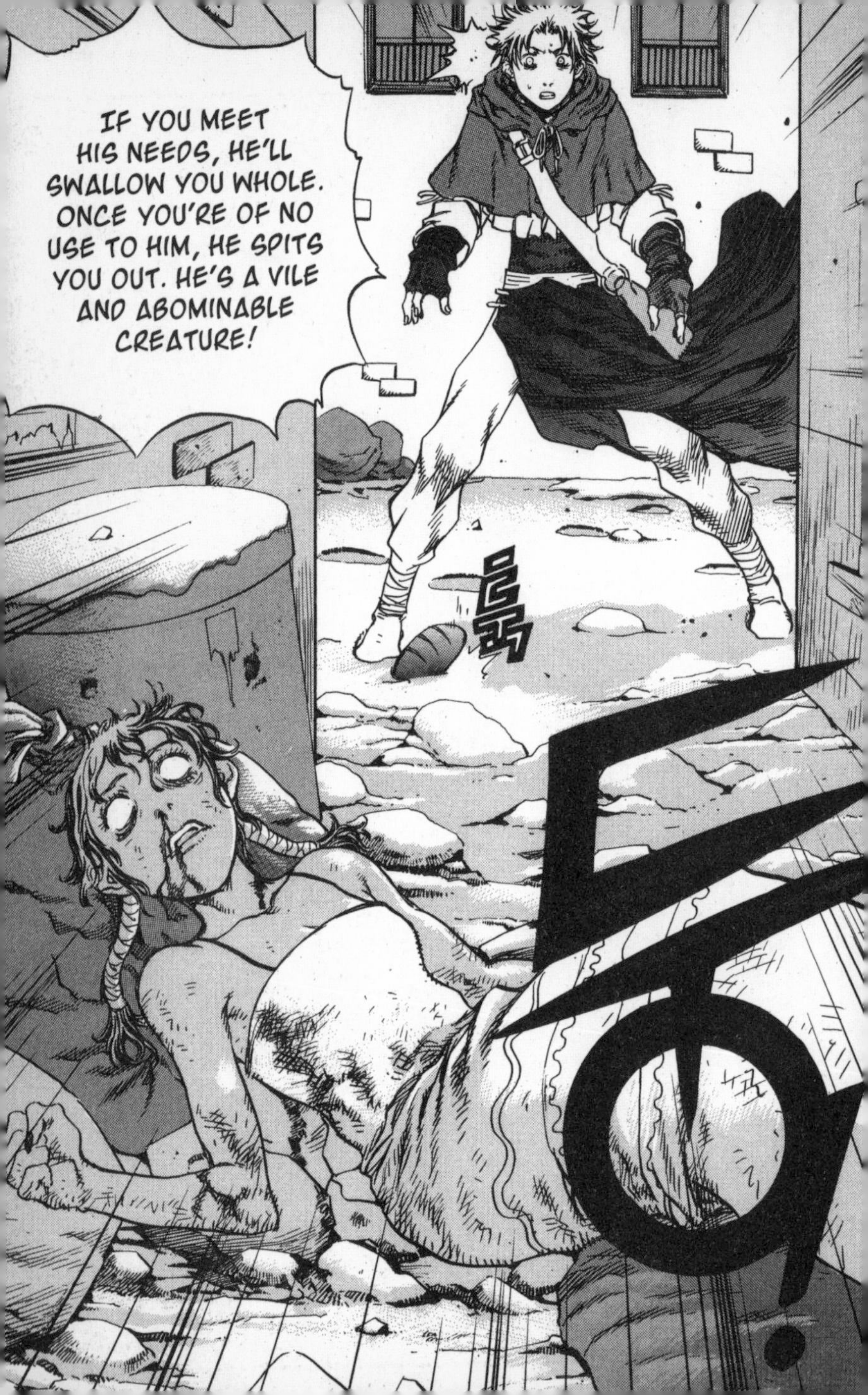
IF YOU MEET HIS NEEDS, HE'LL SWALLOW YOU WHOLE. ONCE YOU'RE OF NO USE TO HIM, HE SPITS YOU OUT. HE'S A VILE AND ABOMINABLE CREATURE!

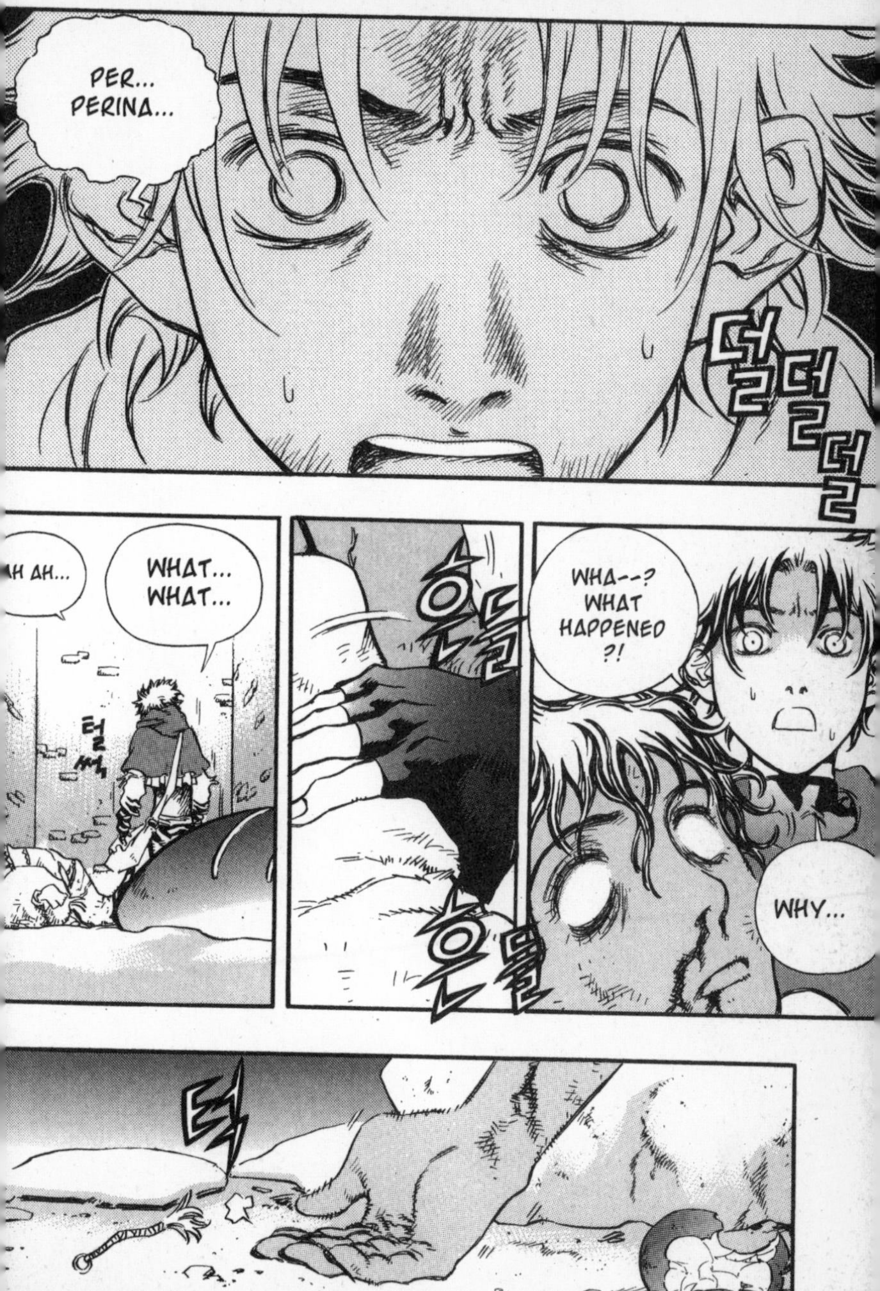
PER...
PERINA...
덜덜덜덜
AH AH...
WHAT...
WHAT...
털썩
WHA--?
WHAT
HAPPENED
?!
WHY...

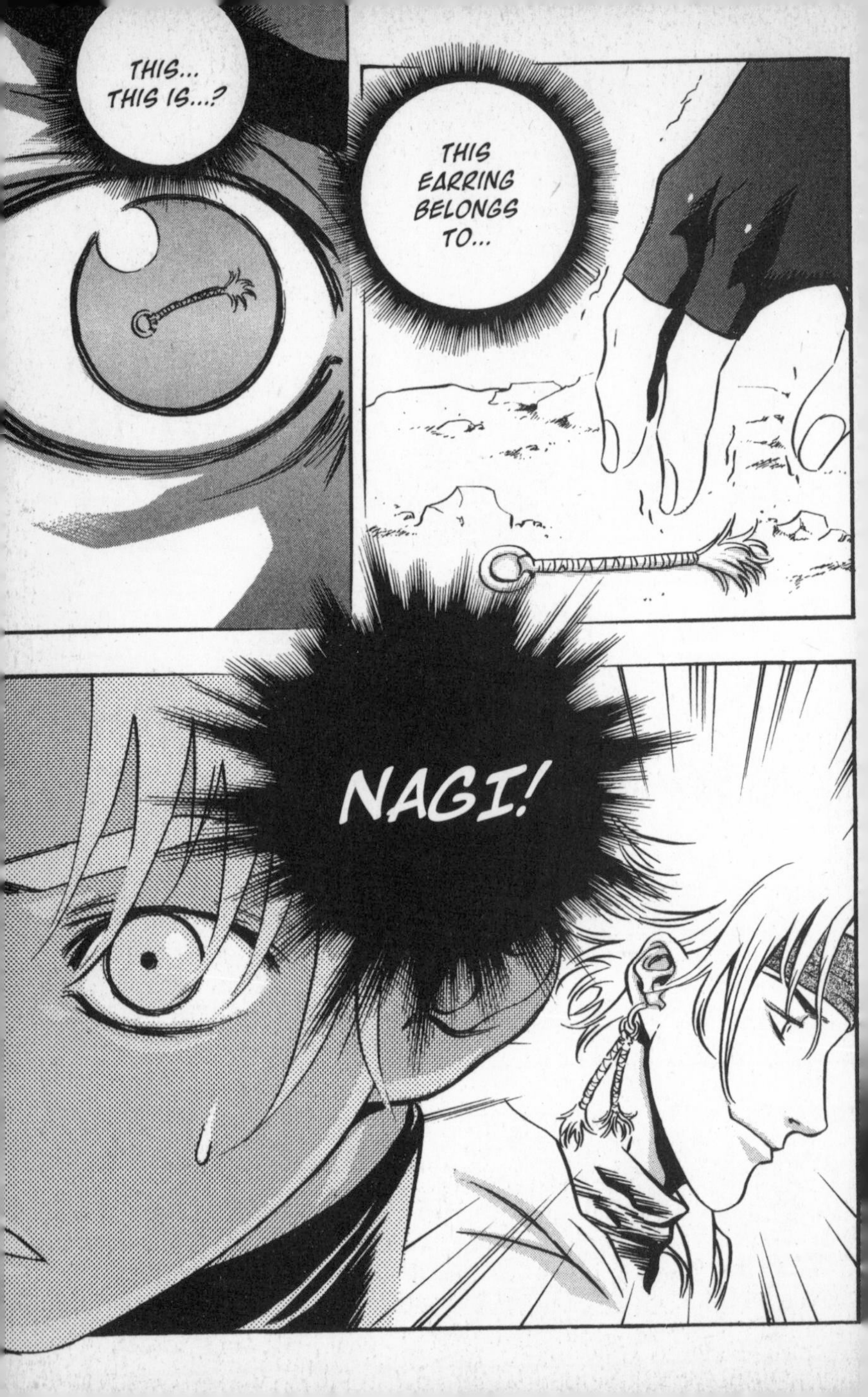
THIS EARRING BELONGS TO...
THIS... THIS IS...?
NAGI!

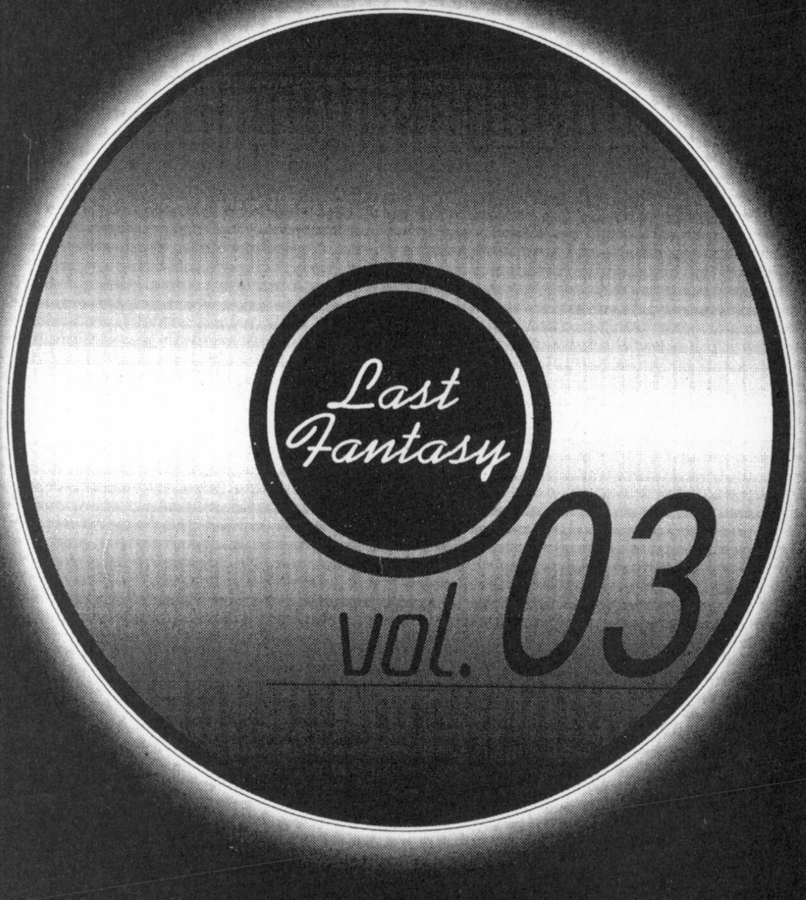
Last Fantasy
vol. 03

BONUS TRACK

What Though Life Conspire To Cheat You
삶이 그대를 속일지라도

- Aleksandr Sergeyerich Pushkin -
푸슈킨

What though life conspire to cheat you,
삶이 그대를 속일지라도,

Do not sorrow or complain.
슬퍼하거나 노여워말라.

Lie still on the day of pain,
슬픈 날엔 참고 견뎌라,

And the day of joy will greet you.
이제 곧 기쁨의 나날이 오리니.

Hearts live in the coming day.
마음은 미래에 사는 것.

There's an end to passing sorrow.
현재는 한없이 우울한 것.

Suddenly all flies away,
모든 것이 하염없이 날아가버려도,

And delight returns tomorrow.
내일은 기쁨으로 돌아오리라.

JUST LIKE THE WORLD IN WHICH WE ARE LIVING, LIFE ITSELF CAN BE A BIT MUCH TO HANDLE IN THE FANTASY WORLD OF TIAN AND DREI. ONE NEEDS THE INNOCENT DREAMS AND YOUTHFUL VIGOR TO GET THROUGH THE CHALLENGES OF EVERYDAY LIFE. TIAN AND DREI ARE A DEPICTION OF OUR OWN SELVES. ALTHOUGH THEY WORK HARD AND DILIGENTLY, THEIR INTRICATELY-LAID PLANS ARE SABOTAGED BY MISTAKE AFTER MISTAKE. SOMETIMES, WE FALL INTO A DESPAIR BECAUSE WE'RE OVERWEIGHED WITH LIFE'S BURDENS. OTHER TIMES, WE FIND OURSELVES IGNORING OR RUNNING AWAY FROM OUR RESPONSIBILITIES. A TRUE WARRIOR FINDS HIMSELF DUSTING OFF, STANDING UP ONCE AGAIN WITH CLENCHED FISTS, AND RUNNING TOWARDS TOMORROW. DON'T LET THESE CHALLENGES GET YOU DOWN. THE WORLD COULD USE A FEW WARRIORS LIKE YOURSELF.

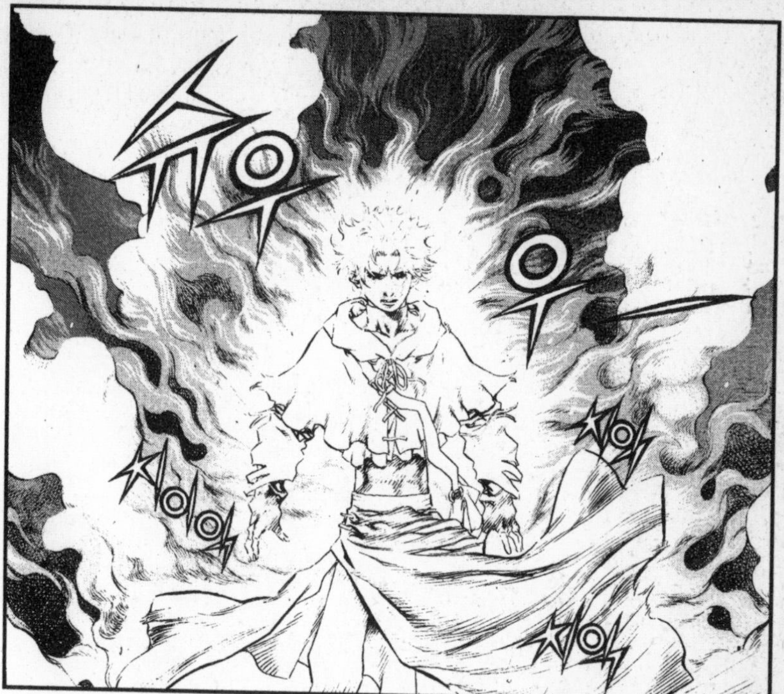

A STRANGE FURY...
THE NIGHTMARE ARRIVED, LIKE A CURSE FROM THE GODS,
WITH SCREAMS AND CRIES OF PAIN FROM THE CORPSES.

BURNING WITH VENGEANCE AT THE DEATH OF PERINA, TIAN
DECLARES THAT HE WILL SHOW NAGI THE FIRE OF HELL...

TIAN AND DREI ARE TRAPPED IN THE VILLAGE, COMPLETELY
SURROUNDED DURING A SIEGE.
WHAT DRAMATIC DECISION WILL TIAN MAKE WHEN FACED
WITH THIS AGONIZING DISASTER?

<THAT WAS THE BIRTH OF THE MESSIAH!> CONTINUED IN
VOLUME 4.
WE CALL THIS THE LAST FANTASY.

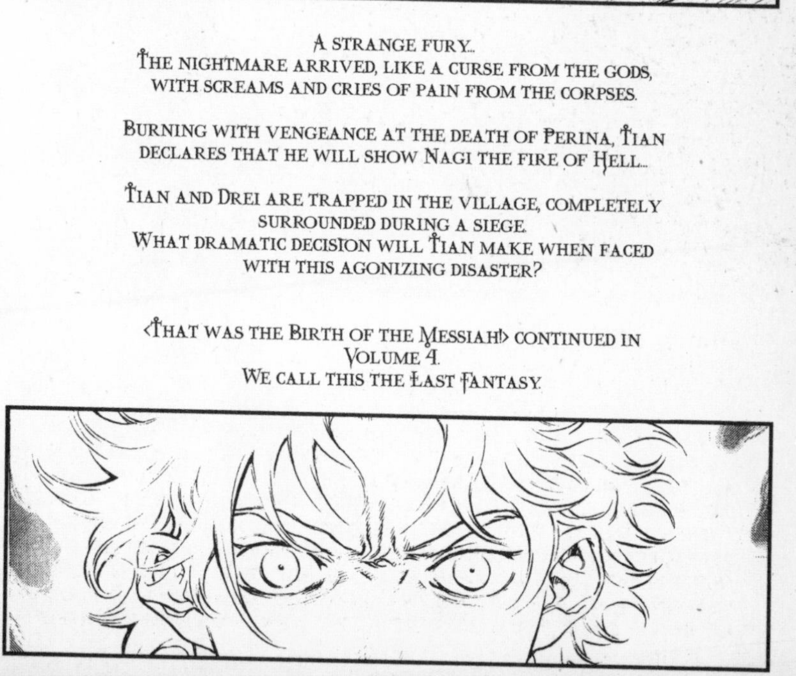

LAST FANTASY CHARACTER FILE 1

Tian

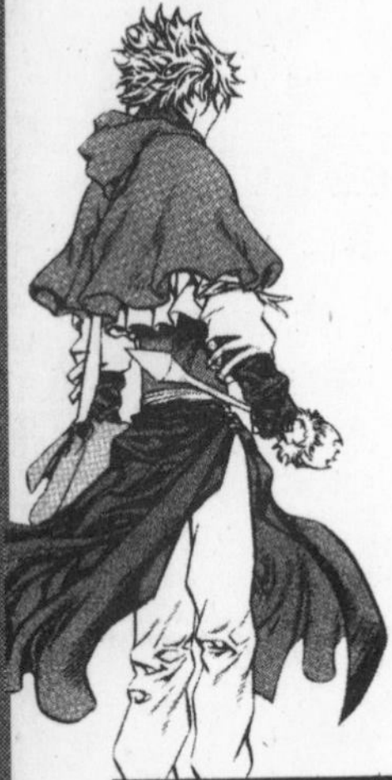

Strength 힘	120
Dexterity 민첩	110
Constiution 건강	80
Intelligence 지능	510
Wisdom 지혜	480
Charisma 매력	170

23 YEARS OLD (MALE)
CURRENTLY ENROLLED IN A WORLD-RENOWNED SCHOOL OF MAGIC AFTER TAKING SOME TIME OFF DUE TO HIS INABILITY TO PAY HIS REGISTRATION FEES. A GENIUS, CALLED BY SOME THE "DARK MAGICIAN," WITH JUST A BASIC KNOWLEDGE OF CIRCLE ONE MAGIC. WHILE HE NORMALLY TRIES TO UPHOLD JUSTICE, HIS IMPOVERISHED BACKGROUND CAUSES HIM TO BECOME POWERLESS WHEN FACED WITH MONEY.

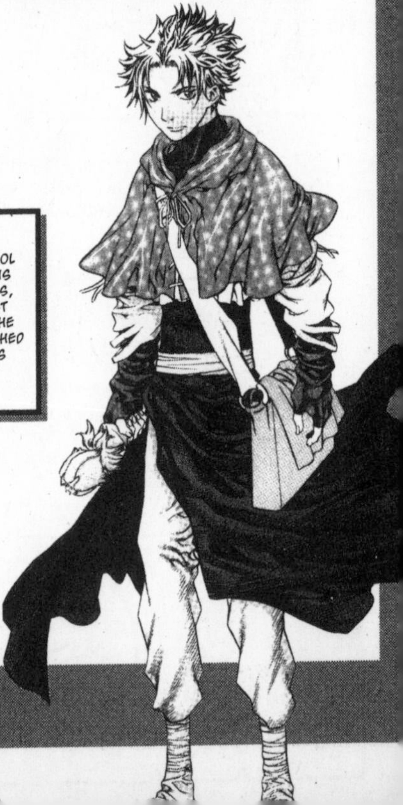

LAST FANTASY CHARACTER FILE 2

Drei

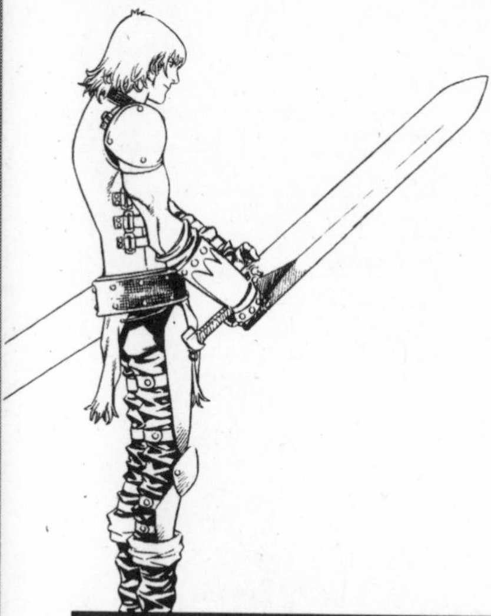

Strength 힘	530
Dexterity 민첩	310
Constiution 건강	470
Intelligence 지능	50
Wisdom 지혜	60
Charisma 매력	260

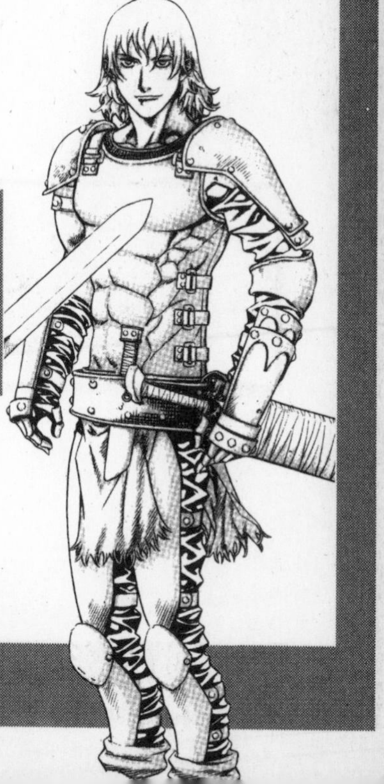

23 YEARS OLD (MALE)
ALTHOUGH HE MAY LOOK LIKE A NOBLE WARRIOR, DREI VON RICHENSTEIN (A RATHER EXTENSIVE NAME) IS A SHAMELESS, HAPPY-GO-LUCKY KNIGHT WHO BOASTS OF HIS TREMENDOUS STENGTH. BEWARE, THOUGH--HIS MENTAL I.Q. MEASURES AT AROUND 50. DREI IS A BUNDLE OF TROUBLE WHO DRIVES TIAN CRAZY WITH HIS PRECARIOUS FINANCIAL DECISIONS WHEN IT COMES TO GOLD AND USELESS ITEMS.

Kremhilt

Strength	힘	70
Dexterity	민첩	140
Constiution	건강	90
Intelligence	지능	160
Wisdom	지혜	210
Charisma	매력	650

18 YEARS OLD (FEMALE)
THE PRINCE OF THE MOST POWERFUL
NATION ON THE CONTINENT, AMERIA.
ALTHOUGH A WOMAN, SHE WAS RAISED AS A MAN
FOR POLITICAL REASONS. AT A YOUNG AGE, SHE HAS
ALREADY PROVEN HER COMPETENCY AS A MONARCH,
BUT DUE TO HER NAIVETE IN REGARDS TO THE WAYS
OF THE WORLD, IS OFTENTIMES TREATED AS A DITZ.

Nagi

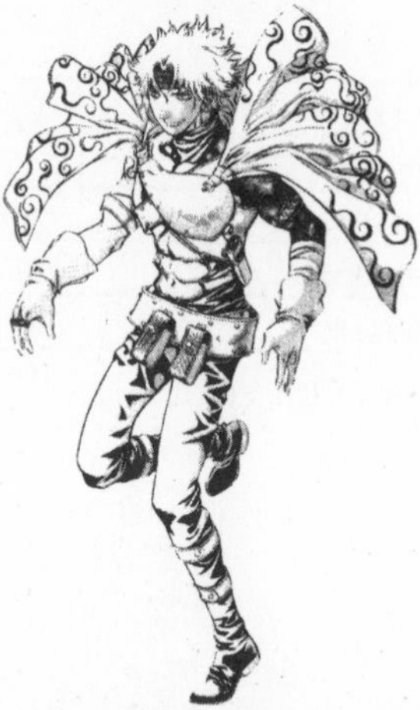

Strength 힘	140
Dexterity 민첩	360
Constiution 건강	110
Intelligence 지능	190
Wisdom 지혜	610
Charisma 매력	580

25 YEARS OLD (MALE)
A MYSTERIOUS THIEF WHO, FOR NO KNOWN REASON, HAS COME TO BE CALLED THE "ROGUE MASTER." HE HAS DONE NOTHING TO EARN THE TITLE AND SEEMS TO BE ADEPT ONLY AT UNLOCKING DOORS, HIDING AND ESCAPING IN ORDER TO FILL HIS DARK MOTIVES OF GREED. NAGI HAS A COLLECTION OF VARIOUS MAGIC ITEMS.

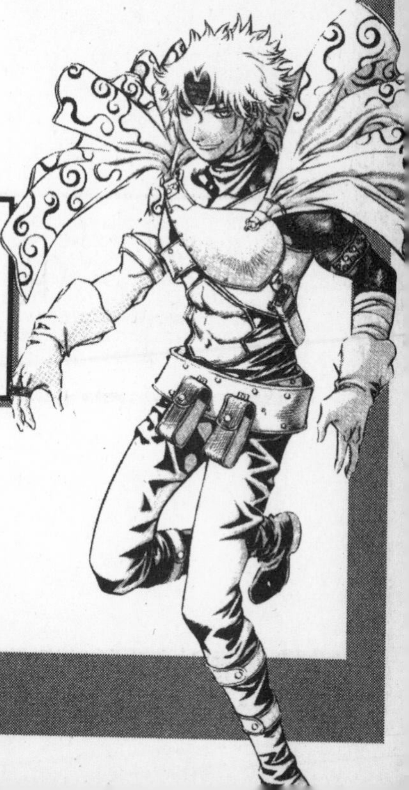

LAST FANTASY CHARACTER FILE 5

Agrippa

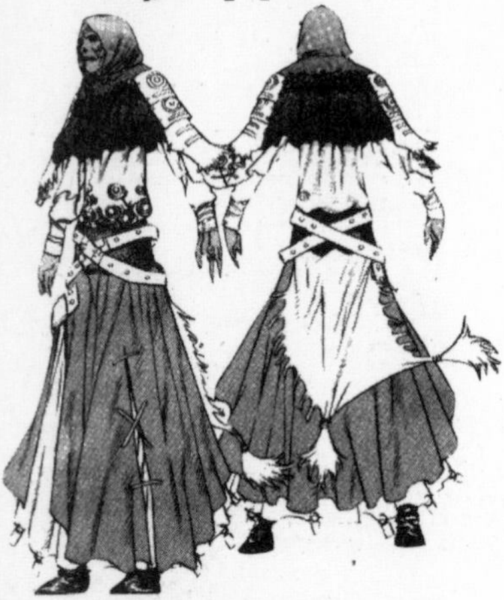

Strength 힘	210
Dexterity 민첩	80
Constiution 건강	950
Intelligence 지능	8470
Wisdom 지혜	3620
Charisma 매력	2100

APPROXIMATELY 500 YEARS OLD (MALE) MYSTERIOUS FIGURE WHO IS SEEN AS THE GREATEST MAGICIAN OF ALL TIME. TRANSFORMED HIMSELF INTO A SKELETON IN ORDER TO GAIN ETERNAL LIFE. CURRENTLY WORKING WITH TWO COMRADES TO RESURRECT THE DEMON KING.

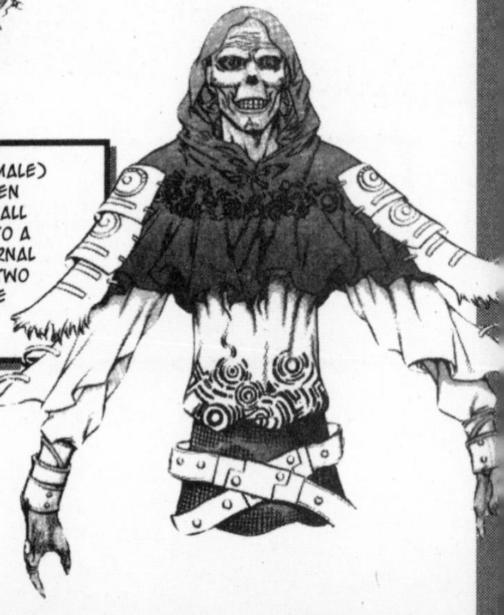

LAST FANTASY CHARACTER FILE 6

Glacier

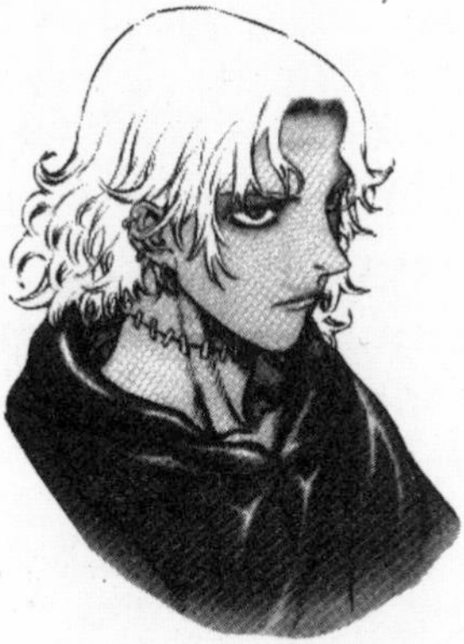

Strength 힘	340
Dexterity 민첩	90
Constiution 건강	510
Intelligence 지능	830
Wisdom 지혜	290
Charisma 매력	110

24 YEARS OLD (MALE)
ONCE A COLLEAGUE OF TIAN, HAS NOW BEEN ON BAD TERMS WITH HIM FOR A VERY LONG TIME. AFTER BEING PUT TO DEATH BY AGRIPPA, GLACIER WAS CONSEQUENTLY RESURRECTED AND NOW SERVES AS AGRIPPA'S SUBORDINATE.

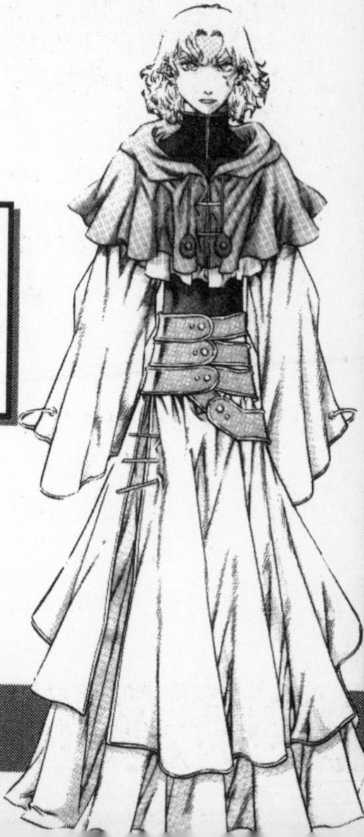

Note of Apology

UNFORTUNATELY, LAST FANTASY VOLUME 2 WAS
PUBLISHED WITHOUT CORRECTING A FEW MISTAKES.
DUE TO MISTAKES MADE IN EDITING, THE PUBLISHED
VERSION HAD A SLIGHT DISCREPANCY WITH THE AUTHOR'S
INTENTIONS. WE APOLOGIZE TO ALL OF OUR READERS
FOR PUBLISHING A BOOK THAT WAS NOT FINISHED.

THE FOLLOWING PAGES ARE THE MOST IMPORTANT
PART OF THE CLIMAX OF VOLUME 2. IF MISUNDERSTOOD,
THE READER'S INTERPRETATION OF THE STORY COULD BE
HINDERED. ALTHOUGH WE ARE NOW PUBLICLY DISPLAYING
OUR ERRORS IN DOING SO, WE FELT THAT SUPPLYING OUR
READERS WITH A PRODUCT OF SUPERIOR QUALITY WAS FAR
MORE IMPORTANT. WITH OUR HEARTS SET ON FIXING THE
STABLE EVEN AFTER ALL THE COWS HAVE LEFT, WE CAME
TO THE DIFFICULT DECISION OF PROVIDING YOU WITH THE
REVISIONS. WE WILL TRY HARDER IN THE FUTURE TO
PREVENT MISTAKES LIKE THIS FROM RECURRING.
THANK YOU.

--CREATIVE HON

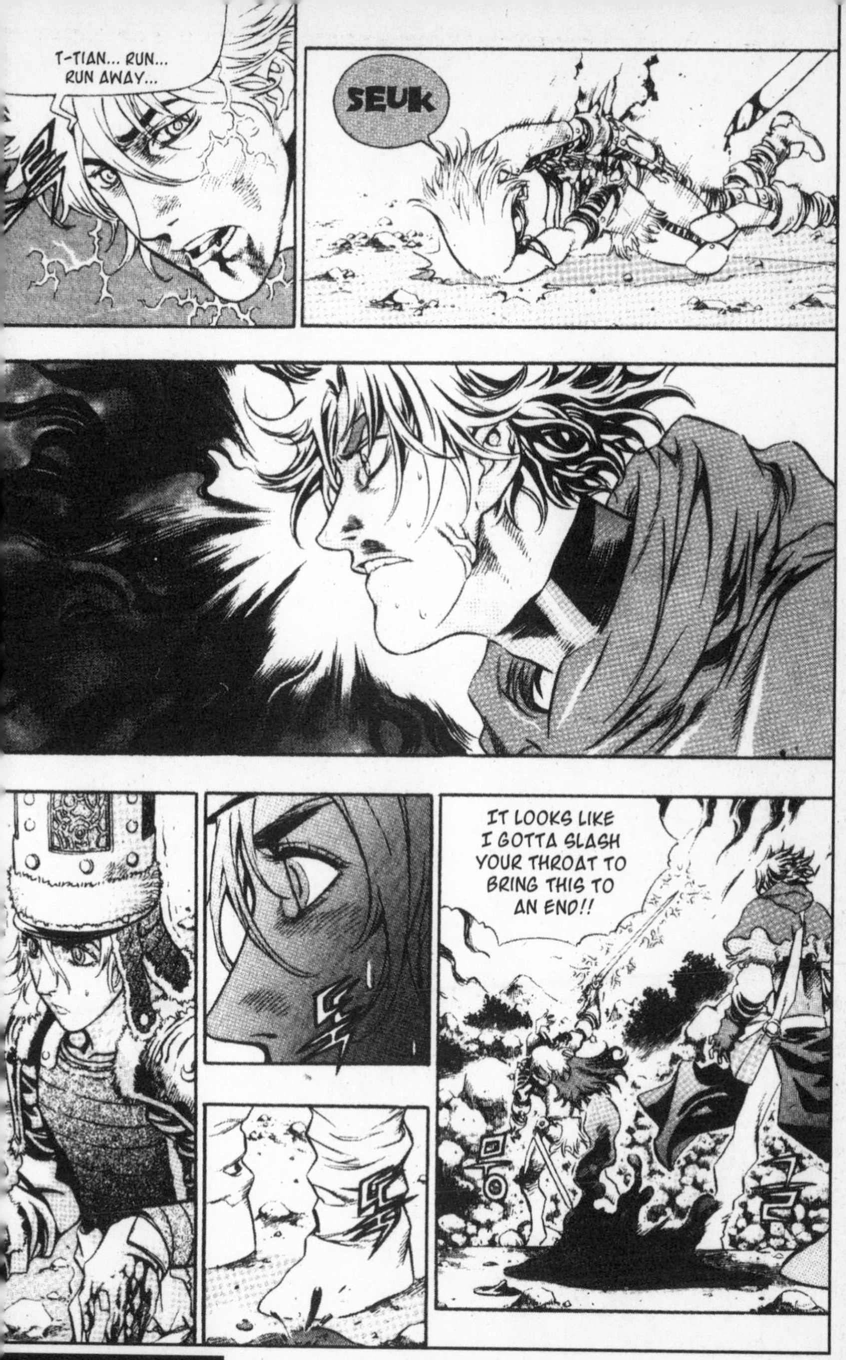
T-TIAN... RUN... RUN AWAY...
SEUK
IT LOOKS LIKE I GOTTA SLASH YOUR THROAT TO BRING THIS TO AN END!!

VOLUME 2, PAGE 103

R...RUN AWAY... => T-TIAN... RUN... RUN AWAY...
OBSTINATE FOOL-- I'LL END THIS NOW! => IT LOOKS LIKE I GOTTA SLASH YOUR THROAT TO BRING THIS TO AN END!!

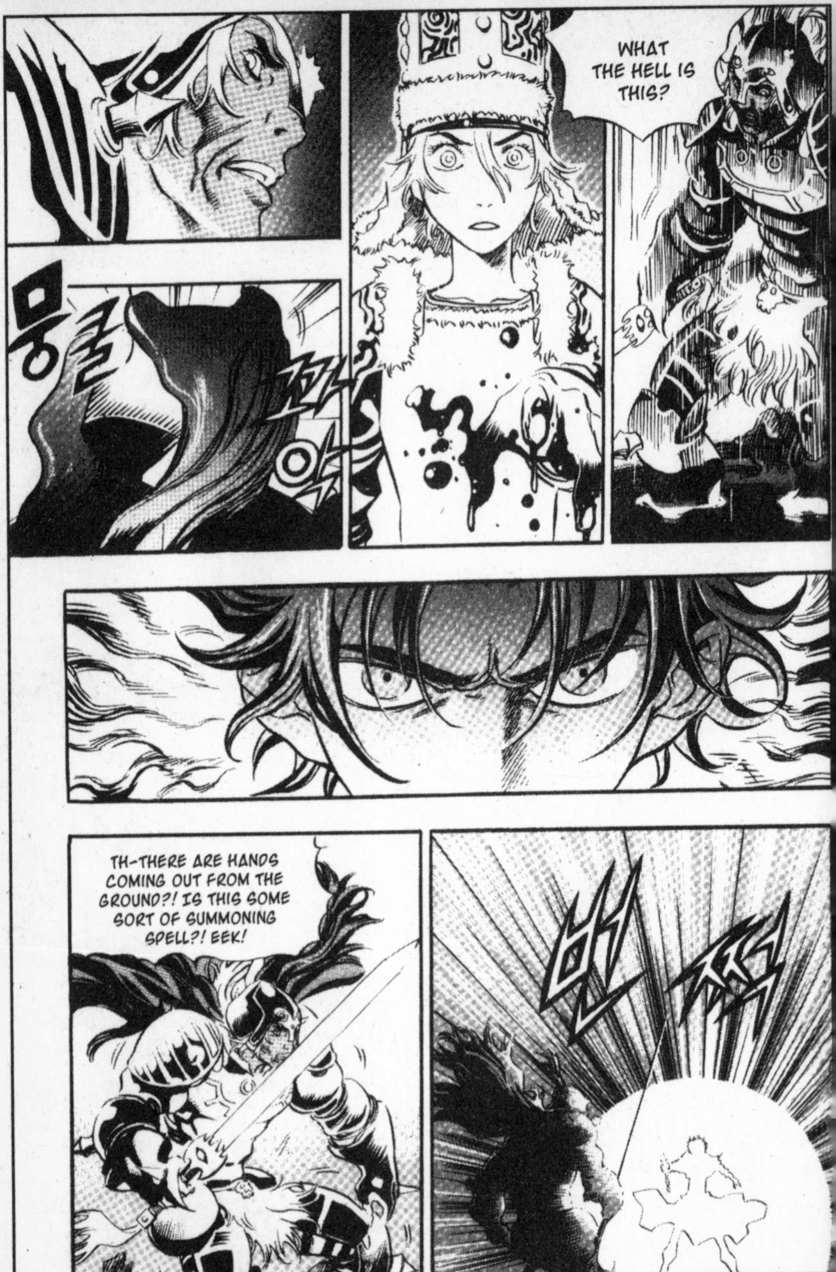
WHAT THE HELL IS THIS?
TH-THERE ARE HANDS COMING OUT FROM THE GROUND?! IS THIS SOME SORT OF SUMMONING SPELL?! EEK!

VOLUME 2, PAGE 104

STOP WITH THIS BOTHERSOME ACT =>
TH-THERE ARE HANDS COMING OUT FROM THE GROUND?! IS THIS SOME SORT OF SUMMONING SPELL?! EEK!

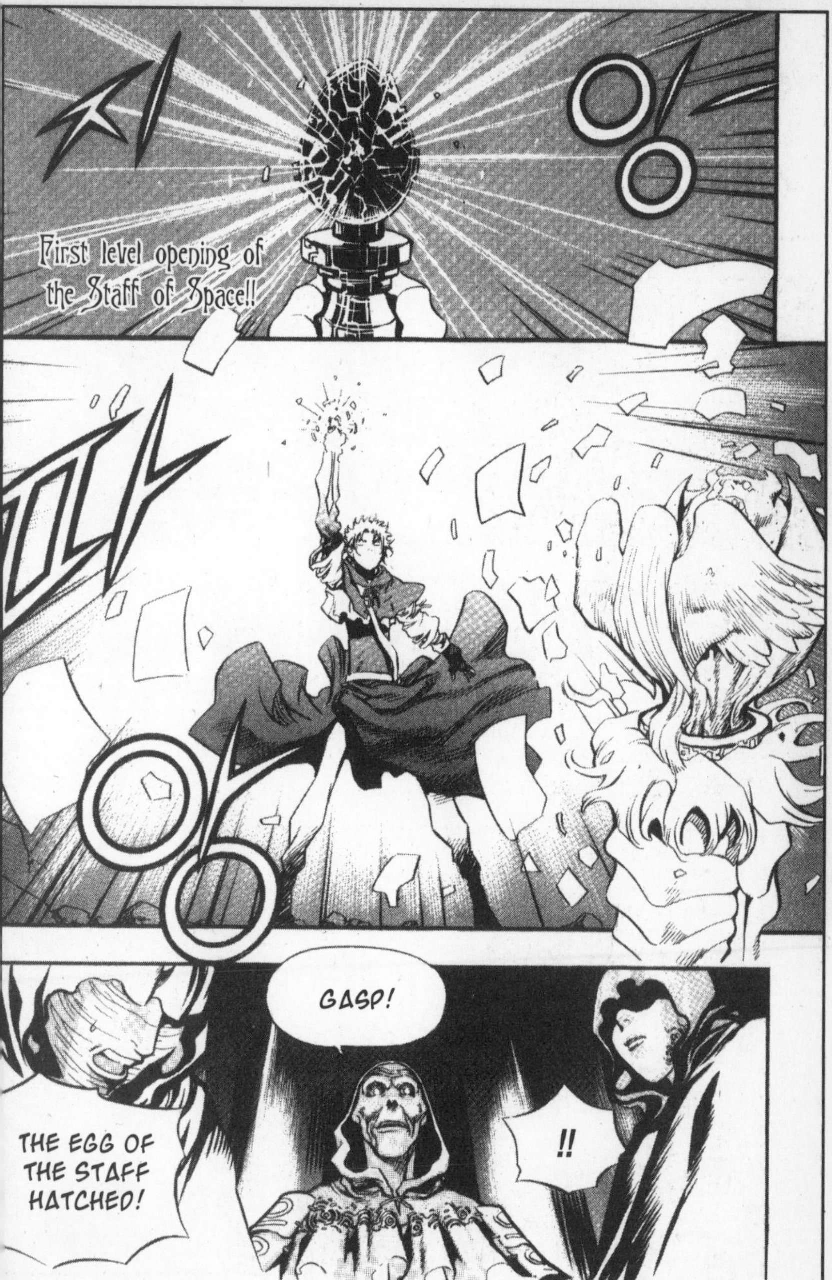
First level opening of the Staff of Space!!
THE EGG OF THE STAFF HATCHED!
!!
GASP!

VOLUME 2, PAGE 105

FIRST LEVEL OPENING OF THE STAFF OF SPACE!! / DID IT CHANGE? => THE EGG OF THE STAFF HATCHED!
... => GASP

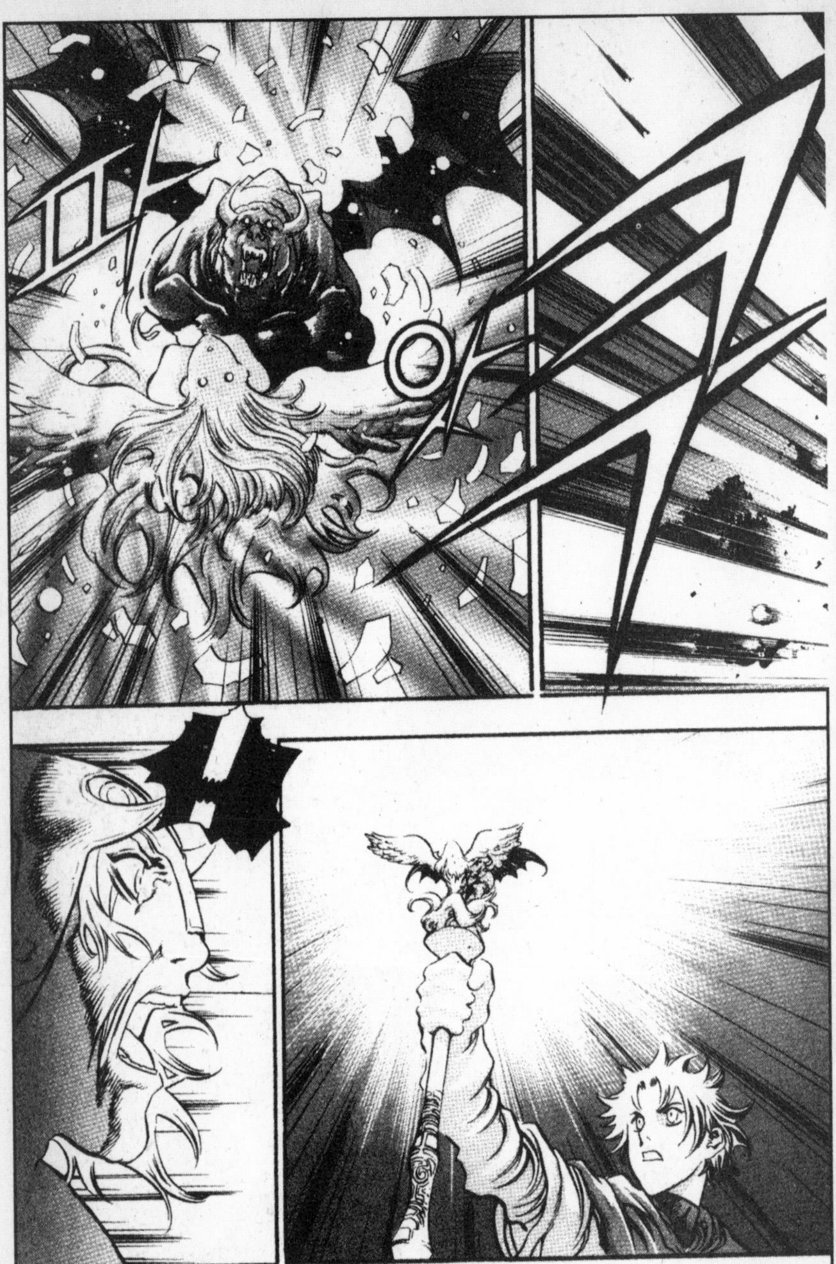

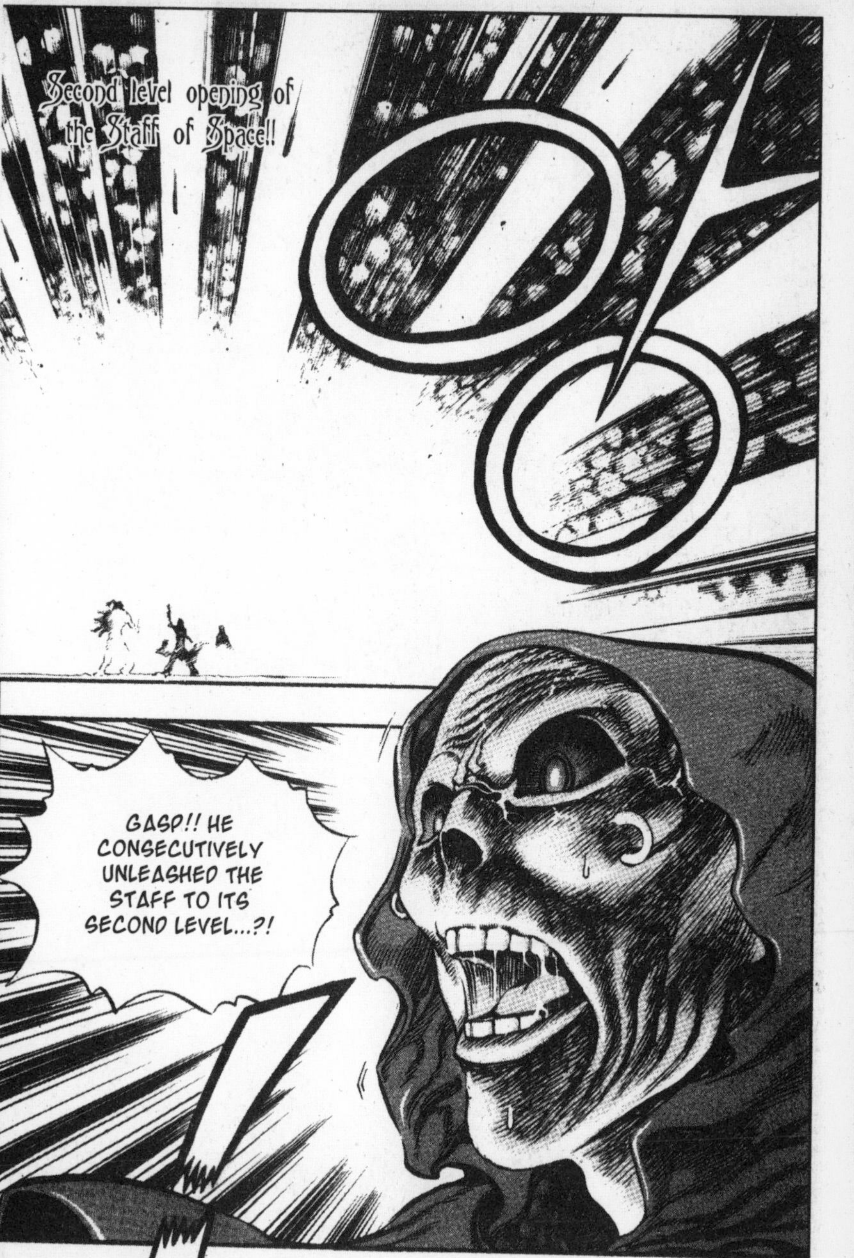
Second level opening of the Staff of Space!!
GASP!! HE CONSECUTIVELY UNLEASHED THE STAFF TO ITS SECOND LEVEL...?!

VOLUME 2, PAGE 107

ACK! SECOND LEVEL OPENING => GASP!! HE CONSECUTIVELY UNLEASHED THE STAFF TO ITS SECOND LEVEL...?!
SECOND LEVEL OPENING OF THE STAFF OF SPACE!!

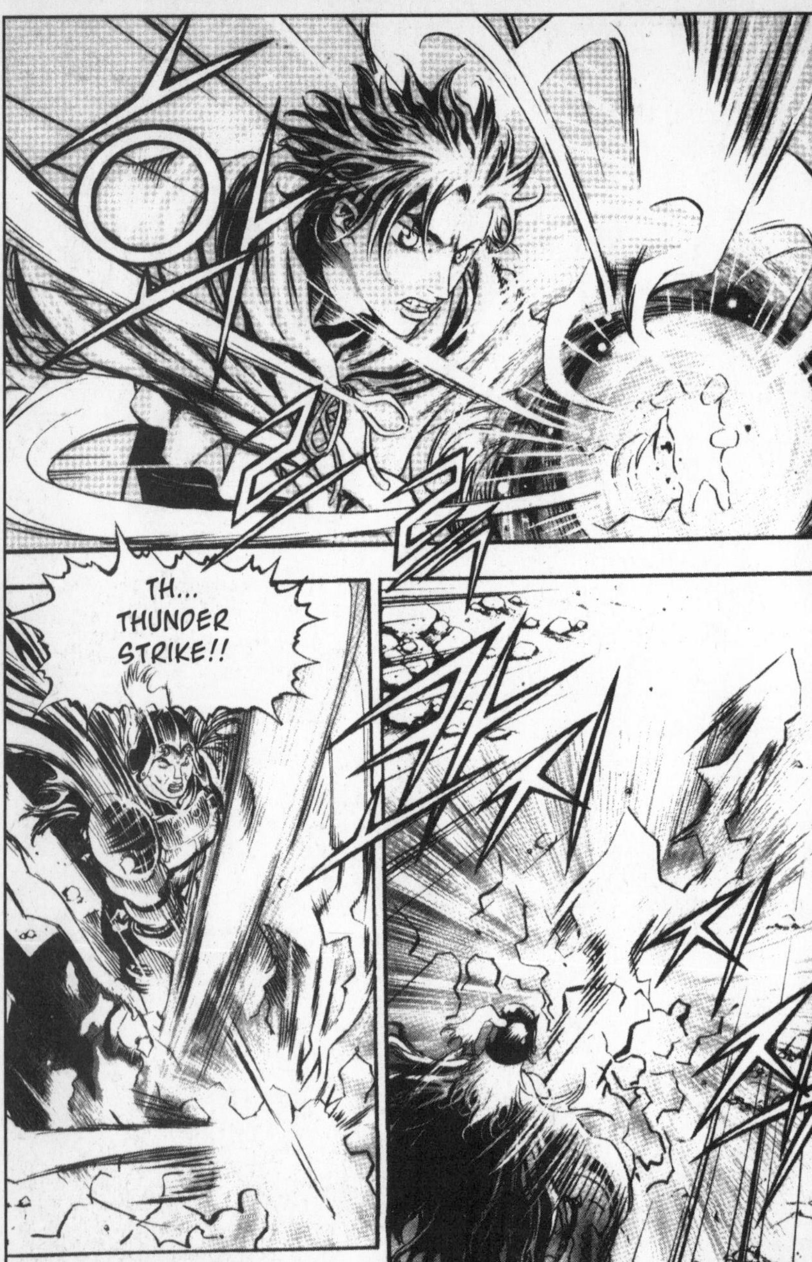
TH...
THUNDER
STRIKE!!

SU, SUNDER STRIKE! => TH-THUNDER STRIKE!!

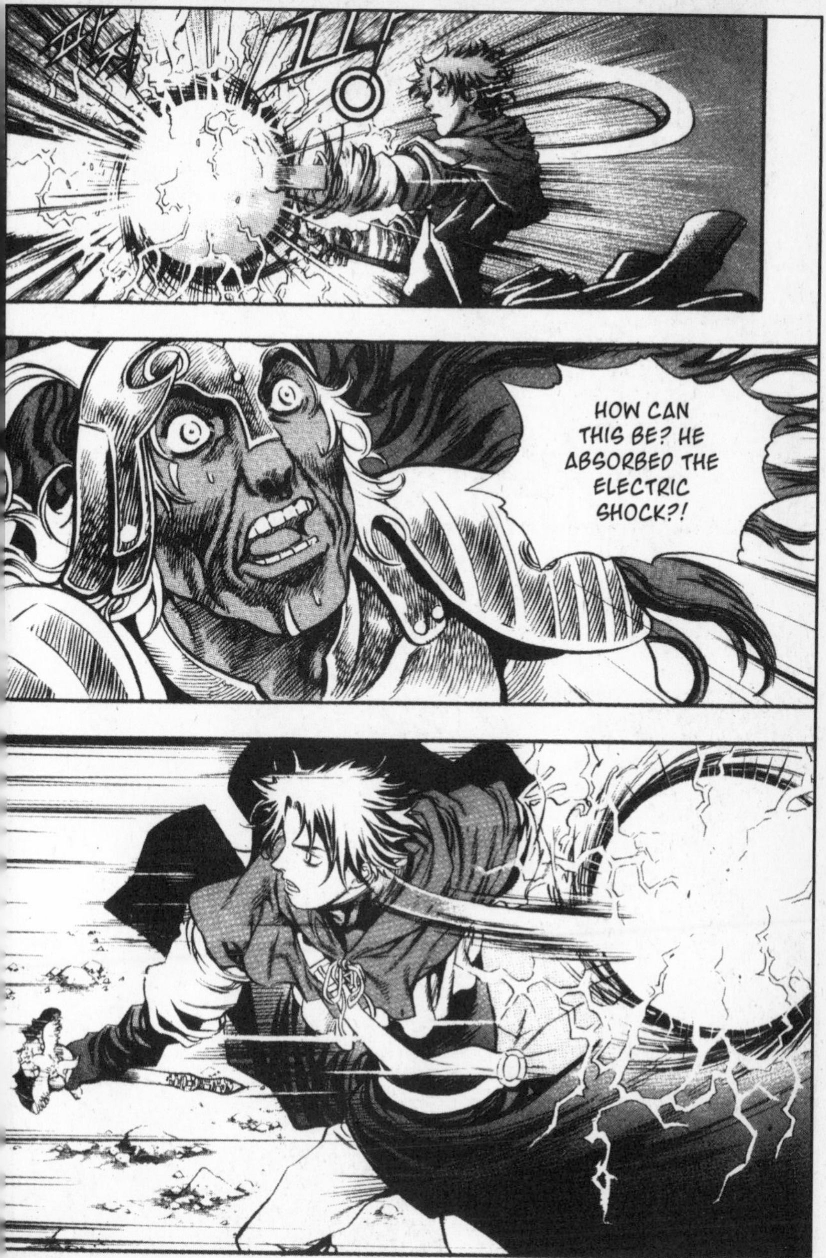
HOW CAN THIS BE? HE ABSORBED THE ELECTRIC SHOCK?!

HOW... HOW CAN THIS BE => HOW CAN THIS BE? HE ABSORBED THE ELECTRIC SHOCK?!

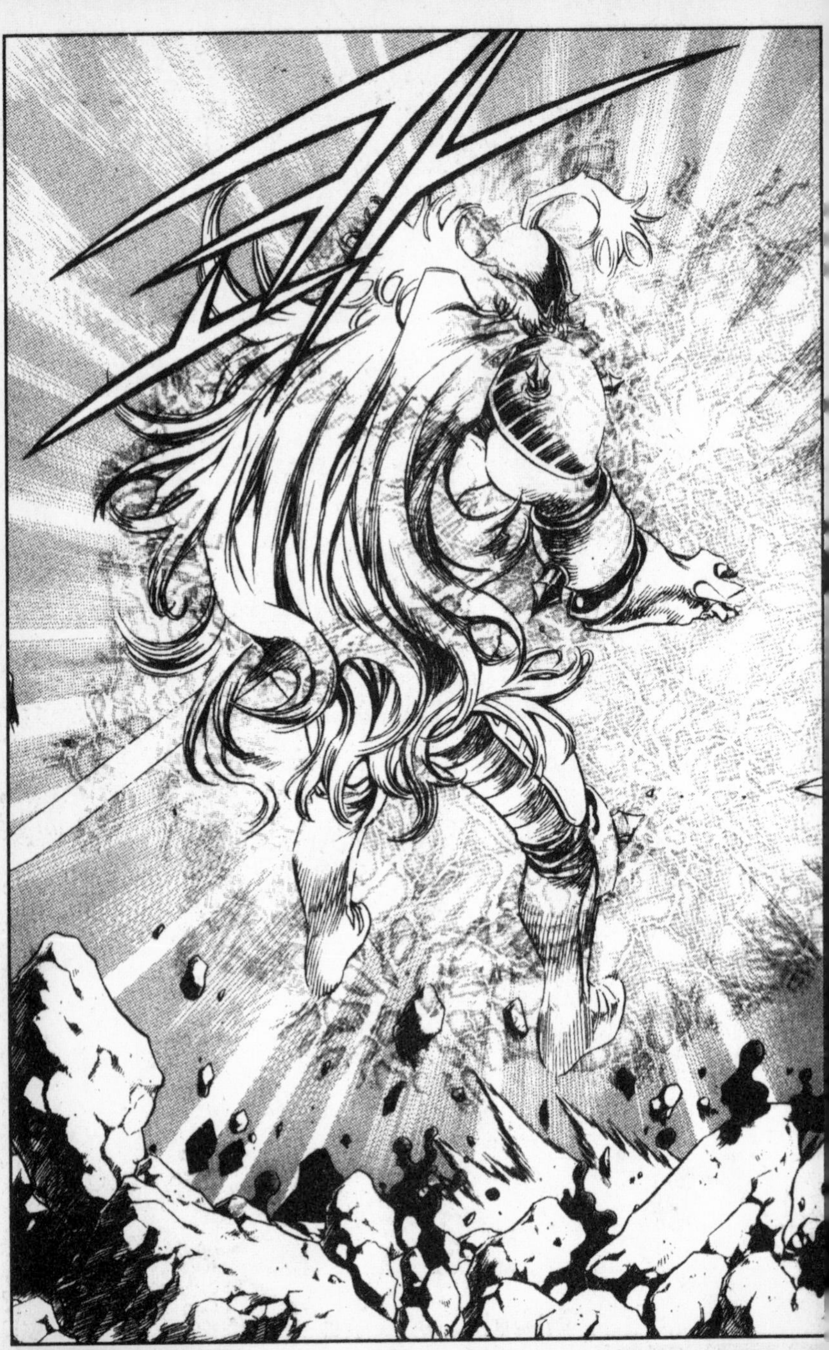

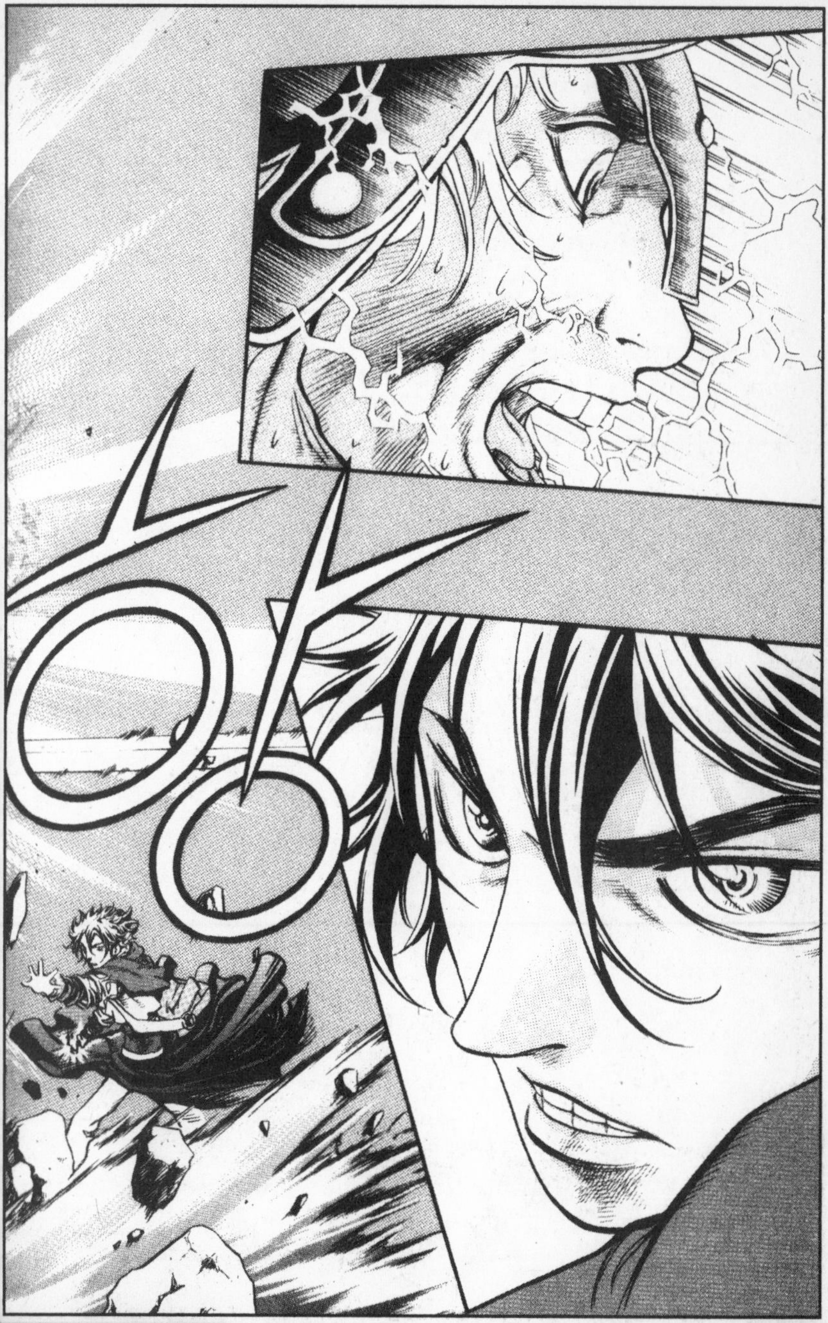

VOLUME 2, PAGE 111

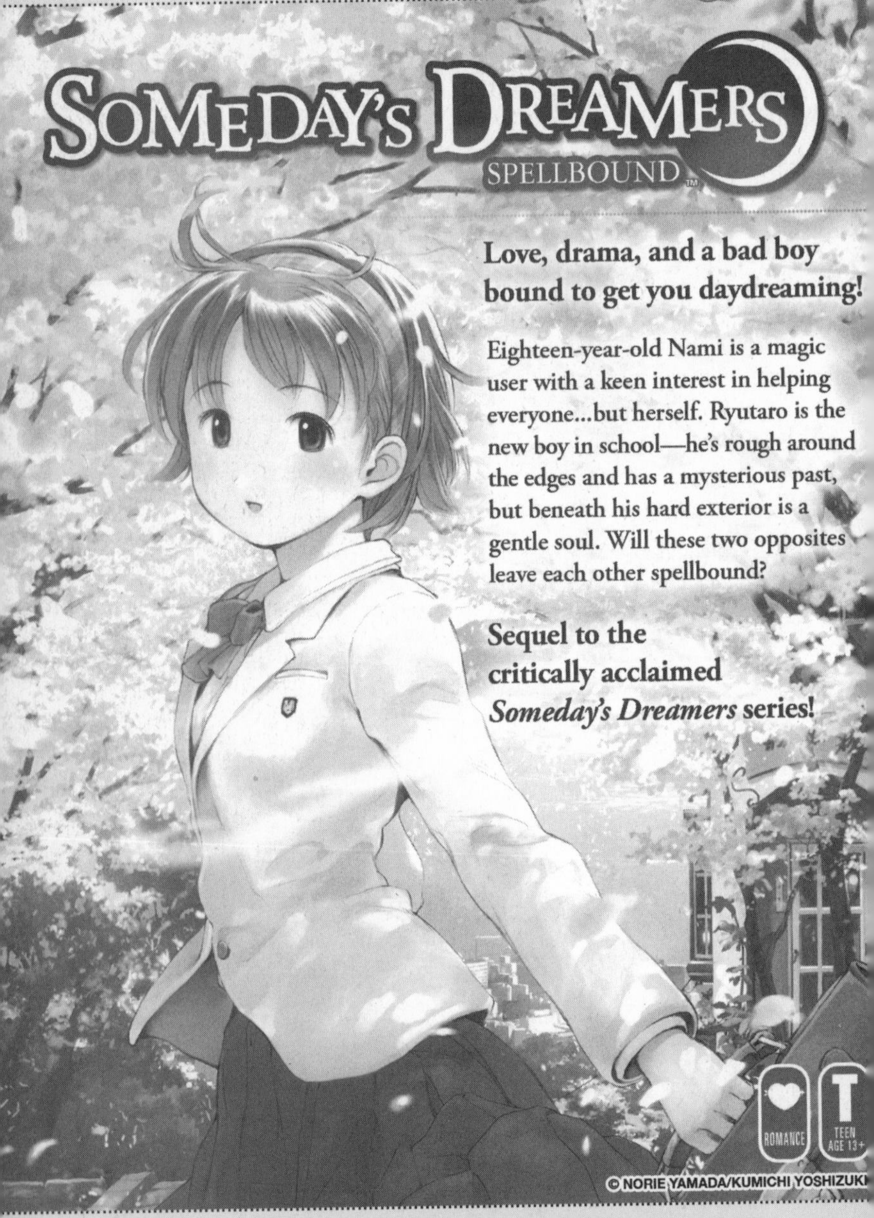
SOMEDAY'S DREAMERS
SPELLBOUND™
Love, drama, and a bad boy bound to get you daydreaming!
Eighteen-year-old Nami is a magic user with a keen interest in helping everyone...but herself. Ryutaro is the new boy in school—he's rough around the edges and has a mysterious past, but beneath his hard exterior is a gentle soul. Will these two opposites leave each other spellbound?
Sequel to the critically acclaimed *Someday's Dreamers* series!
ROMANCE
T
TEEN AGE 13+
© NORIE YAMADA/KUMICHI YOSHIZUKI

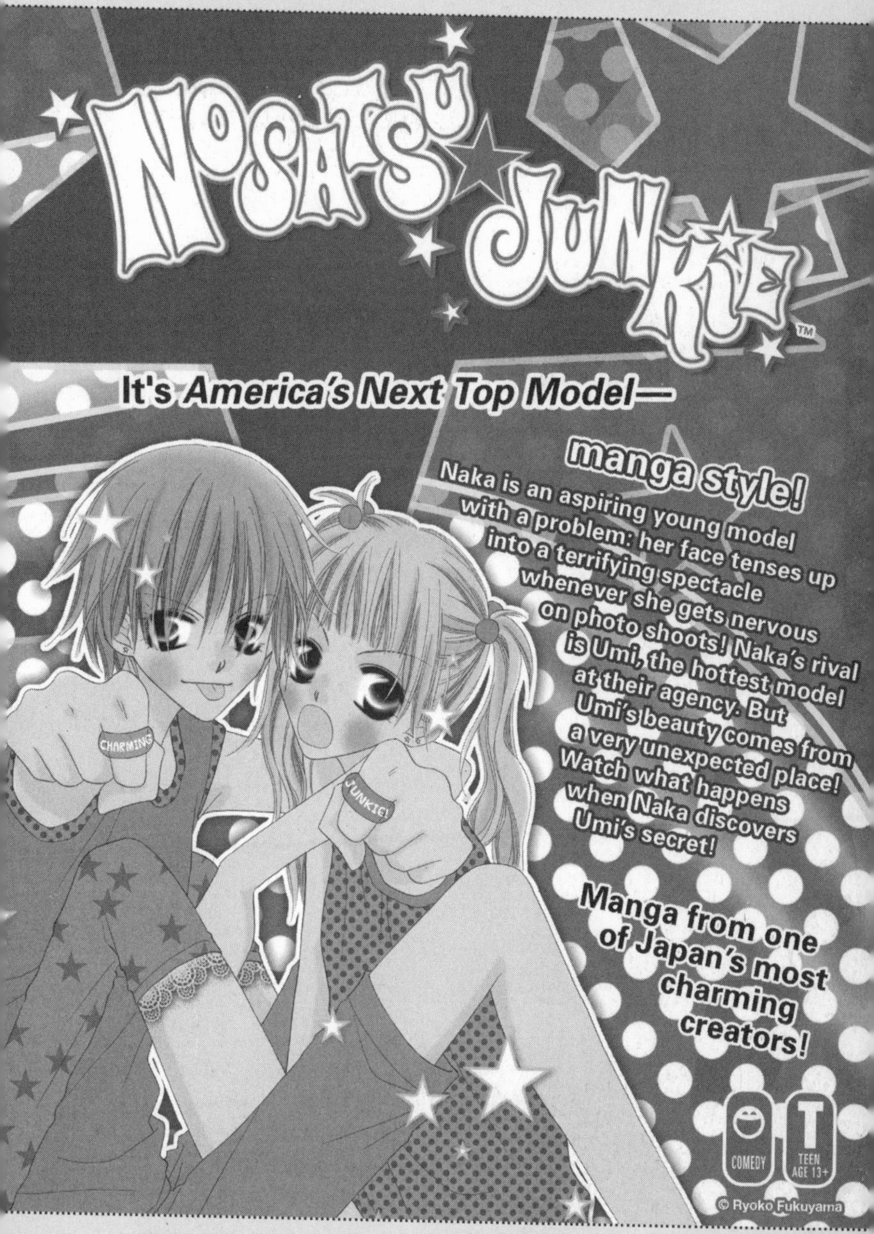
NOSATSU JUNKIE™
It's America's Next Top Model—
manga style!
Naka is an aspiring young model with a problem: her face tenses up into a terrifying spectacle whenever she gets nervous on photo shoots! Naka's rival is Umi, the hottest model at their agency. But Umi's beauty comes from a very unexpected place! Watch what happens when Naka discovers Umi's secret!
Manga from one of Japan's most charming creators!
CHARMING
JUNKIE!
COMEDY
T
TEEN AGE 13+
© Ryoko Fukuyama